Stock Index Futures

Stock Index Futures

Edited by
Frank J. Fabozzi
and
Gregory M. Kipnis

Dow Jones-Irwin
Homewood, Illinois 60430

© DOW JONES-IRWIN, 1984

This publication is designed to provide accurate and
authoritative information in regard to the subject matter
covered. It is sold with the understanding that the
publisher is not engaged in rendering legal, accounting, or
other professional service. If legal advice or other expert
assistance is required, the services of a competent
professional person should be sought.

*From a Declaration of Principles jointly adopted by a Committee
of the American Bar Association and a Committee of Publishers.*

ISBN 0-87094-424-X
Library of Congress Catalog Card No. 83–70863

Printed in the United States of America

1 2 3 4 5 6 7 8 9 0   K   1 0 9 8 7 6 5 4

FJF's corner
    To my sister, Lucy

GMK's corner
    To my tolerant wife,
    Claire, and my
    patient children,
    Christine and Pascale

Foreword

Stock index futures are here. Innovators are finding and exploiting opportunities to use them to increase profits or reduce risk—with encouragingly good results.

But most of us are not. We hold back from this new departure, reluctant to invest the time and attention needed to obtain the necessary knowledge and understanding. We are "waiting to see" how others do.

Our caution or reluctance is not surprising: It is a normal part of the social process through which the diffusion of any innovation must go. The speed of that process varies from innovation to innovation. Teenage girls are notoriously quick to adopt new ways. Conservative farmers are notoriously slow to adopt new ways. (It took over 20 years to win acceptance for hybrid seed corn despite clear and substantial and highly visible evidence that crop yields were much better.)

It takes time—and motivation—to change our ways. In retrospect, we amuse ourselves with tales of how reluctantly the infantry accepted tanks, how unhappily the Navy recognized the role of air power, how long the cavalry held on to horses, and so forth. The time absorbed by the diffusion of any particular innovation is a function of several key variables: How visible is the benefit? How large is the benefit? How great is the risk of error? How costly is the change? What are the social pressures pro and con the change? How easily can the change be reversed? How accessible is the change? How easy is it to make the change? How unfamiliar is the change?

Judging by our experience with options, it is not likely that the acceptance of stock index futures (by institutional investors as a whole) will be rapid. If so, this graceful gradualism will leave opportunities for those who do take the plunge to develop advantages for themselves and for their clients.

Stock index futures are almost certain to give a "high tech" flavor to investment management, accelerating the experience of risk and return.

As professionals, we owe it to ourselves and to our clients to know how to use this important new technology. This book gives each of us the chance to make our start.

Charles D. Ellis, *Ph.D., C.F.A.*
President
Greenwich Research Associates

Contributors

Andrew G. Balbus, J.D., *Paul, Weiss, Rifkind, Wharton & Garrison*

Frank J. Fabozzi, Ph.D., C.F.A., *Professor of Economics, Fordham University*

David C. Fisher, Partner, *Arthur Andersen & Co., New York*

T. Dessa Garlicki, Instructor, *The College of Staten Island, CUNY*

Gary L. Gastineau, Manager of the Options Portfolio Service, *Kidder, Peabody & Co., Inc.*

H. Nicholas Hanson, Ph.D., Vice President, *Salomon Brothers Inc*

Jonathan C. Jankus, Vice President, *Kidder, Peabody & Co., Inc.*

Frank J. Jones, Ph.D., Executive Vice President, *New York Futures Exchange*

Ira G. Kawaller, Ph.D., Director, *New York Office, Chicago Mercantile Exchange*

Gregory M. Kipnis, Vice President, *Donaldson, Lufkin & Jenrette, Inc.*

Stanley J. Kon, Ph.D., Associate Professor of Finance, *Graduate School of Business Administration, University of Michigan*

Robert W. Kopprasch, Ph.D., C.F.A., Vice President, *Salomon Brothers Inc*

Albert Madansky, Ph.D., Professor of Business Administration, *University of Chicago*

Fred M. Santo, Partner, *Rosenman Colin Freund Lewis & Cohen*

Howard Schneider, Partner, *Rosenman Colin Freund Lewis & Cohen*

Stephen F. Selig, LL.B., Partner, *Baer Marks & Upham*

Steve Tsang, Ph.D., Analyst, *Donaldson, Lufkin & Jenrette, Inc.*

Benjamin Wolkowitz, Ph.D., Vice President, *Citicorp Futures Corporation*

R. Steven Wunsch, Vice President, *Kidder, Peabody & Co., Inc.*

Contents

SECTION TWO
Pricing and Performance Characteristics

SECTION THREE
Applications

CHAPTER 1

Introduction

Frank J. Fabozzi, Ph.D., C.F.A.
Professor of Economics
Fordham University

Gregory M. Kipnis
Vice President
Donaldson, Lufkin & Jenrette, Inc.

During the past century and a quarter, futures instruments have aided commodity producers and customers in two vital ways. They have facilitated the price discovery process, and they have provided the means for efficient and economic transfer of risk. In the past decade innovations in the futures industry have resulted in instruments that have extended these functions to financial markets, namely fixed income and foreign exchange. In 1982 a third financial market was opened up with the creation of stock index futures. While it is not yet clear whether stock index futures will improve the price discovery process in an already very efficient market, it is clear that they will provide a powerful, broad spectrum tool for transferring price risk. A likely derivative benefit will be a smoother functioning of the capital markets as the routine use of futures by market makers reduces risk and thereby makes possible increased productivity of capital.

With the advent of futures contracts on stock indexes, active and offensively minded portfolio risk management, in its broadest sense, became practicable. In effect, the risk manager and the individual investor gained new degrees of freedom. He or she can now economically and quickly alter the market risk profile of a stock portfolio. He or she can now consider opportunistic strategies rather than only defensive strategies. This will be true because stock index futures help solve three real-world

1

problems that have made alternative risk management techniques cumbersome and costly, namely the comprehensiveness, the timeliness, and the cost effectiveness of altering the degree of market exposure.

The remarkable growth in the trading volume of stock index futures indicates the extent of the void that needed to be filled. Of course, only part of the volume is associated with hedging, arbitrage, and market-making functions; the rest is the usual trading found in futures markets, including that of speculators and traders.

By any measure, stock index futures have been a success. Particularly impressive has been the rapid climb in trading volume relative to that of the New York Stock Exchange. Astonishing though it may seem, during the month of June 1983, futures trading in the three stock index futures contracts (Standard & Poor's 500 Composite Index, New York Stock Exchange Composite Index, and Value Line Average Composite), expressed on a share equivalent basis, surpassed the volume of trading on the New York Stock Exchange by more than 11 percent.[1] On a typical day during the month, 58,432 contracts were traded, which roughly equalled 103.1 million shares. This compared to a daily average volume on the NYSE of 93.3 million shares. Ever since March 1983, stock index futures trading has exceeded NYSE volume on a fairly regular basis.

Definition and Evolution

A futures contract is a firm legal agreement between a buyer (or seller) and an established exchange or its clearinghouse in which the parties agree to take (or make) delivery of *something* at a specified price at the end of a designated period of time. Prior to 1972, the *something* that the parties agreed to take or make delivery of was traditional agricultural commodities (such as meat and livestock), imported foodstuffs (such as coffee, cocoa, and sugar), or industrial commodities. Collectively, such futures contracts are known as *commodities futures.*

Futures contracts based on a financial instrument or a financial index are known as *financial futures* and referred to by some as "pork bellies in pinstripes." It was not until 1972 that financial futures contracts were introduced. In that year, the International Monetary Market of the Chicago Mercantile Exchange initiated trading in several foreign currencies. In 1975 the Chicago Board of Trade pioneered trading in a futures contract based on a fixed-income instrument. Financial futures contracts in which the underlying financial instrument is a fixed-income security are known as *interest rate futures.*

---

[1] Since futures are traded in terms of contracts (each of which roughly equals 2,000 shares in the case of the S&P 500 and Value Line Average contracts and 1,200 shares in the case of the NYSE Composite contract), an adjustment must be made to put contracts on an equivalent basis with shares.

The latest entrant into the financial futures market was a futures contract based on a common stock index. In 1982 three futures contracts on a broadly based common stock index made their debut. The Kansas City Board of Trade, a commodity exchange that had long been the world's largest center for hard red winter wheat, was the first entrant into the stock index futures market. In February 1982, almost four years after the KCBT announced its intent to trade a stock index futures contract, it obtained approval to begin trading in a futures contract based on the Value Line Average. Two months later, the Chicago Mercantile Exchange began trading futures contracts based on the Standard & Poor's 500 stock index. In May 1982 the New York Futures Exchange started trading futures contracts based on the New York Stock Exchange Composite Index, and subsequently it attempted trading in a subindex based on financial stocks.

Some of the early press publicity relating to stock index futures markets characterized these markets as "legalized gambling." However, though much of the initial trading activity in these markets was for speculation, arbitrage, or spreading, the chief purpose of the markets, like that of all futures markets, is to facilitate price discovery and economic and efficient transfer of risk. As the stock index futures market comes to be better understood by investors, portfolio managers, and regulators, more trading activity will occur whose underlying motivation is risk transfer.

Users and Uses

For the first time, equity managers will have a tool with which they can hedge market-related portfolio risks and rapidly implement changes in market strategy without having to buy or sell securities. From the point of view of plan sponsors, fiduciaries, and beneficiaries, stock index futures should result in an improvement in overall portfolio performance. At the same time stock index futures should allow the market maker (such as the block trader, specialist, or syndicate manager), to increase the productivity of his capital and reduce his capital exposure risks. In this way the fund-raising functions of the equity markets should be enhanced.

Stock index futures will never be a long-term substitute for stocks, nor will they obviate the need for market judgment. They will, however, allow the equity manager to more rapidly correct errors in market judgment and to make a quicker entry into or exit from the market than has hitherto been possible.

An equity manager is always at risk, both as to his basic market judgments and as to his market timing. Stock index futures provide the means whereby market timing can be significantly modified. It can take weeks for a sizable buying or selling program to be completed. In some cases this may be especially difficult, since some thinly traded securities are particularly hard to find or liquidate. Instead, an equity manager can now hedge market risks with stock index futures while preserving the core stock position. In many cases this would be far more desirable than the "lump it or dump it" approach brought about by adverse market swings.

Additional uses (and advantages) of stock index futures include the following:

To quickly implement a market position at low transaction costs.

To protect against market risks in uncovered option positions.

To improve market timing, when accumulation or distribution problems are expected, by buying or selling the market when it seems right rather than when the program is completed.

To unbundle and manage stock selection and market timing sources of return.

To alter a market position, in anticipation of cash inflows or outflows, if a market move is expected in the interim.

To reduce the market risk associated with an undesired short or long position acquired in the course of underwriting, block trading, or market timing.

To hedge a desired portfolio position from mark-to-market exposure during intervals when market weakness is anticipated, for example, prior to statement closing dates.

To create an index fund that will be less costly to construct than one constructed by means of the traditional index fund approach and that under certain pricing conditions will outperform the market index.

Overview of Book

Although the advent of stock index futures contracts is an epochal event in the evolution of money management, there is a need to bridge the gap between actual practice and the theory of how they can be employed. This book attempts to bridge that gap.

Following the discussion of the historical development of financial futures, and stock index futures contracts in particular, in Chapter 2, Chapters 3 through 5 of Section One provide background information that the investor should be familiar with before trading stock index futures. Chapter 3 reviews the major features (contract size, margin, leverage, and other contract and trading details) differentiating the various stock index futures contracts currently traded. The mechanics of trading stock index futures are discussed in Chapter 4. Since the success of any strategy employing stock index futures will depend to some extent on the nature of the underlying index, the characteristics of the currently traded indexes are explained in Chapter 5.

The pricing of stock index futures is the subject of Section Two. Applications (hedging, creating an index fund, uses in active portfolio management, speculating, and spreading) are discussed in Section Three.

In 1983 options on stock index futures and on stock indexes were introduced. The first chapter in Section Four, Chapter 17, presents the basic information about these option contracts and the risk-reward relationships for basic option positions. Chapter 18 explains how these contracts can be employed in portfolio management as well as the difficulties in applying to options on stock index futures and options on stock indexes the option pricing models developed for options on common stock.

The final section, Section Five, deals with the tax treatment (Chapter 19), regulation of institutional users (Chapter 20), and accounting treatment (Chapter 21) of stock index futures and with the regulation of stock index futures trading (Chapter 22).

SECTION ONE

Background Information

CHAPTER 2

Stock Index Futures in Historical Perspective

Benjamin Wolkowitz, Ph.D.
Vice President
Citicorp Futures Corporation*

The Statistical Case against Success

A significant event in the development of futures contracts occurred in February 1982, when the Kansas City Board of Trade initiated trading in stock index futures contracts. Shortly afterward, the Chicago Mercantile Exchange and the New York Futures Exchange introduced their entries in the new stock index futures market. The reception received by these contracts was immediate and enthusiastic, motivating some observers to predict that stock index futures contracts would become the hot new market of the 1980s. Such a prediction, though seemingly premature, was not without foundation, given the early experience with these contracts.

Reviewing the usual record of new futures contracts underscores the truly outstanding nature of the reception given stock index contracts. A recent and extensive study by Professor William L. Silber indicated that from 1960 to 1977 only 31.8 percent of new contracts were traded in an annual volume of more than 10,000 after three years and that only 20.9 percent of contracts representing competitive modifications of existing contracts were traded in that volume.[1] By contrast, all three stock

---

* I would like to acknowledge the helpful comments of Mark Powers of Powers Research, Inc., and the editors.

[1] William F. Silber, "Innovation, Competition, and New Contract Design in Futures Markets," *Journal of Futures Markets* 1 (Summer 1981).

index futures contracts were trading in excess of 10,000 contracts a week shortly after their introduction. In fact, by mid-1982 the average daily trading volume for the three contracts was 35,000.

As Professor Silber's data suggest, the proliferation of contracts infrequently leads to successful trading in competing markets. Moreover, Professor Holbrook Working, long a prominent and incisive analyst of futures markets, observed some time ago that duplicative contracts are unlikely to be successful.[2] Yet all three stock index contracts have been trading successfully, a situation replicated by no other duplicative contracts. It could be argued that the three stock index contracts are in fact different contracts because the underlying indexes are different (more on this later). Indeed, differences in indexes and contract design affect the behavior of these contracts, but any reasonable measure of relationships, such as coefficients of correlation, shows a close association among the three indexes, indicating that in many respects they are substantially the same.[3] In summary, from the perspectives of both volume and contract proliferation the experience with stock index contracts has been an impressive departure from previously established norms.

Elements of Success

In concept, an equity-based contract should have long seemed a likely candidate for a futures contract. The significant liquidity and depth of the underlying equity markets should have suggested the potential for a derivative contract for the same reasons that liquid cash markets in various agricultural products and financial instruments suggested the development of other derivative futures contracts. Besides the liquidity of the underlying cash market, many of the other preconditions associated with successful futures contracts have been characteristic of the equity markets as well. In particular, there is sufficient price volatility so that an equity-based futures contract would hold interest for both hedgers and speculators. Moreover, equity cash prices are competitively determined in markets that disseminate price information widely, quickly, and accurately. In addition, there exist a number of widely recognized and easily understood indexes of equity prices that provide an adequate basis on which to price and settle a contract.

Given that equities have many of the characteristics needed for a successful derivative instrument and given the enthusiastic reception of such instruments, in retrospect it seems odd that it took so long for these instruments to be introduced. Indeed, from a business perspective it could

---

[2] Holbrook Working, "Whose Markets? Evidence of Some Aspects of Futures Trading," *Journal of Marketing* 19 (July 1951).

[3] Correlation coefficients between various market indexes are presented in Chapter 5.

be argued that the introduction of this product was long overdue. But from the perspective of contract design and the historical development of futures markets, the introduction of stock index futures contracts occurred at an appropriate time and in many respects at the earliest possible time. To appreciate this seeming contradiction requires reviewing selectively the history of futures trading and contract development in the United States, starting with the very first agriculture-based contracts.

Agricultural Heritage

Futures markets had their start in agriculture, where they provided a method of insulating farmers, distributors, and processors of agricultural produce from the risk of unanticipated price changes. Farmers were seeking a way to secure a price that would yield a spread over their costs early in the harvest cycle, while processors and distributors were interested in guaranteeing an adequate supply of produce at a price that would ensure them a profit. Enabling farmers to contract with distributors and processors to make delivery at a prearranged price, well in advance of the actual delivery date, would satisfy the needs of both farmers and their direct customers. The economic need for such contracts was sufficiently strong that prior to the introduction of exchange-traded agriculture-based futures, off-exchange substitutes, which were in effect forward contracts (also known as "to arrive" contracts), had already developed.

   In some ways these off-exchange contracts served the same purpose as futures contracts. They were an inferior substitute, however, and the inadequacies inherent in forward contracts contributed to the development of futures contracts. One of the key problems with forward contracts was that they carried no assurance of reliability or performance. They were essentially a customized transaction between two parties operating on the basis of trust. If one party to the contract reneged, the other party had no way of being compensated for attendant losses except to take the matter to litigation; obviously, this would have been an unsatisfactory climax to a transaction initiated as a method of minimizing exposure to price risk. In addition, each forward contract had its own method of determining payment and price. Since price information was not generally available, the participants to a contract could never be certain of receiving the best terms. Besides lack of standardization of payment, there was no standardization of the quality of the commodities to be delivered. Consequently, there was no method of easily reselling a contract, even though various potential applications of forward delivery-type contracts do not actually require the delivery of the commodity. For example, speculators interested in profiting from price movements certainly do not need to make or take delivery of the underlying commodity; nor, in fact, do many types of hedgers.

In spite of the shortcomings of forward contracts, until the latter part of the 19th century they were the only available method of arranging for the future delivery of an agricultural commodity. When the Chicago Board of Trade, the first commodity exchange in the United States, was organized in 1848, the objective was largely to locate the forward contracting activity in one central place. Not until 1865 were the first standardized futures contracts in the United States traded at the Chicago Board of Trade. Their introduction revolutionized the process of arranging for forward delivery of a commodity.

The obvious advantages of futures trading compared with off-exchange forward arrangements were apparent, ensuring the success of the concept. Throughout the latter part of the 19th century, a number of exchanges that are still active today were developed.[4] The development of competitive exchanges and the growth of interest in futures contracts encouraged the proliferation of different types of futures contracts. These ultimately spanned a range of "commodities" extending from the original Chicago Board of Trade grain contracts to the recent stock index futures contracts. Unfortunately, the majority of new contracts have always failed to create sustainable trading interest at the outset. Exchanges have been energetic, however, both in designing new contracts based on different cash market instruments and in altering the basic structure of contracts so as to make them better suited to particular trading needs and particular cash instruments. As a result of these efforts, there are now 41 actively traded contracts. These contracts differ not only in the terms of the cash instrument on which they are based but also in key design characteristics. They reflect the evolutionary process that has led up to stock index contracts.

Contract Development Issues—Storability

As previously noted, the first futures contracts were based on grains. Because grains are storable and the contracts are standardized instruments, a trader could take delivery of a futures contract, store the grain, and redeliver the grain on the next contract. The following hypothetical example illustrates the delivery aspect of these futures contracts.

Step 1   Long 10 December wheat contracts (50,000   Short 10 March wheat contracts.
          bushels).
                              ↓
Step 2   December 27, take delivery.
                              ↓

---

[4] These include the Mid-America Commodity Exchange (1868); the New York Cotton Exchange (1870); the Kansas City Board of Trade (1871); the New York Mercantile Exchange (1872); the Minneapolis Grain Exchange (1881); the Coffee, Sugar, and Cocoa Exchange (1882); and the Chicago Mercantile Exchange (1898). Exchanges continued to be developed in the 20th century, principally the Commodity Exchange (1933) and the New York Futures Exchange (1980).

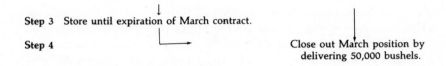

Step 3   Store until expiration of March contract.

Step 4   Close out March position by
                                                          delivering 50,000 bushels.

During the period between the two contract maturity dates, the commodity must be stored at a cost that includes the cost of actual physical storage and insurance and the cost of financing. The total of these costs is referred to as the cost of carry. This concept is at the core of a large number of trading strategies for financial as well as nonfinancial futures contracts and is also a major factor in explaining the prices for different months for the same contract. A primary example of a financial futures contract with this cost of carry aspect is the Treasury bond contract. Since insurance and storage costs are minimal for a Treasury bond, most of the cost of carry for Treasury bonds is the short-term financing rate incurred in taking delivery of a bond and redelivering it on a distant contract. As a consequence, there are a number of trading strategies based on the recognition that the cost of carry for a bond contract is a short-term interest rate.

Of course, many commodities are perishable; that is, they have a limited storage life. Such commodities could not be as easily carried from one futures contract to another as commodities with a long storage life. Introducing futures contracts based on limited or noncarry commodities was a major departure from the original design of futures contracts. The Chicago Mercantile Exchange (CME) opened its operations with a futures contract based on butter. Because of the perishability of butter, this was a noncarry contract. Interestingly, all subsequent CME contracts have been of a limited carry or noncarry variety.

Financial Instruments with and without Forward Markets

The next major contract development leading to the introduction of stock index futures contracts was the opening of the International Monetary Market (IMM), a wholly owned subsidiary of the CME, in 1972.[5] This exchange was developed to offer an entirely new type of futures contract: futures based on financial instruments. The first listed contracts were based on foreign exchange. Foreign currencies were a logical choice for the first financial futures contracts for much the same reason that futures contracts began with grains. There was already a well-developed off-exchange forward market. Thus the process of agreeing to make or take

---

[5] Although there were a number of significant steps between the opening of the CME in 1898 and that of the International Monetary Market in 1972, from the perspective of this discussion they are of a lesser order of importance.

delivery at some future time was an established part of the domestic foreign exchange market in the United States prior to the introduction of currency futures. And as with grains, currency futures provided an exchange-traded substitute for what had previously been conducted off-exchange. The usefulness of these contracts is evidenced by the growing trading success of futures contracts in British pounds, Canadian dollars, Japanese yen, Swiss francs, and West German marks.

The Chicago Board of Trade was next with a financial futures contract, introducing the Government National Mortgage Association (GNMA) contract in 1975. This contract was based on a government-guaranteed debt obligation. The GNMA had also been traded in a well-developed forward market and thus was a natural choice for a futures contract.

Logically, the next step in the development of financial futures was to offer a contract based on a financial instrument for which there was no forward market. The IMM took this step in 1976, when it introduced the Treasury bill futures contract. In 1977 the Chicago Board of Trade followed with the introduction of the Treasury bond futures contract. Both contracts have been highly successful, with the Treasury bond contract becoming the most actively traded futures contract in any market. In both cases these contracts trade a larger daily dollar value of commitments than does the underlying cash market. Curiously, a number of efforts at developing a Treasury note contract have not met with the same degree of success, although exchanges continue to experiment with different types of note contracts.

Quality Distinctions

One characteristic that all government security futures contracts have in common is the uniform and negligible credit risk of the underlying cash instrument. Government securities are differentiated by other characteristics, namely maturity and coupon (for issues of longer original maturity than one year). Indeed, in fulfillment of the obligation under the contract, the Treasury bond futures contract permits delivery of any U.S. Treasury bond with 20 years or more to maturity. To determine the invoice price of a deliverable security requires a simple mathematical transformation from the contract price to the invoice price of an eligible deliverable bond.

When several eligible deliverable securities differ in such characteristics as coupon and maturity, but not in quality, they are likely to be priced in a stable relationship to one another, a situation that is not likely to prevail when quality differences exist. Consequently, if the quality of deliverables were not standardized and controlled, the usefulness of the contracts in hedging, investing, and arbitraging applications would be seriously diminished, and such a contract would be unlikely to succeed.

This system of effecting deliveries has worked well, causing no unique problems or customer abuses. Interestingly, the London International Financial Futures Exchange (LIFFE) had among its first contracts a Eurodollar deposit contract that also settled in cash based on a quote derived by sampling prime Eurobanks.[9]

An Index of Prices of Heterogeneous Items

After the principle of cash delivery had been successfully established for the Eurodollar deposit contract, it could be applied to other contracts in which delivery of the physical instrument was impractical. The only prerequisite was that there exist a reliable widely disseminated and easily understood "price" on which to settle the contract price in order to conduct a delivery.

With the cash delivery issue resolved, the equity market was the logical next focus for a futures contract. Although equity indexes themselves had been published for some time and could have been used as the basis for futures contracts before Eurodollars, the progression from CD to Eurodollar and then to stock index futures was orderly and appeared to suit the regulatory community. Basing a contract on a deliverable bank liability, the CD, and then going to a nondeliverable bank liability, the Eurodeposit, in a sense made the regulatory step to stock index futures with cash delivery less precipitate than it would have been if stock indexes had come immediately after U.S. Treasury obligations contracts. In fact, the Kansas City Board of Trade had proposed its Value Line Stock Index Futures Contract before either the CD or Euro-deposit futures had been proposed, but the Value Line contract was placed in regulatory limbo, receiving serious consideration only after the CD and Euro-deposit contracts establishing the cash settlement arrangements had been approved.

It was logical to approve cash settlement in the Euro-deposit futures contract before considering stock index futures. Although Euro-deposit futures represented a departure from traditional contract design, stock index futures were a yet further departure since these contracts sanctioned the concept of averaging together the prices of related but dissimilar items. The items comprised by the indexes were all securities, but they differed widely as to quality.

The introduction of stock index futures required not only a resolution of the cash settlement issue but also a clarification of the regulatory environment. Commodity trading activity, including trading in financial fu-

---

[9] The United Kingdom also had to contend with laws that restricted the use of cash settlement contracts. In particular, there was a question as to the legal enforceability of a contract that settled in cash.

tures, is regulated by the CFTC, whereas equity trading is regulated by the Securities and Exchange Commission (SEC). Stock index futures contracts posed a jurisdictional issue since the underlying instrument was regulated by one agency and the derivative contract would presumably be regulated by a different agency. To further complicate matters, at about the same time consideration was also being given to trading options both on physical instruments other than individual equity issues (i.e., options on physicals) and on futures contracts (i.e., futures options). The SEC had been regulating equity options since their inception and was therefore a natural candidate to regulate the proposed new option contracts. Because of its responsibility for futures, however, the CFTC was the natural choice as the regulator of commodity options.

This potential regulatory dispute was rather amiably resolved by the chairmen of the two regulatory agencies, Philip Johnson (CFTC) and John Shad (SEC).[10] Under what has become known as the Johnson-Shad Agreement, the regulators decided that regulating futures contracts and options on futures, regardless of the underlying instrument, would be the responsibility of the CFTC, while the SEC would have jurisdiction over options on any security, including certificates of deposit, Treasury bills, bonds and notes, and groups or indexes of securities.[11] This agreement, which was publicly announced in December 1981, clarified the regulatory environment, so that the development of stock index futures contracts, commodity options, and options on physicals could proceed in an hospitable environment.

Stock Indexes

In designing stock index futures, there was no shortage of widely quoted, reliable and familiar indexes on which to base a contract. The Kansas City Board of Trade specified a contract having a size of $500 times the Value Line Index, a comprehensive geometric average of 1,683 stocks. The Chicago Mercantile Exchange established the value of its contract as equal to $500 times the Standard & Poor's 500 Composite Index, which is a value-weighted index. The New York Futures Exchange specified the value of its contract as $500 times the New York Stock Exchange Composite Index, which is a value-weighted index of over 1,500 NYSE-listed stocks. Basing the contracts on different indexes not only affects the size of the contracts, and consequently the required margin on each contract, but also their price volatility.

The most volatile contract and the largest contract in terms of value

---

[10] The regulation of stock index futures trading is discussed in Chapter 22.

[11] The one area of overlap in jurisdiction is options on foreign currencies.

is the Value Line Average Composite. In the middle, in terms of both volatility and size, is the S&P contract. The NYSE contract is the smallest, and it tends to be the least volatile. Thus, unlike CD and Euro-deposit contracts, where the differences in indexes have less to do with the composition of the indexes than with the date and time they are constructed, competing stock index contracts have more significant distinctions. One might expect that the more volatile the contract, the more it will appeal to floor traders, whereas the less volatile the contract, the more it will appeal to institutional users. However the early trading in these contracts offers little evidence in support of this conjecture.

Regardless of the relative volatility of a particular contract, stock index futures permit equity investors to effectively accomplish two objectives; they can buy the market, and they can hedge against market risk. Speculators in equities have had as one objective profiting from general price movement in the markets by buying a bullish market or selling a bearish one. Until the introduction of stock index futures, speculators could satisfy this objective only by dealing in stocks whose price movements were closely related to the general market. This strategy can be unsatisfactory, however, since the prices of individual stocks are continually being influenced by specific information that does not necessarily affect the entire market in the same way. There are mutual funds that comprise groups of stocks selected because their price behavior closely tracks an index of overall market movement. But mutual funds are not particularly well suited to speculation, largely because of their slowness in completing a transaction. Thus stock index futures provided a unique instrument for buying or selling the market.

The introduction of stock index futures contracts also presented hedgers with a unique opportunity. The concern of hedgers is in a sense the opposite of the concern of speculators, since instead of being interested in profiting from general moves in market prices, hedgers are interested in insulating portfolios or individual stocks from such moves. For example, suppose an equity portfolio manager anticipates a bearish period in the market that could erode the value of a fundamentally sound portfolio that the manager is unable or unwilling to sell. Stock index futures provide such a manager with the option of shorting the market. If the manager's expectations are correct, the profit on futures will compensate for the loss on the portfolio. Such a strategy is also applicable when a manager has a portfolio that is anticipated to outperform the market but that the manager would like to insulate from possible adverse market moves. In such a case, if the market does deteriorate, the gain in futures will compensate for the loss in portfolio value. These examples of hedger and speculator strategies are indications of the possible applications unique to stock index futures that in part explain their immediate success.

These basic applications suggest the logical direction of continued developments in stock index futures. Hedgers and speculators may have a narrower focus than the entire market; they may be interested in a subset of the market. Evidence that investor attention is frequently focused on segments of the market is suggested by the existence of a variety of subindexes constructed by the New York Stock Exchange and Standard & Poor's. Both the New York Futures Exchange and the International Monetary Market have proposed trading in several subindexes. In particular, the NYFE has proposed trading futures contracts based on NYSE indexes of industrials, transportation, and utility stocks, and in early November it initiated trading in a futures contract based on the NYSE financial index. Moreover, the NYSE is developing a subindex of energy stocks that could also be used as the basis for a futures contract. The IMM has proposed trading futures contracts based on the Standard & Poor's finance, utilities, and transportation indexes. Because of the potential for successful futures contracts, Standard & Poor's has agreed to develop three additional indexes based on stocks characterized as high technology, energy, and consumer staples.

The likelihood of success for these subindex futures contracts would be in part a function of their uniqueness. A subindex behaving in a distinct manner is more likely to trade successfully than is a contract based on an index closely correlated to other indexes for which contracts exist. In hedging, for example, using a contract based on a given instrument (for example, T bill futures) to hedge a different cash instrument (for example, banker's acceptances) is a well-established futures trading technique known as cross-hedging. The possibility of successful cross hedges with various subindex futures contracts diminishes the likelihood that they will all succeed. Speculative interest will similarly be determined by the uniqueness of the subindexes. Although not all subindex contracts will behave distinctively, there is probably a need for more than just a composite stock index contract. Certainly, at least some of the proposed subindex contracts should eventually establish themselves along with the composite index contracts.

Options on Futures

Another development in financial futures that is likely to have a direct effect on stock index futures is trading in commodity options, which was introduced in the fall of 1982. The CFTC in 1981 approved a limited pilot program authorizing each designated contract market to trade one option based on a futures contract, subject to CFTC approval. The fact that the IMM, NYFE, and Kansas City Board of Trade all proposed options on their stock index futures testifies to the dramatic early success of these futures.

Options on the cash instrument rather than the futures contract have also been proposed, subject to SEC authorization. Stock index options will also appear in this market. The New York Stock Exchange has proposed options on its composite index, its four subindexes, and its newly developed energy index. Both the American Stock Exchange and the Chicago Board Options Exchange also intend to trade stock index options based on their own constructed indexes.

Options on stock index futures and on the indexes themselves may attract to these markets participants who find options better suited to their needs than futures. Moreover, options on stock index futures contracts may serve to further attract participants in equity markets to futures markets. Option trading has become a firmly established adjunct to equity trading since it was introduced in the early 1970s. Equity traders who understand options but have shied away from futures because of a lack of experience with these instruments, may be attracted to this market by the introduction of options on stock indexes. What remains to be seen is which variant, options on cash contracts or options on futures contracts, will dominate. Each has apparent relative advantages and disadvantages, making it difficult to predict which will be successful or whether they can both generate a reasonable market.

One other development that has the potential to significantly affect financial futures trading generally is the increasing overseas involvement with financial futures. In some cases, commodity trading conducted outside the United States has been evolving in much the same way that such trading evolved in the United States. Starting with contracts based on indigenous agricultural products, there has been an evolution to financial instruments. This has been particularly the case in Australia and Canada. Moreover, new exchanges are being developed, notably the London International Financial Futures Exchange (LIFFE), which opened in 1982 offering only financial futures contracts. Similar financial futures exchanges are also in the planning stage for Singapore, Hong Kong, and Brazil.

With the advent of overseas trading in financial futures, trading in a futures contract beyond the closing time of one exchange becomes a very real possibility. The advantage of extended trading hours is that it enables a trader to lay off risk in another market if cash market prices move dramatically after a given exchange has closed. Cash market trading in certain instruments, particularly precious metals and foreign exchange, already goes on around the clock. Consequently, traders in one country can either cover their positions by taking offsetting positions in other countries or take advantage of rallies that gravitate from one time zone to another as markets close for the day. Moreover, a possible outgrowth of having more than one exchange offer the same or a similar contract is arbitrage trading opportunities. A primary example of such a trading possibility is the Eurodollar futures contract offered at the IMM and the LIFFE. Although their relative prices are affected by some differences in the contract, it is still possible to effectively arbitrage these contracts, and indeed a growing proportion of the volume in these contracts is the result of such trading.

The obvious products for trading in several countries are those for which active cash markets already exist. This is perhaps best exemplified by the gold market. Gold futures are currently offered on exchanges in New York, Chicago, London, Singapore, Hong Kong, and Tokyo, all of which have active cash markets trading gold both spot and forward. By contrast, although foreign exchange is a worldwide cash market, foreign exchange futures are not yet as widely offered. Since all of the above-mentioned locations are centers for foreign exchange trading, but only Chicago and London currently have exchange-traded futures contracts in foreign exchange, it seems likely that the futures market for foreign exchange contracts will expand. Another potential candidate for simultaneous trading in several countries is Euro-deposit contracts, which were first offered in the United States and are now also offered in London. The universality of the Eurodollar cash market makes it likely that other developing futures markets will also offer contracts based on this instrument.

Whether stock index futures contracts will attract sufficient interest to justify a market outside the United States is problematic. There is, however, active interest in U.S. equities outside the United States, and it is therefore conceivable that an overseas futures market in stock indexes will develop.

The Prognosis for Financial Futures

The probable development of futures markets has aspects of both widening and deepening participation—widening in the sense of additional trading vehicles and deepening in the sense of additional traders. Additional trading vehicles will be motivated by the same concern and objective that has motivated the development of every contract from the very first one offered at the Chicago Board of Trade in 1865: risk transfer. Commercial users, whether farmers, financial institutions, or corporations, have been well served by financial futures that have enabled them to transfer risk to willing speculators. This same objective has been behind the development of subindex contracts on stock index futures, and it will no doubt lead to a variety of other instruments.

The menu of financial futures contracts based on cash market debt instruments, both public and private, is large but not yet complete. There are still gaps at the middle and very short end of the maturity spectrum.

It is likely that additional contracts to fill these gaps will soon be added. Moreover, the full range of private-debt instruments has yet to be adequately covered with futures contracts, and developments in this direction are likely as well.

When cash settlement was accepted by the CFTC as an admissible method of delivery on a contract, the possibility of a whole new class of contracts was introduced. There are numerous measurable risks that could certainly be the basis for a contract but for which physical delivery would be either awkward or impossible. The stock index futures contract is a perfect example of a contract that would not have materialized without the cash settlement option. A number of other indexes representing measurable risks rather than physical commodities could also become the basis for futures contracts. Among the many candidates for such contracts are the Consumer Price Index, the prime rate, freight rate charges, and ocean shipping rates. The possibilities are extensive for contracts satisfying the objective of transferring quantifiable risks in combination with cash settlement based on a reliable, understandable index.

The deepening of the futures markets comes in part as a function of these products. Institutional investors for the most part watched the early development of financial futures from the sidelines. Institutional investors who had not previously been participants in futures markets were reluctant to become involved. The trading environment and the instruments themselves were alien to cash market traders. Over time, however, these markets gained acceptance as they grew in size and diversity. Government dealers were quick to incorporate financial futures on government obligations into their trading strategies. In turn, their customers, financial intermediaries, money managers, and financial managers generally have begun to rely increasingly on financial futures.

To a lesser degree nonfinancial corporations have begun to consider the futures markets. Although they control large portfolios and could quickly become a significant factor in the futures markets, their potential still remains unrealized. In a similar category are pension and trust managers who for the most part have made little use of futures. This has in part been a consequence of a restrictive regulatory environment. In 1982, however, some liberalization began to be noticed. A Department of Labor opinion letter eased up somewhat on the restrictions on using futures in ERISA portfolios. In addition, the New York State insurance commissioner also indicated a willingness to reexamine a long-standing prohibition against the use of futures by insurance companies.[12]

One final development worth mentioning, particularly as it applies to institutional investors, is the development of bank futures commission merchants (FCMs). In 1982 a number of banks and bank holding compa-

---

[12] Regulation of users of stock index futures trading is discussed in Chapter 20.

nies, including J. P. Morgan, Inc., North Carolina National Bank, Bankers Trust Corporation, and Citicorp, received authorization to act as FCMs. These emerging FCMs should not only provide competition for the existent futures customer base but also add to the investor population by bringing to the market investors who have been unable or unwilling to deal with traditional FCMs but will be comfortable dealing with bank FCMs. Moreover, bank FCMs, because of their substantial resources, should be able to attract institutional investors to the market by providing them with services not otherwise available.

In summary, the outlook seems bright for financial futures in general and for stock indexes in particular. The rapid annual growth rate of financial futures trading volume should continue and perhaps even accelerate as new contracts and new participants join these markets. In the midst of this active environment, it is clear that the rather remarkable early success of stock index futures is likely to be sustained.

CHAPTER 3

Comparative Guide to Stock Index Futures Contracts

R. Steven Wunsch
Vice President
Kidder, Peabody & Co., Inc.

This chapter reviews the major features differentiating the stock index futures contracts traded at the time of this writing—the Value Line Average Composite, the Standard & Poor's 500 Composite Index and the New York Stock Exchange Composite Index. The features compared include contract size, margin, leverage, and other contract and trading details. In the next chapter the mechanics of trading stock index futures are explained. Chapter 5 discusses the characteristics of the indexes underlying the futures contracts.

Whether used for hedging or speculative purposes, stock index futures contracts are different not only from traditional equity investment vehicles but also, in some respects, from other futures contracts. Stock index futures differ from equity investments primarily in their concept of margin, which leads to the greater leverage and risk common to all futures markets. The most significant practical difference between traditional commodity and interest rate futures contracts and stock index futures contracts is the substitution of cash settlement for the traditional delivery mechanism.

Stock Index Futures Contract

A stock index futures contract is an agreement to pay or receive $500 times the difference between the initial futures transaction price and (1) the offsetting futures transaction price, (2) the daily futures settlement price, or (3) the final settlement price of the underlying index on the day the contract expires. Positive differences are paid by sellers and received by buyers. Negative differences are paid by buyers and received by sellers. Stock index futures positions are marked-to-market and settled in cash daily. Contract specifications and trading information for the three stock index futures contracts traded at the time of this writing are summarized in Exhibits 3–1 through 3–3.

Exhibit 3–1

Standard & Poor's 500 Stock Index Futures Contract Summary*

Exchange: Chicago Mercantile Exchange.

Trading Hours: 9 A.M.–3:15 P.M. (Central time), 10 A.M.–4:15 P.M. (New York).

Contract Unit: The value of a contract will be $500 times the quoted futures price (at a futures price of 130.15, that would be $65,075).

Price Quotation: Futures prices are quoted on the same index basis as Standard & Poor's 500 Composite Index. The S&P 500 index is made up of 400 industrial, 40 public utilities, 20 transportation, and 40 financial companies. Stocks in the index are weighted according to their aggregate market value.

Minimum Price Change: 0.05 or $25 per contract unit ($500 × 0.05 = $25).

Daily Price Change Limit: None.

Delivery Months: March, June, September, and December. Four contracts will be trading at any given point in time, the most distant being nine months farther out than the nearby contract.

Contract Trading Termination: Trading in the expiring contract ends at the close of trading on the third Thursday of the contract month.

Cash Settlement: No delivery of or payment for stocks is called for. Positions held through the close of the final day of trading will be settled by cash transfer based on the final settlement price, just as they are settled using daily settlement prices on any other day on which a position is held.

Final Settlement Price: The final settlement price will be the closing S&P 500 composite index at the close on the last day of trading.

Margin Requirements
Speculative
Initial	$6,000
Maintenance	2,500

Hedge
Initial	2,500
Maintenance	1,500

Spread
Initial	400
Maintenance	200

* As of April 1983.

Exhibit 3–2

New York Stock Exchange Composite Index Futures Contract Summary*

Exchange: New York Futures Exchange.

Trading Hours: 10 A.M.–4.15 P.M. (New York).

Contract Unit: The value of a contract will be $500 times the quoted futures price (at a futures price of 64.50, that would be $32,250).

Price Quotation: Future prices are quoted in terms of the NYSE Composite Index. The index is a market-weighted average of the value of all common stock issues listed on the NYSE (approximately 1,500 issues).

Minimum Price Change: 0.05, or $25 per contract unit ($500 × 0.05 = $25).

Daily Price Change Limit: None.

Delivery Months: March, June, September, and December.

Contract Trading Termination: Trading in the expiring contract ends at 4:00 P.M. (New York) on the second to last business day of the contract month.

Cash Settlement: No delivery of or payment for stocks is called for. Positions held through the close of the final day of trading will be settled by cash transfer on the settlement day (the last business day of the month) based on the final settlement price, just as they are settled using daily settlement prices on any other day on which a position is held.

Final Settlement Price: The final settlement price will be the closing value of the New York Stock Exchange Composite Index on the last day of trading.

Margin Requirements

Speculative	
Initial	$3,500
Maintenance	1,500
Hedge	
Initial	1,500
Maintenance	750
Spread	
Initial	200
Maintenance	100

* As of April 1983.

Contract Value

The above definition implies that all stock index futures contracts have a value equal to their price times their specified dollar multiple. Therefore, each stock index futures contract is equivalent in value to $500 times the quoted futures price. For example, if the VLA future is 160, the value of the contract is $80,000 ($500 times 160).

Similarly, the final settlement value of a stock index futures contract is equal to $500 times the closing price of the actual index on the last day of trading. Each contract also covers the same March-June-September-December expiration month cycle, though stipulated settlement days

Exhibit 3–3

Value Line Average Stock Index Futures Contract Summary*

Exchange: Kansas City Board of Trade.

Trading Hours: 9 A.M.–3.15 P.M. (Central time), 10 A.M.–4:15 P.M. (New York).

Contract Unit: The value of a contract will be $500 times the quoted future price (at a futures price of 120.00, that would be $60,000).

Price Quotation: Future prices are quoted on the same index basis as the Value Line Average (VLA) composite stock index, an equally weighted geometric average of approximately 1,700 actively traded stocks.

Minimum Price Change: 0.01, or $5 per contract unit ($500 × 0.01 = $5). Generally, however, trading takes place in increments of 0.05, or $25.

Daily Price Change Limit: None

Delivery Months: March, June, September, and December. Six contracts will be trading at any given point in time, the most distant being 15 months farther out than the nearby contract.

Contract Trading Termination: Trading in the expiring contract ends at 3:10 P.M. (Central) on the last business day of the contract month.

Cash Settlement: No delivery of or payment for stocks is called for. Positions held through the close of the final day of trading will be settled by cash transfer based on the final settlement price, just as they are settled using daily settlement prices on any other day on which a position is held.

Final Settlement Price: The final settlement price will be the closing VLA composite index on final settlement day.

Margin Requirements

Speculative	
Initial	$6,500
Maintenance	2,000
Hedge	
Initial	3,250
Maintenance	1,625
Spread	
Initial	400
Maintenance	200

* As of April 1983.

within those months vary.[1] Thus, at the close of trading on June 29, 1984, the June '84 contract will cease trading and its final settlement price will be equal to $500 times the closing value of the actual VLA Composite Index.

---

[1] The last day of trading is somewhat arbitrarily determined by the exchange. It should be noted that the settlement data has implications for arbitrage and intermarket spreading due to different holding periods for each contract. (See Chapter 16, where this point is addressed as a risk in certain intermarket spreads.)

Minimum Price Change

For each contract, a minimum price change is specified by the exchange. For each stock index futures contract the minimum price change or "tick" is 0.05.

A one-point movement (1.00) in the price of the future means a gain or loss equivalent to the dollar multiple specified in the contract. For example, a one-point change is equal to a gain or loss of $500 per contract. Therefore, the minimum price change or "tick" is worth $25 (0.05 times $500) per contract.

Although futures exchanges may impose daily maximum price change limits, none are currently doing so for stock index futures (or stock index futures options). Limits did exist for S&P 500 and VLA Composite Index contracts through late 1982.

Margin Requirements

Both futures markets and stock markets share the concept of required *initial* and *maintenance* margin levels. Initial margin is the minimum amount of investor equity in an account required to initiate a position. Maintenance margin is the minimum level to which an investor's account equity may fall as a result of adverse market action before he receives a margin call. Beyond this similarity the concept of margin in futures and stock markets diverges in several significant respects.

To begin with, when stocks are purchased on margin, the investor puts up only part of the purchase price and the balance is borrowed from the broker, with the stock serving as collateral for the loan. Interest is charged on the amount borrowed. Futures transactions, in contrast, are not purchases or sales. In the case of traditional futures contracts that are settled at expiration by delivery, they are agreements to purchase or sell in the future. In the case of stock index futures that are settled at expiration in cash (see below under "Cash Settlement"), they are agreements to pay or receive the difference in price in accordance with our definition earlier in this chapter. Therefore, margins on futures contracts do not function as "down payments" and money need not be borrowed or interest paid to complete a futures transaction. Futures margins are, in effect, "good faith" money indicating that contractual obligations under the terms of delivery or cash settlement will be honored.

Second, when an investor's equity in a stock account falls below the maintenance level, he will receive a margin call for sufficient funds to bring the account equity up to the maintenance level. In contrast, when the investor's equity in a futures account falls below the maintenance level, he will receive a margin call for sufficient funds to bring the account equity all the way up to the initial margin level.

Third, the exchange on which a futures contract trades is responsible for setting that contract's minimum initial and maintenance margin requirements, whereas the Federal Reserve Board establishes those requirements for stock positions.[2] Although brokerage firms are free to charge their customers higher than required minimum margins for both stock and futures positions, this is generally not done for stock index futures or stocks.

Fourth, the futures exchanges set minimum margin levels at fixed dollar amounts (which may be changed, however, at an exchange's discretion). Currently, initial speculative margin requirements have been set at $6,500, $6,000, $3,500 for VLA, S&P 500, and NYSE Composite contracts, respectively. Although the margin levels were initially intended to be about 10 percent of contract value, the market's rise since the margin levels were established has resulted in margin levels of about 7 percent of contract value. Maintenance speculative margin levels are less than half of initial margin levels: $2,000, $2,500, and $1,500 for VLA, S&P 500, and NYSE Composite contracts, respectively.

In contrast to the fixed dollar amount of futures margins, the current minimum initial and maintenance margin requirements for stock positions have been set at 50 percent and 25 percent, respectively, by the Federal Reserve Board. Since the required minimum investor equity for holding stock positions is about five times greater than the required minimum for holding futures positions, the leverage and risk of futures positions are about five times greater than the maximum allowable leverage and risk of stock positions—a point to which we shall return.

As mentioned earlier, futures account positions are marked-to-market daily according to closing prices. Because margin must be maintained at specified levels, adverse price movement will require additional margin to be posted, while excess margin resulting from favorable price movement may be withdrawn.

Minimum initial margin and minimum maintenance margin are different for hedgers, speculators, and spreaders. Hedge margins are set lower than speculative margins, primarily because there is less risk in a hedged position than in a speculative position, as will be explained below. To qualify for hedge margin requirements, an investor must own or expect to own a position of underlying value equivalent to that of the futures contracts in which he holds an opposite position. In the case of stock index futures, this means owning or expecting to own a diversified equity portfolio. For example, an investor who owns $635,000 worth of stocks would qualify for hedge margins if he sold short $635,000 worth of futures

---

[2] Only stocks listed on an exchange and regulated over-the-counter stocks may be purchased on margin. Other over-the-counter stock may not be purchased on margin.

contracts. An investor who expects to own a $635,000 diversified portfolio would qualify for hedge margins if he bought $635,000 worth of futures contracts. Since it is difficult to determine the legitimacy of such a claimed "anticipatory hedge," many brokerage firms will automatically classify individuals as speculators to be on the safe side, unless such individuals can make a very good case for hedge designation. Institutions, however, generally have an easier time justifying hedge designation. The margin for hedgers is granted at the discretion of the brokerage firm. Spread margins are the lowest. Spreaders are explained in Chapter 16.

Exhibit 3–1 shows the minimum initial maintenance margins for hedgers, speculators, and spreaders for each contract traded. In the next chapter the different types of margin will be illustrated and the mark-to-market procedure will be explained. Here we will discuss the impact of margin on risk.

To see the leverage created by futures margin, consider the minimum initial margin requirements on VLA futures of $6,500 per contract for speculative positions. At a futures price of 160, for example, this margin requirement is only 8 percent of the value of the contract (160 × $500 = $80,000 contract value; $6,500 ÷ 80,000 is 8.125 percent). Assuming a 50 percent margin requirement for stock market purchases or short sales, the $6,500 speculative margin means that the leverage of a position in VLA futures is more than five times as great as the maximum allowable leverage in stock market positions.

The high degree of leverage characteristics of all futures markets is an essential component of their efficient operation. Such leverage enables both hedgers and speculators (risk reducers and risk assumers) to carry substantial positions when measured in terms of the underlying commodity, interest rate, or stock index while tying up relatively small amounts of capital in margin deposits. Without this feature hedgers might find risk reduction too expensive, while speculators might be unable to trade sufficient volume measured in terms of the underlying commodity, interest rate, or stock index to take the other side of hedgers' trades. *However, the greater leverage of futures markets implies greater risk as well. Not only is it possible for the speculator or hedger to lose his entire margin deposit, but his risk of loss is in no way limited to the amount of his margin deposit.*

Although the risk associated with leverage is substantial, it is worth noting that, compared with margins for commodity and interest rate futures, margins for stock index futures are higher and thus more conservative relative to the volatility of the underlying commodity or debt instrument.[3] For example, the VLA has never moved as much as eight

---

[3] In the political process of getting stock index futures contracts approved by the Commodities Futures Trading Commission, the exchanges agreed to make the initial margins higher for these futures contracts than for other futures contracts. This concession was due to Fed pressure. For Treasury bill futures, for example, the initial margin is $2,500 for $1 million of face value.

points in a single day and has registered single-day changes of more than four points only about five times between 1973 and 1981. In contrast, many commodity margin requirements are set so low that it is not uncommon to lose or double an initial margin deposit in one day.

It is important for the speculator who seeks the maximum leverage per margin dollar and the hedger who seeks to reduce risk at the lowest possible cost to look not just at the dollar margins required but at the margin as a percentage of contract value. This is discussed in Chapter 15. However, speculators and hedgers will also look at other characteristics of the underlying index in deciding which stock index futures contract to use. These considerations are discussed in Chapter 4.

Cash Settlement

The movement of futures contract prices in commodity markets has traditionally conformed closely to price movements in the underlying "cash" commodity because the futures contracts call for actual delivery of some fixed amount of the cash commodity when the contracts expire. As delivery approaches, therefore, the cash and futures prices must converge. Although only a very small percentage of positions are actually held to delivery, any significant difference between cash and futures prices results in arbitrage activity that moves prices back into line. Those engaging in such arbitrage are generally the commercial users of the markets—persons who are financially and, in the case of commodities that require warehousing facilities, physically capable of making and taking delivery of the large quantities of the underlying commodities or financial instruments stipulated in the contracts. Most speculators, in contrast, close out positions well in advance of delivery because they usually do not have the resources necessary to participate in delivery.

Futures contracts on stock indexes function much like other commodity contracts with one important exception: no delivery of or payment for actual stocks (the cash commodity) is called for at any time. Instead, convergence of cash and futures prices at expiration is accomplished simply by settling the price of an expiring futures contract on the last day of trading at the closing level of the actual underlying index. This system is called "cash settlement" because cash is transferred into or out of a customer's margin account on the basis of that final settlement price. The procedure is no different from the daily cash settlements that occur when customers' margin accounts are debited or credited according to daily settlement prices used to mark customers' positions to market. From the point of view of the hedger or speculator holding a position in stock index futures, the only significant difference between final cash settlement and the cash settlement that occurs on any other day on which a position is held is that, after final settlement, the investor no longer holds a position.

This straightforward cash settlement system has several advantages over the traditional delivery procedures for commodity futures contracts. First, there is no two-tiered class of participation, with those who are physically and financially capable of making and taking delivery seeming to have an advantage over those who are not, particularly as delivery time nears. Second, because those holding short positions do not have to purchase the cash commodity (stocks) to make delivery, the possibility of a "short squeeze" is eliminated. Third, convergence of the basis (the difference between the spot price and the futures price) to zero must, by definition, occur when the final settlement price equals the underlying index, regardless of the number of bids or offers in the pit at the time. These features of cash settlement will bring some relief to many commodity market participants who may heretofore have felt pressed to take premature action by an approaching delivery.

Trading Hours

All stock index futures and futures options close 15 minutes after the 4:15 P.M. (New York) close of the New York Stock Exchange. This closing time was originally intended to capture the excitement of the few minutes after the 4:10 money supply release on Friday. However, the Federal Reserve foiled this effort by delaying that release until 4:15.

Although some traders have thought that futures movement between 4 and 4:15 would prove a reliable leading or contrary indicator of the next morning's stock opening, there is no statistically reliable evidence at this time to support either case. For what it is worth, during a 241-day period the stock market opening was in the same direction as the last 15 minutes' futures change 79 times and in the opposite direction 153 times.

CHAPTER 4

Mechanics of Stock Index Futures Trading

Frank J. Fabozzi, Ph.D., C.F.A.
Professor of Economics
Fordham University

This chapter will discuss the mechanics of stock index futures trading. An understanding of these mechanics is absolutely essential if one intends to employ these contracts in an investment strategy.

Selecting a Brokerage Firm and a Broker

The first step after deciding to use stock index futures contracts is to select the organization that will execute the transactions. All brokers executing futures transactions for the public, known as futures commission merchants, must register with the Commodity Futures Exchange Commission. A commodity futures merchant need not be a member of a futures exchange. Some organizations deal exclusively in future transactions. Other organizations handle securities transactions as well as futures transactions.

The selection of a broker depends on what the investor wants from the relationship. Just as with securities trading, some organizations provide research information and supporting services as well as execution, while others provide only the execution function. Because the latter organizations, often called "discount brokers," offer "no frills," they generally charge lower commissions. Commission costs are discussed later in this chapter.

The investor who wants research information and other assistance should examine the line of services provided by the organization under consideration. As in any service industry, the quality of the services rendered varies and is often difficult to measure. One brokerage firm may provide a particular service that is better than the service provided by another firm but may fall short in different types of service.

A consideration directly related to transaction costs is the margin requirements established by the organization. As explained in the previous chapter, although the exchange establishes the minimum initial and maintenance margin requirements, brokerage firms are free to set their own minimum as long as it is not less than that set by the exchange. Although competition keeps the minimum margin requirements from varying substantially from firm to firm, the investor should compare the margin requirements established by the brokerage firms that he or she is considering to execute transactions.

The selection of an account representative at the brokerage firm is an even more important consideration if the investor intends to rely on the account representative's recommendations. Inquiry into the background and performance of the account representative should be made by the investor. The account representative should be registered with the CFTC and should have successfully completed the National Commodity Representatives Examination. This inquiry should be undertaken even if the investor selected a particular account representative based on a recommendation made by a friend or relative. The account representative should fully understand the investor's trading philosophy.

Types of Orders

When an investor wishes to buy or sell a futures contract, the price and conditions under which the order is to be executed must be communicated to the account representative.

The simplest type of order, yet the most dangerous from the investor's perspective, is the *market order*. When a market order is placed, it is executed at the best price available as soon as it reaches the trading pit.[1] Market orders are fine for security trades because security prices usually do not fluctuate substantially between the time the investor decides to trade and the time the order reaches the trading floor. Over 75 percent of stock transactions are placed as market orders. However, stock index futures prices jump around a great deal during short intervals of time. Coupled with the higher leverage associated with stock index futures, an adverse movement of just a few ticks between the time the investor

---

[1] The trading pit is the trading area on the floor of a futures exchange where all transactions for a specific contract are made.

decides to transact based on prevailing market prices and the time the order reaches the trading pit could make the difference between a successful strategy and a disastrous one.

To avoid the dangers associated with market orders, the investor can place a *limit order*. With a limit order the investor may designate a price limit for the execution of the transaction. A buy limit order indicates that the futures contract may be purchased only at the price designated or at a lower price. A sell limit order indicates that the futures contract may be sold at the price designated or at a higher price.

The danger with a limit order is that there is no assurance that it will be executed. The designated price may not be reached. Even if it is reached at a later time, the order may not be fulfilled because there is no one on a futures exchange to assure the role of the specialist on a stock exchange, who keeps a book on unfilled limit orders and executes them when the designated price is reached. Nevertheless, the dangers of a limit order are far less than the dangers of a market order. The investor can exert greater control with a limit order than with a market order because he or she can always revise the price designated in the limit order based on prevailing market prices.

The limit order is a conditional order: it is executed only if the limit price or a better price can be obtained. Another type of conditional order is the *stop order*. A stop order specifies that a transaction is not to be executed until the market price reaches a designated price at which point it becomes a market order. A buy stop order specifies that the order is not to be executed until the market price rises to a designated price. A sell stop order specifies that the order is not to be executed until the market price falls below a designated price.

A stop order can be employed by an investor to protect a profit or to limit a loss. To understand how a stop order can be used and how it differs from a limit order, consider the following examples. Suppose that an investor purchased an S&P 500 futures contract for 126 and that the futures price is now 139. The investor wants to protect the paper profit. To do so, the investor could place a sell stop order at, say, 132. This means that when the futures price falls to 132 or lower, the futures contract is to be sold at the best price possible. To see how an investor can use a sell stop order to limit a loss, suppose that the investor purchased a NYSE Composite Index futures contract for 80 and that the position was taken in the expectation that the futures price would increase. To limit the loss should the futures price decline instead, the investor could place a sell stop order at, say, 75.

The two examples of a sell stop order show how it can be used by an investor in a long position. An investor in a short position can utilize a buy stop order to protect a paper profit or limit a loss.

Notice that in a sell stop order the designated price is less than the current market price of the futures contract. In a sell limit order, however, the designated price is above the market price of the futures contract. In a buy stop order the designated price is above the market price. In a buy limit order it is below the market price.

There are two dangers associated with stop orders. First, since the stock index futures market exhibits abrupt price changes, it is possible that the direction of the change in the futures price may be only temporary, resulting in the premature closing of a position. Second, once the designated price is reached, the stop order becomes a market order and is subject to the uncertainty of the execution price noted earlier for market orders.

A *stop-limit order,* a hybrid of a stop order and a limit order, is a stop order that designates a price limit. For example, in our example of the S&P 500 futures contract that was purchased at 126 and is now priced at 139, the investor can place a sell stop-limit order that goes into effect at a futures price of 132 and has a limit price of 129. The stop-limit order has the same potential problem as the one we noted for a limit order. That is, the limit price may never be reached and therefore the order will not be executed. This defeats the purpose of the stop order, which is to protect a paper profit or limit a loss.

Spreaders are interested, not in the price of a futures contract, but in the difference between the prices of two contracts. A spreader can place an order that is to be executed when two designated stock index futures contracts differ in price by at least a designated amount.

Conditional orders such as the limit order or the buy order must designate the time period for which the order is effective. The order may be designated as good for a day, week, or month. An *open order,* on the other hand, is good until the order is canceled.

Taking and Liquidating a Position

Once an account has been opened, the trader may take a position in the market. If the trader does this by buying a futures contract, the trader is said to be in a *long position.* If, instead, the trader's opening position is the sale of a futures contract, the trader is said to be in a *short position.*

The trader can liquidate a position in one of two ways. One way is to liquidate a position prior to the final settlement date. To do this, the trader must take an offsetting position. For a long position, this means selling an identical number of contracts; for a short position, it means buying an identical number of contracts. The other way is to wait until the final settlement date. At that time the trader liquidates his or her position by cash settlement.

The broker is required to provide confirmation of the execution of an order as soon as possible. The confirmation form that is filled out when a position is taken indicates all the essential information about the trade. When the order involves the liquidation of a position, the confirmation form shows the profit and loss on the position and the commission costs.

It is not uncommon to purchase a security through one brokerage firm and sell it through another. However, this is usually not done with futures contracts. The brokerage firm that executes the order to establish the initial position also executes the order to liquidate the position.

When a trader takes a position in the market, another party is taking the opposite position and agreeing to satisfy the commitment set forth in the contract. But what if that party defaults on the obligation? Is the trader's only recourse to sue the defaulting party? If so, does that mean a trader must be concerned with who the other party is before taking a position in the futures market? Moreover, if the trader wants to liquidate a position before the final settlement date, must the trader do so only with that party?

The answer to those questions is that the trader need not worry about the financial strength and integrity of the other party to the contract. Once the order is executed, the direct relationship between the two parties is severed. A *clearing corporation* associated with each exchange interposes itself as the buyer to every sale and the seller to every purchase. Thus each of the parties to the contract is free to liquidate his position without being concerned about the other party.

Margin Requirement

In the previous chapter the various margin requirements for trading stock index futures contracts were explained. These margin requirements will now be illustrated.

Suppose that Trader X purchased four S&P 500 contracts on Day 1 for 140. If Trader X is a speculator, the minimum initial margin requirement for this contract is $6,000 per contract, or $24,000 for four contracts.[2] If the brokerage firm that Trader X is using for this transaction does not have a higher initial margin requirement, then Trader X must deposit $24,000 in cash or its equivalent. We will assume that Trader X deposits $24,000 in cash but will return later to alternative deposits that Trader X could make. The maintenance margin for this transaction, assuming that the brokerage firm does not require a higher one than that specified by the IMM, is $10,000, since the maintenance margin for each contract is $2,500.

---

[2] See Exhibit 3–1 of the previous chapter.

Exhibit 4–1 presents the assumed settlement price of the S&P 500 futures contract and the value of four contracts for eight trading days following the purchase of the contracts by Trader X. Let us examine each trading day following Day 1. Trader X's account for each trading day is summarized in Exhibit 4–2.

Day 2 The futures price increased from 140 to 144, resulting in a gain of $8,000. The increase in the contract value is added to the equity in Trader X's account. This is what is meant by "marked-to-market." The equity in Trader X's account is the initial margin plus the $8,000 gain. The equity in excess of the initial margin requirement is $8,000. *Trader X may withdraw the $8,000 from the account.*

If Trader X withdraws the entire excess of $8,000 in Day 2 and on Day 3 the equity in the account falls below $24,000, the initial margin requirement, there will be no margin call as long as the equity is at least $10,000, the minimum maintenance margin requirement. This will reduce the amount of funds tied up by the trader from $24,000 to $20,000.

Day 3 Although the futures price is higher than it was when Trader X purchased the contracts, it closed lower than on the previous trading day. Trader X lost $4,000 from the previous trading day's settlement

Exhibit 4–1

Assumed Futures Price and Value of Four Contracts for Margin Requirement Illustration

Day 1: Trade price = 140
Value of four contracts
  = 140 × $500 × 4
  = $280,000

Trading days 2 through 9:

Day	Settlement Price	Value of Four Contracts
2	144	$288,000
3	142	284,000
4	137	274,000
5	138	276,000
6	133	266,000
7	130	260,000
8	128	256,000
9	134	268,000

Note: The contract value is $500 times the futures price. Since there are four contracts, the per contract value is multiplied by 4.

Exhibit 4–2

Margin Requirements and Account Equity for the Purchase of Four S&P 500 Contracts

Initial margin per S&P 500 contract = $6,000.
Initial margin for four S&P 500 contracts = $24,000 (4 × $6,000).

Maintenance margin per S&P 500 contract = $2,500.
Maintenance margin for four S&P 500 contracts = $10,000.

Day	Settlement Price	Value of Four Contracts	Mark-to-Market	Equity in Account	Equity in Excess of Initial Margin	Variation Margin
1	140	$280,000	—	$24,000	—	—
2	144	288,000	$ 8,000	32,000	$ 8,000	—
3	142	284,000	−4,000	28,000	4,000	—
4	137	274,000	−10,000	18,000	−6,000	—
5	138	276,000	2,000	20,000	−4,000	—
6	133	266,000	−10,000	10,000	−14,000	—
7	130	260,000	−6,000	4,000	−20,000	$20,000
8	128	256,000	−4,000	20,000	−4,000	—
9	134	268,000	12,000	32,000	8,000	—

price. The equity in Trader X's account declined from $32,000 to $28,000. The equity in excess of the initial margin is now $4,000 if Trader X did not withdraw any cash from the account in Day 2. Now $4,000 may be withdrawn from the account.

Day 4 The futures price closed below the purchase price on this trading day. The result is a loss of $6,000 from the purchase price and a further decrease in the equity in the account from that of the previous trading day. The $10,000 loss on this trading day reduced the equity to $18,000, assuming that no withdrawals of cash were made at the close of the two previous trading days. Although the equity in the account declined to a value that is less than the initial margin of $24,000, it is not less than the $10,000 maintenance margin. Hence there is no margin call.

Day 5 The increase in the settlement price from 137 to 138 added $2,000 to the equity account. Since the equity in the account is still greater than the maintenance margin required, no margin call is required.

Day 6 The decline in the futures price to 133 reduced the equity in the account to $10,000. The equity is now equal to the maintenance margin requirement. Any further decline in the settlement price will result in a margin call.

Day 7 The settlement price of the futures contract fell to 130. The loss of $6,000 from the previous day's settlement price reduced the equity to $4,000. This is less than the maintenance margin requirement of $10,000. Consequently, there is a margin call to bring the equity in the account up to the *initial margin* of $24,000. This means that Trader X must deposit an additional $20,000 or its equivalent.

If Trader X fails to do so, the contracts will be sold and Trader X will realize a loss of $20,000 ($280,000 − $260,000). Since Trader X deposited $24,000, $4,000, the amount of equity in the account at the close of Day 7, is available to Trader X.

Let us assume that Trader X deposits $20,000 into the account. The $20,000 is the *variation margin*. Note how the amount of the margin call differs for stock index futures compared to stocks purchased on margin. In the latter case the amount of the call margin would be the amount necessary to bring the equity into the account up to the *maintenance margin*, not the initial margin.

To avoid bringing the equity up to the initial maintenance margin, a trader could *voluntarily* deposit funds if he or she anticipates that the equity will fall below the maintenance margin. For example, if Trader X had deposited $6,000 in the account on Day 7, the equity in the account on Day 8 would have been $10,000. Hence, there would not have been a margin call of $20,000.

Day 8   After the $20,000 variation margin was deposited, the settlement price declined further, to 128. This reduces the equity in the account

Exhibit 4–3

Margin Requirements and Account Equity for the Sale of Four S&P 500 Contracts

Initial margin per S&P 500 contract = $6,000.
Initial margin for four S&P 500 contracts = $24,000 (4 × $6,000).

Maintenance margin per S&P 500 contract = $2,500.
Maintenance margin for four S&P 500 contracts = $10,000.

Day	Settlement Price	Value of Four Contracts	Mark-to-Market	Equity in Account	Equity in Excess of Initial Margin	Variation Margin
1	140	$280,000	—	$24,000	—	—
2	144	288,000	−$ 8,000	16,000	−$ 8,000	—
3	142	284,000	4,000	20,000	−4,000	—
4	137	274,000	10,000	30,000	6,000	—
5	138	276,000	−2,000	28,000	4,000	—
6	133	266,000	10,000	38,000	14,000	—
7	130	260,000	6,000	44,000	20,000	—
8	128	256,000	4,000	48,000	24,000	—
9	134	268,000	−12,000	36,000	12,000	—

by $4,000, to $20,000. Since the equity in the account is greater than the $10,000 maintenance requirement, there is no margin call.

Day 9   The settlement price increased to 134, increasing the equity in the account to $32,000. Since the equity in the account is $8,000 greater than the initial margin, Trader X may withdraw the excess.

The foregoing illustrated the purchase of a stock index futures contract. Exhibit 4–3 shows what would happen if four S&P 500 contracts were sold rather than purchased. Notice that the excess equity in the account is the opposite of that shown in Exhibit 4–2. In this illustration there would be no variation margin. *However, a trader must always make provision for the possibility of variation margin, lest he or she be forced to close a position at an inopportune time.*

In our illustration we have assumed that Trader X deposited cash to meet the initial and variation margins. As an alternative, Treasury bills or letters of credit may be used for initial margin. Variation margin must be satisfied with cash.

Commissions

Like the commissions on common stock transactions, the commissions on executions of stock index futures contracts are fully negotiable. The commissions charged on stock index futures contracts are based on a round trip. For individual traders, these commissions range from $40 per contract to $100 at full service brokerage firms. For institutional traders, the typical commission per contract is under $40.

Assuming a round-trip commission of $50 per contract, the cost of transacting is typically less than 0.1 percent (0.001) of the contract value. A round-trip commission for a portfolio consisting of the underlying stocks would be roughly 1 percent of the value of the stocks.

CHAPTER 5

Stock Market Indicators

Frank J. Fabozzi, Ph.D., C.F.A.
Professor of Economics
Fordham University

Jonathan C. Jankus
Vice President
Kidder, Peabody & Co., Inc.

Stock market averages and indexes have come to perform a variety of functions, from serving as benchmarks for sophisticated performance analyses to answering the question "How did the market do today?" Thus the averages and indexes have become a part of everyday life for the investment practitioner. Even though many of the market indicators are used interchangeably, each measures a quite different facet of the "market." Understanding the differences is essential for investors who contemplate the use of futures contracts based on these indicators.

The success of hedging strategies that employ stock index futures contracts will depend to some extent on the nature of the average or index. Therefore, in this chapter we will explain the nature of the various averages and indexes on which major futures contracts are currently traded—the New York Stock Exchange (NYSE) Composite Index, the Standard & Poor's (S&P) 500 Composite Index, and the Value Line Average Composite (VLA). We also discuss the Dow Jones Industrial Average, the American Stock Exchange Market Value Index, the NASDAQ Composite Index, and the Wilshire 5000 Equity Index. Although a survey of pension fund managers taken by the *Institutional Investor* in September 1982 found that only 4.4 percent of the respondents would be interested in using stock index futures contracts based on the Dow Jones Industrial Average, it is discussed in detail because it has been studied extensively and because it allows us to illustrate how different approaches to constructing an index or average affect its performance.[1]

Construction of Stock Market Averages and Indexes

In general, the indicators rise and fall in unison. There are, however, important differences in the magnitude of these moves. To understand the reasons for these differences, it is necessary to understand how indicators are constructed.

Three factors differentiate stock market averages and indexes:

1. The universe of stocks represented by the indicator.
2. The relative weights given to the stocks.
3. The method of averaging used.

Each of these factors is discussed below.

The Universe of Stocks Represented

An index or average can be designed from all publicly traded stocks or from a sample of publicly traded stocks. No index or average currently traded is based on all publicly traded stocks. For the three contracts currently traded, the NYSE Composite Index consists of about 1,520 stocks, the S&P 500 consists of 500 stocks, and the VLA consists of about 1,700 stocks. The breadth of coverage differs for each market indicator. The NYSE Composite Index, first computed in 1966, reflects the market value of all issues traded on the NYSE. Table 5–1 presents summary information on the composition of the stocks in this index.

The indicator series computed by Standard & Poor's represents selected samples of stocks chosen from both the major exchanges—NYSE and the American Stock Exchange (AMEX)—and the over-the-counter market. The universe represented is determined by a committee, which may occasionally add or delete individual stocks or entire industry groups from the universe. The aim of the committee is to capture present overall stock market conditions representing a very broad range of economic indicators. Table 5–1 compares the composition of this index with that of three other broad market indexes.

The VLA, produced by Arnold Bernhard & Co., covers a broad range of widely held and traded issues selected by Value Line. Table 5–1 gives

---

[1] "Wary About Stock Futures: Stock-Index Futures May Catch Fire, but Pension Officers Aren't Sold Yet," *Institutional Investor*, September 1982, p. 117.

Table 5–1

Composition of Indexes (percentage weighting) as of September
1982

	S&P 500	NYSE	Value Line	Wilshire 5000
Consumer non-durables	28%	26%	29%	25%
Consumer durables	3	3	6	3
Materials and services	10	11	20	11
Raw materials	5	5	9	5
Technology	14	12	10	12
Energy	19	18	8	17
Transportation	2	3	5	3
Utilities	13	15	11	13
Finance	6	7	2	10

Source: Wilshire Associates.

summary information about the composition of the stocks in this market
indicator.

There are other market indicators of which the reader should be aware.
The most commonly quoted indicator, the Dow Jones Industrial Average
(DJIA), monitors 30 of the largest blue-chip companies traded on the
NYSE. Table 5–2 shows the companies included in the DJIA. These companies change over time as companies are dropped due to mergers, bank-
ruptcy, or a very low level of trading activity.[2] When a company is replaced
by another company, the average is readjusted in such a way as to provide
comparability with earlier values. We will have more to say about the
adjustment process later in this chapter.

The American Stock Exchange Market Value Index, introduced in September 1973, reflects the market value of all issues traded on that exchange.
This index generally includes companies with smaller capitalization than
the universe of companies traded on the NYSE and has a proportionally
greater foreign and energy-related orientation.

The NASDAQ Composite Index, introduced in February 1971, reflects
changes in the market value of the over-the-counter stocks traded by
the National Association of Securities Dealers (NASD). The NASDAQ
Composite Index represents companies with much smaller capitalization
than that of the companies represented by the two exchange indexes
and has proportionally greater representation of banks and insurance companies.

---

[2] When the DJIA was originally published, in 1897, it was based on 12 stocks. Eight
stocks were added in 1916, and in October 1928 the DJIA was expanded to 30 stocks. Of
the original 12 stocks comprised by the DJIA, only two are now included—American Brands
(formerly American Tobacco) and General Electric. Of the 30 companies in the DJIA in
1928, when the sample was expanded to its present size, only 15 are now included.

Table 5–2

The 30 Stocks in the Dow Jones Industrial Average (as of September 1983)

Allied Corporation	International Business Machines Corp.
Aluminum Co. of America	International Harvester Co.
American Brands, Inc.	International Paper Co.
American Can Company	Merck & Co., Inc.
American Express Company	Minnesota Mining & Manufacturing Co.
American Telephone & Telegraph Company	Owens-Illinois, Inc.
Bethlehem Steel Corp.	The Procter & Gamble Co.
Du Pont	Sears Roebuck & Co.
Eastman Kodak Co.	Standard Oil Co. of California
Exxon Corporation	Texaco Inc.
General Electric Co.	Union Carbide Corp.
General Foods Corp.	United States Steel Corporation
General Motors Corporation	United Technologies Corp.
The Goodyear Tire & Rubber Company	Westinghouse Electric Corporation
Inco	F. W. Woolworth Co.

The Wilshire 5000 Equity Index, created in 1974, is a comprehensive index that represents all actively traded companies. The index is published daily by Wilshire Associates of Santa Monica, California. Approximately 31 percent of the pension officers surveyed by the *Institutional Investor* indicated that they would be interested in a stock index based on the Wilshire 5000. Table 5–1 compares the industry distribution of the firms in the Wilshire 5000 index as of September, 1982, to that of the three comprehensive indexes that are currently the basis of futures contracts.

Relative Weights

The stocks comprised by an indicator must be combined to construct the index or average. Each stock, therefore, must be assigned some relative weight. There are three ways in which weights can be assigned: (1) weighting by the market value of the company, (2) weighting by the price of the company's stock, and (3) weighting each company equally, regardless of its price or value.

With the exception of the VLA, the currently traded market indicators are market value–weighted. The American Stock Exchange Market Value Index, the NASDAQ Composite Index, and the Wilshire 5000 Equity Index are also market value–weighted.[3] The VLA is an equally weighted index. The DJIA is a price-weighted indicator.

Each of these relative weighting schemes will be illustrated later in this chapter.

---

[3] The Wilshire 5000 Equity Index is computed on a daily basis based on market value weights. Wilshire Associates also publishes an equally weighted index on a monthly basis.

Method of Averaging

Given the stocks that will be used to create the sample and the relative weights to be assigned to each stock, it is then necessary to average the individual components. Two methods of averaging are possible—arithmetic and geometric. With the exception of the VLA, all of the market indicators discussed in this chapter are based on an arithmetic mean.

Although the computation of an index based on the geometric averaging technique will be demonstrated in the next section, a brief discussion of the mathematical properties of the geometric mean is appropriate. The arithmetic mean of multiple returns will always be greater than their geometric mean. Consequently, as long as there is any variability of returns among the stocks comprised by the index, an index constructed by using geometric averaging will always grow more slowly, or decline more rapidly, than an index constructed by using arithmetic averaging. As Paul Cootner stated in 1966 in explaining the downward bias resulting from an index constructed by using a geometric mean:

> I would like to stress that this is a *mathematical theorem*. It does not depend upon any particular facts about the stock market. It will always be true. I stress this because some analysts I know have tried to "disprove" it by pointing out that over some recent periods the Value Line 1100 stock index has outperformed the 30 stock Dow-Jones. The moral behind this is quite clear. In those particular periods, the 1070 stocks which are not in the Dow have performed so well that they have overcome the natural downward bias of a geometric index. The point is that an 1100 stock *arithmetic* index would have done even better.[4]

Selecting the Base Year Value for the Indicator

To gauge the movements in the stocks comprised by the indicator, some time period must be designated as the base period and a value assigned to the indicator at that time. For example, the base period for the Consumer Price Index is 1967. The value of the index assigned for the base period is 100. The CPI in March 1983 was 293. This means that the CPI was 193 percent greater in March 1983 than it was in the base period, 1967.

However, the value assigned to the base year of an index need not be 100. For the NYSE Composite Index, the base year is 1965 and the value assigned to the index for that year is 50. Since the value of the NYSE Composite Index was 81.03 on December 31, 1982, this means that the value of the index increased by 62 percent compared to 1965.

---

[4] Paul Cootner, "Stock Market Indexes—Fallacies and Illusions," *Commercial and Financial Chronicle,* September 29, 1966.

Table 5–3

Summary Information for S&P 500, NYSE Composite, and VLA

	S&P 500	*NYSE Composite*	*VLA*
Coverage	500 major companies	1,520 NYSE-listed companies	1,700 selected companies
Relative weighting scheme	Market-weighted	Market-weighted	Equally weighted
Method of averaging	Arithmetic	Arithmetic	Geometric
Base year	1941–43	1965	1961
Value of index in base year	10	50	100

The base selected for the S&P 500 is the period 1941–43. The average prices over that period are assigned an index value of 10.

Although an arbitrary value can be assigned to the base year of a value-weighted and equally weighted index, this cannot be done with a price-weighted market indicator such as the DJIA. This is so because price-weighted indicators are not really indexes. A price-weighted market indicator is an average of the prices included in the indicator after making adjustments for stock splits.

Table 5–3 summarizes for the S&P 500, the NYSE Composite, and the VLA coverage, type of relative weighting scheme, method of averaging, base year, and value of index or average in the base year.

Illustration of Index Construction and the Effects of Computational Differences

To illustrate the construction of an index based on the three relative weighting schemes and the two methods of averaging and the computational effects on the various indexes, we use a hypothetical example. We begin by assuming that the various indexes reflect the same population of stocks, so that we may focus on the biases produced by computational differences, as opposed to differences in the stocks comprised by the index.

We begin with three stocks, A, B, and C, whose prices in the base or initial period (0) and some future time period (t) are given in Table 5–4. The value assigned to the index in the base year is 100 for all but the price-weighted index.

Market Value–Weighted Index

The total market value of each stock in the index is computed by simply multiplying the price of each by the corresponding number of

Table 5-4

The Effect of Various Computational Techniques on Index Values

Stock:	Base Year Price (0)	No. of Shares	Market Value	Price at Time t	Price Change (%)	New Market Value	Percent Change in Market Value
A	$100	50	$ 5,000	$110.00	10%	$ 5,500	10%
B	20	400	8,000	21.00	5	8,400	5
C	50	200	10,000	50.00	0	10,000	0
Total			$23,000			$23,900	

	Base Year Index (0)			Value of Index at Time t	Change in Index (%)		
Market value–weighted index	100			103.91	3.91%		
Price-weighted index	56.67			60.33	6.47		
Equally weighted arithmetic index	100			105.00	5.00		
Equally weighted geometric index	100			104.92	4.92		

shares outstanding. The market value–weighted index is then computed by dividing the current total market value of all the stocks used to construct the index by the total market value of all these stocks in the initial or base period. The quotient is then multiplied by the value assigned to the index in the base period. Mathematically, this is expressed as follows:

Market-value-weighted index

$$= \frac{\text{Total market value in period } t}{\text{Total market value in base period}} \times \frac{\text{Index value}}{\text{in base period}}$$

Using the data for the hypothetical three-stock index given in Table 5–4, the total market value is $23,000 in the base year and $23,900 in time period t. Assuming that the index value in the base year is set at 100, then the market value–weighted index in time period t is 103.91, as shown below:

$$\frac{\$23,900}{\$23,000} \times 100 = 103.91$$

Had the value of the index in the base period been set at 40 instead of 100, the market value–weighted index in period t would be 41.57. Regardless of the value assigned to the index in the base period, the percentage change is 3.91 percent, which reflects an increase from $23,000 to $23,900 in the aggregate wealth in this hypothetical market portfolio.

In the preceding computation, the arithmetic mean was used to construct the index.

Price-Weighted Index

A price-weighted index reflects changes in the average price of the stocks used to construct the index, adjusting for stock splits. Assuming no stock splits between the base period and period t for any of the three stocks in Table 5–4, the average price of the three stocks changed from $56.67 [(100 + 20 + 50)/3] to $60.33 [(110 + 21 + 50)/3], or an increase of 6.47 percent.

Note that relative to the market value–weighted index, the price-weighted index considerably overstates the overall market portfolio change in this illustration. The reason is that the price-weighted index overweights the movement of stock A, simply because stock A had the highest price. Aggregate market value is not considered.

In this illustration the method of averaging is the arithmetic average. This is the method used to compute the DJIA, which is a price-weighted index. Alternatively, a price-weighted average based on the geometric mean of the prices could be computed.

Let's drop the assumption that all three stocks in Table 5–4 did not have a stock split between the base period and time period t. Instead, assume that in time period t stock A split 2 for 1 and the market price of stock A fell from $110 per share, the price it would have had in the absence of the stock split, to $55 per share. The average price in time period t is $42 [(55 + 21 + 50)/3] as a result of the stock split. This is less than the base period average price of $56.67 and implies that the average stock price has declined. Of course, this is ridiculous. An adjustment is required so that the indicator will not be misleading as a result of the stock split.

The adjustment is made by changing the divisor that is used to compute the average. In the absence of the stock split, the sum of the three prices in time period t is divided by 3, the number of stocks in our hypothetical index. The average price is $60.33. The sum of the three prices in time period t after the stock split is $126. If the divisor is 2.089 (126 divided by 60.33), the average price would be $60.33 and the index in time period t would be 106.47, just as before the stock split.

Revising the divisor is the procedure currently employed by Dow Jones to adjust for stock splits. Consequently, the computation of the DJIA can be expressed mathematically using the following formula:

$$DJIA = \frac{\text{Sum of the price of the 30 industrials}}{\text{Divisor}}$$

The divisor takes into consideration not only stock splits but also changes in the composition of the stocks used to compute the DJIA. As noted earlier, occasionally companies are dropped from the DJIA and replaced by other companies. For example, in 1979 Chrysler was replaced by IBM and Esmark was replaced by Merck.

Notice that an adjustment for stock splits is not necessary for a market value–weighted index. The market value–weighted index would still be 103.91 after the 2 for 1 split of stock A.

It would seem that the adjustment factor can be relied on to provide comparability with previous years after a stock split. This, however, would not be a proper conclusion. Recall that the adjustment factor is computed by looking for the value that will preserve the average price after the stock split. An alternative approach is to reweight the price of the split stock. For example, in our illustration of a 2 for 1 stock split for stock A, the weight for stock A would be doubled in determining the numerator of the price-weighted index, leaving the numerator unchanged before and after the stock split. This approach was in fact used for the DJIA prior to 1928.[5]

Although the two approaches will give identical results at the time of the stock split, critics of the way in which Dow Jones currently adjusts for stock splits argue that this method produces a downward bias in subsequent years. As Hartman L. Butler, Jr., and J. Devon Allen point out:

> The new procedure reduces the importance of a successful company by reducing its weighting in the average every time expanding earnings occasion a stock split. Conversely, a laggard company with a disappointing earnings record (hence no split) receives increased arithmetic importance for at least a few years, although over time this bias will be at least partially offset as earnings disappointment reduces market price, hence weighting in the index.[6]

Equally Weighted Arithmetic Index

In an equally weighted arithmetic index, an equal dollar amount is assumed to be invested in each stock comprised by the index. For example, suppose that in the base year $1,000 is invested in each of the three

---

[5] The approach was dropped by the successor of Charles H. Dow, first editor of *The Wall Street Journal* (Robert D. Milne, "The Dow Jones Industrial Average Re-examined," *Financial Analysts Journal,* December 1966).

[6] Hartman L. Butler, Jr., and J. Devon Allen, "The Dow Jones Industrial Average Re-Reexamined," *Financial Analysts Journal,* November–December 1979, pp. 24 and 26.

stocks in Table 5–4. Given the same prices in the base year as used in the example above (i.e., 100, 20, and 50), the number of shares of stocks A, B, and C that could be purchased for $1,000 each is 10, 50, and 20, respectively. Thus the investment in the base year is $3,000. In time period t, as prices changed to 110, 21, and 50, respectively, the portfolio value of those shares would be equal to $3,150 [(110 × 10) + (21 × 50) + (50 × 20)]. The value of the portfolio therefore increased by 5 percent [(3,150/3,000) − 1]. If the base year index was 100, the index at time period t would be 105 (100 × 1.05).

An alternative way of viewing the construction of this index is to note that the index percentage change equals the arithmetic average of the percentage changes in the prices of each of the three stocks, which is also 5 percent [(10 percent + 5 percent + 0 percent)/3]. This property will always be true when the current period is compared to the base period, but not for subsequent period-to-period comparisons.

Equally Weighted Geometric Index

As just noted, the equally weighted arithmetic index reflects the arithmetic average percentage change in the stocks comprised by the index calculated between the current period and the base period. The equally weighted geometric index has a similar interpretation. The difference is that the geometric mean is used to compute the average percentage change in the stocks comprised by the index.

The following steps are used to compute the geometric mean of the percentage change in the price of N stocks comprised by an index.

Step 1. Compute the ratio of the price in period t to the base period price for each of the N stocks comprised by the index. (Prices must be adjusted for stock splits and dividends. Notice that the ratio represents 1 plus the percentage price change.)

Step 2. Multiply the ratios obtained from Step 1.

Step 3. Find the Nth root of the product computed in Step 2. (The Nth root is the value that produces the value computed in Step 2 if multiplied by itself N times.)

Step 4. Subtract 1 from the value found in Step 3.

Using the three stocks in Table 5–4, the geometric mean return is found as follows:

Step 1. The ratio for each stock is:

$$A = 110/100 = 1.10$$
$$B = 21/20 \quad = 1.05$$
$$C = 50/50 \quad = 1.00$$

Step 2. Multiply the three ratios:

$$1.10 \times 1.05 \times 1.00 = 1.155$$

Step 3. Find the third root of 1.155, that is, $(1.155)^{1/3}$. The value we seek is 1.0492 since

$$1.0492 \times 1.0492 \times 1.0492 = 1.155$$

Step 4. Subtract 1 from the value found in Step 3:

$$1.0492 - 1 = .0492, \text{ or } 4.92 \text{ percent}$$

Notice that the geometric mean return is less than the arithmetic mean return of 5 percent. This is consistent with the mathematical property of the geometric mean discussed earlier in this chapter. The small difference between the geometric mean and the arithmetic mean in this illustration is due to the relatively small variation in the individual returns.

The equally weighted geometric index is found by multiplying 1 plus the geometric mean return by the value of the index in the base period. Assuming the value of the index in the base period to be 100, then the equally weighted geometric index for our hypothetical three-stock index would be 105 (1.05 × 100).

A property of the geometric index is that both the period-to-period and the current period–to–base period percentage changes will be the same for the index and the individual stocks.

The VLA is the only index discussed in this chapter that is an equally weighted geometric index.

Reworking the DJIA

The DJIA is a popular stock market indicator often quoted in the financial press.[7] A psychologically significant value for the DJIA is 1000. Some of the best parties on Wall Street have followed a market closing above 1000. The DJIA broke 1000 for the first time on January 18, 1966, when it reached 1001. Not until November 14, 1972, did it break the 1000 barrier again, closing at 1003.16.

Let us look at what would have happened if the DJIA were computed using the three other approaches discussed in this section instead of being price-weighted.

---

[7] Hartman L. Butler, Jr., and J. Devon Allen relate an anecdote about a successful stock trader who when asked why the DJIA was always mentioned when people talked about the recent behavior of the stock market, replied: "The Dow Jones has been around a long time. It is literally available at my fingertips. *It is the only stock average I understand"* (emphasis added) (Butler and Allen, "The Dow Jones Industrial Average Re-Reexamined," p. 23).

At the end of 1965, the DJIA was 969.26. Had the market value–weighted index approach been used to compute the index for the 30 industrials in the DJIA since 1945, the index would have had a value of 1026.84 at the end of 1965. The equally weighted arithmetic index and the equally weighted geometric index approaches would have resulted in 1965 year-end DJIAs of 1096.92 and 813.40, respectively.[8] The lower value for the equally weighted geometric index compared to the equally weighted arithmetic index should not be surprising. It follows from the mathematical property of the geometric mean discussed earlier.

We also mentioned the downward bias that results from the practice employed by Dow Jones to adjust the divisor. If the constant-divisor approach had been used instead of the current approach from the end of 1945 to the end of 1965, the DJIA would have been 1086.59 rather than 969.26.[9]

Substitution of companies also had an impact on the DJIA. In 1939 IBM was removed from the DJIA and replaced by AT&T. Had this substitution not taken place, the DJIA would have been 1017.39 in December 1961 rather than 734.91![10]

Implications for Asset Allocation Strategy

An important consideration for the hedger is the asset allocation strategy that corresponds to each of the computational methods discussed in this chapter.

A value-weighted index is an appropriate benchmark for an index fund that attempts to invest in "the market." Certainly, all investors in aggregate define the market. With commissions ignored, a value-weighted index represents the performance achievable by investing in all possible stocks in proportion to their market value.

A price-weighted index is an appropriate benchmark for an investor who apportions his or her wealth among stocks in ratios that correspond to their current prices. For the example in Table 5–4, the investor would invest five times as much in stock A as in stock B, simply because the price of stock A is five times that of stock B. Equivalently, this strategy implies that the investor invests in an equal number of shares of each stock, regardless of the price.

The equally weighted arithmetic index is an appropriate benchmark for an investor who apportions his or her wealth in equal dollar amounts among all stocks selected.

[8] Milne, "The Dow Jones Industrial Average Re-examined," p. 86.
[9] Ibid.
[10] Ibid.

Table 5–5

Correlation among Selected Indexes*

Composites	NYSE	DJC	S&P 500	NASDAQ Composite	AMEX Composite	Value Line Average Composite
NYSE	1.000	0.964	0.996	0.931	0.837	0.908
Dow Composite	0.964	1.000	0.962	0.898	0.807	0.898
S&P 500	0.996	0.962	1.000	0.902	0.805	0.875
NASDAQ Composite	0.931	0.898	0.902	1.000	0.892	0.952
AMEX Composite	0.837	0.807	0.805	0.892	1.000	0.878
Value Line Average Composite	0.908	0.898	0.875	0.952	0.878	1.000
Industrials	NYSI	DJIA	S&P 400	NASDI	VLI	
NYSI	1.000	0.934	0.995	0.911	0.880	
Dow Industrials	0.934	1.000	0.947	0.819	0.862	
S&P 400	0.995	0.947	1.000	0.881	0.861	
NASDAQ Industrials	0.911	0.819	0.881	1.000	0.932	
Value Line Industrials	0.880	0.862	0.861	0.932	1.000	

* Based on monthly percentage changes from 1975 to 1981.
Source: *Quantitative Research Notes,* May 12, 1982, The Research Department, Kidder, Peabody & Co., Inc. Reprinted with permission.

These examples cannot be extended to a comparable asset allocation strategy for the equally weighted geometric index. Proponents of this type of index claim that arithmetic averages overstate attainable results.[11] However, it is important to understand that the results described by a geometric index are simply unattainable by means of any portfolio strategy. That is, an investor could not (ex ante) construct a portfolio of stocks whose total appreciation would equal the geometric mean of the percentage appreciation of all.

Comovements of Stock Market Indicators

Table 5–5 presents the correlation coefficients among various indexes based on monthly price changes for the seven-year period 1975 to 1981. The results are portrayed for both composite indexes and industrials.

[11] Since it is common practice for portfolio managers to compare their performance to some market indicator, adjusting of course, for risk, a portfolio manager may look better compared to an index that is constructed using geometric averaging as opposed to one constructed using arithmetic averaging. As Paul Cootner facetiously stated in 1966: "If there were a *Society for the Protection of Security Analysts*, it should lobby for legislation to make such an index [geometric] mandatory."

Overall, the correlations are quite high. Indeed, it is almost surprising that the relationship should be so close, in particular for the Dow Jones averages, in light of the sizable computational differences in a few cases. A moment's reflection on the universe biases involved gives some explanation. At present, the Dow Jones Industrials, although only 30 companies, represent approximately 21 percent of the total capitalization of NYSE stocks and approximately 28 percent of the total capitalization of the S&P 500. These are precisely the huge issues that have the heaviest impact on the value-weighted NYSE and Standard & Poor's indicators. This makes it easier to understand why these indicators should follow each other so closely.

A matter of great interest to the potential hedger or speculator using stock index futures contracts should certainly be the *relative volatility* of the various indexes. To examine that relative volatility, a simple linear regression was run between the monthly percentage changes in the values of each pair of indexes. The simple linear regression estimated can be expressed as follows:

$$y_t = \alpha + \beta x_t$$

where:

y_t = Percentage change in the value of index y in month t
x_t = Percentage change in the value of index x in month t

and α and β are the values estimated by using least squares regression analysis.[12]

The estimate of β is the measure of the relative volatility of index y with respect to the monthly percentage changes in the value of index x and is commonly referred to as the "beta coefficient," or simply "beta." Table 5–6 presents the beta between each pair of indexes, while Table 5–7 presents the intercept term, or "alpha."[13]

If we use the S&P 500 Composite Index as a benchmark portfolio (index x in the regression), for example, we can see that the index with the highest beta relative to this portfolio would be the NASD Industrial Index with a beta of 1.30. The index with the lowest beta relative to the S&P 500 is the Dow Jones 65-Stock Composite, with a beta of 0.99.

---

[12] The procedure for computing a least squares regression is discussed in all statistics textbooks.

[13] Notice that the "beta" when the benchmark is switched for a given pair of indexes is not the reciprocal. That is, β estimated from

$$y_t = \alpha + \beta x_t$$

is not equal to $1/\beta$ when

$$x_t = \alpha' + \beta' y_t$$

is estimated. The reason is that the correlations between the indexes are not perfect (i.e., equal to one) and the alphas are not equal to zero.

Table 5-6

Regression Estimates of Relative Volatility (Beta) for Selected Indexes*

| | Index Used as Benchmark Portfolio | | | | | | | | | | |
	NYSE	NYSI	DJC	DJIA	S&P 500	S&P 400	NASDAQ	NASDI	VLA	VLI	AMEX
NYSE	1.00	0.91	0.97	0.93	1.03	1.00	0.78	0.64	0.68	0.65	0.55
NYSI	1.08	1.00	1.04	1.00	1.12	1.09	0.84	0.70	0.72	0.68	0.59
DJC	0.96	0.87	1.00	0.94	0.99	0.96	0.75	0.61	0.67	0.64	0.53
DJIA	0.95	0.87	0.98	1.00	1.00	0.97	0.72	0.58	0.66	0.62	0.49
S&P 500	0.96	0.88	0.93	0.90	1.00	0.97	0.73	0.60	0.63	0.60	0.51
S&P 400	0.98	0.91	0.95	0.93	1.03	1.00	0.75	0.62	0.64	0.61	0.52
NASDAQ	1.11	1.01	1.07	0.99	1.11	1.07	1.00	0.82	0.85	0.81	0.70
NASDI	1.29	1.19	1.25	1.15	1.30	1.26	1.17	1.00	0.99	0.94	0.83
VLA	1.21	1.08	1.20	1.13	1.21	1.15	1.06	0.87	1.00	0.95	0.77
VLI	1.27	1.14	1.26	1.19	1.27	1.21	1.12	0.92	1.05	1.00	0.81
AMEX	1.28	1.17	1.24	1.11	1.27	1.23	1.14	0.96	1.01	0.98	1.00

Legend:
NYSE   New York Stock Exchange Composite
NYSI   New York Stock Exchange Industrials
DJC   Dow Jones 65-Stock Composite
DJIA   Dow Jones 30 Industrials
S&P 500 Standard & Poor's 500-Stock Composite
S&P 400 Standard & Poor's 400 Industrials
NASDAQ NASD Composite
NASDI   NASD Industrials
VLA   Value Line Average Composite
VLI   Value Line Industrials
AMEX   American Stock Exchange Market Value Index

* Based on monthly percentage changes from 1975 to 1981.
Source: *Quantitative Research Notes*, May 12, 1982, The Research Department, Kidder, Peabody & Co., Inc. Reprinted with permission.

Table 5-7

Regression Estimates of Intercept (Alpha) for Selected Indexes*

	Index Used as Benchmark Portfolio										
	NYSE	NYSI	DJC	DJIA	S&P 500	S&P 400	NASDAQ	NASDI	VLA	VLI	AMEX
NYSE	0.00	0.01	0.18	0.45	0.10	0.12	-0.31	-0.29	-0.04	-0.05	-0.31
NYSI	0.00	0.00	0.20	0.48	0.10	0.12	-0.32	-0.32	-0.01	-0.02	-0.33
DJC	-0.11	-0.10	0.00	0.29	-0.02	0.00	-0.41	-0.39	-0.18	-0.18	-0.41
DJIA	-0.36	-0.35	-0.24	0.00	-0.28	-0.26	-0.62	0.59	-0.41	-0.42	-0.59
S&P 500	-0.09	-0.08	-0.08	0.34	0.00	0.02	-0.35	-0.33	-0.10	-0.10	-0.34
S&P 400	-0.10	-0.10	0.07	0.33	-0.02	0.00	-0.37	-0.36	-0.10	-0.11	-0.37
NASDAQ	0.56	0.57	0.75	1.07	0.69	0.72	0.00	0.02	0.37	0.36	0.01
NASDI	0.70	0.71	0.93	1.31	0.86	0.88	0.05	0.00	0.50	0.48	0.03
VLA	0.30	0.35	0.49	0.84	0.45	0.49	-0.26	-0.22	0.00	-0.01	-0.31
VLI	0.33	0.38	0.53	0.89	0.49	0.53	-0.27	-0.23	0.01	0.00	-0.31
AMEX	1.08	1.09	1.30	1.69	1.24	1.27	0.46	0.45	0.83	0.82	0.00

Legend:
NYSE	New York Stock Exchange Composite
NYSI	New York Stock Exchange Industrials
DJC	Dow Jones 65-Stock Composite
DJIA	Dow Jones 30 Industrials
S&P 500	Standard & Poor's 500-Stock Composite
S&P 400	Standard & Poor's 400 Industrials
NASDAQ	NASD Composite
NASDI	NASD Industrials
VLA	Value Line Average Composite
VLI	Value Line Industrials
AMEX	American Stock Exchange Market Value Index

* Based on monthly percentage charges from 1975 to 1981.
Source: *Quantitative Research Notes*, May 12, 1982, The Research Department, Kidder, Peabody & Co., Inc. Reprinted with permission.

Because of the differences among the indexes discussed earlier in this chapter, relative rankings are not necessarily the same when different portfolios are used as benchmarks. For example, the results in Table 5–6 indicate that had we chosen to use the Value Line Average Composite as a benchmark (understanding that this series is not describable by any real portfolio), we would have found that the index with the lowest relative beta was the S&P 500, with a value of 0.63, and that the index with the highest relative beta was the Value Line Industrial Index, with a value of 1.05.

There are, of course, ranges of uncertainty in these statistical data, and the betas computed in Table 5–6 are subject to sampling error over the period of the study. Nevertheless, some obvious differences do appear.

As expected, the NASD indexes are quite volatile relative to the NYSE and S&P indexes. This is not the case relative to the Value Line indexes, however. Part of the explanation is the fact that any equally weighted index will give small companies relatively greater weight than would a market value–weighted index and therefore should be expected to reflect more closely the price action of smaller companies (such as many of those traded in the over-the-counter market). As the betas and the data discussed below make clear, small-capitalization stocks tend to be more volatile than large-capitalization stocks.

Thus far we have been considering monthly price changes. However, it is worthwhile to investigate the price changes of various stock market indicators over different periods of time in the recent past. Table 5–8 shows the percentage changes in the various indexes over recent 1-month, 3-month, 12-month, and 2-year periods ending in February 1982.

It is apparent from the results reported in Table 5–8 that over time considerable differences arise among the selected indicators. Moreover, these differences increase with time, to the point where over the two-year period half of the indicators show positive returns and half show

Table 5–8

Performance of Selected Indexes (percent change in price)*

	1 Month	3 Months	12 Months	2 Years
S&P 500	−6.1%	−10.5%	−13.8%	−0.6%
S&P 400	−6.7	−10.9	−15.9	−2.8
DJIA	−5.4	−7.3	−15.4	−4.5
NYSE Composite	−5.9	−11.0	−13.0	0.6
AMEX Composite	−10.0	−20.0	−21.5	−12.4
NASDAQ OTC Industrials	−6.8	−13.6	−18.1	5.7
Value Line Average Composite	−5.0	−10.3	−11.8	2.0

* For periods ended February 26, 1982.
Source: *Current Investment Policy and Strategy Implementation*, April 1982, Kidder, Peabody Investment Policy Group.

negative returns. Even over the 12-month period, although all returns are negative, the relative magnitudes of the differences are dramatic.

The speculator will no doubt be interested in the percentage changes in the indexes during market cycles. These results are reported in Table 5–9 for the NYSE Composite Index, the S&P 500, the VLA and the DJIA for successive intermediate peaks and troughs from February 1966 through December 1980.

Although the geometric averaging process understates the percentage changes compared to arithmetic averaging, the VLA, which is an equally weighted geometric index, usually shows greater percentage swings in market cycles compared to the other three indexes. The reason is that the VLA consists of a greater portion of more volatile small-company stocks whose prices are generally more sensitive to market direction. Consequently, the VLA tends to move up farther when the market rises and to move down farther when the market declines.

Summary

In a popular investment management textbook, the author begins the chapter on stock market indicator series with the following statement: "A fair statement regarding stock market indicator series is that everybody

Table 5–9

Comparison of Cyclical Percentage Changes for Selected Indexes:
Major Stock Market Indicators, 1966 through 1980*

Cycle Period	VLA	NYSE	S&P 500	DJIA
2/66–10/66	−24.7%	−22.7%	−22.7%	−24.7%
10/66–10/67	47.2	37.3	32.9	24.8
10/67– 3/68	−10.7	−9.3	−9.1	−11.1
3/68–12/68	35.4	24.3	21.7	18.8
12/68– 7/70	−54.1	−35.0	−32.2	−29.8
7/70– 4/71	43.6	44.5	42.6	36.7
4/71–11/71	−20.3	−11.7	−11.6	−13.3
4/71– 4/72	26.8	21.2	19.5	18.5
4/72– 1/73	−7.6	6.7	9.1	8.2
1/73–12/74	−58.9	−45.6	−44.0	−42.5
12/74– 2/76	87.7	54.4	52.1	64.0
2/76– 3/78	1.2	−10.9	−14.3	−24.3
3/78– 9/78	31.6	23.8	22.1	21.5
9/78–12/78	−17.8	−11.0	−10.0	−11.3
12/78–10/79	27.8	18.2	15.8	11.5
10/79–11/79	−11.6	−8.9	−8.8	−10.2
11/79– 2/80	18.3	17.0	16.2	11.1
2/80– 3/80	−20.1	−15.9	−14.6	−13.2
3/80–12/80	37.9	37.8	35.6	24.3

* Based on end-of-week closing values.
Source: *Value Line Composite Average: The Index behind the Futures* by the Kansas City Board of Trade.

talks about them, but few people know how they are constructed and what they represent."[14] In view of this observation, the successful use of stock index futures contracts by both hedgers and speculators requires an understanding of how stock indicators are constructed and what they represent. In this chapter we discussed the various factors that differentiate stock indexes and provided some empirical evidence on the comovements of the various major stock indexes.

---

[14] Frank K. Reilly, *Investment Analysis and Portfolio Management* (Hinsdale, Ill.: Dryden Press, 1979), p. 119.

SECTION TWO

Pricing and Performance Characteristics

CHAPTER 6

Pricing of Stock Index Futures

H. Nicholas Hanson, Ph.D.
Vice President
Salomon Brothers Inc

Robert W. Kopprasch, Ph.D., C.F.A.
Vice President
Salomon Brothers Inc

When stock index futures first began trading, in February 1982, professional market participants began to transfer the pricing knowledge accumulated (sometimes the hard way) in earlier financial futures. Investors found that the basic *logic* used in pricing Treasury bond futures, for example, was equally applicable to stock index futures. But just as debt *options* players found that they could not directly transfer the equity option experience because of structural differences in the markets, so too did equity players find that certain peculiarities of their market required adjustments to the standard pricing "rules" of interest rate futures. In this chapter we will examine the pricing logic of futures (and other forward commitments) and then discuss the specific unique features of equity index contracts that require some alteration of previously developed debt futures pricing. Recognizing that some readers may already be familiar with interest rate futures, some sections will be followed by comparisons with GNMA or Treasury bond futures.

We will first develop an arbitrage pricing model by example. Next we will present a more formal derivation using an "equivalent portfolio" approach. Happily, both lead to the same pricing equation. Technically, the equations developed are for forward contracts as opposed to futures contracts. We will later show that there is little theoretical difference between forwards and futures *in terms of pricing*, despite the margin flows inherent in futures.

The Arbitrage Approach

Cost of Carry

Most forward commitments are priced on the basis of net "cost of financing." The cost of financing refers to the rate that would have to be paid to borrow funds to buy the asset, or the rate that could be earned on the funds if the asset were sold. *Net* financing adjusts the cost for any monetary benefits received as a result of holding the asset. Holders of Treasury bonds receive coupon income; holders of gold find that they can "lend" their gold and receive a fee, say 2 percent; and holders of stock portfolios receive dividends. In any model of pricing, these "yields" must be considered.

The term *cost of carry* (or "carry" for short) is used to refer to the net financing cost after consideration of the yield on the asset. Thus, while financing cost is always referred to as negative because it represents a cash outflow to the asset holder, carry can be positive or negative. Positive carry implies that the yield on the asset is greater than the financing cost, while negative carry implies the opposite.

Arbitrage Pricing

Let us develop the valuation methodology of forward commitments by example. Consider an asset that has a market value of $100 and that offers a yield of 5 percent (earned evenly throughout the year but paid at the end of the period). If the financing rate is 8 percent (also accumulating evenly throughout the year), what should the forward price be? Any investor can buy the asset for $100 (which he borrows) and knows that by the end of the year he will have accumulated a yield of $5 (i.e., 5 percent × $100) and a financing cost of $8. This results in a net carry of negative $3 (a cost). Thus he must receive at least $103 in order to break even. If the forward price is any higher, say $105, an arbitrageur will engage in this transaction and will risklessly earn $2 on every unit asset in the trade.[1] He would buy for 100 (borrowed), sell forward at 105. At the end of the period, he would collect his "yield" of $5, deliver

---

[1] The arbitrage is riskless only if the credit of the contra party in the trade (the forward buyer) is impeccable. The clearing organizations in futures and the mark-to-market margin mechanism combine to reduce the credit problem to a minor consideration.

the asset to the forward buyer at 105, and simultaneously repay his loan of $100 plus $8 interest (5 + 105 − 108 = $2). Note that the profit (at the *end* of the period) equals the excess of the forward price of $105 over the theoretical price of $103.

This example is one of negative carry, and the theoretical forward price (103) is above the current or spot price (100). If the example had involved positive carry, the theoretical forward price would have been lower than the spot price. Note that the "expected" future price never enters into the forward price. The reason for this is arbitrage, which will bring the prices back into line until no further arbitrage profits are available. In order to demonstrate this, let us assume that short selling is permitted and that the short seller has use of the funds raised. If bearish forward sellers drove the one-year forward price down to 101, here is how arbitrage would enter into the market. Arbitrageurs would buy forward at 101 and sell the asset short at today's spot price of 100. They would earn 8 percent on the $100 raised and would have to pay the $5 yield to the lender of the asset. This would leave them with $103, only $101 of which is required to take delivery of the asset on the forward settlement date. The asset thus purchased is used to settle the short positions. This would result in a profit of $2, the difference between the theoretical forward price ($103) and the actual forward price ($101). As expected, when the forward price is too low, the arbitrageur buys the contract because it is too cheap.

In symbolic form, we can write the arbitrage pricing equation as follows:

$$F_0 = S_0 + rS_0 - S_0y \qquad (6\text{--}1)$$

where

F_i = Forward price at time i
S_i = Spot price at time i (i.e., price of asset)
r = Cost of financing (expressed in decimal form)
y = Yield on asset (expressed in decimal form)

The forward price, as discussed above and as shown in Equation (6–1), should equal the spot price today plus the financing cost minus the yield on the asset. Note that r and y represent periodic rates, not annualized rates. Note also that S_0y represents the dollar dividend paid at the end of the forward period. Using D to represent this dividend, we can rewrite Equation (6–1) as

$$F_0 = S_0 + rS_0 - D \qquad (6\text{--}2)$$

We can also rearrange Equation (6–1) to

$$F_0 \quad = \quad S_0 \;+\; S_0(r - y) \qquad (6\text{--}3)$$
$$\text{Forward} = \text{Spot} + \text{Net carry}$$
$$\text{price} \qquad \text{price} \quad \text{adjustment}$$

When r is greater than y, the futures price should be above the spot price, or "trade at a premium to cash." When r is less than y, the futures price should be below spot, that is, it should "trade at a discount."

Several assumptions were made in the simple model described above. We will mention them here only because many of them are also required for the "equivalent portfolio" derivation. Following that derivation, we will examine the conformance of the real world to the assumptions.

1. The nature of the asset at delivery is identical to its current form. This assumption is necessary to allow the arbitrageur to use the asset purchased forward to cover his short sale, or, in the opposite transaction, to allow him to deliver the asset purchased today to satisfy his forward sale.
2. The asset price is known (we need the asset price to derive the theoretical forward price).
3. The asset can be sold short at any time.
4. The proceeds from the short sale are either available to the investor or "invested" for him to provide a return.
5. The yield on the security is known, and paid at the end of the forward period.
6. The term financing rate is known, and paid at the end of the forward period (5 and 6 together determine carry).
7. There are no transaction costs.

The Equivalent Portfolio Approach

Let us now look at a more formal derivation of the valuation equation. Until now, we have referred to "the asset," "the yield," and so on, without limiting the discussion to equities. At this point we will assume that we are pricing a forward on *one stock* rather than a portfolio. Then we will expand the discussion to include consideration of a portfolio as "the asset."

Consider the following two investment strategies.

Strategy 1 Buy one share of stock XYZ for S_0 dollars. The return (in dollars) over a holding period ending at time T will be

$$\tilde{R}_1 = \tilde{S}_T - S_0 + D \qquad (6\text{–}4)$$

where $\tilde{R}_1$ = dollar return at time T and the other notation is as defined earlier. The tilde (˜) over a variable indicates that it is a random variable and cannot be known in advance. $\tilde{R}_1$ is a random variable because it depends on the value of XYZ at the end of the period, $\tilde{S}_T$.

Strategy 2 Invest S_0 dollars in the risk-free asset (e.g., Treasury bills) and enter into a forward commitment to take delivery of one share of stock *XYZ* at time T in the future for a dollar amount F_0, the current forward price. In this case the dollar return will be

$$\tilde{R}_2 = \tilde{F}_T - F_0 + rS_0 \qquad (6\text{--}5)$$

Since $\tilde{F}_T = \tilde{S}_T$ (that is, the forward price when there is no time left before delivery equals the spot price)

$$\tilde{R}_2 = \tilde{S}_T - F_0 + rS_0 \qquad (6\text{--}6)$$

Under our assumptions, the two strategies are equivalent in risk and therefore, in equilibrium, should provide the same return. Hence

$$\tilde{R}_1 = \tilde{R}_2$$

Setting the right-hand sides of Equations (6–4) and (6–6) equal, we have

$$\tilde{S}_T - S_0 + D = \tilde{S}_T - F_0 + rS_0,$$

and

$$F_0 = S_0 + rS_0 - D \qquad (6\text{--}7)$$

This is the same result as Equation (6–2).

Since S could represent the market value of a portfolio of stocks, the same result holds for the price of a forward contract on a portfolio. For example, S could be the price of a share of an open-end mutual fund. In a frictionless world (one without transaction costs) a stock market index can in most cases be duplicated by a portfolio, so that Equation (6–4) is also the correct pricing formula for a forward contract on a stock index. Indexes such as the Standard and Poor's 500 Composite, the New York Stock Exchange Composite, and the Dow Jones Industrial Average can be duplicated by a portfolio. The Value Line Average Composite, however, because of its computational procedure, cannot be, so that Equation (6–4) does not give the correct pricing for a forward contract on it.[2]

To this point we have referred to *forward* contracts instead of futures contracts. Although we have not yet established that future prices should be the same as those derived for forwards, further reference to forwards in the sections that follow would appear artificial because generally such contracts do *not* exist. We will discuss theoretical futures prices as if they were interchangeable with forward prices. The final section of this

---

[2] Because of the geometric averaging procedure used, the Value Line Average Composite will always have a lower return than an equally weighted portfolio of its component stocks. See Chapter 5.

chapter will discuss the relationship between theoretical forward and futures prices.

The two approaches used to obtain the pricing model above suggest that two different actions (similar in effect) will take place whenever there is a discrepancy between the market price of the futures contract and the theoretical price. For example, if the actual futures price is *lower* than the theoretical price, the equivalent portfolio approach holds that investors who are not constrained should sell their portfolios and replace them with Treasury bills and futures contracts.[3] The selling activity should result in lower equity prices, which would lower the theoretical futures price toward the actual futures price. The buying of the futures should drive the futures price higher, so that the gap between actual and theoretical will be further narrowed or eliminated.

The arbitrage model goes even further. The potential participants are not limited to those with equity portfolios. Pure arbitrageurs, having no equity position to begin with, engage in the same transactions (with the same directional effects) by buying futures and selling stock short. Thus the magnitude of trading could conceivably exceed the size of the portfolios of those following the equivalent portfolio logic. These powerful forces should combine to drive the actual and theoretical prices together if the assumptions of the model are not overly simplified or restrictive.

Examining the Assumptions

Let us return to the list of assumptions given earlier. For convenience, we will examine them in the order shown, although no ranking of importance is meant to be implied.

The Nature of the Asset at Delivery

There are several aspects of reality that conflict with this assumption. First, stock index futures do not have a simple asset underlying the contract. The stock index is a concept more than an asset, though it can be approximated by a diversified portfolio. Due to the large number of securities needed, it is difficult to buy (or short) an exact duplicate of the asset. In addition, changes in the index to reflect stock splits, stock dividends, or changes in the securities that the index comprises further complicate the matching process. This is not to say that the approximation cannot be close, but the holder (or seller) will have a small amount of uncertainty introduced by this mismatch.[4]

---

[3] Constraints such as statutory prohibition, loss recognition, tax effects, and imperfect information would prevent some investors from engaging in the strategy.

[4] Traders of GNMA futures will understand the significance of this section, because the underlying GNMA security can change during the holding period due to prepayments that differ from the expected rate. Thus, while the required delivery item does not change, the asset held may change.

Of potentially greater importance is the contract specification that calls for cash settlement of the contract instead of delivery of the asset by the seller and payment by the purchaser. Even if the investor is able to match the index exactly, the underlying portfolio cannot be delivered, resulting in transactions costs that may be significant, especially since the entire portfolio would have to be liquidated (or repurchased if short) simultaneously if the investor did not want any unhedged long or short position.

The Price of the Underlying Asset

In order to evaluate the potential arbitrage transactions, the value of the stock index must be available during the trading hours of the futures contracts. The values of the S&P 500, the NYSE Composite, and the Value Line Average Composite are available during trading hours, but they may lag market movements. This is because they are based on the last sale of the component stocks and not on the current bid/ask. As such, the last trade may be somewhat lower (or higher) than where the stock would trade at the time the arbitrage is being evaluated. Thus, while a trade may look attractive—perhaps the index looks "cheap" relative to the futures—the arbitrageur might find that his surrogate portfolio would be more expensive than the index indicated. This may not seem like a large factor, but it may explain in part why there is much greater intraday volatility of the futures than of the indexes.

Short Sales of the Asset

Because the index is difficult to duplicate, and because its price may not reflect the current market, it is difficult to short, even in theory, the exact asset underlying the contract. Market practitioners do not need to be told of the difficulty of shorting an entire portfolio. The requirement that stocks (but not futures) be shorted only on an uptick also complicates the potential arbitrage.[5] An uptick occurs when a stock trades at a price higher than the previous transaction.

As an example of how the uptick rule affects arbitrage, consider the following example. Suppose we have two stocks, A and B, that make up an index. Initially, A and B are each priced at $50 a share, so that the index, which comprises one share of each, is $100. An arbitrageur, detecting cheap futures, wishes to sell A and B short and buy the futures. Suppose that A then trades at $50\frac{1}{8}$ and B at $49\frac{7}{8}$, the index remaining

---

[5] An uptick occurs when a stock trades at a price higher than the previous transaction. A short sale is also permitted on a zero uptick, that is, when the last price change was up but the current trade is at the same price as that of the previous trade.

at 100. The arbitrageur can short A (at $50\frac{1}{8}$) but not B (at $49\frac{7}{8}$), because of the uptick rule. What does he do? Does he go ahead and short A, hoping for an uptick on B? This could be very risky, since the market may drift downward and the uptick on B may not come until B is much lower, and by then he may have a loss on the futures. The "pure arbitrage" is thus very difficult, and certainly not riskless.

However, the marginal pricer in this case need not be the pure arbitrageur. Suppose a portfolio manager already owns A and B. He may sell them out of his portfolio (sell long) and buy the cheap futures, capturing the mispricing in this manner. This type of arbitrage is much easier to do because long sales are not subject to the uptick rule, so that it is much easier to get the trades off simultaneously, or nearly simultaneously.

Proceeds of the Short Sale

When the proceeds of the short sale are available to the investor, he can invest these proceeds to earn the short-term rate until he "unwinds" the trade. In reality, there are varying degrees of availability of these proceeds to different classes of investors. Retail investors will find that not only are the proceeds not available but that Regulation T requires an additional deposit of at least 50 percent of the value at the time of the short sale.[6] Thus the model described earlier does not accurately reflect the constraints of the retail investor and his theoretical price would vary from the theoretical price determined by less constrained investors.

Broker-dealers find that the proceeds are basically available to them when selling short. The shares are borrowed in any one of three basic methods described below.

Borrow versus cash   The shares are borrowed from a customer who has a long position, and the cash proceeds are given to the customer as collateral for the loan. Because the customer continues to earn the yield on the equity, he must offer a return on the cash, usually 75 percent of the broker call rate. Because the customer can earn more than this on the cash, he is being compensated for the extra credit risk and the service of lending securities.

Borrow versus collateral   The borrower of the shares places other collateral (securities) with the lender to eliminate the credit risk and pays a

---

[6] Under Regulation T, the Federal Reserve Board controls credit in the securities industry. At the time this book went to press, Regulation T required a minimum deposit of 50 percent, but this *initial margin requirement is subject to change.*

fee of 1 to 2 percent (annual rate) of the value of the shares to the lender for the service.

Borrow versus letter of credit   In this case the letter of credit eliminates the credit risk and the lender receives a 1 to 2 percent (annual) fee for the service of lending the shares.

The net effect of these implicit and explicit fees is to reduce the price at which the futures become an attractive substitute for the shares; that is, the break-even theoretical bid price is lowered because of the fees, though the asked price is not similarly lowered. Thus there is frequently a range of prices that offers no arbitrage. When the price exceeds that range, one would sell the futures; and when the price is lower than that range, one would buy the futures.

Dividend Known and Paid at End of Period

One of the assumptions made in the derivation of Equation (6–7) was that the dividend pay date coincided with the settlement date of the contract. This assumption is not necessary and was included only for mathematical simplicity, so that D could be the actual dividend. However, the dividend can be adjusted for the time value of money between the pay date and the settlement date. That is, if the dividend were to be received before settlement, it could be reinvested at the risk-free rate until settlement, in which case D would be larger than the actual dividend received. If the dividend were to be received after settlement, it should be discounted at the risk-free rate. In mathematical terms,

$$F_0 = S_0 + rS_0 - D'$$

where

$D' = D (1 + r)^n$ (pay date n days before settlement)

$D' = D/(1 + r)^n$ (pay date n days after settlement)

and D is the actual dividend paid. Unless n and/or r is large, the error made by assuming that D' and D are equal is negligible. For example, with a 10 percent annual risk-free rate and a dividend of $1.75 that is received 91 days before or after settlement, D' and D differ by only about four cents. Thus we will continue to use the approximation that $D' = D$. The reader, however, should be aware of this effect and check its size, particularly in the case of futures with a long time until settlement.

A much more important effect when valuing futures contracts on stock indexes is the seasonality in the dividends. Even though an index may contain several hundred stocks, the dividend yield until settlement may

Exhibit 6–1

Percent of Quarterly Dividend Remaining S&P 500

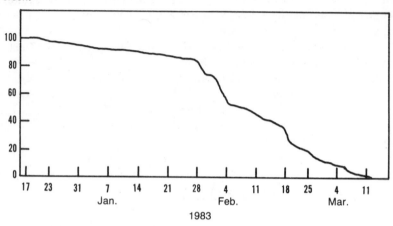

1983

vary in a nonlinear way with time. This is illustrated in Exhibit 6–1, which depicts this nonlinearity for the S&P 500 for the 91-day period ending March 17, the last day of trading of the S&P 500 March 1983 futures contract. From Exhibit 6–1 it is apparent that during the first half of the "settlement quarter," stocks accounting for only about 15 percent of the total dollar dividends for the quarter have gone ex-dividend. Thus the holder of the S&P 500 over the second half of the settlement quarter will receive about 85 percent of the quarter's dividends.[7] Naturally, this makes the effective annual dividend considerably larger, as shown in Exhibit 6–2. An interesting result of this is that a properly priced futures contract can sell at a discount to the index if the dividend yield until settlement exceeds the risk-free rate until settlement. This becomes immediately obvious if Equation (6–7) is rearranged so that

$$\frac{F_0 - S_0}{S_0} = r - y$$

where the dividend yield $y = D/S_0$. If y is greater than r, then the basis, $(F_0 - S_0)/S_0$, is negative.

In the case of Treasury bond futures, the underlying bonds accrue coupon income evenly within each semiannual period. This results in a

---

[7] The recent change in the ex dividend date of AT&T has changed this to about 75 percent. The charts reflect the statement in the text.

Exhibit 6–2

Annualized Dividend until March Settlement

Annualized dividend ($)

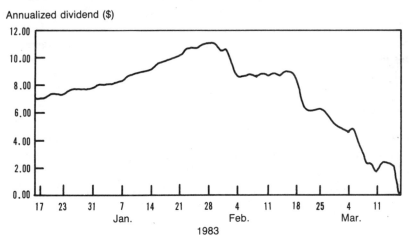

constant "effective semiannual coupon" that does not depend on the cal-culation data. (If the coupon date falls before the settlement date for the futures contract the actual/actual date arithmetic used for Treasury bonds causes a slight change in the "effective semiannual coupon," but the impact is small.) The exact cash flows associated with GNMA securities are not known and must be estimated.

The Relationship between Forwards and Futures

The major difference between a futures contract and a forward contract results from variation margin, the daily mark-to-the-market of an open futures position.[8] If an investor is long a futures contract and its settlement price on a given day is below that of the previous day, he is required to post the price difference in cash. If the price rises, he will receive the price difference, again in cash. With forward contracts, only paper profits or losses occur daily. No cash changes hands until expiration of the contracts. Thus an investor who purchases Treasury bills and fairly valued forward contracts on the S&P 500 (such that his beta is 1) will realize exactly the same return as an investor who purchases the S&P 500 if the position is held until expiration of the contracts. In fact, the requirement that these two returns be identical led to the pricing equations for the forward contract, Equations (6–2) and (6–7).

---

[8] See Chapter 4.

Now consider the investor who has purchased Treasury bills and futures contracts. If the futures price drops, he will have to meet the variation margin by liquidating some of his Treasury bills. He thus loses the interest on these funds. Of course, if the futures price rises, cash will flow into his account and he will gain interest by investing these funds in Treasury bills. The net effect of these daily cash flows is to alter the return on his position by the net interest gained or lost. Summarizing in mathematical terms,

a. T-bills and forward contracts: $R_A = R_{500}$
b. T-bills and futures contracts: $R_B = R_{500} + i_M$

where i_M is the net interest gained or lost from variation margin.

If the overnight rate of interest, r, remains constant, there exists an adjustment to the number of futures contracts purchased that will make the term i_M equal to zero. To illustrate this, suppose that three days are left until expiration of the futures, as depicted below.

Day	0	1	2	3
Settlement price	F_0	F_1	F_2	F_3

F_3 is the value at expiration of the futures on Day 3. Since the futures contract is marked to the index at expiration, $F_3 = I_3$.

Suppose we buy a futures contract at some time during Day 0 for price F. At the close of Day 0, we will have a dollar return equal to $(F_0 - F)$. If F_0 is greater than F, we can invest this money at the overnight rate of interest for three days. At the end of Day 3, we will have $(F_0 - F)(1 + r)^3$ dollars. If F_0 is less than F, we will liquidate $(F - F_0)$ T-bills, thus losing an amount of interest equal to $(F - F_0)(1 + r)^3$. Each day we repeat this procedure, which is illustrated in Table 6–1. The dollar total return to the holder of the *futures* contract is the sum of the terms in column 4 of Table 6–1.

$$R_{fut} = (F_0 - F)(1 + r)^3 + (F_1 - F_0)(1 + r)^2 \\ + (F_2 - F_1)(1 + r) + (I_3 - F_2) \quad (6\text{--}8)$$

which depends on the daily settlement prices. The total return to the holder of a *forward* contract is given by the sum of the terms in the third column of Table 6–1.

Table 6–1

Day	Settlement Price	Variation Margin	Variation Margin plus Interest at Expiration
0	F_0	$F_0 - F$	$(F_0 - F)(1 + r)^3$
1	F_1	$F_1 - F_0$	$(F_1 - F_0)(1 + r)^2$
2	F_2	$F_2 - F_1$	$(F_2 - F_1)(1 + r)$
3	I_3	$I_3 - F_2$	$I_3 - F_2$

$$R_{fwd} = (F_0 - F) + (F_1 - F_0) + (F_2 - F_1) + (I_3 - F_2) = I_3 - F \quad (6\text{--}9)$$

Thus the return depends only on the initial and final prices and is independent of the intermediate daily settlement prices.

Suppose that rather than holding one futures contract for the three-day period, the investor holds n_i contracts on Day i. Equation (6–8) may then be rewritten

$$R_{fut} = n_0(F_0 - F)(1 + r)^3 + n_1(F_1 - F_0)(1 + r)^2$$
$$+ n_2(F_2 - F_1)(1 + r) + n_3(I_3 - F_2) \quad (6\text{--}10)$$

By inspection, we see that if

$$n_0 = \frac{1}{(1 + r)^3}, \; n_1 = \frac{1}{(1 + r)^2}, \; n_2 = \frac{1}{(1 + r)}, \text{ and } n_3 = 1,$$

Equation (6–10) reduces to $R_{fut} = I_3 - F = R_{fwd}$.

Thus the return on the futures position is identical to that on the forward position. There is no net interest gained or lost due to the variation margin. Embodied in Equation (6–10) is the assumption that the daily adjustment to the number of contracts, n_i, is implemented by buying futures at the opening the next day at a price equal to the previous day's settlement price. Note that this procedure does not eliminate the daily cash flows. It just assures that no net interest will be gained or lost due to meeting them. We have created a "forward equivalent." In general, if there are N days left until expiration of the futures, the appropriate number of futures contracts to purchase is

$$n = \frac{1}{(1 + r)^N} \quad (6\text{--}11)$$

and

$$\text{One forward equivalent} = \frac{1}{(1 + r)^N} \text{ futures contract} \quad (6\text{--}12)$$

Note that as the number of days until expiration decreases, n increases, approaching unity as N approaches zero. Table 6–2 gives the number of futures contracts required to be in the equivalent position of 1,000 forward contracts, assuming an annual interest rate of 10 percent.[9]

Even if this position is closed out before expiration of the futures, the return is still the same as that which would be obtained with a forward. For example, suppose n_0 contracts were purchased initially during Day 0 at Price F and sold at the close at Price F_0. The return would be

$$n_0(F_0 - F) = \frac{F_0 - F}{(1 + r)^3} \quad (6\text{--}13)$$

[9] One thousand forward contracts at an S&P 500 price of 170 represents an $85 million ($500 × 170 × 1,000) position in the index.

Table 6–2

Time until Expiration	No. of Forwards	No. of Futures
1 year	1,000	909
6 months	1,000	953
3 months	1,000	976
2 months	1,000	984
1 month	1,000	992
1 week	1,000	998
1 day	1,000	1,000

Had this been a forward contract, in order to close out the position, the investor would have to sell a forward at F_0. Since no money would change hands until delivery, his return today would be the present value of the difference in the two prices, or $(F_0 - F)/(1 + r)^3$, identical to that in Equation (6–13).

While this procedure is applicable to futures contracts on any commodity, in the real world it will only allow a futures position to approximate a forward position. Varying interest rates intraday, correlation between spot price changes and interest rate changes, the inability to purchase futures contracts in the morning at the previous day's settlement price, and the inability to purchase fractions of a contract introduce frictions that prevent creation of a perfect "forward equivalent." Nevertheless, for stock index futures this procedure is quite effective in reducing i_M to an essentially negligible amount.

The bottom line on this forward-futures equivalence argument is that if short-term rates are stable or reasonably so, the prices of futures contracts and forward contracts with identical delivery dates should be nearly equivalent. Note that this does not mean that futures and forwards are equivalent in terms of actual price volatility *per contract*. For contracts of identical size, futures are more volatile than forwards because of the immediate mark-to-market on the futures. As shown above, the profit on a forward position is the present value of the difference in purchase and sale prices, while the profit on a futures contract is the undiscounted difference between the prices. Thus, if a strategy is conceived in terms of forwards, and then implemented with futures, the number of contracts must be adjusted to reflect the difference in volatility.[10] When futures

---

[10] One might also think of the futures contract as having the volatility of a forward contract of greater size than the futures. This greater size is simply the compounded value of the nominal amount, found by multiplying the nominal amount by $(1 + r)^n$, where r and n are as defined earlier. Thus, if one buys 1,000 units of the underlying instruments, one might sell futures contracts on 900 units if the 900 units have the volatility of 1,000 forward units. As this position moved through time, the futures position would be increased because $(1 + r)^n$ (the volatility factor) declines as n declines.

positions and forward positions are weighted this way, there is no difference in economic profit between them.

As an example, consider spot silver at $4 per ounce and one-year futures (and forwards) trading at $5 per ounce. If one buys spot and sells it forward (using either futures or forwards), the position established is like a one-year fixed-income instrument with a 25 percent yield. If that *yield* remains constant, the investor should be indifferent to the actual price of silver. Let us look at a scenario in which silver explodes overnight to $40, but the 25% market doesn't change, leaving forwards and futures at $50. Assume the investor desires to liquidate his position.

If the investor had used forwards, he would have sold forward an amount equal to his spot holdings. The change in the spot price from $4 to $40 would give him a cash profit of $36. A new forward can now be bought at 50, and when the long and short forward positions settle one year hence, the investor will lose $45 (buy at 50, sell at 5). But $45 one year hence in a 25 percent market is worth $36 today. Thus the investor has no profit or loss despite the large change in price. (And, if his position were held to delivery, the investor would earn the original 25 percent.)

If the trade were done with futures, one would sell $1/(1 + r)^N$ futures contracts. In this case, $1/(1 + 0.25)^1 = 1/1.25 = 0.8$. Thus, when the contract moved from $5 to $50, each contract would provide a $45 loss and 0.8 contracts would lose $36, identical to the gain on the spot silver. This quick example should highlight the price change similarity but volatility differences between forwards and futures.[11]

---

[11] Readers interested in more advanced treatments of this subject are referred to the following articles:

B. Cornell and M. R. Reinganum. "Forward and Futures Prices: Evidence from the Foreign Exchange Markets," *Journal of Finance* 36 (1981), pp. 1035–45.

J. C. Cox, J. E. Ingersoll and S. A. Ross. "The Relation between Forward and Futures Prices," *Journal of Financial Economics* 9 (1981), pp. 321–46.

E. Elton, M. Gruber and J. Rentzler. "Intra-day Tests of the Efficiency of the Treasury Bill Futures Market," working paper, New York University, 1982.

K. R. French. "The Pricing of Futures and Forward Contracts," Ph.D. dissertation, University of Rochester, 1982.

K. R. French. "A Comparison of Futures and Forward Prices," working paper, UCLA, 1982.

R. A. Jarrow and G. S. Oldfield. "Forward Contracts and Futures Contracts," *Journal of Financial Economics* 9 (1981), pp. 373–82.

R. J. Rendleman and C. E. Carabini. "The Efficiency of the Treasury Bill Futures Market," *Journal of Finance* 34 (1979), pp. 895–914.

S. F. Richard and M. Sundaresan. "A Continuous Time Equilibrium Model of Forward Prices and Futures Prices in a Multigood Economy," *Journal of Financial Economics* 9 (1981), pp. 347–72.

CHAPTER 7

Classical Theory, Dividend Dynamics, and Stock Index Futures Pricing

Gregory M. Kipnis
Vice President
Donaldson, Lufkin & Jenrette, Inc.

Steve Tsang, Ph.D.
Analyst
Donaldson, Lufkin & Jenrette, Inc.

The hedger, arbitrageur, spread trader, or speculator should have a clear understanding of the determinants of the spreads between futures contracts and stock index prices. Only when rational futures prices are defined can the risks and opportunities of using futures be identified.

In this chapter we define the determinants of expected return for a stock index futures portfolio and how this differs from expected returns to a stock portfolio. A stock portfolio realizes price appreciation plus dividends and reinvestment. The stock index futures contract portfolio, on the other hand, will realize an interest rate of return (Treasury bill rate) plus price appreciation. Since like things should yield like returns, then in equilibrium, assuming no leverage, futures will price themselves in such a way that the two returns must be equal. For example, when interest rates exceed dividend yields, the futures contract's appreciation will be less than the stock price gain by the difference between the interest rate and the dividend yield. The theoretically correct futures price cannot be known exactly. However, to obtain the most nearly correct estimate, one must not confuse futures prices with forward or expected prices. Numerical examples are given throughout.

In this chapter we also discuss several important issues related to the correct measurement of dividend yields. This seemingly simple concept must be looked at entirely differently when evaluating a maturing asset such as a futures contract. Utilizing yield-to-maturity calculations and incorporating the unique features of the seasonal dividend distribution lead to important discoveries about how different futures maturities and different stock index futures markets should behave in relation to their underlying market index.

We end by showing an actual example of the calculations for the theoretical price for the December 1982 S&P 500 futures contract.

Relationship between Expected, Forward, Futures, and Spot Stock Prices

Classical Theory of Expected Prices

According to classical stock valuation theory, the *expected price of stocks should always be higher than the current price level* unless the market discount rate is lower than the expected dividend yield. This pricing relationship simply implies that the current stock price is the equilibrium price of the collective market assessment, which always reflects the expected dividend flows and stock appreciation in relation to the investment risk over a holding period. If the collective assessment lowered the expected price and dividend flows, the present value stock price would have to be adjusted downward accordingly. Spot market price movements, therefore, continuously reflect the market assessment process. Since equity markets are liquid and efficient, any short-term shocks will be discounted quickly by the market.

The classical stock pricing theory is sound because no rational investor would buy equity securities at the current price if the expected return, that is, price appreciation plus dividends yield, were less than the cost of equity capital for a specific holding period. Based on this formulation, the link between the current (spot) market price and the expected price, for a fixed holding period, would be as follows:

$$P_0 = \frac{D}{(1 + k)} + \frac{P_t}{(1 + k)} \qquad (7\text{--}1)$$

The two prices should relate as follows:

$$P_t = (1 + k - d)P_0 = (1 + i + e - d)P_0 \qquad (7\text{--}2)$$

where:

P_0 = Present (spot) price of the stock
P_t = Expected price of the stock at the end of holding period t

$D =$ Expected dividend at the end of holding period
$k =$ Market discount rate for the stock $= i + e$
$i =$ Risk-free interest
$e =$ Equity risk premium
$d =$ Expected dividend yield, i.e., D/P_0.

If the dividend yield (d) is 6 percent for a selected stock and the relevant market discount rate (k) is 21 percent per year, then the expected stock price (P_t) should be 15 percent higher than the present price (P_0) one year from now to justify the investment.

The Expected Price Is Not a Forward Price

It is essential to understand that the expected price differs significantly from the forward price for the same time horizon. They differ because the actual price in the future is unknown; it can only be forecast. The expected price for a future date only represents the most likely market expectation at the moment in time. A forward price, on the other hand, is a carrying cost concept; that is, it is a cost accounting calculation for holding the asset.

As indicated in Equation (7–2), the expected price (P_t) is dependent on the difference between the market discount rate (k) and the dividend yield (d) for the holding period. The market discount rate has two major components: the riskless interest rate (i) and the equity risk premium (e). The risk premium is compensation for the investment risk (uncertainty) of holding equities.

The forward price for a storable asset, such as gold, silver, or stocks, on the other hand, is theoretically bounded by the net cost of carry for a predetermined holding period. Cost of carry normally includes net capital costs, insurance, storage, commissions, and so forth. In other words, the forward price is an accounting estimate of the cost of inventorying the item. Therefore, the equity risk premium is not a factor in estimating the forward price.[1] By dropping out the risk premium (e) component from the market discount rate in Equation (7–2), the link between the present (spot) price and the forward price for a stock would be as follows:[2]

$$FP_t = (1 + i - d)P_0 \qquad (7\text{–}3)$$

where

---

[1] For nonstorable assets, the forward price is not bounded by the cost of carry. Thus the difference between the expected price and the forward price diminishes.

[2] This equation holds if borrowing and lending rates are equal to the riskless interest rate.

FP_t = Forward price for holding period t
  i = Riskless interest rate, i.e., the market discount rate less the equity risk premium $(k - e)$.

Equation (7–3) indicates that the forward price of a stock is dependent on the difference between the riskless interest rate and the dividend yield. If the dividend yield is 6 percent and the riskless rate is 12 percent per annum, then the one-year forward price should be 6 percent higher than the present stock price to prevent arbitrage opportunities. This result is quite different from that of the previous example, where the premium for the expected price is 15 percent because of the inclusion of the equity risk premium (e).

Another implication of Equations (7–2) and (7–3) is that the expected price is always higher than the forward price, because the expected risk premium must be positive. Furthermore, although the forward price premium can be negative, the expected price premium for all practical cases must be positive as long as earnings growth is anticipated.

A Futures Contract Is Not a Forward Contract

One might think that Equation (7–3) is an appropriate pricing formula for stock index futures contracts. This formula was in fact the general consensus of the futures industry in early 1982, before the Standard & Poor's 500 Composite Index futures started trading.[3] This view, though seemingly close to being correct, fails to give proper consideration to the potentially large risk differences between a futures contract and a forward contract.[4, 5]

While both a futures contract and a forward contract represent an agreement to exchange a commodity at a specific future date, the futures contract is different from a forward contract in two important ways that relate to risk, both of which are associated with the daily mark-to-the-market rule for the futures contract. According to this rule, the daily trading gains and losses are settled up as adjustments to the equity positions of both parties, that is, long and shorts (see Chapter 4). Since the gains and losses to equity can be invested or must be financed at the short-term rate of interest, the actual changes in the equity positions of both parties are not identical to the difference between contract initiation

---

[3] G. M. Kipnis and S. Tsang, "Stock Index Futures—From Contango to Backwardation," *ACS Futures Research,* ACLI International, March 1982.

[4] G. M. Kipnis and S. Tsang, "Determinants of Stock Index Futures Prices and Spreads," *ACS Futures Research,* ACLI International, April 1982.

[5] G. M. Kipnis and S. Tsang, "A Conceptual Trap in the Stock Index Pricing Model," *ACS Futures Research,* ACLI International, August 1982.

and settlement prices. This difference is generally referred to as the *margin variation risk.*

The feature of margin variation risk does not exist in a forward contract because such a contract generally does not involve payments until the maturity date. At that date the short delivers the commodity and receives the agreed-upon price from the long. Therefore, the forward price can be viewed as a "riskless" expected price.

The second difference between futures and forwards, associated with the mark-to-the-market rule, is referred to as capital exposure risk. Since a futures position is marked-to-the-market daily, the contract value is always treated at its full face value, not the cash value of the spot price.

For example, if the spot price of a commodity, say silver, trades at $40 per ounce and a deferred futures contract at $50 (a 25 percent carry cost), using $40 to buy the deferred futures contract could result in a loss larger than the investment capital. This would be the case if the spot price for silver tumbled suddenly to, say, $4 per ounce and futures to $5 (maintaining the same 25 percent carry). Futures would fall by $45, or $5 more than the original equity. This example clearly illustrates that the capital exposure risk in a futures contract is equivalent to the full face value of the futures contract. This consequence is not found in a forward contract because losses associated with sharp swings are not debited to the buyer.

However, the mark-to-the-market risk can be attenuated through a number of trading techniques. Also, the daily margin variation effects may be random at times; thus the net effect over time could be offsetting. In any case, the price for a futures contract is not a true "expected" price as defined in Equation (7–1), because the risk associated with such a contract is not the same as the equity risk premium.

Failure to recognize the margin variation risk may be beneficial if future prices move favorably. Failure to recognize the capital exposure risk can mislead traders into overlooking the need to weight their trade properly and into believing that Equation (7–3) is the correct pricing formula for stock index futures contracts.

In the following sections we develop a formal price model for stock index futures contracts based on an equivalent portfolio approach; that is, the investment capital must carry an identical risk for both portfolios.

Stock Portfolio Return Must Equal Futures Portfolio Return

The components of the investment returns for a stock index futures portfolio differ significantly from a stock portfolio because the futures contract is trading against the stock index rather than a stock portfolio. The stock portfolio return includes stock price appreciation and dividend yield plus reinvestment returns, whereas the stock index only tracks the price appreciation. The difference between investment returns for a stock portfolio and a futures index contract is illustrated in Equations (7–4) and (7–5). The total expected holding period return for an S&P 500 indexed stock portfolio (TRS) would be as follows and must equal the implied market discount rate.

$$TRS = a + d + r = k \qquad (7\text{–}4)$$

where:

$a =$ Stock price *a*ppreciation
$d =$ Stock *d*ividend yield
$r =$ Stock dividend *r*einvestment return

$k = \frac{p_t}{p_0} - 1 + d$, from Equation (7–2), which is the same as appreciation
   plus dividend yield (and reinvestment) for a continuous investment

However, the stock index futures contract can be bought by posting interest earning assets, such as T bills, for the margin requirement. Thus the total expected return for a futures/bills portfolio (TRF) would be as follows:

$$TRF = f + i \qquad (7\text{–}5)$$

where:

$i =$ T bill yield
$f =$ Expected return on the stock index futures contract $(F_t - F_0)/P_0$,
   where $F =$ futures price and $P =$ stock index price

The rate of return of a futures/bills portfolio can be related to a market portfolio return through the capital asset pricing model (CAPM) as follows:

$$f = \text{Beta}(a + d + r - i) \qquad (7\text{–}6)$$

where beta is the sensitivity (risk) of futures relative to the market and the term in the right-hand bracket is the equity risk premium, that is, the market return less the T bill rate. The equilibrium equation, based on CAPM, simply states that the risk level associated with a futures/bills portfolio determines whether the TRF is greater or smaller than the TRS.

Since the stock index futures contract is new, its risk-return characteristics, relative to the market portfolio, cannot yet be reliably estimated. However, the S&P 500 futures contract is designed to track the Standard & Poor's 500 Composite Index. It is reasonable to expect that the risk level of this contract, on a 100 percent equity basis, should approximately equal that of the S&P 500 index, and its beta value, therefore, should approach unity in the long run. Also, the beta value for the S&P 500 index is approximately equal to unity, relative to the market portfolio, due to significantly more stable dividend yields. Therefore, the beta value for the futures/bills portfolio in Equation (7–6) can be reasonably expected to approximate unity.

If we assume that the beta is exactly equal to one, then Equation (7–6) would be reduced to the following:

$$\begin{aligned} f &= a + d + r - i \\ &= k - i \\ &= e \text{ [see Equations (7–3) and (7–4)]} \end{aligned} \tag{7–7}$$

Simply stated, this result means that the price appreciation of a futures position should be equal to the equity risk premium. Rearranging terms, Equation (7–7) can be written as follows:

$$a - f = i - (d + r) \tag{7–8}$$

Equation (7–8) simply states that the expected return on a stock index futures contract must be less than the stock index appreciation by the difference between riskless interest income and dividend return. In other words, the futures price appreciation is equal to the risk premium of the market portfolio (e).

The price relationship between the current stock index value and the stock index futures price is graphically shown in Exhibit 7–1. The expected price (P_t) and the expected futures price converge at time t. The futures

Exhibit 7–1

Relationship between Futures, Expected, and Spot Stock Index Prices

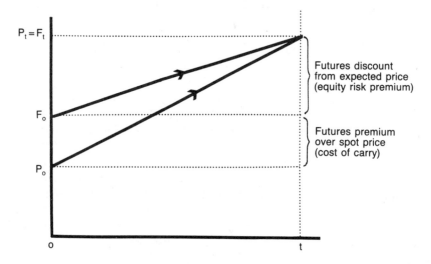

price line indicates the theoretical path that futures will travel from F_0 to P_t. The vertical difference between P_t and F_0 represents the expected return to a stock index futures contract (f). Since f equals the risk premium (e) and thus must be positive, the spot futures price (at time 0) must be at a discount to the expected stock price (P_t) and the expected futures price (F_t) at time t.

In addition, from Equation (7–8), Exhibit 7–1 shows that futures price and the cash index can be linked as follows:[6]

$$F_0 = (1 + i - d - r)P_0 \qquad (7\text{–}9)$$

It is clear that this result is identical to the pricing formula derived for a forward contract in Equation (7–3). Since there are risk differences between futures and forward contracts, the beta for the futures/bills portfolio in Equation (7–6) may not equal one. It has been demonstrated that this difference associated with variation margin flows cannot be hedged away if future interest rates are not deterministic. Also, it can be shown that the expected gains associated with variation margin flows on a futures contract tend to be negative if interest rates are negatively correlated with stock prices. Since this negative relationship generally holds in the case of stocks, it is reasonable to expect that the futures price should trade at a discount to the forward price.[7] Thus we conclude that the theoretical futures value can be best approximated by the following formula:

$$F_0 = \frac{(1 + i)}{(1 + d)} \times P_0. \qquad (7\text{–}10)$$

Five Important Cash/Futures Price Relationships

Equations (7–7) and (7–8) reveal several important relationships between the stock index values and the stock index futures values.

1. If the T bill yield is higher than the expected dividend yield (plus the reinvestment return), the stock index futures value will be higher

---

[6] This result follows from an equilibrium model that sets the total cash flows from each portfolio equal to one another without regard for the implied leverage in the futures portfolio. Thus:

$$P_0 + (P_t - P_0) + (d + r)P_0 = P_0 + (F_t - F_0) + iP_0$$

where P_0 equals both the initial capital and the cash price of the stock index.
Solving this equation for F_0 leads to:

$$F_0 = P_0 + iP_0 - (d + r)P_0$$
$$= (1 + i - d - r)P_0.$$

[7] The negative effects of variation margin flows may not hold for the shorter term.

than the current stock index value. This is called a premium, or positive carrying cost market.

2. If the T bill yield is less than the dividend yield (plus the reinvestment return), the futures price would trade below the spot index. This is called a discount, or negative carrying cost market.

3. If the T bill yield is higher than the dividend yield (plus the reinvestment return), the implied equity risk premium would be less than the expected stock price appreciation.

4. If the T bill yield is less than the dividend yield (plus the reinvestment return), the implied equity risk premium would be higher than the expected stock price appreciation.

5. The price of a futures contract is always lower than the expected future price because the equity risk premium is always positive.

Dividend Dynamics of Stock Index Futures Prices

Earlier in this chapter we established the theoretical determinants of stock index futures prices under simplified conditions. In this section we deal with several real-world issues related to the correct measurement of dividend yields. Critical to this measurement issue is an understanding of the differences between the yield-to-maturity concepts for fixed-income instruments and the constant holding period concepts generally used in equity analysis.

In effect, a stock index futures/T bill portfolio is a fixed-income-type instrument. When comparing its return to that of a stock portfolio, the dividend yield for the portfolio should be recalculated to a yield-to-maturity basis, that is, for a fixed-maturity holding period rather than the usually reported annual yield.

Proper recognition of this distinction, and other factors, leads to some important conclusions about how different futures maturities and different stock index contracts should behave in relation to their underlying market index. At certain times it is perfectly rational for some contracts to trade at a discount while others are at a premium to the market. It is also rational for the same contract month for the S&P and NYSE futures to trade at significantly different spreads to their underlying indexes.

Fixed-Maturity versus Constant Holding Period Yields

In an earlier section we demonstrated that a stock market portfolio and a stock index futures/T bill portfolio will provide equal total returns when the futures price is at a full carry premium to the cash index value. Full carry is roughly equal to the ratio difference between the riskless interest rate (T bill rate) and the dividend yield for a fixed holding period. The fixed-maturity holding period used for the computation *must* correspond to the maturity date of a futures contract because only on that date will the futures price necessarily converge to the underlying stock index value.

It is essential that the importance of the concept of a fixed-maturity holding period be fully understood. For example, in most cases dividend yields for a fixed-maturity holding period will differ significantly, not only for each of the corresponding futures contracts, but also from the conventionally calculated dividend yields for constant holding periods, such as quarterly or annual yields. A fixed-maturity holding period means that the maturity date is fixed; thus each passing day shortens the duration of the next fixed holding period calculation. By contrast, a constant holding period means that the holding interval does not change over time. Virtually all statistical services report dividend yields based on the constant holding period concept.

To graphically demonstrate the differences in dividend yield calculations for a fixed-maturity holding period and a constant holding period, we first analyze the dividend distribution pattern for the Dow Jones 30 stocks for the period from January 1, 1981, to December 31, 1981. We then look at the dynamic effect on yields that comes from shifting the maturity date from December 31 to December 16 (a shift of only 15 days). Finally, we illustrate the dynamic dividend yield pattern corresponding to the maturity date of each of the four S&P 500 Composite Index futures contracts. Since the record date is used as the basis for dividend disbursements, the actual timing of dividend flows is largely irrelevant in determining a fixed-maturity holding period dividend yield. (The payment date normally lags the ex-dividend date by about three to four weeks.) In present value terms this lag is of little importance to the yield calculation and is therefore ignored.

Dividend Yield Dynamics

Exhibit 7–2 illustrates the quarterly dividend distribution for the 30 Dow Jones Industrials. It is clear that most of the ex-dividend dates tend to concentrate in February, May, August, and November. Except for a few dividend changes, the pattern of quarterly distribution is quite consistent over the year.

Exhibit 7–3 illustrates the declining balance of the total 1981 dividends a DJ stock portfolio holder would have received during the fixed holding period, with December 31, 1981, as the maturity date. For example, if the DJ stock portfolio were initiated on December 31, 1980, the investor would have received $72.22 by the end of 1981. Note that there are

Exhibit 7–2

Dividend Distribution, Dow Jones 30 Industrials

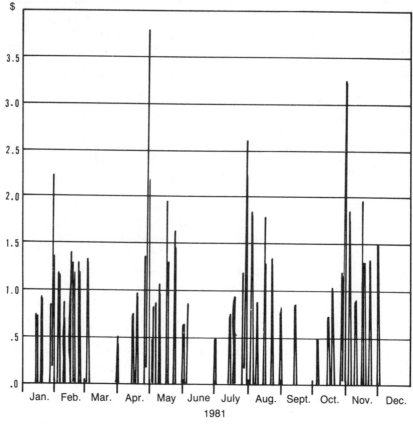

Source: DLJ.

periods when the remaining balance holds constant. For example, if the stock portfolio were initiated on any date between June 4 and June 29, the investor would have received the same dividend amount of $37.53 through the end of the year. After the last ex-dividend date, on December 1, 1981, the investor would not receive any dividends for the remainder of the holding period.

The dividend yield calculations for both a fixed-maturity holding period and a constant holding period are shown in Exhibit 7–4. The solid line in the chart indicates the annualized yield for the declining balance for the dividends to be received over the remainder of the fixed-maturity holding period. The dotted line represents the dividend yield for a con-

Exhibit 7-3

Declining Balance of 1981 Dividends, DJ 30 Stock Industrials

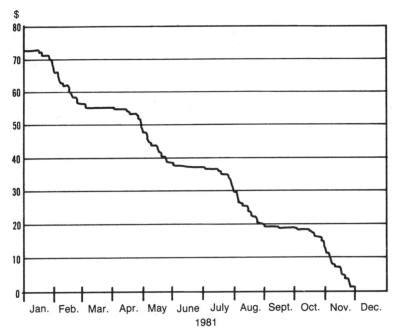

Source: DLJ.

stant, one-year holding period. It is clear from the chart that the fixed-maturity holding period dividend yield is much more volatile than the constant holding period yield. The divergence is even more pronounced during the third and fourth quarters of the dividend cycle.

Exhibit 7-5 illustrates the annualized fixed-maturity dividend yield with the maturity date shifted from December 31 to December 16. This shift is made to conform with the expiration date of the December S&P stock index futures contract (which by formula is the third Thursday of the expiry month). The shift of maturity date of the holding period, however, does not change the dollar amount of dividend distribution to be received. As a result, the fixed-maturity yield differs significantly from the December 31 maturity yield, particularly in the later part of the year. For example, the December 31 dividend yield peaks at 8.5 percent in late October (see Exhibit 7–4), compared with more than 11 percent (see Exhibit 7–5) for the December 16 maturity. The shift in the maturity date, however, does not change the timing of quarterly highs and lows in the yield.

Exhibit 7–4

Fixed Maturity and Constant (One-Year) Holding Period Dividend Yields, at
Annual Rates, January 1 to December 31, 1981

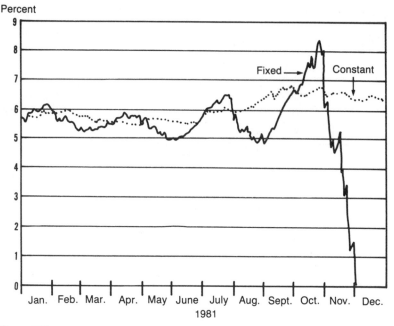

Percent

Source: DLJ.

Dividend distributions for the S&P 500 Composite Index generally
follow the same pattern as that of the 30 DJ Industrials. Based on a
historical dividend distribution pattern for S&P 500 stocks, we calculated
the fixed-maturity dividend yields corresponding exactly to the maturity
dates of each of the four futures contracts—March, June, September,
and December. As shown in Exhibit 7–6, the differences in the fixed-
maturity dividend yields for the different futures contract maturities will
be considerably different at certain times of the year. Note the tiering
of yields in late July and early August. At the widest point the September
maturity yield was about 3 percent higher than the June maturity yield.
Dividend yields always peak at about six weeks prior to the contract
expiration. For example, the fixed-maturity dividend yield for the December contract maturity date peaked in early November at about 10.5 percent.
At that time the yield for the March maturity was about 7 percent. By
early February the yield for a March maturity reached its high of about
9 percent.

Exhibit 7–5

Fixed-Maturity Dividend Yields for DJ 30 Industrials, at Annual Rate, with Maturity Shifted to December 16, 1981

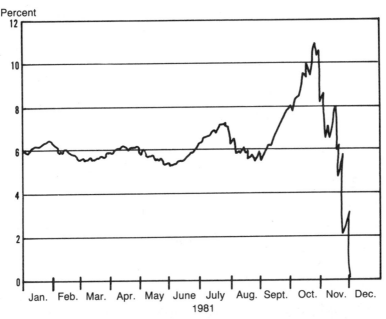

Percent

Source: DLJ.

Major Conclusions

The existence of both tiering and seasonality for the fixed-maturity portfolio dividend yield, for the different futures contract maturity dates, leads to interesting and important conclusions about how futures prices should trade in relation to the market index. It is entirely rational for the two following situations to occur:

1. The nearby futures contracts could sell at discounts to the market index whenever the fixed-maturity yield exceeds the T bill rate, while the other contracts still sell at a premium.

2. The futures contract premiums, or discounts, will vary both between contracts and over time even if the T bill rate does not change over time.

It should be pointed out that the fixed-maturity dividend yield curves portrayed in Exhibit 7–6 were based on an assumed 6 percent dividend yield for the year ahead (note that each yield curve begins at the 6 percent line). In the real world, however, expected dividend yields change over time. Therefore:

Exhibit 7–6

Fixed-Maturity Dividend Yield for S&P 500 at Annual Rates

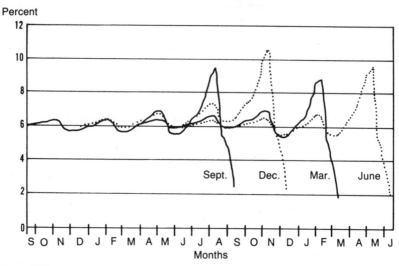

Source: DLJ.

3. Changes and differences in expected dividend yields will cause the magnitude and variability of futures prices to be different for each contract.

Another factor that can alter the expected dividend yields to maturity would be major changes in the ex-dividend dates. We have noted that the ex date has changed for several securities by one to two weeks from time to time.

4. It is important to know the exact schedule of record dates for dividend disbursements before one can correctly calculate dividend yields to maturity.

Finally, when comparing futures spreads for different stock index futures contracts, one should adjust for the different contract expiration dates. The NYSE contract for the New York Stock Exchange Composite Index expires on the next to last business day of the contract month, whereas the IMM contract for the S&P 500 Composite Index expires on the third Thursday of the contract month. This difference in contract specification could result in a difference of up to 14 days in the maturity dates. As a result, at today's dividend yields the fixed-maturity dividend yield could differ between the S&P and NYSE contract by as much as 3 percentage points, at annual rates, during the months prior to contract expiration.

5. Given the difference in the S&P and NYSE contract expiration dates, it would be possible for the expiring S&P contract to trade at a discount to its market index while the expiring NYSE contract was at a premium to its market index.

Putting It All Together: Example of Theoretical Prices for a Futures Contract

As demonstrated earlier, a stock portfolio and a stock index futures/T bill portfolio will provide equal returns when the futures prices are at a full carry to the cash index value. Full carry is roughly equal to the ratio difference between the riskless interest rate and the dividend yield, measured on a yield-to-maturity basis. In Exhibit 7–7 we show the estimates for the dividend yield to maturity and the T bill interest rate for

Exhibit 7–7

Dividend Dynamics: T Bill Yield (Line) versus December Maturity Dividend Yield (Dot)

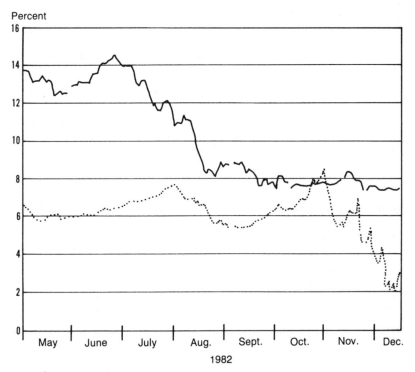

Source: DLJ.

valuing the S&P 500 December 82 futures contract, which had an expiration date of December 16.

The chart has a number of noteworthy features. For example, the estimate of the dividend yield to maturity for late October and early November was greater than the T bill yield. This would indicate that the December contract should have been trading at a discount at that time. It is also worthy of note that the dividend yield did not reach the high level projected earlier and as shown in Exhibit 7–6. The market rally that started in mid-August was so strong that it offset the seasonal increase in dividends, so that the dividend yield to maturity was held down. Even on a constant (one-year) maturity basis, dividend yields were held to below 5 percent.

Based on these two series, the theoretical futures prices are calculated and contrasted with the actual S&P December 82 futures prices in Exhibit 7–8. Whenever the futures price (solid line) was below the theoretical price (dotted line), the futures contract was undervalued. Conversely,

Exhibit 7–8

S&P December Futures (Line) versus Theoretical Index Value (Dot)

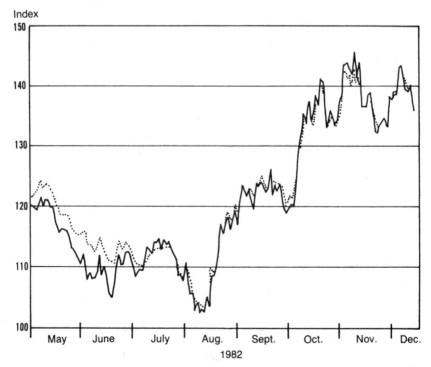

Source: DLJ.

Exhibit 7-9

The Spreads: Theoretical (Line) versus Actual (Dot)—Theoretical Futures less S&P 500
Index (Line), December 82 Futures less S&P 500 Index (Dot)

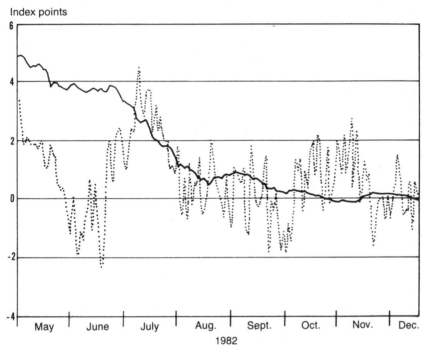

Index points

Source: DLJ.

whenever the futures price was above the theoretical price, the futures
contract was overvalued.

Exhibit 7-9 magnifies the relationship between theoretical and actual
December futures prices by showing both of them relative to the actual
index values. For example, on June 18, 1982, the S&P 500 index closed
at 107.28 and the S&P December futures closed at 104.90, or at a 2.38-
point discount from the spot index. On the same date the theoretical
price for the futures contract was 111.03, or 3.75 points above the actual
index. It was possible on that date for an investor to establish a futures
position that would outperform the S&P 500 stock index by about 11.8
percent, at an annual rate, for the six-month period June 18–December
16, 1982. This was an unusual day; opportunities of this magnitude rarely
occur. But this example does underscore the fact that stock index futures
can provide an alternative market for developing strategies to outperform
the market.

From Exhibit 7-9, it can be seen clearly that the market was not very efficient in pricing the new futures contract during the first two months of trading—May and June 1982. Since early July, however, the futures contract has traded within a reasonably close range of the theoretical prices. This strongly suggests that the external efficiency of the futures market improved very rapidly. However, there is still room for improvement in the internal efficiency of the market. The trading range will not narrow until the transaction costs and arbitrage risks are reduced further. In Chapter 10 the costs of arbitraging departures from theoretical value are examined closely and it is pointed out that most of the time futures trade well within a rational band defined by transaction costs.

CHAPTER 8

Standard & Poor's 500 Composite Index Futures Evaluation Tables

Gary L. Gastineau
Manager of the Options Portfolio Service
Kidder, Peabody & Co., Inc.

Albert Madansky, Ph.D.
Professor of Business Administration
University of Chicago

The Pricing Relationship[1]

The appropriate price for a stock index futures contract is relatively straightforward in concept and is totally consistent with the principles of the capital asset pricing model. The stock index futures pricing model is based on the neutral hedge or riskless arbitrage concept that has been so important in the development of option theory and pricing models for most financial futures contracts. Suppose an investor creates a portfolio whose composition and weighting are exactly equal to those of the Standard & Poor's 500 Composite Index. If the same investor sold S&P 500 futures contracts with a face value equal to the market value of the portfolio, he would have eliminated all stock market risk from the portfolio. The expected return for the period that the hedge is in place should equal the "risk-free" rate of portfolio theory. Market friction and complications in handling variation margin are neither trivial nor of overwhelming significance in limiting the usefulness of this approach.

---

[1] See the two previous chapters for an expanded treatment of the theoretical pricing relationship.

99

The major consideration that keeps the valuation of the futures contract from being a simple calculation based on this cost of carry or arbitrage model is the timing of dividend payments. Holders of the stock portfolio will obtain all dividends due on the underlying stocks from the time the position is initiated. If these dividends flow in a steady stream and if the dividend yield on the index happens to be equal to the risk-free rate of return, the futures price and the current index value should be equal. Because dividends yields in recent years have been below short-term interest rates, we might expect the futures price to be greater than the current value of the index under normal circumstances.

However, we cannot simply take the dividend yield on the S&P 500 Composite Index and subtract it from the Treasury bill yield to get the annualized difference between the current value of the S&P 500 Composite Index and the appropriate futures price. We must take into account the fact that dividends are not paid in equal amounts each day. Typically, each company will make a lump-sum dividend payment once during a quarter. Table 8–1 shows the pattern of ex-dividend amounts during a typical calendar quarter for all stocks in the S&P 500 Composite Index.[2] Of the total dividends credited during this quarter, 10.7 percent were credited during the month of January, 55.4 percent during the month of February, and 33.9 percent during the month of March. The period is broken down further into 15-day segments and individual dates. It is interesting to note that nearly 75 percent of all S&P 500 company ex-dividend amounts fell during the 45-day period beginning February 1 and ending March 15. Since this pattern is typical of other quarters and since the settlement date for the S&P 500 futures contract falls in the middle of the third month of each calendar quarter, the dividend rate during the 45-day period before settlement is far higher than would be indicated by a simple calculation based on the indicated yield of the index. If during the last 45 days of its life an S&P 500 futures contract sells below the current quotation for the index, this does not necessarily mean that the futures contract is underpriced. To the extent that the dividend *rate* during the last 45 days of the life of the futures contract exceeds the short-term risk-free rate, it might be entirely appropriate for the index to sell at an apparent discount.

In the valuation tables we have incorporated the dividends for the first quarter of 1982 (adjusted for the AT&T policy change) and assumed that they are typical of other quarters. The tables would have to be modified if major corporations such as General Motors and Du Pont once again pay sizable year-end extra dividends. Likewise, a change will be

---

[2] Table 8–1 is based on the first quarter of 1982 with an important adjustment to reflect the dividend policy change made in early 1983 by American Telephone & Telegraph to delay its dividend by one month in preparation for divestiture.

Table 8–1

Daily Ex-Dividend Record, First Quarter, 1982

January	Daily Dividend	February	Daily Dividend	March	Daily Dividend
1	$ –0–	1	$1,014,522,892	1	$ 475,481,425
2	–0–	2	620,986,860	2	233,877,935
3	–0–	3	706,450,730	3	211,252,855
4	244,450,655	4	1,083,636,845	4	226,646,535
5	84,333,375	5	760,013,549	5	46,388,835
6	–0–	6	–0–	6	–0–
7	–0–	7	–0–	7	–0–
8	–0–	8	302,863,260	8	221,314,295
9	–0–	9	77,539,835	9	456,911,665
10	–0–	10	79,395,850	10	12,290,885
11	125,031,970	11	493,953,535	11	160,487,000
12	14,781,315	12	–0–	12	132,207,945
13	–0–	13	–0–	13	–0–
14	77,423,915	14	–0–	14	–0–
15	1,493,800	15	–0–	15	93,392,590
16	–0–	16	147,042,660	16	24,396,600
17	–0–	17	175,652,290	17	–0–
18	110,004,260	18	229,103,820	18	77,890,880
19	56,192,560	19	33,335,295	19	–0–
20	–0–	20	–0–	20	–0–
21	–0–	21	–0–	21	–0–
22	36,231,630	22	243,098,250	22	1,156,973,290
23	–0–	23	388,689,790	23	–0–
24	–0–	24	100,333,870	24	106,333,017
25	122,280,645	25	59,752,500	25	79,197,416
26	299,047,115	26	59,209,980	26	64,933,420
27	6,999,970	27	–0–	27	–0–
28	11,502,180	28	–0–	28	–0–
29	78,875,975			29	14,167,000
30	–0–			30	236,973,000
31	–0–			31	23,754,500

	Percent of Total Dividend
January 1–15	4.6
16–31	6.1
January total	10.7
February 1–14	43.3
15–28	12.1
February total	55.4
March 1–15	18.9
16–31	15.0
March total	33.9

necessary when the AT&T divestiture leads to a major change in the composition of the S&P 500 or if there is some other reason to expect a different quarterly pattern of dividends. For the present, however, this pattern provides a reasonable point of departure for valuation of stock index futures contracts.

Using the Tables

To prepare the valuation tables, shown as Tables 8–2 through 8–6, the dividends from Table 8–1 were systematically "spread out" over the month in which they fell. While the pattern of dividends in some future quarter will not correspond perfectly due to changes in ex dates, any error will almost certainly be less than the error in estimating the true current value of the index, as discussed later in this chapter. *Please keep in mind that we are trying to adjust for the appropriate pattern of ex-dividend dates, not to give the user of these tables misleading confidence in the precision of the number.* To retain the pattern as well as possible, the end of each calendar month approximates the 30-, 60-, and 91-day points in the first column of Tables 8–2 through 8–6. The second column shows the days until expiration of the contract based on the premise that, on average, the contract will settle in the middle of the third month of the calendar quarter. The third column shows the fraction of total dividends to be paid during the quarter that will fall between that day and the settlement date of the futures contract.

To select the appropriate table, an investor must obtain estimates of (1) the dividend yield on the S&P 500 Composite Index and (2) the discount yield for the Treasury bill maturing closest to the settlement day of the stock index futures contract. Estimates of the S&P dividend are available from most brokerage firms, and Treasury bill yields appear daily in most major newspapers.

Actually, the bond equivalent yield of a Treasury bill is the appropriate interest rate measurement. Because the Treasury bill discount yield is so universally quoted, however, the tables are designed to use discount yield as the interest rate input. The corresponding bond equivalent yield was used to calculate the coefficients. Tables are provided for S&P dividend returns of 3 percent through 7 percent and for Treasury bill discount yields of 4 percent through 14 percent. To use these tables, an investor selects the table for the appropriate S&P dividend rate, say 4 percent, which is Table 8–5. The column to be used will be that of the discount return available on the Treasury bill maturing closest to the settlement date of the stock index futures contract. In this example we assume that the Treasury bill discount rate is 7 percent. If there are 36 days before settlement, the figure on the 4 percent S&P return, Table 8–5, in the 7

Table 8-2   S&P 500 Futures Evaluation Table (S&P Dividend Return = 7%)

		4%	5%	6%	7%	8%	9%	10%	11%	12%	13%	14%
75	.84217	-0.0063	-0.0042	-0.0020	0.0001	0.0023	0.0044	0.0066	0.0088	0.0110	0.0133	0.0155
74	.84217	-0.0064	-0.0043	-0.0022	-0.0001	0.0020	0.0042	0.0063	0.0085	0.0107	0.0129	0.0151
73	.82948	-0.0063	-0.0042	-0.0022	-0.0001	0.0020	0.0042	0.0063	0.0084	0.0106	0.0127	0.0149
72	.82948	-0.0064	-0.0044	-0.0023	-0.0003	0.0018	0.0039	0.0060	0.0081	0.0102	0.0124	0.0145
71	.82239	-0.0064	-0.0044	-0.0024	-0.0003	0.0017	0.0038	0.0058	0.0079	0.0100	0.0121	0.0142
70	.82239	-0.0065	-0.0045	-0.0025	-0.0005	0.0015	0.0035	0.0056	0.0076	0.0097	0.0117	0.0138
69	.81188	-0.0065	-0.0045	-0.0025	-0.0006	0.0014	0.0034	0.0055	0.0075	0.0095	0.0115	0.0136
68	.81188	-0.0066	-0.0046	-0.0027	-0.0008	0.0012	0.0032	0.0052	0.0072	0.0092	0.0112	0.0132
67	.81064	-0.0067	-0.0048	-0.0028	-0.0009	0.0010	0.0029	0.0049	0.0069	0.0088	0.0108	0.0128
66	.81064	-0.0068	-0.0049	-0.0030	-0.0011	0.0008	0.0027	0.0046	0.0066	0.0085	0.0104	0.0124
65	.80413	-0.0068	-0.0049	-0.0031	-0.0012	0.0007	0.0026	0.0044	0.0064	0.0083	0.0102	0.0121
64	.80413	-0.0069	-0.0051	-0.0032	-0.0014	0.0004	0.0023	0.0042	0.0060	0.0079	0.0098	0.0117
63	.80401	-0.0070	-0.0052	-0.0034	-0.0016	0.0002	0.0020	0.0039	0.0057	0.0076	0.0094	0.0113
62	.80401	-0.0071	-0.0054	-0.0036	-0.0018	0.0000	0.0018	0.0036	0.0054	0.0072	0.0091	0.0109
61	.79476	-0.0071	-0.0053	-0.0036	-0.0018	-0.0001	0.0017	0.0035	0.0053	0.0071	0.0089	0.0107
60	.79476	-0.0072	-0.0055	-0.0038	-0.0020	-0.0003	0.0014	0.0032	0.0049	0.0067	0.0085	0.0103
59	.79476	-0.0073	-0.0056	-0.0039	-0.0022	-0.0005	0.0012	0.0029	0.0046	0.0064	0.0081	0.0099
58	.79004	-0.0073	-0.0057	-0.0040	-0.0023	-0.0007	0.0010	0.0027	0.0044	0.0061	0.0078	0.0095
57	.79004	-0.0074	-0.0058	-0.0042	-0.0025	-0.0009	0.0008	0.0024	0.0041	0.0058	0.0074	0.0091
56	.78699	-0.0075	-0.0059	-0.0043	-0.0027	-0.0011	0.0005	0.0022	0.0038	0.0055	0.0071	0.0088
55	.78699	-0.0076	-0.0060	-0.0045	-0.0029	-0.0013	0.0003	0.0019	0.0035	0.0051	0.0068	0.0084
54	.77672	-0.0075	-0.0060	-0.0045	-0.0029	-0.0013	0.0002	0.0018	0.0034	0.0050	0.0066	0.0082
53	.77672	-0.0076	-0.0061	-0.0046	-0.0031	-0.0016	0.0000	0.0015	0.0031	0.0046	0.0062	0.0078
52	.75159	-0.0073	-0.0058	-0.0044	-0.0029	-0.0014	0.0001	0.0017	0.0032	0.0047	0.0063	0.0078
51	.75159	-0.0074	-0.0060	-0.0045	-0.0031	-0.0016	-0.0001	0.0014	0.0029	0.0044	0.0059	0.0074
50	.75100	-0.0075	-0.0061	-0.0047	-0.0032	-0.0018	-0.0004	0.0011	0.0026	0.0040	0.0055	0.0070
49	.75100	-0.0076	-0.0063	-0.0049	-0.0034	-0.0020	-0.0006	0.0008	0.0023	0.0037	0.0051	0.0066
48	.75003	-0.0077	-0.0064	-0.0050	-0.0036	-0.0022	-0.0008	0.0005	0.0020	0.0034	0.0048	0.0062
47	.75003	-0.0079	-0.0065	-0.0052	-0.0038	-0.0025	-0.0011	0.0003	0.0016	0.0030	0.0044	0.0058
46	.74340	-0.0078	-0.0065	-0.0052	-0.0039	-0.0026	-0.0012	0.0001	0.0014	0.0028	0.0042	0.0055
45	.65814	-0.0065	-0.0052	-0.0039	-0.0026	-0.0013	0.0000	0.0013	0.0026	0.0039	0.0053	0.0066
44	.65814	-0.0066	-0.0053	-0.0041	-0.0028	-0.0015	-0.0003	0.0010	0.0023	0.0036	0.0049	0.0062
43	.60595	-0.0058	-0.0046	-0.0033	-0.0021	-0.0009	0.0004	0.0016	0.0029	0.0042	0.0054	0.0067
42	.60595	-0.0059	-0.0047	-0.0035	-0.0023	-0.0011	0.0001	0.0014	0.0026	0.0038	0.0051	0.0063
41	.54658	-0.0050	-0.0038	-0.0026	-0.0015	-0.0003	0.0009	0.0021	0.0033	0.0045	0.0057	0.0070
40	.45552	-0.0035	-0.0023	-0.0012	-0.0001	0.0011	0.0023	0.0034	0.0046	0.0058	0.0070	0.0081
39	.45552	-0.0036	-0.0025	-0.0014	-0.0003	0.0009	0.0020	0.0031	0.0043	0.0054	0.0066	0.0077
38	.39164	-0.0026	-0.0015	-0.0004	0.0007	0.0018	0.0029	0.0040	0.0051	0.0062	0.0073	0.0085
37	.39164	-0.0027	-0.0016	-0.0006	0.0005	0.0015	0.0026	0.0037	0.0048	0.0059	0.0070	0.0081
36	.36619	-0.0024	-0.0013	-0.0003	0.0007	0.0018	0.0028	0.0038	0.0049	0.0060	0.0070	0.0081
35	.35968	-0.0024	-0.0014	-0.0004	0.0006	0.0016	0.0027	0.0037	0.0047	0.0057	0.0068	0.0078
34	.35968	-0.0025	-0.0015	-0.0005	0.0004	0.0014	0.0024	0.0034	0.0044	0.0054	0.0064	0.0074
33	.35300	-0.0025	-0.0015	-0.0006	0.0004	0.0013	0.0023	0.0032	0.0042	0.0052	0.0061	0.0071
32	.35300	-0.0026	-0.0017	-0.0008	0.0002	0.0011	0.0020	0.0029	0.0039	0.0048	0.0058	0.0067
31	.31149	-0.0020	-0.0011	-0.0002	0.0007	0.0016	0.0025	0.0034	0.0043	0.0052	0.0061	0.0070
30	.31149	-0.0021	-0.0012	-0.0004	0.0005	0.0014	0.0022	0.0031	0.0040	0.0049	0.0057	0.0066
29	.29913	-0.0020	-0.0012	-0.0003	0.0005	0.0013	0.0022	0.0030	0.0039	0.0047	0.0056	0.0065
28	.28437	-0.0018	-0.0010	-0.0002	0.0006	0.0014	0.0022	0.0030	0.0038	0.0046	0.0055	0.0063
27	.28437	-0.0019	-0.0012	-0.0004	0.0004	0.0011	0.0019	0.0027	0.0035	0.0043	0.0051	0.0059
26	.26512	-0.0017	-0.0010	-0.0002	0.0005	0.0013	0.0020	0.0028	0.0035	0.0043	0.0051	0.0058
25	.26512	-0.0018	-0.0011	-0.0004	0.0003	0.0010	0.0018	0.0025	0.0032	0.0040	0.0047	0.0054
24	.26232	-0.0019	-0.0012	-0.0005	0.0002	0.0009	0.0015	0.0022	0.0030	0.0037	0.0044	0.0051
23	.24189	-0.0017	-0.0010	-0.0003	0.0003	0.0010	0.0016	0.0023	0.0030	0.0037	0.0044	0.0050
22	.24189	-0.0018	-0.0011	-0.0005	0.0001	0.0008	0.0014	0.0020	0.0027	0.0033	0.0040	0.0046
21	.20922	-0.0013	-0.0007	-0.0001	0.0005	0.0011	0.0017	0.0023	0.0029	0.0036	0.0042	0.0048
20	.20922	-0.0014	-0.0008	-0.0003	0.0003	0.0009	0.0015	0.0020	0.0026	0.0032	0.0038	0.0044
19	.20079	-0.0014	-0.0008	-0.0003	0.0002	0.0008	0.0013	0.0019	0.0025	0.0030	0.0036	0.0041
18	.19577	-0.0014	-0.0009	-0.0004	0.0001	0.0007	0.0012	0.0017	0.0022	0.0028	0.0033	0.0038
17	.19577	-0.0015	-0.0010	-0.0005	-0.0001	0.0004	0.0009	0.0014	0.0019	0.0024	0.0029	0.0034
16	.19079	-0.0014	-0.0011	-0.0006	-0.0002	0.0003	0.0008	0.0012	0.0017	0.0022	0.0026	0.0031
15	.15083	-0.0010	-0.0005	-0.0001	0.0003	0.0008	0.0012	0.0016	0.0021	0.0025	0.0030	0.0034
14	.13118	-0.0007	-0.0003	0.0001	0.0005	0.0009	0.0013	0.0017	0.0021	0.0025	0.0029	0.0033
13	.13118	-0.0008	-0.0005	-0.0001	0.0003	0.0007	0.0010	0.0014	0.0018	0.0022	0.0026	0.0029
12	.11342	-0.0006	-0.0003	0.0000	0.0004	0.0007	0.0011	0.0014	0.0018	0.0021	0.0025	0.0029
11	.09438	-0.0004	-0.0001	0.0002	0.0005	0.0008	0.0012	0.0015	0.0018	0.0021	0.0025	0.0028
10	.09438	-0.0005	-0.0002	0.0000	0.0003	0.0006	0.0009	0.0012	0.0015	0.0018	0.0021	0.0024
9	.09048	-0.0006	-0.0003	-0.0001	0.0002	0.0005	0.0007	0.0010	0.0012	0.0015	0.0018	0.0020
8	.07188	-0.0004	-0.0001	0.0001	0.0003	0.0006	0.0008	0.0010	0.0013	0.0015	0.0017	0.0020
7	.07188	-0.0005	-0.0003	-0.0001	0.0001	0.0003	0.0005	0.0007	0.0009	0.0011	0.0014	0.0016
6	.03348	0.0001	0.0003	0.0004	0.0006	0.0008	0.0009	0.0011	0.0013	0.0015	0.0017	0.0018
5	.03348	0.0000	0.0001	0.0003	0.0004	0.0005	0.0007	0.0008	0.0010	0.0011	0.0013	0.0014
4	.03348	-0.0001	0.0000	0.0001	0.0002	0.0003	0.0005	0.0006	0.0007	0.0008	0.0009	0.0010
3	.01896	0.0000	0.0001	0.0002	0.0003	0.0003	0.0004	0.0005	0.0006	0.0007	0.0008	0.0009
2	.01896	-0.0001	-0.0001	0.0000	0.0001	0.0001	0.0002	0.0002	0.0003	0.0004	0.0004	0.0005
1	.00785	0.0000	0.0000	0.0000	0.0001	0.0001	0.0001	0.0001	0.0002	0.0002	0.0002	0.0003
0	.00000	0.0000	0.0000	0.0000	0.0000	0.0000	0.0000	0.0000	0.0000	0.0000	0.0000	0.0000
90	1.00000	-0.0074	-0.0048	-0.0023	0.0003	0.0029	0.0055	0.0081	0.0106	0.0134	0.0161	0.0188
89	.99795	-0.0075	-0.0049	-0.0024	0.0001	0.0027	0.0053	0.0079	0.0105	0.0131	0.0158	0.0184
88	.99140	-0.0075	-0.0050	-0.0025	0.0001	0.0026	0.0052	0.0077	0.0103	0.0129	0.0155	0.0181
87	.99140	-0.0076	-0.0051	-0.0026	-0.0001	0.0024	0.0049	0.0074	0.0100	0.0125	0.0151	0.0177
86	.89417	-0.0060	-0.0036	-0.0011	0.0014	0.0039	0.0063	0.0089	0.0114	0.0139	0.0165	0.0190
85	.89417	-0.0061	-0.0037	-0.0013	0.0012	0.0036	0.0061	0.0086	0.0111	0.0136	0.0161	0.0186
84	.88523	-0.0061	-0.0037	-0.0013	0.0011	0.0036	0.0060	0.0084	0.0109	0.0134	0.0159	0.0184

Table 8-2 (concluded)

		4%	5%	6%	7%	8%	9%	10%	11%	12%	13%	14%
84	83	.87858	-0.0061	-0.0037	-0.0013	0.0011	0.0034	0.0059	0.0083	0.0107	0.0131	0.0156	0.016
85	82	.87858	-0.0062	-0.0038	-0.0015	0.0009	0.0032	0.0056	0.0080	0.0104	0.0128	0.0152	0.017
86	81	.87312	-0.0062	-0.0039	-0.0016	0.0008	0.0031	0.0054	0.0078	0.0102	0.0126	0.0150	0.017
87	80	.87193	-0.0063	-0.0040	-0.0017	0.0006	0.0029	0.0052	0.0075	0.0099	0.0122	0.0146	0.017
88	79	.87193	-0.0064	-0.0041	-0.0019	0.0004	0.0027	0.0049	0.0072	0.0096	0.0119	0.0142	0.016
89	78	.85202	-0.0062	-0.0039	-0.0017	0.0005	0.0028	0.0050	0.0073	0.0096	0.0119	0.0142	0.016
90	77	.85002	-0.0062	-0.0040	-0.0018	0.0004	0.0026	0.0048	0.0071	0.0093	0.0116	0.0139	0.016
91	76	.85002	-0.0063	-0.0042	-0.0020	0.0002	0.0024	0.0046	0.0068	0.0090	0.0112	0.0135	0.015

Table 8-3   S&P 500 Futures Evaluation Table (S&P Dividend Return = 6%)

		4%	5%	6%	7%	8%	9%	10%	11%	12%	13%	14%
1	75	.84217	-0.0042	-0.0021	0.0001	0.0022	0.0044	0.0065	0.0087	0.0109	0.0131	0.0154	0.017
2	74	.84217	-0.0043	-0.0022	-0.0001	0.0020	0.0041	0.0063	0.0085	0.0106	0.0128	0.0150	0.017
3	73	.82948	-0.0042	-0.0022	-0.0001	0.0020	0.0041	0.0062	0.0084	0.0105	0.0126	0.0148	0.017
4	72	.82948	-0.0044	-0.0023	-0.0003	0.0018	0.0039	0.0060	0.0081	0.0102	0.0123	0.0144	0.016
5	71	.82239	-0.0044	-0.0023	-0.0003	0.0017	0.0038	0.0058	0.0079	0.0100	0.0121	0.0142	0.016
6	70	.82239	-0.0045	-0.0025	-0.0005	0.0015	0.0035	0.0056	0.0076	0.0097	0.0117	0.0138	0.015
7	69	.81188	-0.0044	-0.0025	-0.0005	0.0015	0.0035	0.0055	0.0075	0.0095	0.0115	0.0136	0.015
8	68	.81188	-0.0045	-0.0026	-0.0007	0.0013	0.0032	0.0052	0.0072	0.0092	0.0112	0.0132	0.015
9	67	.81064	-0.0046	-0.0027	-0.0008	0.0011	0.0030	0.0050	0.0069	0.0089	0.0109	0.0128	0.014
10	66	.81064	-0.0048	-0.0029	-0.0010	0.0009	0.0028	0.0047	0.0066	0.0086	0.0105	0.0125	0.014
11	65	.80413	-0.0048	-0.0029	-0.0011	0.0008	0.0027	0.0046	0.0065	0.0084	0.0103	0.0122	0.014
12	64	.80413	-0.0049	-0.0031	-0.0012	0.0006	0.0025	0.0043	0.0062	0.0080	0.0099	0.0118	0.013
13	63	.80401	-0.0050	-0.0032	-0.0014	0.0004	0.0022	0.0041	0.0059	0.0077	0.0096	0.0115	0.013
14	62	.80401	-0.0051	-0.0033	-0.0016	0.0002	0.0020	0.0038	0.0056	0.0074	0.0092	0.0111	0.012
15	61	.79476	-0.0051	-0.0033	-0.0016	0.0002	0.0019	0.0037	0.0055	0.0072	0.0090	0.0108	0.012
16	60	.79476	-0.0052	-0.0035	-0.0018	-0.0000	0.0017	0.0034	0.0052	0.0069	0.0087	0.0105	0.012
17	59	.79476	-0.0053	-0.0036	-0.0019	-0.0002	0.0015	0.0032	0.0049	0.0066	0.0084	0.0101	0.011
18	58	.79004	-0.0053	-0.0037	-0.0020	-0.0004	0.0013	0.0030	0.0047	0.0064	0.0081	0.0098	0.011
19	57	.79004	-0.0055	-0.0038	-0.0022	-0.0006	0.0011	0.0027	0.0044	0.0061	0.0077	0.0094	0.011
20	56	.78699	-0.0055	-0.0039	-0.0023	-0.0007	0.0009	0.0025	0.0041	0.0058	0.0074	0.0091	0.010
21	55	.78699	-0.0056	-0.0041	-0.0025	-0.0009	0.0007	0.0023	0.0039	0.0055	0.0071	0.0087	0.010
22	54	.77672	-0.0056	-0.0041	-0.0025	-0.0010	0.0006	0.0022	0.0037	0.0053	0.0069	0.0085	0.010
23	53	.77672	-0.0057	-0.0042	-0.0027	-0.0012	0.0004	0.0019	0.0034	0.0050	0.0066	0.0081	0.009
24	52	.75159	-0.0054	-0.0040	-0.0025	-0.0010	0.0005	0.0020	0.0035	0.0051	0.0066	0.0081	0.009
25	51	.75159	-0.0055	-0.0041	-0.0026	-0.0012	0.0003	0.0018	0.0033	0.0048	0.0063	0.0078	0.009
26	50	.75100	-0.0057	-0.0042	-0.0028	-0.0014	0.0001	0.0015	0.0030	0.0044	0.0059	0.0074	0.008
27	49	.75100	-0.0058	-0.0044	-0.0030	-0.0016	-0.0002	0.0013	0.0027	0.0041	0.0056	0.0070	0.008
28	48	.75003	-0.0059	-0.0045	-0.0031	-0.0018	-0.0004	0.0010	0.0024	0.0038	0.0052	0.0067	0.008
29	47	.75003	-0.0060	-0.0046	-0.0033	-0.0019	-0.0006	0.0008	0.0021	0.0035	0.0049	0.0063	0.007
30	46	.74340	-0.0060	-0.0047	-0.0034	-0.0020	-0.0007	0.0006	0.0020	0.0033	0.0047	0.0060	0.007
31	45	.65814	-0.0048	-0.0035	-0.0023	-0.0010	0.0003	0.0016	0.0029	0.0043	0.0056	0.0069	0.008
32	44	.65814	-0.0049	-0.0037	-0.0024	-0.0012	0.0001	0.0014	0.0027	0.0040	0.0052	0.0066	0.007
33	43	.60595	-0.0043	-0.0030	-0.0018	-0.0006	0.0007	0.0019	0.0032	0.0044	0.0057	0.0070	0.008
34	42	.60595	-0.0044	-0.0032	-0.0020	-0.0008	0.0004	0.0017	0.0029	0.0041	0.0053	0.0066	0.007
35	41	.54658	-0.0036	-0.0024	-0.0013	-0.0001	0.0011	0.0023	0.0035	0.0047	0.0059	0.0071	0.008
36	40	.45552	-0.0023	-0.0012	-0.0001	0.0011	0.0022	0.0034	0.0046	0.0057	0.0069	0.0081	0.009
37	39	.45552	-0.0025	-0.0013	-0.0002	0.0009	0.0020	0.0031	0.0043	0.0054	0.0066	0.0077	0.008
38	38	.39164	-0.0016	-0.0005	0.0006	0.0016	0.0027	0.0038	0.0050	0.0061	0.0072	0.0083	0.009
39	37	.39164	-0.0017	-0.0007	0.0004	0.0014	0.0025	0.0036	0.0047	0.0058	0.0068	0.0079	0.009
40	36	.36619	-0.0015	-0.0004	0.0006	0.0016	0.0027	0.0037	0.0048	0.0058	0.0069	0.0079	0.009
41	35	.35968	-0.0015	-0.0005	0.0005	0.0015	0.0025	0.0036	0.0046	0.0056	0.0066	0.0077	0.008
42	34	.35968	-0.0016	-0.0006	0.0004	0.0013	0.0023	0.0033	0.0043	0.0053	0.0063	0.0073	0.008
43	33	.35300	-0.0016	-0.0007	0.0003	0.0012	0.0022	0.0031	0.0041	0.0051	0.0060	0.0070	0.008
44	32	.35300	-0.0017	-0.0008	0.0001	0.0010	0.0020	0.0029	0.0038	0.0048	0.0057	0.0066	0.007
45	31	.31149	-0.0012	-0.0003	0.0006	0.0015	0.0024	0.0033	0.0042	0.0051	0.0060	0.0069	0.007
46	30	.31149	-0.0013	-0.0005	0.0004	0.0013	0.0021	0.0030	0.0039	0.0048	0.0056	0.0065	0.007
47	29	.29913	-0.0012	-0.0004	0.0004	0.0013	0.0021	0.0029	0.0038	0.0046	0.0055	0.0063	0.007
48	28	.28437	-0.0011	-0.0003	0.0005	0.0013	0.0021	0.0029	0.0037	0.0045	0.0054	0.0062	0.007
49	27	.28437	-0.0012	-0.0005	0.0003	0.0011	0.0019	0.0026	0.0034	0.0042	0.0050	0.0058	0.006
50	26	.26512	-0.0011	-0.0003	0.0004	0.0012	0.0019	0.0027	0.0034	0.0042	0.0050	0.0057	0.006
51	25	.26512	-0.0012	-0.0005	0.0003	0.0010	0.0017	0.0024	0.0031	0.0039	0.0046	0.0054	0.006
52	24	.26232	-0.0012	-0.0006	0.0001	0.0008	0.0015	0.0022	0.0029	0.0036	0.0043	0.0050	0.005
53	23	.24189	-0.0010	-0.0004	0.0003	0.0009	0.0016	0.0023	0.0029	0.0036	0.0043	0.0050	0.005
54	22	.24189	-0.0012	-0.0005	0.0001	0.0007	0.0014	0.0020	0.0026	0.0033	0.0039	0.0046	0.005
55	21	.20922	-0.0008	-0.0002	0.0004	0.0010	0.0016	0.0022	0.0028	0.0035	0.0041	0.0047	0.005
56	20	.20922	-0.0009	-0.0003	0.0002	0.0008	0.0014	0.0020	0.0026	0.0031	0.0037	0.0043	0.004
57	19	.20079	-0.0009	-0.0003	0.0002	0.0007	0.0013	0.0018	0.0024	0.0030	0.0035	0.0041	0.004
58	18	.19577	-0.0009	-0.0004	0.0001	0.0006	0.0011	0.0017	0.0022	0.0027	0.0032	0.0038	0.004
59	17	.19577	-0.0010	-0.0005	-0.0001	0.0004	0.0009	0.0014	0.0019	0.0024	0.0029	0.0034	0.003
60	16	.19079	-0.0011	-0.0006	-0.0002	0.0003	0.0008	0.0012	0.0017	0.0022	0.0026	0.0031	0.003
61	15	.15083	-0.0006	-0.0002	0.0003	0.0007	0.0011	0.0016	0.0020	0.0025	0.0029	0.0033	0.003
62	14	.13118	-0.0004	0.0000	0.0004	0.0008	0.0012	0.0016	0.0020	0.0024	0.0028	0.0033	0.003
63	13	.13118	-0.0005	-0.0001	0.0002	0.0006	0.0010	0.0014	0.0017	0.0021	0.0025	0.0029	0.003
64	12	.11342	-0.0004	0.0000	0.0003	0.0007	0.0010	0.0014	0.0017	0.0021	0.0024	0.0028	0.003
65	11	.09438	-0.0002	0.0001	0.0004	0.0008	0.0011	0.0014	0.0017	0.0020	0.0024	0.0027	0.003
66	10	.09438	-0.0003	0.0000	0.0003	0.0006	0.0009	0.0011	0.0014	0.0017	0.0020	0.0023	0.002
67	9	.09048	-0.0003	-0.0001	0.0002	0.0004	0.0007	0.0009	0.0012	0.0015	0.0017	0.0020	0.002
68	8	.07188	-0.0002	0.0000	0.0003	0.0005	0.0007	0.0010	0.0012	0.0014	0.0017	0.0019	0.002

Table 8–3 (concluded)

	4%	5%	6%	7%	8%	9%	10%	11%	12%	13%	14%
7	.07188	-0.0003	-0.0001	0.0001	0.0003	0.0005	0.0007	0.0009	0.0011	0.0013	0.0015	0.0017
6	.03348	0.0002	0.0003	0.0005	0.0007	0.0009	0.0010	0.0012	0.0014	0.0016	0.0017	0.0019
5	.03346	0.0001	0.0002	0.0003	0.0005	0.0006	0.0008	0.0009	0.0011	0.0012	0.0014	0.0015
4	.03245	0.0000	0.0001	0.0002	0.0003	0.0004	0.0005	0.0007	0.0008	0.0009	0.0010	0.0011
3	.01896	0.0001	0.0001	0.0002	0.0003	0.0004	0.0005	0.0006	0.0007	0.0007	0.0008	0.0009
2	.01896	-0.0001	0.0000	0.0001	0.0001	0.0002	0.0002	0.0003	0.0003	0.0004	0.0005	0.0005
1	.00785	0.0000	0.0000	0.0001	0.0001	0.0001	0.0001	0.0002	0.0002	0.0002	0.0003	0.0003
0	.00000	0.0000	0.0000	0.0000	0.0000	0.0000	0.0000	0.0000	0.0000	0.0000	0.0000	0.0000
90	1.00000	-0.0049	-0.0023	0.0002	0.0028	0.0054	0.0080	0.0106	0.0133	0.0159	0.0186	0.0213
89	.99795	-0.0050	-0.0025	0.0001	0.0026	0.0052	0.0078	0.0104	0.0130	0.0156	0.0182	0.0209
88	.99140	-0.0050	-0.0025	0.0000	0.0025	0.0051	0.0076	0.0102	0.0128	0.0154	0.0180	0.0206
87	.99140	-0.0051	-0.0026	-0.0002	0.0023	0.0049	0.0074	0.0099	0.0125	0.0150	0.0176	0.0202
86	.89417	-0.0038	-0.0013	0.0011	0.0036	0.0061	0.0086	0.0111	0.0136	0.0161	0.0187	0.0212
85	.89417	-0.0039	-0.0015	0.0010	0.0034	0.0059	0.0083	0.0108	0.0133	0.0158	0.0183	0.0208
84	.86523	-0.0039	-0.0015	0.0009	0.0033	0.0058	0.0082	0.0107	0.0131	0.0156	0.0181	0.0206
83	.87858	-0.0039	-0.0015	0.0009	0.0032	0.0056	0.0080	0.0105	0.0129	0.0153	0.0178	0.0203
82	.57858	-0.0040	-0.0016	-0.0007	0.0030	0.0054	0.0078	0.0102	0.0126	0.0150	0.0174	0.0199
81	.87312	-0.0040	-0.0017	0.0006	0.0029	0.0053	0.0076	0.0100	0.0124	0.0147	0.0171	0.0195
80	.87193	-0.0041	-0.0018	0.0005	0.0028	0.0051	0.0074	0.0097	0.0121	0.0144	0.0168	0.0192
79	.87193	-0.0042	-0.0020	0.0003	0.0026	0.0048	0.0071	0.0094	0.0117	0.0141	0.0164	0.0188
78	.85202	-0.0040	-0.0018	0.0004	0.0027	0.0049	0.0072	0.0094	0.0117	0.0140	0.0163	0.0187
77	.85002	-0.0041	-0.0019	0.0003	0.0025	0.0047	0.0069	0.0092	0.0114	0.0137	0.0160	0.0183
76	.85002	-0.0042	-0.0021	0.0001	0.0023	0.0045	0.0067	0.0089	0.0111	0.0134	0.0156	0.0179

Table 8–4   S&P 500 Futures Evaluation Table (S&P Dividend Return = 5%)

	4%	5%	6%	7%	8%	9%	10%	11%	12%	13%	14%
75	.64217	-0.0021	0.0000	0.0022	0.0043	0.0065	0.0087	0.0108	0.0130	0.0152	0.0175	0.0197
74	.84217	-0.0022	-0.0001	0.0020	0.0041	0.0063	0.0084	0.0106	0.0127	0.0149	0.0171	0.0193
73	.82948	-0.0022	-0.0001	0.0020	0.0041	0.0062	0.0083	0.0104	0.0126	0.0147	0.0169	0.0191
72	.82948	-0.0023	-0.0002	0.0018	0.0039	0.0060	0.0080	0.0101	0.0123	0.0144	0.0165	0.0186
71	.82239	-0.0023	-0.0003	0.0017	0.0038	0.0058	0.0079	0.0099	0.0120	0.0141	0.0162	0.0183
70	.82239	-0.0024	-0.0004	0.0016	0.0036	0.0056	0.0076	0.0097	0.0117	0.0138	0.0158	0.0179
69	.81188	-0.0024	-0.0004	0.0015	0.0035	0.0055	0.0075	0.0095	0.0115	0.0136	0.0156	0.0177
68	.81188	-0.0025	-0.0006	0.0014	0.0033	0.0053	0.0072	0.0092	0.0112	0.0132	0.0152	0.0173
67	.81064	-0.0026	-0.0007	0.0012	0.0031	0.0051	0.0070	0.0090	0.0109	0.0129	0.0149	0.0169
66	.81064	-0.0027	-0.0009	0.0010	0.0029	0.0048	0.0067	0.0087	0.0106	0.0125	0.0145	0.0165
65	.80413	-0.0028	-0.0009	0.0009	0.0028	0.0047	0.0066	0.0085	0.0104	0.0123	0.0142	0.0161
64	.80413	-0.0029	-0.0011	0.0008	0.0026	0.0045	0.0063	0.0082	0.0101	0.0119	0.0138	0.0157
63	.80401	-0.0030	-0.0012	0.0006	0.0024	0.0042	0.0061	0.0079	0.0097	0.0116	0.0135	0.0153
62	.80401	-0.0031	-0.0013	0.0004	0.0022	0.0040	0.0058	0.0076	0.0094	0.0113	0.0131	0.0149
61	.79476	-0.0031	-0.0014	0.0004	0.0021	0.0039	0.0057	0.0074	0.0092	0.0110	0.0128	0.0146
60	.79476	-0.0032	-0.0015	0.0002	0.0019	0.0037	0.0054	0.0072	0.0089	0.0107	0.0125	0.0142
59	.79476	-0.0033	-0.0016	0.0000	0.0017	0.0034	0.0052	0.0069	0.0086	0.0103	0.0121	0.0138
58	.79004	-0.0034	-0.0017	-0.0001	0.0016	0.0033	0.0050	0.0066	0.0083	0.0101	0.0118	0.0135
57	.79004	-0.0035	-0.0019	-0.0002	0.0014	0.0030	0.0047	0.0064	0.0080	0.0097	0.0114	0.0131
56	.78699	-0.0036	-0.0020	-0.0004	0.0012	0.0029	0.0045	0.0061	0.0078	0.0094	0.0111	0.0127
55	.78699	-0.0037	-0.0021	-0.0005	0.0010	0.0026	0.0042	0.0058	0.0074	0.0091	0.0107	0.0123
54	.77672	-0.0036	-0.0021	-0.0006	0.0010	0.0025	0.0041	0.0057	0.0073	0.0088	0.0104	0.0121
53	.77672	-0.0038	-0.0023	-0.0007	0.0008	0.0023	0.0038	0.0054	0.0069	0.0085	0.0101	0.0116
52	.75159	-0.0036	-0.0021	-0.0006	0.0009	0.0024	0.0039	0.0054	0.0069	0.0085	0.0100	0.0116
51	.75159	-0.0037	-0.0022	-0.0008	0.0007	0.0022	0.0036	0.0051	0.0066	0.0081	0.0096	0.0112
50	.75100	-0.0038	-0.0024	-0.0009	0.0005	0.0020	0.0034	0.0049	0.0063	0.0078	0.0093	0.0108
49	.75100	-0.0039	-0.0025	-0.0011	0.0003	0.0017	0.0031	0.0046	0.0060	0.0075	0.0089	0.0104
48	.75003	-0.0040	-0.0026	-0.0013	0.0001	0.0015	0.0029	0.0043	0.0057	0.0071	0.0085	0.0100
47	.75003	-0.0041	-0.0028	-0.0014	-0.0001	0.0013	0.0026	0.0040	0.0054	0.0068	0.0082	0.0096
46	.74340	-0.0041	-0.0028	-0.0015	-0.0002	0.0011	0.0025	0.0038	0.0052	0.0065	0.0079	0.0092
45	.65814	-0.0032	-0.0019	-0.0006	0.0007	0.0020	0.0033	0.0046	0.0059	0.0072	0.0086	0.0099
44	.65814	-0.0033	-0.0020	-0.0008	0.0005	0.0018	0.0030	0.0043	0.0056	0.0069	0.0082	0.0095
43	.60595	-0.0027	-0.0015	-0.0003	0.0009	0.0022	0.0034	0.0047	0.0059	0.0072	0.0085	0.0098
42	.60595	-0.0029	-0.0017	-0.0005	0.0007	0.0019	0.0032	0.0044	0.0056	0.0069	0.0081	0.0094
41	.54658	-0.0022	-0.0011	0.0001	0.0013	0.0025	0.0037	0.0048	0.0060	0.0073	0.0085	0.0097
40	.45552	-0.0012	-0.0001	0.0011	0.0022	0.0034	0.0045	0.0057	0.0069	0.0081	0.0092	0.0104
39	.45552	-0.0013	-0.0002	0.0009	0.0020	0.0031	0.0043	0.0054	0.0066	0.0077	0.0089	0.0100
38	.39164	-0.0006	0.0004	0.0015	0.0026	0.0037	0.0048	0.0059	0.0070	0.0082	0.0093	0.0104
37	.39164	-0.0007	0.0003	0.0014	0.0024	0.0035	0.0046	0.0056	0.0067	0.0078	0.0089	0.0100
36	.36619	-0.0005	0.0005	0.0015	0.0025	0.0036	0.0046	0.0057	0.0067	0.0078	0.0089	0.0099
35	.35968	-0.0006	0.0004	0.0014	0.0024	0.0034	0.0045	0.0055	0.0065	0.0075	0.0086	0.0096
34	.35968	-0.0007	0.0003	0.0013	0.0022	0.0032	0.0042	0.0052	0.0062	0.0072	0.0082	0.0092
33	.35300	-0.0007	0.0002	0.0012	0.0021	0.0031	0.0040	0.0050	0.0060	0.0069	0.0079	0.0089
32	.35300	-0.0008	0.0001	0.0010	0.0019	0.0028	0.0038	0.0047	0.0056	0.0066	0.0075	0.0085
31	.31149	-0.0004	0.0005	0.0014	0.0022	0.0031	0.0040	0.0049	0.0058	0.0068	0.0077	0.0086
30	.31149	-0.0005	0.0003	0.0012	0.0020	0.0029	0.0038	0.0047	0.0055	0.0064	0.0073	0.0082
29	.29913	-0.0005	0.0003	0.0012	0.0020	0.0028	0.0037	0.0045	0.0054	0.0062	0.0071	0.0079
28	.28437	-0.0004	0.0004	0.0012	0.0020	0.0028	0.0036	0.0044	0.0052	0.0061	0.0069	0.0077
27	.28437	-0.0005	0.0002	0.0010	0.0018	0.0026	0.0034	0.0041	0.0049	0.0057	0.0065	0.0073
26	.26512	-0.0004	0.0003	0.0011	0.0018	0.0026	0.0033	0.0041	0.0049	0.0056	0.0064	0.0072
25	.26512	-0.0005	0.0002	0.0009	0.0016	0.0024	0.0031	0.0038	0.0045	0.0053	0.0060	0.0068
24	.26232	-0.0006	0.0001	0.0008	0.0015	0.0022	0.0029	0.0036	0.0043	0.0050	0.0057	0.0064
23	.24189	-0.0004	0.0002	0.0009	0.0015	0.0022	0.0029	0.0035	0.0042	0.0049	0.0056	0.0062

Table 8–4 (concluded)

			4%	5%	6%	7%	8%	9%	10%	11%	12%	13%	14%
54	22	.24189	-0.0006	0.0001	0.0007	0.0013	0.0020	0.0026	0.0032	0.0039	0.0045	0.0052	0.005
55	21	.20922	-0.0003	0.0003	0.0009	0.0015	0.0021	0.0028	0.0034	0.0040	0.0046	0.0052	0.005
56	20	.20922	-0.0004	0.0002	0.0008	0.0013	0.0019	0.0025	0.0031	0.0037	0.0043	0.0048	0.005
57	19	.20079	-0.0004	0.0002	0.0007	0.0013	0.0018	0.0023	0.0029	0.0035	0.0040	0.0046	0.005
58	18	.19577	-0.0004	0.0001	0.0006	0.0011	0.0016	0.0022	0.0027	0.0032	0.0037	0.0043	0.004
59	17	.19577	-0.0005	-0.0001	0.0004	0.0009	0.0014	0.0019	0.0024	0.0029	0.0034	0.0039	0.004
60	16	.19079	-0.0006	-0.0001	0.0003	0.0008	0.0012	0.0017	0.0022	0.0026	0.0031	0.0036	0.004
61	15	.15083	-0.0002	0.0002	0.0007	0.0011	0.0015	0.0020	0.0024	0.0028	0.0033	0.0037	0.004
62	14	.13118	-0.0001	0.0003	0.0007	0.0011	0.0015	0.0019	0.0023	0.0028	0.0032	0.0036	0.004
63	13	.13118	-0.0002	0.0002	0.0006	0.0009	0.0013	0.0017	0.0021	0.0024	0.0028	0.0032	0.003
64	12	.11342	-0.0001	0.0003	0.0006	0.0010	0.0013	0.0017	0.0020	0.0024	0.0027	0.0031	0.003
65	11	.09438	0.0001	0.0004	0.0007	0.0010	0.0013	0.0016	0.0020	0.0023	0.0026	0.0029	0.003
66	10	.09438	-0.0001	0.0002	0.0005	0.0008	0.0011	0.0014	0.0017	0.0020	0.0023	0.0026	0.002
67	9	.09048	-0.0001	0.0001	0.0004	0.0007	0.0009	0.0012	0.0014	0.0017	0.0020	0.0022	0.002
68	8	.07188	0.0000	0.0002	0.0005	0.0007	0.0009	0.0011	0.0014	0.0016	0.0019	0.0021	0.002
69	7	.07188	-0.0001	0.0001	0.0003	0.0005	0.0007	0.0009	0.0011	0.0013	0.0015	0.0017	0.001
70	6	.03348	0.0003	0.0004	0.0006	0.0008	0.0009	0.0011	0.0013	0.0015	0.0016	0.0018	0.002
71	5	.03348	0.0001	0.0003	0.0004	0.0006	0.0007	0.0009	0.0010	0.0012	0.0013	0.0014	0.001
72	4	.03245	0.0000	0.0002	0.0003	0.0004	0.0005	0.0006	0.0007	0.0009	0.0010	0.0011	0.001
73	3	.01896	0.0001	0.0002	0.0003	0.0004	0.0004	0.0005	0.0006	0.0007	0.0008	0.0009	0.001
74	2	.01896	0.0000	0.0000	0.0001	0.0002	0.0002	0.0003	0.0003	0.0004	0.0005	0.0005	0.000
75	1	.00785	0.0000	0.0000	0.0001	0.0001	0.0001	0.0001	0.0002	0.0002	0.0002	0.0003	0.000
76	0	.00000	0.0000	0.0000	0.0000	0.0000	0.0000	0.0000	0.0000	0.0000	0.0000	0.0000	0.000
77	90	1.00000	-0.0024	0.0002	0.0027	0.0053	0.0079	0.0105	0.0131	0.0158	0.0184	0.0211	0.023
78	89	.99795	-0.0025	0.0000	0.0026	0.0051	0.0077	0.0103	0.0129	0.0155	0.0181	0.0207	0.023
79	88	.99140	-0.0025	0.0000	0.0025	0.0050	0.0076	0.0101	0.0127	0.0153	0.0178	0.0205	0.023
80	87	.99140	-0.0026	-0.0002	0.0023	0.0048	0.0073	0.0099	0.0124	0.0149	0.0175	0.0201	0.022
81	86	.89417	-0.0015	0.0009	0.0034	0.0058	0.0083	0.0108	0.0133	0.0158	0.0184	0.0209	0.023
82	85	.89417	-0.0016	0.0008	0.0032	0.0056	0.0081	0.0106	0.0130	0.0155	0.0180	0.0205	0.023
83	84	.88523	-0.0016	0.0007	0.0031	0.0031	0.0056	0.0080	0.0104	0.0129	0.0153	0.0178	0.0203	0.022
84	83	.87858	-0.0017	0.0007	0.0031	0.0054	0.0078	0.0102	0.0127	0.0151	0.0175	0.0200	0.022
85	82	.87858	-0.0018	0.0006	0.0029	0.0052	0.0076	0.0100	0.0124	0.0148	0.0172	0.0196	0.022
86	81	.87312	-0.0018	0.0005	0.0028	0.0051	0.0075	0.0098	0.0122	0.0145	0.0169	0.0193	0.021
87	80	.87193	-0.0019	0.0004	0.0026	0.0049	0.0072	0.0096	0.0119	0.0142	0.0166	0.0190	0.021
88	79	.87193	-0.0020	0.0002	0.0025	0.0047	0.0070	0.0093	0.0116	0.0139	0.0162	0.0186	0.020
89	78	.85202	-0.0019	0.0003	0.0025	0.0048	0.0070	0.0093	0.0116	0.0139	0.0162	0.0185	0.020
90	77	.85002	-0.0020	0.0002	0.0024	0.0046	0.0068	0.0091	0.0113	0.0136	0.0158	0.0181	0.020
91	76	.85002	-0.0021	0.0001	0.0022	0.0044	0.0066	0.0088	0.0110	0.0133	0.0155	0.0177	0.020

Table 8–5   S&P 500 Futures Evaluation Table (S&P Dividend Return = 4%)

			4%	5%	6%	7%	8%	9%	10%	11%	12%	13%	14%
1	75	.84217	0.0000	0.0021	0.0043	0.0064	0.0086	0.0108	0.0129	0.0151	0.0174	0.0196	0.021
2	74	.84217	-0.0001	0.0020	0.0041	0.0062	0.0084	0.0105	0.0127	0.0148	0.0170	0.0192	0.021
3	73	.82948	-0.0001	0.0020	0.0041	0.0062	0.0083	0.0104	0.0125	0.0146	0.0168	0.0190	0.021
4	72	.82948	-0.0002	0.0018	0.0039	0.0060	0.0080	0.0101	0.0122	0.0143	0.0164	0.0186	0.020
5	71	.82239	-0.0003	0.0018	0.0038	0.0058	0.0079	0.0099	0.0120	0.0141	0.0162	0.0183	0.020
6	70	.82239	-0.0004	0.0016	0.0036	0.0056	0.0076	0.0097	0.0117	0.0138	0.0158	0.0179	0.020
7	69	.81188	-0.0004	0.0016	0.0036	0.0055	0.0075	0.0095	0.0115	0.0136	0.0156	0.0176	0.019
8	68	.81188	-0.0005	0.0014	0.0034	0.0053	0.0073	0.0093	0.0113	0.0132	0.0152	0.0173	0.019
9	67	.81064	-0.0006	0.0013	0.0032	0.0052	0.0071	0.0090	0.0110	0.0129	0.0149	0.0169	0.018
10	66	.81064	-0.0007	0.0012	0.0031	0.0050	0.0069	0.0088	0.0107	0.0126	0.0146	0.0165	0.018
11	65	.80413	-0.0007	0.0011	0.0030	0.0048	0.0067	0.0086	0.0105	0.0124	0.0143	0.0162	0.018
12	64	.60413	-0.0009	0.0010	0.0028	0.0046	0.0065	0.0083	0.0102	0.0121	0.0140	0.0158	0.017
13	63	.80401	-0.0010	0.0008	0.0026	0.0044	0.0062	0.0081	0.0099	0.0118	0.0136	0.0155	0.017
14	62	.80401	-0.0011	0.0007	0.0025	0.0042	0.0060	0.0078	0.0096	0.0114	0.0133	0.0151	0.016
15	61	.79476	-0.0011	0.0006	0.0024	0.0041	0.0059	0.0077	0.0094	0.0112	0.0130	0.0148	0.016
16	60	.79476	-0.0012	0.0005	0.0022	0.0039	0.0057	0.0074	0.0091	0.0109	0.0127	0.0144	0.016
17	59	.79476	-0.0013	0.0004	0.0020	0.0037	0.0054	0.0071	0.0089	0.0106	0.0123	0.0141	0.015
18	58	.79004	-0.0014	0.0003	0.0019	0.0036	0.0053	0.0069	0.0086	0.0103	0.0120	0.0137	0.015
19	57	.79004	-0.0015	0.0001	0.0017	0.0034	0.0050	0.0067	0.0083	0.0100	0.0117	0.0134	0.015
20	56	.78699	-0.0016	0.0000	0.0016	0.0032	0.0048	0.0065	0.0081	0.0097	0.0114	0.0130	0.014
21	55	.78699	-0.0017	-0.0001	0.0014	0.0030	0.0046	0.0062	0.0078	0.0094	0.0110	0.0127	0.014
22	54	.77672	-0.0017	-0.0002	0.0014	0.0029	0.0045	0.0060	0.0076	0.0092	0.0108	0.0124	0.014
23	53	.77672	-0.0018	-0.0003	0.0012	0.0027	0.0043	0.0058	0.0073	0.0089	0.0104	0.0120	0.013
24	52	.75159	-0.0017	-0.0002	0.0013	0.0028	0.0043	0.0058	0.0073	0.0088	0.0104	0.0119	0.013
25	51	.75159	-0.0018	-0.0003	0.0011	0.0026	0.0040	0.0055	0.0070	0.0085	0.0100	0.0115	0.013
26	50	.75100	-0.0019	-0.0005	0.0010	0.0024	0.0038	0.0053	0.0067	0.0082	0.0097	0.0112	0.012
27	49	.75100	-0.0020	-0.0006	0.0008	0.0022	0.0036	0.0050	0.0065	0.0079	0.0093	0.0108	0.012
28	48	.75003	-0.0021	-0.0007	0.0006	0.0020	0.0034	0.0048	0.0062	0.0076	0.0090	0.0104	0.011
29	47	.75003	-0.0022	-0.0009	0.0005	0.0018	0.0032	0.0045	0.0059	0.0073	0.0087	0.0100	0.011
30	46	.74340	-0.0023	-0.0010	0.0003	0.0017	0.0030	0.0043	0.0057	0.0070	0.0084	0.0097	0.011
31	45	.65814	-0.0015	-0.0003	0.0010	0.0023	0.0036	0.0049	0.0062	0.0076	0.0089	0.0102	0.011
32	44	.65814	-0.0016	-0.0004	0.0009	0.0021	0.0034	0.0047	0.0060	0.0072	0.0085	0.0098	0.011
33	43	.60595	-0.0012	0.0000	0.0012	0.0025	0.0037	0.0049	0.0062	0.0075	0.0087	0.0100	0.011
34	42	.60595	-0.0013	-0.0002	0.0010	0.0023	0.0035	0.0047	0.0059	0.0071	0.0084	0.0096	0.010
35	41	.54658	-0.0009	0.0003	0.0015	0.0026	0.0038	0.0050	0.0062	0.0074	0.0086	0.0098	0.011
36	40	.45552	-0.0001	0.0011	0.0022	0.0034	0.0045	0.0057	0.0068	0.0080	0.0092	0.0104	0.011
37	39	.45552	-0.0002	0.0009	0.0020	0.0032	0.0043	0.0054	0.0066	0.0077	0.0088	0.0100	0.011
38	38	.39164	0.0003	0.0014	0.0025	0.0036	0.0047	0.0058	0.0069	0.0080	0.0091	0.0103	0.011

Table 8–5 (*concluded*)

		4%	5%	6%	7%	8%	9%	10%	11%	12%	13%	14%
39	37	.39164	0.0002	0.0013	0.0023	0.0034	0.0045	0.0055	0.0066	0.0077	0.0088	0.0099	0.0110
40	36	.36619	0.0004	0.0014	0.0024	0.0035	0.0045	0.0055	0.0066	0.0076	0.0087	0.0098	0.0108
41	35	.35968	0.0003	0.0013	0.0023	0.0033	0.0043	0.0054	0.0064	0.0074	0.0084	0.0095	0.0105
42	34	.35968	0.0002	0.0012	0.0022	0.0031	0.0041	0.0051	0.0061	0.0071	0.0081	0.0091	0.0101
43	33	.35300	0.0002	0.0011	0.0021	0.0030	0.0040	0.0049	0.0059	0.0068	0.0078	0.0088	0.0098
44	32	.35300	0.0001	0.0010	0.0019	0.0028	0.0037	0.0047	0.0056	0.0065	0.0075	0.0084	0.0094
45	31	.31149	0.0004	0.0012	0.0021	0.0030	0.0039	0.0048	0.0057	0.0066	0.0075	0.0085	0.0094
46	30	.31149	0.0003	0.0011	0.0020	0.0028	0.0037	0.0046	0.0054	0.0063	0.0072	0.0081	0.0090
47	29	.29913	0.0003	0.0011	0.0019	0.0027	0.0036	0.0044	0.0053	0.0061	0.0070	0.0078	0.0087
48	28	.28437	0.0003	0.0011	0.0019	0.0027	0.0035	0.0043	0.0051	0.0060	0.0068	0.0076	0.0084
49	27	.28437	0.0002	0.0010	0.0017	0.0025	0.0033	0.0041	0.0048	0.0056	0.0064	0.0072	0.0080
50	26	.26512	0.0003	0.0010	0.0017	0.0025	0.0032	0.0040	0.0048	0.0055	0.0063	0.0071	0.0078
51	25	.26512	0.0002	0.0009	0.0016	0.0023	0.0030	0.0037	0.0045	0.0052	0.0059	0.0067	0.0074
52	24	.26232	0.0001	0.0008	0.0014	0.0021	0.0028	0.0035	0.0042	0.0049	0.0056	0.0063	0.0070
53	23	.24189	0.0002	0.0008	0.0015	0.0021	0.0028	0.0035	0.0041	0.0048	0.0055	0.0062	0.0068
54	22	.24189	0.0001	0.0007	0.0013	0.0019	0.0026	0.0032	0.0038	0.0045	0.0051	0.0058	0.0064
55	21	.20922	0.0003	0.0009	0.0015	0.0021	0.0027	0.0033	0.0039	0.0045	0.0051	0.0057	0.0064
56	20	.20922	0.0002	0.0007	0.0013	0.0019	0.0024	0.0030	0.0036	0.0042	0.0048	0.0054	0.0060
57	19	.20079	0.0001	0.0007	0.0012	0.0018	0.0023	0.0029	0.0034	0.0040	0.0045	0.0051	0.0056
58	18	.19577	0.0001	0.0006	0.0011	0.0016	0.0021	0.0026	0.0032	0.0037	0.0042	0.0048	0.0053
59	17	.19577	0.0000	0.0004	0.0009	0.0014	0.0019	0.0024	0.0029	0.0034	0.0039	0.0044	0.0049
60	16	.19079	-0.0001	0.0003	0.0008	0.0013	0.0017	0.0022	0.0027	0.0031	0.0036	0.0041	0.0045
61	15	.15083	0.0002	0.0006	0.0010	0.0015	0.0019	0.0023	0.0028	0.0032	0.0036	0.0041	0.0045
62	14	.13118	0.0003	0.0007	0.0011	0.0015	0.0019	0.0023	0.0027	0.0031	0.0035	0.0039	0.0043
63	13	.13118	0.0001	0.0005	0.0009	0.0013	0.0016	0.0020	0.0024	0.0028	0.0032	0.0035	0.0039
64	12	.11342	0.0002	0.0006	0.0009	0.0012	0.0016	0.0019	0.0023	0.0026	0.0030	0.0033	0.0037
65	11	.09438	0.0003	0.0006	0.0009	0.0012	0.0016	0.0019	0.0022	0.0025	0.0028	0.0032	0.0035
66	10	.09438	0.0002	0.0005	0.0007	0.0010	0.0013	0.0016	0.0019	0.0022	0.0025	0.0028	0.0031
67	9	.09048	0.0001	0.0004	0.0006	0.0009	0.0011	0.0014	0.0017	0.0019	0.0022	0.0025	0.0027
68	8	.07188	0.0002	0.0004	0.0006	0.0009	0.0011	0.0013	0.0016	0.0018	0.0020	0.0023	0.0025
69	7	.07188	0.0001	0.0003	0.0005	0.0007	0.0009	0.0011	0.0013	0.0015	0.0017	0.0019	0.0021
70	6	.03348	0.0003	0.0005	0.0007	0.0009	0.0010	0.0012	0.0014	0.0016	0.0017	0.0019	0.0021
71	5	.03348	0.0002	0.0004	0.0005	0.0007	0.0008	0.0009	0.0011	0.0012	0.0014	0.0015	0.0017
72	4	.03245	0.0001	0.0002	0.0004	0.0005	0.0006	0.0007	0.0008	0.0009	0.0011	0.0012	0.0013
73	3	.01896	0.0001	0.0002	0.0002	0.0003	0.0004	0.0005	0.0006	0.0007	0.0008	0.0009	0.0010
74	2	.01896	0.0000	0.0001	0.0001	0.0001	0.0002	0.0003	0.0003	0.0004	0.0005	0.0006	0.0006
75	1	.00785	0.0000	0.0001	0.0001	0.0001	0.0001	0.0001	0.0002	0.0002	0.0003	0.0003	0.0003
76	0	.00000	0.0000	0.0000	0.0000	0.0000	0.0000	0.0000	0.0000	0.0000	0.0000	0.0000	0.0000
77	90	1.00000	0.0001	0.0027	0.0052	0.0078	0.0104	0.0130	0.0156	0.0183	0.0209	0.0236	0.0263
78	89	.99795	0.0000	0.0025	0.0051	0.0076	0.0102	0.0128	0.0154	0.0180	0.0206	0.0232	0.0259
79	88	.99140	0.0000	0.0025	0.0050	0.0075	0.0100	0.0126	0.0152	0.0177	0.0203	0.0229	0.0255
80	87	.99140	-0.0001	0.0023	0.0048	0.0073	0.0098	0.0123	0.0149	0.0174	0.0200	0.0226	0.0251
81	86	.89417	0.0007	0.0032	0.0056	0.0081	0.0106	0.0131	0.0156	0.0181	0.0206	0.0232	0.0257
82	85	.89417	0.0006	0.0030	0.0054	0.0079	0.0103	0.0128	0.0153	0.0178	0.0203	0.0228	0.0253
83	84	.88523	0.0006	0.0030	0.0054	0.0078	0.0102	0.0126	0.0151	0.0175	0.0200	0.0225	0.0250
84	83	.87858	0.0005	0.0029	0.0053	0.0076	0.0100	0.0124	0.0149	0.0173	0.0197	0.0222	0.0247
85	82	.87858	0.0004	0.0027	0.0051	0.0074	0.0098	0.0122	0.0146	0.0170	0.0194	0.0218	0.0243
86	81	.87312	0.0004	0.0027	0.0050	0.0073	0.0096	0.0120	0.0143	0.0167	0.0191	0.0215	0.0239
87	80	.87193	0.0003	0.0025	0.0048	0.0071	0.0094	0.0117	0.0141	0.0164	0.0188	0.0211	0.0235
88	79	.87193	0.0001	0.0024	0.0046	0.0069	0.0092	0.0115	0.0138	0.0161	0.0184	0.0208	0.0231
89	78	.85202	0.0002	0.0025	0.0047	0.0069	0.0092	0.0114	0.0137	0.0160	0.0183	0.0206	0.0229
90	77	.85002	0.0001	0.0023	0.0045	0.0067	0.0090	0.0112	0.0134	0.0157	0.0180	0.0202	0.0225
91	76	.85002	0.0000	0.0022	0.0044	0.0065	0.0087	0.0109	0.0132	0.0154	0.0176	0.0199	0.0221

Table 8–6   S&P 500 Futures Evaluation Table (S&P Dividend Return = 3%)

		4%	5%	6%	7%	8%	9%	10%	11%	12%	13%	14%
1	75	.84217	0.0021	0.0042	0.0064	0.0085	0.0107	0.0129	0.0151	0.0172	0.0195	0.0217	0.0239
2	74	.84217	0.0020	0.0041	0.0062	0.0083	0.0105	0.0126	0.0148	0.0169	0.0191	0.0213	0.0235
3	73	.82948	0.0020	0.0040	0.0061	0.0082	0.0103	0.0124	0.0146	0.0167	0.0189	0.0210	0.0232
4	72	.82948	0.0019	0.0039	0.0060	0.0080	0.0101	0.0122	0.0143	0.0164	0.0185	0.0207	0.0228
5	71	.82239	0.0018	0.0038	0.0058	0.0079	0.0099	0.0120	0.0141	0.0161	0.0182	0.0203	0.0224
6	70	.82239	0.0017	0.0037	0.0057	0.0077	0.0097	0.0117	0.0138	0.0158	0.0179	0.0200	0.0220
7	69	.81188	0.0017	0.0036	0.0056	0.0076	0.0096	0.0116	0.0136	0.0156	0.0176	0.0197	0.0217
8	68	.81188	0.0015	0.0035	0.0054	0.0074	0.0093	0.0113	0.0133	0.0153	0.0173	0.0193	0.0213
9	67	.81064	0.0014	0.0033	0.0053	0.0072	0.0091	0.0111	0.0130	0.0150	0.0169	0.0189	0.0209
10	66	.81064	0.0013	0.0032	0.0051	0.0070	0.0089	0.0108	0.0127	0.0147	0.0166	0.0186	0.0205
11	65	.80413	0.0013	0.0031	0.0050	0.0068	0.0087	0.0106	0.0125	0.0144	0.0163	0.0182	0.0202
12	64	.80413	0.0012	0.0030	0.0048	0.0066	0.0085	0.0103	0.0122	0.0141	0.0160	0.0179	0.0198
13	63	.80401	0.0010	0.0028	0.0046	0.0064	0.0083	0.0101	0.0119	0.0138	0.0156	0.0175	0.0194
14	62	.80401	0.0009	0.0027	0.0045	0.0062	0.0080	0.0098	0.0116	0.0135	0.0153	0.0171	0.0190
15	61	.79476	0.0009	0.0026	0.0044	0.0061	0.0079	0.0096	0.0114	0.0132	0.0150	0.0168	0.0186
16	60	.79476	0.0008	0.0025	0.0042	0.0059	0.0076	0.0094	0.0111	0.0129	0.0147	0.0164	0.0182
17	59	.79476	0.0007	0.0023	0.0040	0.0057	0.0074	0.0091	0.0108	0.0126	0.0143	0.0161	0.0178
18	58	.79004	0.0006	0.0022	0.0039	0.0056	0.0072	0.0089	0.0106	0.0123	0.0140	0.0157	0.0174
19	57	.79004	0.0005	0.0021	0.0037	0.0054	0.0070	0.0087	0.0103	0.0120	0.0137	0.0153	0.0170
20	56	.78699	0.0004	0.0020	0.0036	0.0052	0.0068	0.0084	0.0101	0.0117	0.0133	0.0150	0.0167
21	55	.78699	0.0003	0.0018	0.0034	0.0050	0.0066	0.0082	0.0098	0.0114	0.0130	0.0146	0.0163
22	54	.77672	0.0002	0.0018	0.0033	0.0049	0.0064	0.0080	0.0096	0.0111	0.0127	0.0143	0.0159
23	53	.77672	0.0001	0.0016	0.0031	0.0047	0.0062	0.0077	0.0093	0.0108	0.0124	0.0140	0.0155

Table 8–6 (*concluded*)

		4%	5%	6%	7%	8%	9%	10%	11%	12%	13%	14%
24	52	.75159	0.0002	0.0017	0.0032	0.0047	0.0062	0.0077	0.0092	0.0107	0.0122	0.0138	0.015
25	51	.75159	0.0001	0.0015	0.0030	0.0045	0.0059	0.0074	0.0089	0.0104	0.0119	0.0134	0.014
26	50	.75100	0.0000	0.0014	0.0028	0.0043	0.0057	0.0072	0.0086	0.0101	0.0115	0.0130	0.014
27	49	.75100	-0.0001	0.0013	0.0027	0.0041	0.0055	0.0069	0.0083	0.0098	0.0112	0.0127	0.014
28	48	.75003	-0.0002	0.0011	0.0025	0.0039	0.0053	0.0067	0.0080	0.0095	0.0109	0.0123	0.013
29	47	.75003	-0.0004	0.0010	0.0023	0.0037	0.0050	0.0064	0.0078	0.0091	0.0105	0.0119	0.013
30	46	.74340	-0.0004	0.0009	0.0022	0.0035	0.0049	0.0062	0.0075	0.0089	0.0102	0.0116	0.013
31	45	.65814	0.0001	0.0014	0.0027	0.0040	0.0053	0.0066	0.0079	0.0092	0.0105	0.0119	0.013
32	44	.65814	0.0000	0.0013	0.0025	0.0038	0.0050	0.0063	0.0076	0.0089	0.0102	0.0115	0.012
33	43	.60595	0.0003	0.0015	0.0027	0.0040	0.0052	0.0065	0.0077	0.0090	0.0102	0.0115	0.012
34	42	.60595	0.0002	0.0014	0.0026	0.0038	0.0050	0.0062	0.0074	0.0087	0.0099	0.0111	0.012
35	41	.54658	0.0005	0.0017	0.0028	0.0040	0.0052	0.0064	0.0076	0.0088	0.0100	0.0112	0.012
36	40	.45552	0.0011	0.0022	0.0034	0.0045	0.0057	0.0068	0.0080	0.0092	0.0103	0.0115	0.012
37	39	.45552	0.0010	0.0021	0.0032	0.0043	0.0054	0.0066	0.0077	0.0088	0.0100	0.0111	0.012
38	38	.39164	0.0013	0.0024	0.0035	0.0046	0.0057	0.0068	0.0079	0.0090	0.0101	0.0112	0.012
39	37	.39164	0.0012	0.0023	0.0033	0.0044	0.0055	0.0065	0.0076	0.0087	0.0098	0.0109	0.0120
40	36	.36619	0.0013	0.0023	0.0033	0.0044	0.0054	0.0065	0.0075	0.0086	0.0096	0.0107	0.011
41	35	.35968	0.0012	0.0022	0.0032	0.0042	0.0052	0.0063	0.0073	0.0083	0.0093	0.0104	0.011
42	34	.35968	0.0011	0.0021	0.0031	0.0040	0.0050	0.0060	0.0070	0.0080	0.0090	0.0100	0.011
43	33	.35300	0.0011	0.0020	0.0029	0.0039	0.0048	0.0058	0.0068	0.0077	0.0087	0.0097	0.010
44	32	.35300	0.0009	0.0019	0.0028	0.0037	0.0046	0.0055	0.0065	0.0074	0.0083	0.0093	0.010
45	31	.31149	0.0011	0.0020	0.0029	0.0038	0.0047	0.0056	0.0065	0.0074	0.0083	0.0092	0.0102
46	30	.31149	0.0010	0.0019	0.0027	0.0036	0.0045	0.0053	0.0062	0.0071	0.0080	0.0089	0.009
47	29	.29913	0.0010	0.0018	0.0027	0.0035	0.0043	0.0052	0.0060	0.0069	0.0077	0.0086	0.009
48	28	.28437	0.0010	0.0018	0.0026	0.0034	0.0042	0.0050	0.0058	0.0067	0.0075	0.0083	0.009
49	27	.28437	0.0009	0.0017	0.0024	0.0032	0.0040	0.0048	0.0056	0.0064	0.0071	0.0079	0.008
50	26	.26512	0.0009	0.0017	0.0024	0.0032	0.0039	0.0047	0.0054	0.0062	0.0069	0.0077	0.008
51	25	.26512	0.0008	0.0015	0.0022	0.0030	0.0037	0.0044	0.0051	0.0059	0.0066	0.0073	0.008
52	24	.26232	0.0007	0.0014	0.0021	0.0028	0.0035	0.0042	0.0049	0.0056	0.0063	0.0070	0.007
53	23	.24189	0.0008	0.0014	0.0021	0.0027	0.0034	0.0041	0.0047	0.0054	0.0061	0.0068	0.0075
54	22	.24189	0.0007	0.0013	0.0019	0.0025	0.0032	0.0038	0.0045	0.0051	0.0057	0.0064	0.0077
55	21	.20922	0.0008	0.0014	0.0020	0.0026	0.0032	0.0038	0.0044	0.0050	0.0056	0.0063	0.006
56	20	.20922	0.0007	0.0012	0.0018	0.0024	0.0030	0.0035	0.0041	0.0047	0.0053	0.0059	0.0069
57	19	.20079	0.0006	0.0012	0.0017	0.0023	0.0028	0.0034	0.0039	0.0045	0.0050	0.0056	0.006
58	18	.19577	0.0006	0.0011	0.0016	0.0021	0.0026	0.0031	0.0037	0.0042	0.0047	0.0053	0.0058
59	17	.19577	0.0004	0.0009	0.0014	0.0019	0.0024	0.0029	0.0034	0.0039	0.0044	0.0049	0.005
60	16	.19079	0.0004	0.0008	0.0013	0.0017	0.0022	0.0027	0.0031	0.0036	0.0041	0.0045	0.0050
61	15	.15083	0.0006	0.0010	0.0014	0.0018	0.0023	0.0027	0.0031	0.0036	0.0040	0.0045	0.004
62	14	.13118	0.0006	0.0010	0.0014	0.0018	0.0022	0.0026	0.0030	0.0034	0.0038	0.0042	0.004
63	13	.13118	0.0005	0.0008	0.0012	0.0016	0.0020	0.0023	0.0027	0.0031	0.0035	0.0039	0.004
64	12	.11342	0.0005	0.0008	0.0012	0.0015	0.0019	0.0022	0.0026	0.0029	0.0033	0.0036	0.0040
65	11	.09438	0.0005	0.0008	0.0012	0.0015	0.0018	0.0021	0.0024	0.0027	0.0031	0.0034	0.003
66	10	.09438	0.0004	0.0007	0.0010	0.0013	0.0016	0.0018	0.0021	0.0024	0.0027	0.0030	0.003
67	9	.09048	0.0003	0.0006	0.0008	0.0011	0.0014	0.0016	0.0019	0.0021	0.0024	0.0027	0.0029
68	8	.07186	0.0004	0.0006	0.0008	0.0010	0.0013	0.0015	0.0017	0.0020	0.0022	0.0024	0.002
69	7	.07188	0.0002	0.0004	0.0006	0.0008	0.0010	0.0013	0.0015	0.0017	0.0019	0.0021	0.002
70	6	.03348	0.0004	0.0006	0.0008	0.0009	0.0011	0.0013	0.0015	0.0016	0.0018	0.0020	0.002
71	5	.03348	0.0003	0.0005	0.0006	0.0007	0.0009	0.0010	0.0012	0.0013	0.0015	0.0016	0.001
72	4	.03245	0.0002	0.0003	0.0004	0.0005	0.0007	0.0008	0.0009	0.0010	0.0011	0.0012	0.001
73	3	.01896	0.0002	0.0003	0.0004	0.0005	0.0005	0.0006	0.0007	0.0008	0.0009	0.0010	0.001
74	2	.01896	0.0001	0.0001	0.0002	0.0003	0.0003	0.0004	0.0004	0.0005	0.0005	0.0006	0.000
75	1	.00785	0.0001	0.0001	0.0001	0.0001	0.0001	0.0002	0.0002	0.0002	0.0003	0.0003	0.000
76	0	.00000	0.0000	0.0000	0.0000	0.0000	0.0000	0.0000	0.0000	0.0000	0.0000	0.0000	0.000
77	90	1.00000	0.0026	0.0052	0.0077	0.0103	0.0129	0.0155	0.0181	0.0208	0.0234	0.0261	0.028
78	89	.99795	0.0025	0.0050	0.0076	0.0101	0.0127	0.0153	0.0179	0.0205	0.0231	0.0257	0.028
79	88	.99140	0.0024	0.0049	0.0075	0.0100	0.0125	0.0151	0.0176	0.0202	0.0228	0.0254	0.028
80	87	.99140	0.0023	0.0048	0.0073	0.0098	0.0123	0.0148	0.0174	0.0199	0.0225	0.0250	0.027
81	86	.89417	0.0029	0.0054	0.0078	0.0103	0.0128	0.0153	0.0178	0.0203	0.0228	0.0254	0.028
82	85	.89417	0.0028	0.0052	0.0077	0.0101	0.0126	0.0150	0.0175	0.0200	0.0225	0.0250	0.027
83	84	.88523	0.0028	0.0052	0.0076	0.0100	0.0124	0.0148	0.0173	0.0198	0.0222	0.0247	0.027
84	83	.87858	0.0027	0.0051	0.0075	0.0098	0.0122	0.0146	0.0171	0.0195	0.0219	0.0244	0.026
85	82	.87858	0.0026	0.0049	0.0073	0.0096	0.0120	0.0144	0.0168	0.0192	0.0216	0.0240	0.026
86	81	.87312	0.0025	0.0048	0.0072	0.0095	0.0118	0.0142	0.0165	0.0189	0.0213	0.0237	0.026
87	80	.87193	0.0024	0.0047	0.0070	0.0093	0.0116	0.0139	0.0163	0.0186	0.0210	0.0233	0.0257
88	79	.87193	0.0023	0.0046	0.0068	0.0091	0.0114	0.0137	0.0160	0.0183	0.0206	0.0229	0.025
89	78	.85202	0.0024	0.0046	0.0068	0.0090	0.0113	0.0136	0.0158	0.0181	0.0204	0.0227	0.025
90	77	.85002	0.0023	0.0045	0.0067	0.0089	0.0111	0.0133	0.0156	0.0178	0.0201	0.0224	0.024
91	76	.85002	0.0022	0.0043	0.0065	0.0087	0.0109	0.0131	0.0153	0.0175	0.0197	0.0220	0.024

percent T bill column is 0.0034. To find the appropriate value of the futures contract given an estimate of the current value of the index, 1 is added to this figure and the resulting number, 1.0034, is multiplied by the index. If the Treasury bill return is 6½ percent, the midpoint between the 6 percent and 7 percent columns ((0.0022 + 0.0034)/2 = 0.0028) is used. The result is added to 1, and the resulting factor is 1.0028. A similar interpolation can be made between two tables for different dividend yields. If the figure derived from the table is negative, it is added algebraically to 1. The resulting factor will be less than 1, and the appropriate value of the futures contract will be *less* than the current value of the index. The appropriate value of the futures contract will frequently be less than the current value during the 45 days before settlement, especially when short-term interest rates are low.

More Distant Contracts

A close approximation for the appropriate value of the futures contract settling three months after the nearest settlement date can be obtained by multiplying the value for the nearest contract by 1 plus one quarter of the annualized difference between an appropriate Treasury bill discount rate and the S&P 500 yield.

F_1 = Value of nearest settlement contract

F_2 = Value of next contract

i' = Average of annualized Treasury bill discount rates for bills maturing closest to settlement dates of the two futures contracts (expressed as a decimal)

d = Annualized dividend yield on S&P 500 Composite Index (expressed as a decimal)

$$F_2 = \left[1 + \frac{(i' - d)}{4} \right] F_1 \qquad (8\text{--}1)$$

An even closer approximation for more distant contracts can be obtained by converting the Treasury bill discount rate into a bond equivalent yield and substituting i for i' in Equation (8–1).

$$i = \text{Bond equivalent yield}$$

$$i = \frac{365i'}{360 - 90i'} \qquad (8\text{--}2)$$

Equation (8–2) was the basis for the calculation incorporated in the tables. The relationship between i' and i is as follows:

i' Percent	i Percent
4	4.0965
5	5.1336
6	6.1760
7	7.2236
8	8.2766
9	9.3350
10	10.3989
11	11.4682
12	12.5430
13	13.6233
14	14.7093

Errors in Estimating the True Current Value of the Index (Calculation Lag)

To prepare Tables 8–2 through 8–6, an estimate of the true current value of the index was needed. Unfortunately, the true value of the index is not necessarily the value computed from last sale prices and distributed by electronic quotation systems. The most recent sale price of each stock in the index is used to calculate the published index. For some of the stocks in the index, the last sale price will differ materially from the likely price if the stock were to trade again. If the next trade in some of the stocks in the index will take place at prices materially different from that of the last sale, the true current value of the index will differ correspondingly from the value provided by the quotation services.

The most obvious example of this tendency for the calculated index value to lag changes in the true current value of the index occurs on days when stock prices change dramatically. The last sale value of the index will reflect the previous night's closing price until the stock opens and attains something approximating an equilibrium price. As if the tendency of the calculated value of the index to lag what is going on in the market were not enough, the fact that stock index futures continue to trade after the stock market closes suggests that the true current value of the index at 4:15 P.M. may be different from its last sale value at 4:00 P.M. when the stock market closed.

Shortcomings aside, the reported value of an index is the only value most investors have to go on. During periods when there is a degree of price stability, pluses and minuses stand a reasonable chance of canceling out and the quoted value for the index is probably a good approximation of its true current value. As long as an investor is aware of potential discrepancies, calculation of the appropriate value for the stock index futures contract based on the last sale value of the index provides a useful *starting point* toward estimating any premium or discount at which the futures contract may be selling. Of considerable interest to practitioners would be a technique for estimating the true current value of the index based on price changes in stocks that have traded within the past few minutes or on recent bid-asked spreads quoted on the exchange floor. Whether an investor uses a sophisticated adjustment technique or simply tries to incorporate a rough guess of the extent to which the current quoted value of the index differs from its true current value, he should give some thought to this problem. At the very least, recognition of the problem may prevent some speculation on the significance of stock index futures premiums and discounts.

CHAPTER 9

Performance Characteristics

Gregory M. Kipnis
Vice President
Donaldson, Lufkin & Jenrette, Inc.

Steve Tsang, Ph.D.
Analyst
Donaldson, Lufkin & Jenrette, Inc.

In this chapter we analyze the risk characteristics of the three major stock index futures markets: the Standard and Poor's (S&P) 500 Composite Index, the New York Stock Exchange (NYSE) Composite Index, and the Value Line Average Composite (VLA). The findings are based on daily closing prices for the period of maturity—for the September 82, December 82, March 83, and June 83 contracts.

Based on six months of history, there are sufficient data to evaluate and compare the characteristics of the various stock index futures contracts. Despite conceptual differences in the three major indexes for which there are futures contracts, the following summary findings should be useful for the risk manager:

1. Based on the daily percentage moves, futures contracts tend to behave much more similarly to each other than the underlying indexes do among themselves.
2. Deferred contracts are not more volatile than nearbys.
3. Relative to the underlying index, Value Line (VLA) futures have the greatest volatility, S&P 500 futures the least. On an absolute basis, VLA futures are the least volatile, S&P 500 futures the most.

4. Futures are more volatile on market down days than on market up days.
5. The futures betas are all significantly greater than one relative to their underlying index.
6. Daily futures price moves can be inconsistent with the market. For example, NYSE and S&P futures moved oppositely to the market 15 to 18 percent of the time, whereas VLA was inconsistent with the market 27 percent of the time.
7. In addition to reflecting changes in carrying costs, changes in the premium and discount of futures over their market index also appear to anticipate future directions for the markets.
8. Finally, it should be remembered that futures trading ends 15 minutes after the stock market closes. Thus the link between the cash and futures is broken briefly. Also, the NYSE contract was not subject to limits during the study period, whereas the other contracts were. These special considerations may explain in part some of the unique behavioral characteristics of futures.

Correlations

During the six months of the study period, the three major stock indexes and their various futures contract prices were highly correlated. Despite some countermarket moves (about 17 percent of the time for the S&P and NYSE contracts and 27 percent for the VLA futures contract), the correlation coefficients are all higher than .99, measured using *price-level* data (see upper panel of Table 9–1). However, the correlation between the market indexes and their respective futures prices, based on daily *percentage changes,* is somewhat weaker. For example, as shown in the lower panel of Table 9–1, the correlation coefficients range between .877 and .887 for the S&P 500 index versus the various S&P 500 futures contracts, between .857 and .863 for the NYSE group, and between .744 and .755 for the VLA group.

It is important to note that the daily *percentage changes* of VLA futures prices is more strongly correlated with the S&P 500 and NYSE indexes than with its own market index. For example, the correlation coefficient between VLA December futures and the VLA index is only .744, as compared with .862 against the NYSE index, .875 against the S&P 500 index, and .868 against the DJIA. This result suggests that futures traders in the VLA market tend to follow the lead of the broader market averages in the short term. This may be logical, because many of the stocks in the VLA index are not priced frequently, since many are thinly traded.

Although the daily price *percentage changes* for the VLA futures contracts are heavily influenced by the broad market indexes, the correlation coefficient on *price levels* indicates that each futures contract is more closely correlated with its own cash index. This seemingly contradictory finding should be expected since each futures contract must ultimately converge to its respective market index on maturity.

The extent of inconsistent moves is evident from the results of a simple "sign" test, shown in Table 9–2. During the study period the market, as measured by the S&P 500 Composite Index, was up on 57 days and down or unchanged on 67 days. Of the 57 days when the market was up, the futures prices were up on 49 days for each of the three (S&P 500, NYSE, and VLA) nearby futures contracts. Of the 67 down days, the futures prices were down on 53 days for two of the index futures (S&P 500 and VLA). Thus, of the 124 total trading days, there were 102 consistent daily price moves for the S&P and VLA futures and 105 for the NYSE futures. The NYSE futures were somewhat more consistent with the S&P 500 index on down days than were the other two contracts. When the VLA index was used as the measure of the market, against which futures were compared, daily futures movements were much less consistent in all cases (see lower panel in Table 9–2).

It is especially important to note again that all daily futures price changes are more strongly correlated with each other than with their respective market indexes. Also, all futures price changes are about equally correlated with the popular Dow Jones Industrial Average (DJIA). In fact, the NYSE futures are slightly more correlated with the DJIA (.887) than with the NYSE index (.863), and the VLA futures are very much more correlated with the DJIA (.860) than with their own underlying index (.744).

It is also important to note that the correlation between the market index and futures prices does not decrease with the length of contract maturity. The correlation coefficient, measured either on levels or percentage changes, is about the same for both nearer and deferred contracts (see Table 9–1). This result should be viewed as evidence that the relatively new stock index futures market is maturing very rapidly. If this relationship continues to hold over time, it should help attract more investors to use the deferred positions, thus increasing the overall market liquidity.

Absolute Volatility

To further examine the relative price behavior, we compare, for each market index and futures contract, the volatility among stock index markets based on the mean and the standard deviation of daily percentage changes.

Table 9-1

Correlation Matrix

	(0)	(1)	(2)	(3)	(4)	(5)	(6)	(7)	(8)	(9)	(10)	(11)	(12)	(13)	(14)
(0) DJIA	1.000														
(1) S&P index	.997	1.000													
(2) S&P nearby	.991	.995	1.000												
(3) S&P Dec.	.990	.995	1.000	1.000											
(4) S&P Mar.	.991	.995	1.000	1.000	1.000										
(5) S&P June	.991	.995	1.000	1.000	1.000	1.000									
(6) NYSE index	.996	1.000	.995	.994	.994	.994	1.000								
(7) NYSE nearby	.990	.995	.999	.999	.999	.999	.995	1.000							
(8) NYSE Dec.	.990	.994	.999	.999	.999	.999	.993	1.000	1.000						
(9) NYSE Mar.	.990	.994	.999	.999	.999	.999	.993	1.000	1.000	1.000					
(10) NYSE June	.990	.993	.998	.999	.999	.999	.993	1.000	1.000	1.000	1.000				
(11) VLA index	.979	.985	.979	.979	.979	.979	.989	.982	.980	.981	.981	1.000			
(12) VLA nearby	.982	.984	.986	.986	.986	.986	.988	.988	.988	.989	.989	.996	1.000		
(13) VLA Dec.	.982	.986	.986	.986	.987	.987	.989	.989	.989	.989	.990	.995	1.000	1.000	
(14) VLA Mar.	.981	.985	.985	.985	.986	.986	.988	.988	.988	.988	.989	.995	1.000	1.000	1.000
(15) VLA June	.980	.984	.984	.984	.985	.985	.987	.987	.987	.988	.988	.995	1.000	1.000	1.000

Price Levels

Percent Changes

	(0)	(1)	(2)	(3)	(4)	(5)	(6)	(7)	(8)	(9)	(10)	(11)	(12)	(13)	(14)
(0) DJIA	1.000														
(1) S&P index	.963	1.000													
(2) S&P nearby	.879	.887	1.000												
(3) S&P Dec.	.873	.882	.998	1.000											
(4) S&P Mar.	.870	.877	.996	.998	1.000										
(5) S&P June	.869	.877	.993	.995	.998	1.000									
(6) NYSE index	.957	.998	.871	.865	.862	.861	1.000								
(7) NYSE nearby	.887	.883	.968	.966	.962	.957	.863	1.000							
(8) NYSE Dec.	.881	.879	.968	.967	.962	.957	.857	.998	1.000						
(9) NYSE Mar.	.885	.880	.968	.967	.962	.958	.859	.997	.999	1.000					
(10) NYSE June	.887	.882	.967	.966	.962	.957	.861	.996	.998	1.000	1.000				
(11) VLA index	.864	.919	.734	.728	.728	.729	.942	.707	.697	.699	.701	1.000			
(12) VLA nearby	.860	.868	.962	.962	.961	.961	.857	.936	.938	.939	.940	.744	1.000		
(13) VLA Dec.	.868	.875	.967	.967	.966	.964	.862	.946	.949	.950	.950	.744	.985	1.000	
(14) VLA Mar.	.874	.879	.965	.965	.964	.962	.867	.941	.944	.945	.945	.748	.979	.996	1.000
(15) VLA June	.873	.880	.959	.959	.959	.958	.869	.933	.935	.936	.936	.753	.971	.990	.994

Source: DLJ.

Table 9–2

Consistent Daily Price Movements: Market Indexes versus Futures Prices

S&P 500 Composite Index

	Up Days	Down Days	Total
S&P index	57	67	124
S&P futures	49	53	102
NYSE futures	49	56	105
VLA futures	49	53	102

Value Line Average Composite

	Up Days	Down Days	Total
VLA index	65	59	124
S&P futures	46	42	88
NYSE futures	45	44	89
VLA futures	47	43	90

Source: DLJ.

As shown in Table 9–3, the mean of the absolute daily percentage changes and the standard deviation of those changes are significantly higher for the futures contracts than for their respective cash market indexes. However, the mean and the standard deviation for futures contracts with different maturities, against the same market index, differ only slightly from one another.

Among the three major market indexes, the least volatile index is the VLA index, with a daily absolute mean percentage change of 0.77 and a standard deviation of 1.00. Similar comparisons can be found for the futures contracts as well. This result is expected because the geometric averaging technique used to calculate the VLA index tends to dampen the effect of large percentage changes. Because of the broader market base, the NYSE index is slightly less volatile than the S&P 500 index. Curiously, however, the NYSE futures contracts are more volatile than the S&P 500 futures contracts.

These tendencies also hold if price changes are classified into two groups: up days and down days. Again, the VLA index is less volatile than the other two indexes. For example, the average daily changes for the VLA index were 0.96 on up days and −0.56 on down days, versus 1.34 and −0.74 for the S&P 500 index and 1.24 and −0.68 for the NYSE index.

Table 9–3

Daily Price Volatility of Stock Indexes and Futures Values (measured from daily percentage changes, June–December 1982)

	Index	Nearby	December 82	March 83	June 83
S&P 500					
Mean (absolute)	1.02%	1.45%	1.47%	1.49%	1.49%
Standard deviation	1.34	1.79	1.82	1.83	1.83
Mean (+ days)	1.34	1.61	1.62	1.62	1.60
Standard deviation	1.05	1.39	1.40	1.42	1.41
Mean (− days)	−0.74	−0.98	−0.99	−1.00	−1.04
Standard deviation	0.65	1.11	1.13	1.14	1.12
NYSE					
Mean (absolute)	0.94	1.57	1.61	1.63	1.62
Standard deviation	1.25	1.96	2.02	2.05	2.05
Mean (+ days)	1.24	1.68	1.70	1.73	1.74
Standard deviation	0.98	1.70	1.76	1.81	1.82
Mean (− days)	−0.68	−1.02	−1.04	−1.06	−1.05
Standard deviation	0.62	1.14	1.19	1.18	1.18
VLA					
Mean (absolute)	0.77	1.39	1.42	1.42	1.41
Standard deviation	1.00	1.70	1.74	1.73	1.72
Mean (+ days)	0.96	1.17	1.19	1.19	1.21
Standard deviation	0.74	1.61	1.63	1.62	1.58
Mean (− days)	−0.56	−0.77	−0.80	−0.80	−0.83
Standard deviation	0.53	1.12	1.17	1.15	1.13

Source: DLJ.

Relative Volatility

The normalized or relative price volatility for each futures contract, calculated in relation to its own market index, is quite different from the absolute volatility of the market index itself. Relative volatility is defined as the ratio of the mean percentage change of the futures prices to the mean percentage change of the underlying market index. Table 9–4 indicates that VLA futures have the greatest relative volatility, followed by NYSE futures and S&P 500 futures. Table 9–4 also shows that the futures prices are relatively more volatile when the market moves down than on up days. For example, the average price increase for the S&P 500 December futures contract was 21 percent higher than the market rises on up days and the decrease was 34 percent greater than the market declines on down days.

Table 9–4

Relative Volatility of Futures Prices to Their Respective Stock Indexes

	Nearby	December 82	March 83	June 83
S&P 500				
Absolute	142%	144%	146%	146%
Up days (+)	120	121	121	119
Down days (−)	132	134	135	141
NYSE				
Absolute	167	171	173	172
Up days (+)	135	137	140	140
Down days (−)	150	153	156	154
VLA				
Absolute	181	184	184	183
Up days (+)	122	124	124	126
Down days (−)	138	143	143	148

Note: Relative volatility is calculated by the ratio of the mean percentage changes of futures contract to the index.
Source: DLJ, table 3.

Futures' Beta Coefficients

The daily price movements for each futures contract, relative to its respective market index, can be analyzed by looking at the beta—a measure of relative price responsiveness. As shown in Table 9–5, the beta coefficients for all futures contracts are greater than one, but the magnitude of the beta does not vary much with the length of contract maturity. For example, the beta is identical for the S&P 500 nearby and June 83 futures contracts (1.17 versus 1.17). The beta for NYSE and VLA futures contracts increased slightly with the length of contract maturity, rising from 1.34 to 1.40 in the case of the former and from 1.26 to 1.30 in the case of the latter. The results also indicate that the S&P 500 futures contracts are by far the least sensitive (lowest beta) relative to the market index. This finding is curious in light of the fact that the NYSE index itself has a relatively low volatility, yet the NYSE futures contracts demonstrate the most price sensitivity (highest beta) in comparison with the other two markets. The fact that there were no limit constraints on the NYSE futures during the test period may have only limited impact on this finding.

It should be pointed out that some of the short-term beta coefficients, measured from daily percentage changes, are far from stable relative to the values obtained from longer-term measurements, that is, weekly or monthly price changes instead of daily changes. In an earlier study we found that the price volatility for the VLA index was less than that of

Table 9–5

Beta Coefficient for Selected Futures Contracts
versus Their Respective Stock Indexes

	Constant	Beta	Standard Error
S&P 500			
Nearby	−0.03	1.17	0.85%
December 82	−0.03	1.18	0.88
March 83	−0.03	1.18	0.89
June 83	−0.04	1.17	0.88
NYSE			
Nearby	−0.05	1.34	1.00
December 82	−0.06	1.37	1.05
March 83	−0.07	1.39	1.06
June 83	−0.06	1.40	1.06
VLA			
Nearby	−0.03	1.26	1.14
December 82	−0.04	1.29	1.17
March 83	−0.05	1.29	1.15
June 83	−0.05	1.30	1.13

Note: The constant and beta are derived from regression analysis of daily percentage changes.
Source: DLJ.

the S&P 500 index on a daily basis.[1] The beta of VLA increased significantly as we lengthened the time interval for measuring relative price changes. For example, the beta for VLA was 0.83 against S&P 500, measured from daily percentage changes between 1971 and 1982. The beta increased to 0.95, measured from weekly percentage changes, and increased further to 1.17, measured from month-to-month percentage changes. The fact that in relation to the S&P 500, the beta of VLA increases with the length of the holding period implies that there is a systematic bias toward more volatile stocks. In other words, the VLA index tended to make larger and longer trend moves than did the market value–weighted S&P 500 index, despite the fact that the geometric weighting in VLA dampens the short-term, day-to-day price changes.

Basis and Theoretical Spread

We found that during the first three months of index futures trading the movement of the basis, that is, the difference between the futures

[1] Gregory M. Kipnis and Steve Tsang, "The New Stock Index Contract—An Important New Hedging Vehicle and Unique Barometer of Market Expectations," *ACS Futures Research Bulletin,* ACLI International, February 1982.

Exhibit 9-1

S&P 500 Composite Index (Line) versus S&P Nearby Futures (Daily Closes)

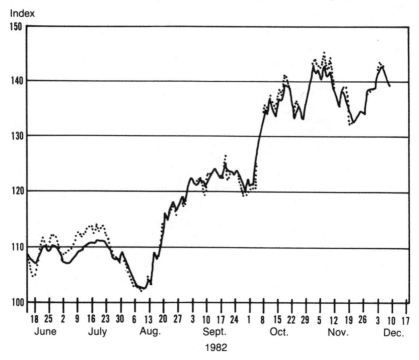

Source: DLJ.

price and the market index, reflected not only changes in carrying charges but also changes in price expectations (sentiment) for the near term.[2] This tendency continued to hold during the present study period, June–December 1982, but to a lesser degree. As shown in Exhibit 9–1, the S&P 500 index nearby futures contract tracked very closely on either side of the S&P 500 nearby index in the six months of the study period. However, despite the close association between futures and market index prices, the basis movement continued to be very volatile (see Exhibit 9–2).

During the first stage of the big market rally between August and September 1982, the basis was quite flat on average, which indicates that many investors were not really convinced that the huge upward move would be sustained. However, during the second leg of the market

---

[2] Gregory M. Kipnis and Steve Tsang, "The Short History of Stock Index Futures: Volatility and Spread Trading Opportunities," *ACS Futures Research Bulletin,* ACLI International, May 1982.

Exhibit 9–2

Basis: S&P 500 Nearby Futures Less S&P 500 Composite Index

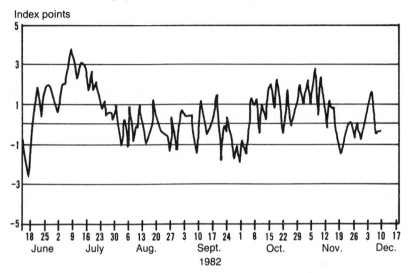

Source: DLJ.

rally, between October and November, the basis also moved upward significantly, which might have reflected a swing to overall market bullishness. After the early November 1982 peak, the basis weakened sharply; and so did the market index.

Since the basis between futures prices and the market index can be arbitraged up to a point (see Chapter 10), the spread between the "theoretical" futures price and actual futures prices should be viewed as a better measure of market sentiment, plus other random factors. The theoretical futures price is roughly equal to the ratio difference between the riskless interest rate and the dividend yield to contract maturity. As shown in Exhibit 9–3, the pattern of spread movement is quite similar to that of the basis movement seen in Exhibit 9–2. This result seems to suggest that changes in market sentiment continue to dominate futures price levels. The extent of this influence may have diminished since the early months of the trading in index futures.

Intraday Price Movements

The tendency of the futures market to lead the stock market is even more evident on an intraday basis. This tendency has been consistently

Exhibit 9–3

Spreads: S&P Nearby Futures less Theoretical Prices

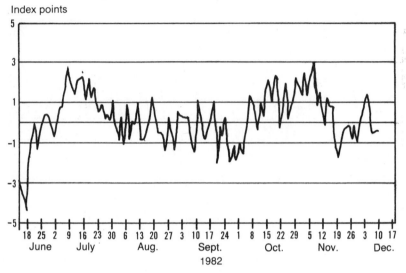

Source: DLJ.

observed on numerous occasions in the past several months. One example is shown in Exhibit 9–4, the trade-by-trade, minute-by-minute price movements for both the futures contract and the stock index on December 8, 1982. The upper panel shows the S&P 500 futures prices and the lower panel shows the actual S&P 500 index. It is easily seen that the peaks and troughs for December futures lead stock market turns by about 5 to 20 minutes. For example, futures prices peaked at 11:50 A.M. before trending lower, while the market index peaked at around 12:10 P.M. This is a very useful finding for market makers and day traders.

Since the stock market and the stock index futures markets both comprise a large number of individuals with similar background information and interests, this phenomenon may be due to the fact that within a very short period of time it is much easier to buy or sell a single price index than the actual 500 individual stocks. Thus, when market sentiment begins to change, the stock index futures market would reflect the impact somewhat sooner than the broader stock market index, which reflects changes in each of 500 stocks. Careful monitoring of the price movement in the futures market could help stock traders determine the timing of buying and selling on an intraday basis. However, since futures prices are more volatile than the market, there are many minor false moves that cannot be easily distinguished from real turns.

Exhibit 9–4

Minute-by-Minute Tick Chart, December 8, 1982 (December futures: upper; S&P index: lower)

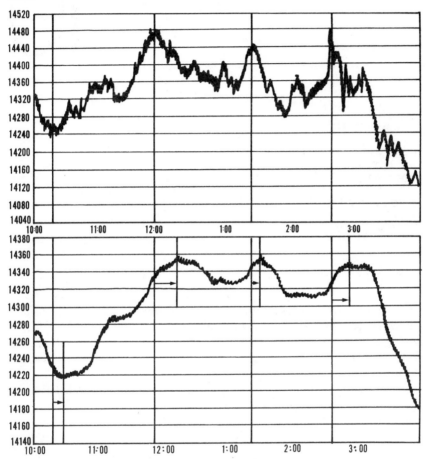

CHAPTER 10

Arbitrage

Gregory M. Kipnis
Vice President
Donaldson, Lufkin & Jenrette, Inc.

Steve Tsang, Ph.D.
Analyst
Donaldson, Lufkin & Jenrette, Inc.

Stock index cash/futures arbitrage is complicated by four major considerations: (1) identifying when futures are over- or undervalued, (2) determining the costs associated with an arbitrage, (3) selecting a small optimal portfolio that tracks a target index, and (4) managing the basis risk of a surrogate portfolio.[1]

In the next section of this chapter we examine the actual arbitrage opportunities under varying assumptions of transaction costs and operation efficiencies, based on a stock portfolio that is perfectly indexed to the market. The results indicate that there have been many arbitrage opportunities even for the less efficient arbitrageurs faced with relatively high transaction costs. Since the S&P 500 Composite Index is a broadly based market index and the weights for each of the stocks constantly change over time, it is impractical to actually arbitrage the market portfolio against the futures contract. The practical alternative would be to use a workable number of stocks to replicate the performance of the market index. However, the performance of sample portfolios often differs randomly from the market; thus a "basis" risk arises. In the third section of this chapter we analyze the arbitrage risks and rewards from using two small sample portfolios. The simulation results strongly suggest that

---

[1] Basis risk is defined in Chapter 12.

124

most of the arbitrage opportunities associated with a sample portfolio can be profitably exploited and that the basis risks, if not correctly managed, could either significantly offset or increase the profits associated with an arbitrage.

The Twilight Zone in Arbitraging Stock Index Futures

There is a zone within which futures prices can freely fluctuate around their "fair," or equilibrium, value as defined in Chapters 6 and 7. The size of this zone is defined by the costs associated with attempting to arbitrage departures from equilibrium values. In this section we define those costs, estimate the twilight (or nonarbitrageable) zone, and identify the frequency and profitability of the trading opportunities that fall outside the twilight zone. The number of opportunities and their profitability are very sensitive to the economic situation of the arbitrageur.

In earlier studies we discussed a simplified method for identifying cash/futures arbitrage opportunities, using the stock index futures contracts.[2] For owners of large portfolios that essentially track the market index or for investors with fresh funds to invest in the stock market, such opportunities could be used very effectively to outperform the market by trading the stock index futures contracts. Basically, an opportunity arises whenever stock index futures trade at a price significantly below "full carrying costs." In such a situation an investor's return could be enhanced by the amount of the differences between theoretical equilibrium futures prices and actual futures prices, adjusted for various costs associated with the transaction.

In addition, for arbitrageurs who must borrow funds and/or stocks to implement the arbitrage, the profitability would be affected significantly by the limitation on the use of the short-sale proceeds of borrowed stocks. For many large traders and brokers, shorting stocks may not be an important constraint because they may have the full use of short-sale funds. For traders with limited use of the short-sale proceeds, the arbitrageur's profitability would be significantly lessened.

To analyze the effect of transaction costs and constraints on the use of short-sale proceeds on arbitrage profitability in the S&P 500 Composite Index futures market, we examined the S&P 500 futures contracts for September 1982, December 1982, March 1983, and June 1983. All data are based on daily closing prices from the first trading day, April 21, 1982, to January 20, 1983. The dividend yield is based on a yield-to-

---

[2] Gregory M. Kipnis and Steve Tsang, "Determinants of Stock Index Future Price Spreads," *ACS Futures Research*, April 1982; and Gregory M. Kipnis and Steve Tsang, "An Opportunity to Outperform the Stock Market," *ACS Futures Research*, August 1982.

maturity measurement (see Chapter 7), and the riskless rate of interest is the T bill yield matched to the maturity of each futures contract.

Arbitrage Costs

Basically, four major costs are associated with an arbitrage: (1) round-trip commission costs for cash and futures positions, (2) bid-ask spreads and/or up-tic costs associated with shorting stocks, (3) margin outflow costs net of margin inflow income, and (4) interest cost (income) net of dividend income (cost) for long (short) stock and short (long) futures positions.

It is fairly easy to determine the total commissions costs on a per futures contract or on the basis of a number of equivalent shares per futures contract. The number of equivalent shares per contract is generally quite stable because the index level moves with share values. Only when the relative weight for a stock changes dramatically would the number of shares per index contract vary. For example, if IBM moved from $60 to $90 per share and AT&T stayed at $60, it would be necessary to sell three AT&T shares and buy two IBM Shares in order to rebalance the portfolio.[3] Furthermore, commission costs vary with the size of the arbitrageur's operation. They can roughly range from below 5 cents per stock share and $15–40 per futures contract for the very largest traders, institutions, or brokerage firms to as high as 10–20 cents per stock share and $50–80 per futures contract for smaller traders.

The second important cost is the bid-ask spread and the up-tic cost for shorting stocks. In order to complete an arbitrage, a small premium is sometimes paid by the arbitrageur for quick executions. Since execution efficiency also varies with the size of the arbitrageur's operation, it is fair to assume that the larger the arbitrageur, the smaller the premiums he must pay.

The third cost associated with an arbitrage is the net margin outflow cost associated with futures positions, since futures contracts are marked-to-the-market daily. Any losses would have to be financed at the prevailing rate of interest. Conversely, all gains could be withdrawn from the account to earn interest income. Since the margin flow income is basically random, that is, stock prices tend to be a random walk, it may be reasonable to assume that the margin inflow/outflow effect should be offsetting over time.

The fourth arbitrage cost is the interest cost net of dividend income, for long-stock/short-futures positions, or the dividend cost net of interest income, for short-stock/long-futures positions. As we have demonstrated

---

[3] Also affecting the number of shares would be stocks splits, new offerings, and so on.

Exhibit 10–1

S&P 500 Composite Index (Line) versus March Futures (Dot)

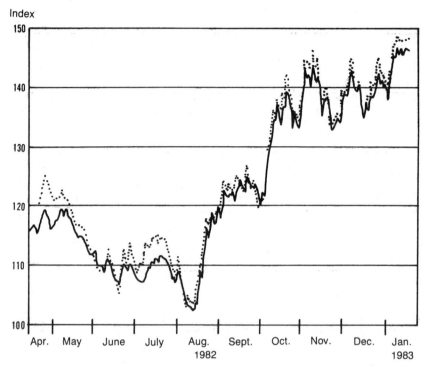

Source: DLJ.

in an earlier writing, dividend and interest income are the two major determinants of stock index prices.[4] Without transaction costs a stock market portfolio and a stock index futures/T bill portfolio would provide equal returns when the futures prices were at a full-carry premium to the cash index value. Full carry is roughly equal to the ratio difference between the riskless T bill rate and the dividend yield, on a yield-to-maturity basis. The dividend yield to maturity and the T bill rate must correspond to the maturity of the futures contract because only on that date will the futures price converge to the actual cash index.

Without limitation on the use of short-sale proceeds, for the most efficient traders, a profitable arbitrage opportunity arises whenever the futures price trades either above or below the full-carry premium by an amount that is greater than the transaction costs (commissions plus

---

[4] Kipnis and Tsang, "Determinants of Stock Index Futures Price Spreads."

Exhibit 10–2

S&P March Futures (Dot), Theoretical Upper and Lower Bounds (Line)
(75 percent use of short proceeds)

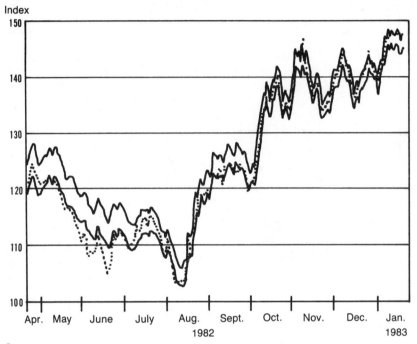

Source: DLJ.

execution inefficiency costs). If the futures price is below the lower boundary, that is, the theoretical equilibrium futures price minus the total transaction costs, a short-cash/long-futures arbitrage should be a profitable
strategy. Conversely, if the futures contract is trading above the upper
boundary, defined as the theoretical value plus the transaction costs, a
long-cash/short-stock arbitrage should be profitable. Thus the arbitrage-
free band, that is, the zone within which futures prices can trade without
yielding any net arbitrage profits, would be nearly symmetrical around
the theoretical futures price. The uptick cost for a short-stock position
is the factor that disturbs the symmetry.

   For the less efficient trader, faced with some limitation on the use of
short-sale proceeds, the arbitrage-free band would be significantly different. The upper boundary is somewhat higher because a larger commission
and execution inefficiency costs must be paid for the long-cash/short-
futures arbitrage. The lower boundary, however, could be significantly

Exhibit 10–3

Twilight Zone: March Futures less S&P 500 Composite Index (Line), Theoretical Bounds less S&P 500 Composite Index (Dot)

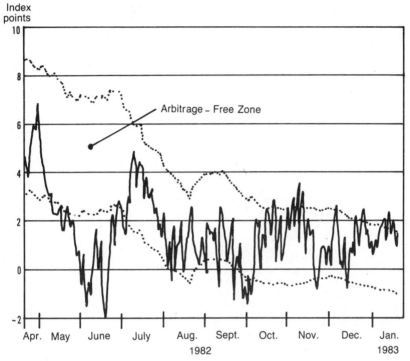

Source: DLJ.

lower because of the reduced interest income from the short-sale proceeds of the borrowed stocks, which significantly raises the total arbitrage costs. From those transaction cost estimates are calculated the total number of arbitrage opportunities and the profitability associated with those opportunities. The results are shown in Table 10–1. To simplify the presentation, several charts are used based on the assumption of 75 percent use of the short-sale proceeds from borrowed stocks. These charts illustrate the theoretical arbitrage-free boundary and the profitability associated with an arbitrage for the March 1983 S&P 500 futures contract.

Quantifying Arbitrage Opportunities and Profitability

As shown in Exhibit 10–1, the March futures prices have been tracking the actual S&P 500 index very closely since the inception of the new

Table 10–1

Summary of Cash/Futures Arbitrage Opportunity and Profitability in the S&P 500 Futures Market

	Contract Maturity			
	September 82	*December 82*	*March 83*	*June 83*
Total trading days	104	168	192	146
100 percent use of short-sale funds				
A. Short-cash/long-futures (days)	43	71	116	101
Average profit ($/contract)	$650	$880	$1,140	$960
Maximum profit ($/contract)	$1,810	$2,690	$3,650	$2,770
B. Long-cash/short-futures (days)	21	30	23	6
Average profit ($/contract)	$370	$320	$241	$160
Maximum profit ($/contract)	$1,040	$1,020	$710	$310
75 percent use of short-sale funds				
A. Short-cash/long-futures (days)	21	30	50	29
Average profit ($/contract)	$515	$560	$600	$320
Maximum profit ($/contract)	$1,290	$1,710	$2,210	$830
B. Long-cash/short-futures (days)	17	25	17	5
Average profit ($/contract)	$340	$280	$210	$80
Maximum profit ($/contract)	$940	$920	$610	$210
50 percent use of short-sale funds				
A. Short-cash/long-futures (days)	9	9	6	0
Average profit ($/contract)	$380	$230	$300	$0
Maximum profit ($/contract)	$770	$720	$770	$0
B. Long-cash/short-futures (days)	12	16	13	1
Average profit ($/contract)	$360	$310	$160	$110
Maximum profit ($/contract)	$840	$820	$510	$110

Source: DLJ.

Exhibit 10–4

Relative Return Enhancement: Short Cash/Long Futures ($ per S&P futures contract, March maturity basis)

$000

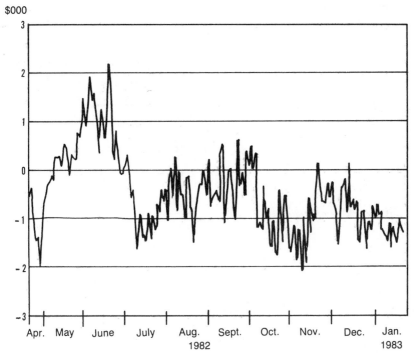

Source: DLJ.

futures market. The theoretically calculated upper and lower bounds for traders with 75 percent use of the short proceeds are shown in Exhibit 10–2. A futures price (dotted line) below the lower boundary indicates a profitable short-cash/long-futures arbitrage opportunity. The converse is true whenever futures prices are above the upper boundary.

Exhibit 10–3 magnifies the arbitrage-free band by recalculating all of the series shown in Exhibit 10–2 as spread differences from the actual index value. In this way one clearly sees that many arbitrage opportunities have been associated with the March 1983 futures contract. On June 18, for example, the March futures contract was 2 points below the cash index and the theoretical lower bound was 2.42 points above the cash index; thus there was a potential arbitrage profit of $2,210 (4.42 points) for the short-cash/long-futures arbitrage. Exhibit 10–4 illustrates the dollar profitability for only the short-cash/long-futures arbitrage opportunities, and Exhibit 10–5 illustrates only the long-cash/short-futures arbi-

Exhibit 10–5

Relative Return Enhancement: Long Cash/Short Futures ($ per S&P futures contract, March maturity basis)

$000

Source: DLJ.

trage opportunities. Shown in Exhibit 10–6 is the relative return enhancement per contract, at annual percentage rates, for the short-cash/long-futures arbitrage.

In Table 10–1 we summarize the arbitrage opportunities for four futures contracts based on three different limitations on the use of short-sale proceeds and transaction costs from April 21, 1982, to January 20, 1983. From the data it is evident that the higher the limitation on the use of short-sale proceeds and total transaction costs, the smaller are the number of arbitrage opportunities and the lower the arbitrage profitability. For example, among a total of 192 trading days for the March 1983 contract, there were 116 short-cash/long-futures opportunities for the most efficient arbitrageurs. The number of opportunities declined to 50 for traders with 75 percent use of the short-sale proceeds and to only 6 for traders who have to give up 50 percent of the short proceeds. The average profit per contract also dropped sharply, from $1,140 for the most efficient trad-

Exhibit 10–6

Relative Return Enhancement in Percentages at Annual Rates (Short Cash/Long
Futures, March maturity basis)

Percent

Source: DLJ.

ers to about $600 for traders with 75 percent use of short proceeds and
to only $300 for traders with 50 percent use of short proceeds.

For the long-cash/short-futures arbitrage, the number of opportunities
also decreased for traders with higher transaction costs. The average profitability per contract, however, did not change very dramatically because
the interest component for short-sale proceeds was not a factor. In fact,
under certain conditions the average profit was somewhat higher because
of the elimination of some of the marginally profitable trades. For example,
looking at the December 1982 contract, the average profit for traders
with 75 percent use of short proceeds was $280 per contract as compared
with $310 for traders with 50 percent limitation on short-sale proceeds.
This was the case because the higher transaction costs associated with
the less efficient traders reduced trading opportunities from 25 to 16.

Conclusion

In conclusion, anyone entertaining the idea of attempting to profit from arbitraging futures prices that appear to be over- or undervalued should first very carefully analyze both his costs and those of the most efficient arbitrageurs to understand where the twilight zone exists; for within that zone almost anything can happen. Furthermore, all of the examples given here assume that an arbitrage is implemented with a cash portfolio that exactly tracks the market index; that is, there is no basis risk. In the following section we will demonstrate that significant basis risks are associated with using small sample portfolios that appear to be highly correlated with the market.

Risks and Rewards Using Small Portfolios

In the following section the potential rewards and problems associated with two small, supposedly optimal stock portfolios are analyzed. The simulation results show that even though there have been many profitable arbitrage opportunities, the basis risk introduced by small, and seemingly optimal, portfolios can significantly increase or offset the arbitrage profits. As a consequence, timing and trading disciplines become necessary additional skills.

Constructing Small Arbitrage Portfolios

In this section we analyze the potential arbitrage risks and rewards from using two small sample stock portfolios, each containing eight identical stocks, but with different weighting schemes. Stock portfolio A was selected from a list of large-capitalization stocks through an optimization process. The weight for each of the eight stocks in the portfolio was determined so as to minimize the variance of the tracking error (basis risk) relative to the S&P 500 index for the period May 1981 to May 1982. Portfolio B was formulated by using the same eight stocks, with the weighting changed to equal share weight. This nonoptimal portfolio was chosen to provide a basis of comparison for portfolio A. The list of stocks and the shares for each of the stocks in the two portfolios are shown in Table 10–2. All of the data used for the analysis are daily market closing prices.

The portfolio beta relative to the S&P 500 index for the sample period is 0.95 for portfolio A and 0.80 for portfolio B.[5] The beta is used to

---

[5] See Chapter 12 for the definition of beta.

Table 10–2

Stock Components in Sample Portfolios

Company	Portfolio A	Portfolio B
Du Pont	35	100
General Electric	35	100
General Foods	95	100
IBM	20	100
AT&T	100	100
U.S. Steel	140	100
Exxon	360	100
United Technologies	65	100
Total shares	850	800
Value on 6/1/82	$28,719	$33,163
Historical beta	0.95	0.80
R^2	0.97	0.83

determine the hedge ratio in the arbitrage analysis. The relative performance of the two portfolios and the S&P 500 index are shown in Exhibit 10–7. Despite the small number of stocks used to construct the sample portfolios, the movements of the three are reasonably related to one another.[6] It is clear that for most of the sample period portfolio A tracked the S&P 500 index much more closely than did portfolio B. It is also important to note that portfolio B underperformed the market by a wide margin for most of 1981 but that it outperformed the market in the first five months of 1982.

Implementing the Arbitrage

In earlier chapters and other writings, it has been demonstrated that a stock portfolio and a stock index futures/T bill portfolio provide equal returns when the futures prices are at a full-carry premium to the cash index value.[7] Full carry is roughly equal to the ratio difference between the riskless interest rate and the stock portfolio's dividend yield for a fixed-maturity holding period. The fixed-maturity holding period must correspond to the maturity date of the futures contract because only on that date will the futures price converge to the price of the actual stock index.

To implement the arbitrage, one would establish a hedged position by going either long futures and short stocks or short futures and long

---

[6] To facilitate comparison, the values of the portfolios are indexed to equal the S&P 500 index on May 1, 1981.

[7] See footnote 2 for citations.

Exhibit 10–7

S&P 500 Composite Stock Index (Line), Price Index for Portfolio A (Dot), and Price
Index for Portfolio B (Dash) (indexes = 133 on 5/1/81)

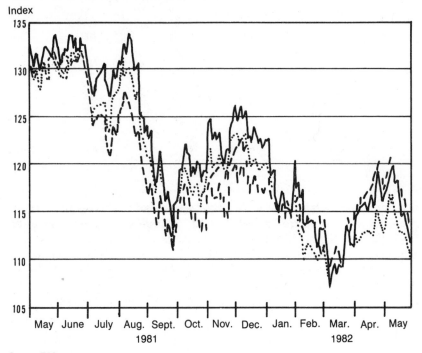

Source: DLJ.

stocks. The trade employed would depend on whether the futures prices
were undervalued or overvalued by an amount which was at least greater
than the transaction costs. For the most efficient arbitrageur, transaction
costs are estimated at about $300 per contract value for the long-futures
hedge and at somewhat less for the short-futures hedge. In the simulations
each arbitrage trade is held to the maturity of the futures contract. The
futures market used in these examples is the S&P 500 September 1982
futures contract, and the test period consists of the 75 trading days from
June 1, 1982, to September 16, 1982. Including weekends, the holding
period for the arbitrage could be as long as 107 days and as short as 1
day.

Simulation Results

For portfolio A, during the 75 trading days of the test period the September futures prices were undervalued on 33 days and overvalued on

Table 10–3

Profit/Loss for Hedged Positions

	Long Futures/ Short Stocks	Short Futures/ Long Stocks	Total
Portfolio A			
Number of trades	27	29	56
Profitable trades	27	8	35
Winning percentage	100%	27.6%	62.5%
Average profit per trade ($/$1,000)	$41.87	−$10.17	$14.92
Average expected arbitrage profit ($/$1,000)	$12.19	$13.72	$12.98
Portfolio B			
Number of trades	25	27	52
Profitable trades	8	26	34
Winning percentage	32.0%	96.3%	65.4%
Average profit per trade ($/$1,000)	−$25.66	$30.60	$3.55
Average expected arbitrage profit ($/$1,000)	$15.14	$14.56	$14.84

42 days. During the 33 days on which the futures prices were undervalued, 27 long-futures/short-stock positions were implemented. All of the trades were profitable! During the 42 days on which the futures prices were overvalued, 29 short-futures/long-stock trades were implemented. Only 8 of these 29 hedged positions were profitable. Thus, of the total 56 trades, 35 were profitable. The average profit per trade, per $1,000 hedged, was $41.87 for the long-futures/short-stock positions and −$10.17 for the short-futures/long-stock positions. The overall average profit for the 56 trades was $14.92 per $1,000 hedged (see Table 10–3). Keep in mind that none of the returns are annualized.

For portfolio B, the trading results were almost completely reversed. Of the 25 long-futures/short-stock trades implemented, only 8 were profitable. Of the 27 short-futures/long-stock trades, 26 were profitable. The average loss for the long-futures hedge was $25.66 per $1,000, and the average profit for the short-futures hedge was $30.66 per $1,000. The arbitrage results are also shown in Exhibit 10–8. The solid line indicates the amount of profit or loss that would result if the hedge position for portfolio A were held from each trading day in the test period until September 16. The dotted line indicates the results for portfolio B. All of the profits and losses shown in Table 10–3 have been adjusted for interest and dividend flows and are net of all commission costs.

Basis Risk

The major risk for an arbitrage trade that uses a sample portfolio rather than the market portfolio is the basis risk. For the long-futures/short-

Exhibit 10–8

Arbitrage Profits/Losses for Portfolio A (Line) and Portfolio B (Dot) (all hedged positions mature on 9/16/82)

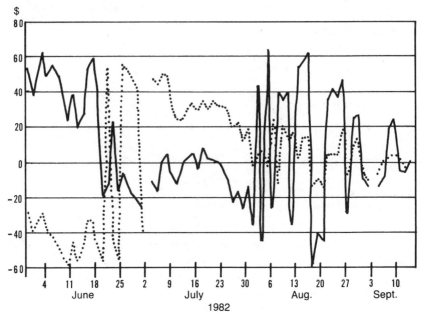

Source: DLJ.

stock positions, based on a sample portfolio, the arbitrage would be profitable if the sample portfolio either underperformed the S&P 500 futures price or outperformed the futures by an amount no greater that the "excess" yield (i.e., the difference between the actual and theoretical full-carry price net of transaction costs). If the basis moved adversely, hedging losses would result. The reverse criteria would be necessary for the short-futures/long-stock positions to be profitable. Thus careful monitoring of the basis movement of the hedged portfolio is essential for the arbitrageur. As shown in Exhibit 10–9, the basis movements for the two portfolios were quite volatile during the three-month test period. For example, portfolio A underperformed the index futures value by 7.3 percent (i.e., 7.1 percent versus 14.4 percent) for the holding period from August 18 until the September 16 maturity date (see solid line).

For the whole test period, portfolio A underperformed the index futures prices. The basis movement for portfolio B, on the other hand, was less consistent. The portfolio outperformed the index futures prices for trades initiated during June and July and underperformed the futures prices

Exhibit 10–9

Posthedge Analysis: Actual Holding Period Basis Movements at Each Date, Portfolio
A (Line) and Portfolio B (Dot) (relative to S&P futures)

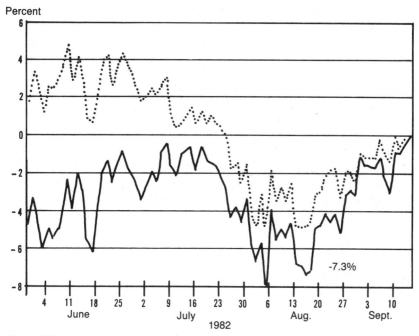

Source: DLJ.

during most of August and September. To a large extent the basis variation
explains why portfolio A and portfolio B achieved almost opposite arbitrage results during the test period.

As shown in Table 10–3, the average expected arbitrage profit would
have been $12.19 per $1,000 if portfolio A had performed exactly with
the market during the entire hedge period for the long-futures/short-
stock positions. The favorable, though unexpected, basis movements improved the average realized profit by $29.68, to $41.87 per $1,000 hedged.
For the short-futures/long-stock positions, on the other hand, the average
profit per $1,000 hedged was reduced from $13.72 to a loss of $10.17
due to the unexpected underperformance of the small stock portfolio.
The impact of the basis movements on arbitrage profitability was as significant for portfolio B as for portfolio A, but the results were almost
completely reversed. The unexpected loss of $25.66 for the long-futures/
short-stock positions was mainly due to the outperformance of the stock
portfolio. Conversely, the average realized profit of $30.60 for the short-
futures/long-stock positions was more than twice the size of the expected

arbitrage profit of $14.56 per $1,000 hedged, due to favorable basis movements.

Improving the Results through Timing

All of the arbitrage results presented above were based on hedged positions for a fixed maturity, that is, expiring on September 16, 1982. However, not all profitable or unprofitable trades based on this fixed maturity date were consistently profitable or unprofitable throughout the holding period.

As shown in Exhibit 10–10, the hedged positions implemented on June 18 and lifted on September 16 resulted in a profit of $58.50 per $1,000 for portfolio A (see ending point of solid line). However, this hedged position (long futures/short stocks) was unprofitable on several occasions during August (e.g., August 17). Furthermore, as shown in Exhibit 10–10, a greater profit of $60 could have been realized on July 20 (see peak

Exhibit 10–10

Tracking a Single Trade: Arbitrage Profit/Loss for Long-Futures/Short-Stocks Position Implemented on June 18 and Matured on September 16, Portfolio A (line) versus Portfolio B (Dot)

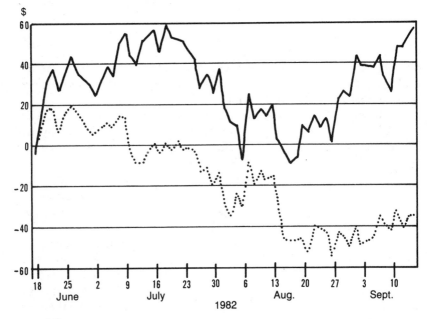

Source: DLJ.

value of solid line). For portfolio B, an early lifting of the hedge on June 28 would have resulted in a profit of $20 per $1,000 rather than the $33.08 loss that would have resulted if it had been held until maturity (see dotted line).

The exercise presented above indicates that just às important as properly selecting a sample portfolio to implement arbitrage trading is determining timing rules for lifting the hedge, especially when markets and the portfolio basis are volatile, which is almost always the case.

The positive arbitrage results from the over 100 trades tested strongly suggest that the relative performance of an existing portfolio could be enhanced by the disciplined use of stock index futures. The key to a profitable hedging or arbitrage operation is to properly manage the portfolio's basis risk during the hedge period.

Conclusion

It is impractical to actually arbitrage using a 500 stock portfolio against the S&P 500 futures contract. A practical alternative is to use a workable number of stocks to replicate the market index. However, the performance of the selected small stock portfolio often differs from that of the market. This exposes the arbitrage to a basis risk. Because the basis movement tends to be unpredictable, that risk can either enhance or detract from the basic arbitrage profitability. Careful trading discipline may help in this regard. The basis risk can also be reduced by increasing the number of stocks used in the portfolio or by reweighting the stocks as appropriate. Should a liquid indexed fund, which can be traded as a security, become available, then the basis problem would be significantly reduced.

SECTION THREE

Applications

The Uses and Users of the Stock Index Futures Markets

Frank J. Jones, Ph.D.
Executive Vice President
New York Futures Exchange

This chapter describes the nature of the users of stock index futures contracts and the purpose of their uses. While the users of the various types of futures markets are not identical in type, they are parallel. For example, professional grain traders and distributors are important users of grain futures contracts, while professional stock traders and distributors, are important users of stock index futures contracts. In general, the users of stock index futures contracts will parallel the users of grain and Treasury security futures contracts.

It is also interesting to note the chronological entry of the various types of users into the futures markets. Again, while the entries of the various types of users into the contracts of the different futures markets are not identical, they are parallel. For example, floor traders and professional upstairs traders always precede commercial hedgers in using the futures markets.

This chapter discusses the various types of users of the stock index futures market in the order in which they have entered the market. Exhibit 11–1 provides the outline for this discussion.

In this regard, even though stock index futures did not begin trading at any exchange until February 1982, and at the third of the three exchanges now trading them until May 1982, stock index futures markets

Exhibit 11-1

The Users of Stock Index Futures Markets

Floor
  Trader (proprietary)
    Scalper
    Day trader
    Position trader
      Technical
      Fundamental
  Broker
    Spot month
    Back months
    Spreads (nearby and deferred)

Professional stock trader

Abritrageur

Retail customer
  Traditional commodity customer
  Stock market customer

Commercial hedger
  Stock firm professional
  Underwriter
  Risk arbitrageur
  Block positioner
  Dealer
  Portfolio manager

---

have developed very quickly with respect to types of uses. Thus the chronology of the users of these markets is as complete as the chronology of the users of futures markets that have existed much longer.

Floor Traders

The first type of user in all futures markets is the floor trader. Floor traders are the source of liquidity in futures markets, and this source of liquidity must exist before most types of nonfloor users can participate in these markets.

Floor traders are typically independent entrepreneurs whose business is to trade futures contracts on an exchange floor. They accept the concomitant risk in order to have the potential to make a substantial income.

When we either think about floor traders or observe them on an exchange floor, it may seem that they are all engaged in the same activity. This, however, is not the case. Many different roles are performed by floor traders. This section describes some of their activities and functions.

The fundamental distinction among floor traders is whether they are trading for their own account, in which case they are called "proprietary traders," or whether they are filling orders for other customers, that is, they are brokers. (These two types are also referred to as "principals" and "agents.")

Even among proprietary traders and brokers, however, there are several different specialties. These specialties are discussed below.

Proprietary Traders

The most important function on an exchange floor is that of the scalper. The scalper (also called a dealer) is the market maker in futures markets.

Every market, in order to have liquidity, needs one or more market makers. In any market, the market maker is an entrepreneur who continually provides bid prices (prices at which he will buy from customers so that customers can sell) and offer prices (prices at which he will sell to customers so that customers can buy). In order to make an income and sustain his participation, the trader will always set his bid price below his offer price. In this way, if the general price level stays constant, the trader will buy at one price and sell at a higher price, thus making a profit by the amount of the difference, called the spread.

However, there can be substantial risk in market making. For example, if the market maker bought and the market price went down, he would experience a capital loss. Similarly, he would lose if he sold and the market price went up. Both types of risk are substantial in the futures markets, since it is as easy to buy and have a long position as it is to sell and have a short position.

The scalper on the exchange floor is the futures market's market maker. Over the entire trading day, the scalper makes bids to buy from customers who want to sell and offers to sell to customers who want to buy, thereby providing liquidity on the exchange floor. In providing liquidity to the market, scalpers necessarily take positions by buying and selling, but they hold these positions for very short periods of time, moments or minutes. And while there is an unavoidable risk associated with taking these positions, many successful scalpers bear little risk, as indicated by the small day-to-day volatility of their income. Soon after they buy a contract, they resell it, and vice versa. In this way they earn a fairly stable income based on the bid-asked spread and risk little capital loss from the movement of prices against their positions. However, many inexperienced or unskilled scalpers bear considerable risk. In fact, the rate of failure among scalpers is relatively high.

Other types of proprietary floor traders take positions and hold them for longer periods of time than scalpers, either for hours within a day or even over several days. Obviously, such floor traders do not provide a continuous source of liquidity on an exchange floor because they are not buying and selling continuously. However, they may provide important sources of orders, at times very large orders.

Traders who take positions (long or short) for a matter of hours during a day but "go home flat" (that is, with no positions overnight) are called "day traders."

Traders who hold positions for more than a day are called "position traders." Day traders or position traders can trade on either a technical basis or a fundamental basis, though most day and position traders are technically oriented. Technical trading bases itself only on an analysis of prices, trading volume, and the open interest of the product in question without trying to explain what caused changes in these. Fundamental analysis, on the other hand, attempts to explain prices by their fundamental determinants, such as the supply and demand for the product.

Traders, particularly scalpers, may also specialize according to the contract month or months in which they concentrate their trading activity. Some scalpers trade in only the spot month, that is, the month with the nearest maturity. Typically, this month is the most active and liquid month (at least until two to four weeks prior to its maturity). Other scalpers trade only the "back months," the months that follow the spot month, which usually have less liquidity than the spot month.

Finally, there are scalpers who trade only spreads, that is, combinations of two or more contract months in which they are long one month and short another month. Spreads are often less risky than long or short positions. Within spreads scalpers may also specialize with respect to nearby spreads (that is, spreads involving contract months close to maturity) and deferred spreads (that is, spreads involving back month contracts). Thus traders who specialize in scalping may further specialize by scalping only spot months, back months, and either nearby or deferred spreads.

Scalpers who trade only specific single months may also develop spread positions in order to limit the risk of the contract month in which they are scalping. For example, assume that a scalper has bought a September 83 contract and that then, either because the contract month is not sufficiently liquid or because the price for the contract is too low and he sees a better price at which to sell the June 83 contract instead of selling back his September 83 contract, he "legs into" a spread by selling a June 83 contract. Thus, instead of being flat, he has a spread that is long September 83 and short June 83. Sometime later, the scalper will either liquidate both of these contracts (that is, sell the September 83 and buy the June 83) or "leg out of" the spread separately by liquidating one contract at a time.

Proprietary floor traders may account for up to 50 percent of the total trading volume, and even more in new futures contracts.

Brokers

Brokers, as indicated, do not trade their own capital but execute customer orders. Brokers, like scalpers, may specialize in the months in which they trade. Thus some brokers fill orders, that is, buy or sell futures contracts based on customer orders, in spot months or back months or for spreads, either nearby or deferred.

An important distinction among brokers is whether they are independent entrepreneurs or employees of specific firms. Independent brokers, that is, brokers who are independent entrepreneurs, may fill orders for several different firms. The firms simply "hand off" their orders to brokers because of the brokers' skill at this function. The broker typically receives a fixed amount of commission for his "floor brokerage" and fills the orders, also called "paper," for as many different firms as will supply him with them.

Some firms use independent brokers as floor brokers, while others use their own employees. And some firms use a combination of independent brokers and their own brokers. There are several considerations for a firm in deciding whether to use independent brokers or its own brokers. By using independent brokers, a firm will get more specialization by contract month; that is, it can use different brokers for spot months, back months, and nearby and deferred spreads. A firm that uses its own brokers would have to use one or a few brokers for all of these months. In addition, firms that trade in large amounts may want to spread their orders among brokers to conceal their trades. Finally, if a firm uses independent brokers, those brokers are liable for all "out-trades," that is, transactions reported to the exchange by the buyer and the seller on the exchange floor and thus not accepted as "good trades" by the exchange, and "trade-throughs," that is, market trading through limit orders held by the broker. If, on the other hand, the firm uses its own brokers, it is responsible for these losses. It is due to out-trades and the market trading through limit orders that brokers also bear risk. Thus, contrary to common perceptions, brokering is not a riskless activity.

This section described the various functions and specializations of floor traders. The existence of scalpers, who are market makers, is essential to initiate any futures market. And a flow of orders into the market is needed to sustain the scalpers. Without an order flow the scalpers would be playing a zero-sum game—that is, the profits of one scalper would have to be derived from the losses of another scalper, so that not all of the scalpers would be able to sustain themselves in addition to scalpers.

Thus, there must be brokers to fill outside paper, that is, execute the orders of outsiders.

Professional Stock Trader

Floor traders are essential to the development of any futures contract and are necessary from the beginning of any futures market. Another class of participants that typically enters the futures market from the very beginning are the professional traders. In the case of agricultural commodities, these could be grain companies; in the case of Treasury security futures market, they are the Treasury security dealers; and in the stock index futures markets, they are the professional stock traders.

Professional stock traders are often traders at large institutions, including investment banks, but there are also smaller stock traders as well. Such traders trade stocks on a continuous basis. With the advent of stock index futures, they can also trade the market as a whole instead of individual stocks. And they can trade stock index futures contracts in much the same way that they trade individual stocks. In this way, however, they would be trading the overall market instead of individual stocks, since stock index futures contracts are based on overall stock market indexes.

If the relationship between futures contract prices and the stock market index were fixed (that is, if the basis were constant), the trading in such contracts would be based completely on perceived changes in the overall stock market as measured by the index underlying the futures contract. However, the basis, or relationship, between the futures price and the underlying index varies substantially over time, between premium and discount. This variable basis adds another dimension to trading stock index futures contracts. Traders may buy or sell futures contracts based on the degree of the basis, whether premium or discount, and on expectations about changes in the basis. Some traders also use the basis as a leading indicator of futures and stock market changes, whether for brief intraday periods or for daily or longer periods. Such traders may follow the futures markets as a guide to trading the stock market.

Professional stock traders have been active in the stock index futures markets from the first day of trading, and they continue to participate in the ways described above. They have contributed significant trading volume to these markets.

Arbitrageur

Arbitrageurs have been important participants in all futures markets and, in particular, in the Treasury securities futures markets that have developed since 1975.

Arbitrageurs typically take one position in the futures market and an opposite or offsetting position in the underlying cash market. For example, an arbitrageur in the Treasury bond futures markets may take a short futures position and a long position in the underlying Treasury bonds. Contrariwise, and less frequently, arbitrageurs may take a long position in the Treasury bond futures markets and a short position in the underlying Treasury bonds.

These arbitrages are low-risk/low-return types of strategies. However, they are often conducted in large quantities and thus can lead to substantial profits. Arbitrage plays a very important role in futures markets. In addition to contributing order flow, it provides these markets with "correct pricing." Since arbitrage is based on futures markets transactions conducted relative to cash market transactions, arbitrage causes the futures contracts to be priced correctly relative to the cash markets. As a result, the futures prices are neither too high nor too low relative to the cash market prices. This correct pricing is important for the effective use of futures markets by nonprofessional users, such as the commercial hedgers and retail participants described below.

Arbitrage with respect to stock index futures contracts has been much more difficult, however, than the arbitrage of other instruments such as Treasury bond futures. The reason for this greater difficulty is that other futures contracts are based on specific tangible deliverables, whereas stock index contracts are based on an index that is simply an average of many stock prices and has no existence of its own.

For example, when doing an arbitrage with Treasury bond futures contracts, an arbitrageur can take either a long or short position in a specific Treasury bond that is deliverable on the contract against the opposite position in the futures contract. The cash market transaction is the purchase or the shorting of a specific Treasury bond. Even though several Treasury bonds are deliverable on the futures contract, at any point in time one bond is the cheapest deliverable and there is a fairly fixed price relationship among all the other bonds. Thus, for Treasury bonds it is quite easy to take a position in the cash market that offsets the futures markets position.

However, for stock index futures contracts there is no specific deliverable. These contracts are based on broad stock market indexes. For example, the New York Stock Exchange Composite Index is a market-weighted average of approximately 1,500 stocks—all the stocks listed and traded on the New York Stock Exchange. In order to have a relatively perfect offsetting cash market position in the stock index futures contract, the arbitrageur would have to construct a portfolio based on a correctly weighted average of these 1,500 stocks. This would obviously require a large amount of capital, and even with a large amount of capital it would require significant transaction costs, particularly if odd lots of many of the stocks were included in the portfolio. This would be necessary to have a more or less perfect arbitrage.

Few or no arbitrageurs have arbitraged stock index futures contracts in this manner. Instead, arbitrageurs have attempted to construct "model portfolios" or "synthetic portfolios." These are portfolios of a relatively small number of stocks (from 15 to 100) that "track" or follow the broad stock market index with a high degree of accuracy. However, particularly at the low end of this range, the model portfolios do not track the indexes perfectly, and this imprecision adds a basis risk to the arbitrage.

Another difficulty with this type of arbitrage is that, unlike Treasury bonds, for which interest is accrued on a daily basis, so that the same interest is paid on a Treasury bond holding every day, dividends on stocks are paid in a very different way. The entire quarterly dividend on a stock is paid to the owner of record on the ex-dividend date. Thus, if a stock is sold one day before the ex-dividend date, the seller receives no dividend for the quarter.

In addition, the dividend payment dates for different stocks differ considerably. Thus the time pattern of dividend payments on different portfolios of stocks varies considerably. Consequently, the temporal dividend pattern of the model portfolio depends on the ex-dividend dates of the specific stocks that are included in the portfolio. This is important because the dividends received on a model portfolio affect the return on the arbitrage.

For these reasons, the arbitrage of stock index futures contracts has been much more difficult than that of Treasury bond futures contracts. As a result, much more analysis has been devoted to the arbitrage of stock index futures contracts. Yet the degree of precision that has been achieved in arbitraging these contracts has been much lower than the degree of precision that has been achieved in arbitraging Treasury bond futures contracts. For this reason, however, the profits to be derived from arbitraging stock index futures may be considerable. And many arbitrageurs have claimed substantial profits in arbitraging model portfolios of stocks against stock index futures contracts.

Arbitrage is an important source of order flow in all futures contracts, particularly the interest rate futures contracts. Arbitrageurs are typically early users of futures contracts, and they have participated in a significant way in stock index futures contracts from their inception.

Retail

Retail participation is essential in any futures contract. While, on the one hand, there are no existing futures contracts without commercial hedge users, on the other hand, there are no existing successful futures contracts without substantial retail participation.

However, retail participation in a futures markets does not usually begin immediately after a futures contract begins trading. Before retail participants enter a futures market, liquidity must be established. This, as indicated, is provided by floor traders with the participation of professional traders and arbitrageurs.

Since futures contracts are high-risk/high-return vehicles, retail participants in stock index futures are typically willing to bear a high degree of risk in return for the possibility of a substantial profit. Due to the high risk, many participants in futures markets lose the entire equity that they initially invest in such markets. Because of the risk/return characteristics of futures markets, the total number of retail participants in such markets at any given time is fairly small. The common estimate is that there are approximately 150,000 participants in the futures markets. This is small compared to the 32 million individuals holding stock at any time, 7 million of whom are regarded as active investors and traders in the stock market. Thus, even though the interest rate futures markets have broadened the overall participation in futures markets substantially beyond the scope of the original agricultural futures market participants, the number of retail users of futures markets remains small.

The advent of stock index futures contracts provided a high-risk/high-return futures contract that was of substantial interest to the traditional futures market participants. Many of the traditional retail futures market participants participated in the stock index futures markets after a relatively short development period.

But in addition to appealing to traditional futures market participants, the new stock index futures contracts also appealed to many retail stock market customers who had never been in the futures market before. Also, many brokers who had never sold futures contracts began brokering in stock index futures for stock customers who had never participated in futures contracts. Thus many new retail customers became active in stock index futures markets. As a result, the stock index futures markets tended to expand the traditional futures markets. Moreover, it appears that in time the stock index futures markets will make a substantial penetration into the 7 million active stock traders.

The early entry of the retail futures market customers into the stock index futures markets, and particularly the entry of the stock and stock options customers who had never traded futures contracts before, has in part resulted from the early development of liquidity in these markets and in part been responsible for the rapid growth and development of these markets. The stock index futures markets have penetrated the broader stock market for several reasons. First, the underlying "product," a stock market index, was familiar to participants in the stock market. But while they could buy and sell individual stocks, they had never had the opportunity to buy and sell the overall stock market in one decision. The availability of a futures contract based on a stock market index provided them with investment opportunities that had not existed prior to the development of a vehicle on the overall stock market.

Second, the size of the stock index futures contracts in dollar terms was sufficiently small that most participants could trade in these contracts with ease. For example, the values of the New York Futures Exchange and the Chicago Mercantile Exchange contracts have been approximately $40,000 and $75,000, respectively, levels that are well within the capacity of most stock market investors, particularly in view of the margin of approximately 10 percent, as discussed next.

Third, while the margin on stocks was 50 percent, the traditional margins on most futures contracts was 2 percent or less. It is the small margins that lead to the high risk of traditional futures contracts. However, the Board of Governors of the Federal Reserve System induced the exchanges trading stock index futures contracts to impose on the stock index futures contracts margins whose dollar value was initially equal to approximately 10 percent of the dollar value of the contracts. The dollar value of these margins has not to date been changed. While these margins are higher than the margins on traditional futures contracts, they are closer to the margin levels to which most stock market investors are accustomed. Thus they effectively reduce the risk of investing in the futures markets and make the stock index futures more comfortable to traditional stock market investors. For these reasons and others, it appears that stock index futures contracts, and the options thereon, will allow the futures markets to continue to penetrate the much broader stock market.

Commercial Hedgers[1]

Typically, the last type of user to use a new futures market is the commercial hedger. As the last entrants into the futures market, commercial hedgers begin to use the market only when it has demonstrated its ability to handle orders continuously and in significant size, that is, when it has liquidity, and when they have become familiar with the market. It is remarkable that after only two months of trading there was already commercial hedge use of stock index futures trading.

While there has already been significant commercial hedge use of the

---

[1] See Paula A. Tosini and Eugene J. Moriarity, "Potential Hedging Use of a Futures Contract Based on a Composite Stock Index," *Journal of Futures Markets* 2, no. 1 (1982), pp. 83–103.

stock index futures markets, it would not be accurate to say at the time of this writing that the stock index futures markets have made a significant penetration into the commercial stock business. Based on the early, significant uses, however, it appears that many or most stock market professionals will soon be using stock index futures to hedge and increase their yields. In that event the stock index futures markets will be very large.

Stock Market Professionals

The first commercial uses of stock index futures were made by firms in the stock business, that is, by stock market professionals. The stock index futures markets have been used particularly by three stock market specialties: stock underwriters, risk arbitrageurs, and block positioners. All three stock market specializations have used stock index futures to hedge their stock holdings.

Two such early uses received considerable publicity. Specifically, during June 1982 Goldman Sachs used the stock index futures contract to hedge $250 million worth of stock trades with International Harvester. International Harvester traded its stock portfolio to Goldman Sachs for a bond portfolio, thus causing Goldman Sachs to have a significant stock holding and a related market risk.

> A short hedge was placed on a "significant" portion of the stock, according to a source.
> Goldman used all three stock index futures now trading "whatever was available," the source said. Stock index futures contracts available are the Kansas City Board of Trade Value Line Composite Index, the NYSE Indexes, the Chicago Mercantile Exchange S&P 500.
> The decision was made to hedge because the transaction was so large, the source said.
> Further, "when you have a program of all buy or all sell, you bear the entire risk of the market," explained the source. "You're able to modify the open-ended risk associated with the one-sided program" with stock index futures.[2]

The second well-publicized use was by Salomon Brothers, which used the stock index futures markets to facilitate a $400 million switch by the New York City Pension Fund from Alliance Capital to an index fund at Bankers Trust. In this case Salomon Brothers essentially guaranteed Bankers Trust and the city certain prices in the stock transactions prior to the actual purchase or sale of the stocks. Had Salomon Brothers been unable to find a buyer or seller at the specified prices, it would have

---

[2] Kimberly Blanton, "Index Futures Contracts Hedge Big Block Trades," *Pensions & Investments Age,* July 19, 1982, pp. 1, 38.

had to become a principal in the trade, meaning that it would have been subject to the risk of later market fluctuations.

> [Salomon head trader Stanley] Shopkorn confirmed that to guard against trading risks, Salomon also was trading in stock options and the relatively new stock index futures contracts on market indexes, such as the Standard & Poor's 500 and the NYSE Composite Index. . . . Similarly by selling stock index futures, Salomon could protect itself against losses from broad moves down in the market, which would deteriorate the value of its holding. This hedging use for futures is especially useful for the index fund holding, because of the breadth of stocks in the fund.[3]

The hedge uses of stock index futures for stock market specializations, mainly underwriting, risk arbitrage, and block positioning, have become considerable. Such hedging is increasingly becoming an essential part of these specializations.

In addition, stock market dealers, such as specialists on the New York Stock Exchange and other exchanges, including odd-lot dealers, and dealers in over-the-counter markets, have used the stock index futures markets to hedge their stock portfolios, although only to a limited extent to date.

Portfolio Managers

Another class of commercial hedgers consists of managers of stock portfolios. While these managers can be considered stock market professionals, they tend to be somewhat less active in their stock market transactions than are the stock market specialists considered in the previous section. However, in the dollar size of their stockholdings, and thus in the risk borne due to declining stock prices, this class of commercial participants in the stock market is far larger than any other. Table 11–1 provides a list of the types of institutions that hold stock portfolios and the magnitude of their holdings.

Despite the large risk of changes in the value of their stock portfolios, portfolio managers are expected to be the last entrants into the stock index futures markets. The basis for this expectation is that even though the Treasury bond futures market has existed for seven years and is highly liquid, bond portfolio managers have to date made limited use of the Treasury bond futures contract for hedging. However, it may turn out that stock portfolio managers will make more use of the futures market to hedge their portfolios than have bond portfolio managers. The early evidence supports this outcome.

In fact, at least three pension funds have already used stock index

---

[3] "Salomon Guides Portfolio Shift of $400 Million," *The Wall Street Journal,* July 1, 1982, p. 2.

Table 11-1

Market Value of Common Stockholdings of Major Institutional Groups*

	1977	1978	1979	1980
Private noninsured pension funds	$100.9	$106.7	$122.7	$174.4
Investment companies†	38.6	36.3	34.3	43.4
Life insurance companies‡,§	23.5	24.5	28.5	35.0
Property/liability insurance companies§,‖	13.3	15.2	18.9	25.3
Personal trust funds	92.3	92.7	104.0	131.0
Mutual savings banks #	3.0	3.0	2.9	2.4
State and local retirement funds #	30.0	33.3	37.1	44.3
Foundations	25.7	26.5	39.6	32.4
Educational endowments	9.7	10.1	10.1	10.2
Total	$337.0	$348.3	$398.1	$498.4

* Billions of dollars, end of year.
† Includes open-end, closed-end, face amount, and unit trust companies.
‡ Includes separate accounts, a significant portion of which involves pension plans.
§ Statement value.
‖ Excludes holdings of insurance company stock.
Book value.
Source: SEC *Statistical Bulletin* 40, no. 8. (August 1981).

futures markets, specifically Westinghouse Electric Corporation's $2.5 billion pension fund, the $150 million Public Service Company of Colorado's pension fund and Exxon Corporation's $5 billion pension fund. Two of these have used the stock index futures market to hedge, as indicated below.

Westinghouse Electric Corporation:[4]

Anticipating a continuing market rally, Westinghouse bought 400 stock index contracts worth over $20 million between July 29 and August 11.

It was "an offensive strategy for us since we weren't ready to buy individual stocks in such a short period of time," explained the company source.

Stock index futures provided Westinghouse "a quick way of putting money into the market," and one "much cheaper" than buying the actual stocks.

. . . Westinghouse's strategy may be defined as an "anticipatory long hedge," according to a staff analyst.

Public Service Company of Colorado:[5]

Stuyvesant (Capital Management, the investment management firm for the Colorado Pension Fund) will also hedge the funds equity investments against market drops by selling futures contracts.

If the portfolio value the fund holds declines, some or all of the loss will be recouped by appreciation in the futures contracts.

---

[4] "Stock Futures Used in Rally," *Pensions & Investment Age,* October 25, 1982, pp. 1, 52.
[5] "Utility Hires for Futures," *Pensions & Investment Age,* November 8, 1982, pp. 1, 51.

These and other pension funds have also used stock index futures for purposes other than traditional long or short hedging, specifically for yield improvement. In this regard, consider the following.

Westinghouse Electric Corporation:[6]

A strategy less costly than buying the stocks themselves, buying a futures on a stock market index . . . allows its holder to move into and out of the market without purchasing or selling stock.

Public Service Company of Colorado:[7]

The fund, in anticipation of a stock market rally, can purchase stock index contracts instead of the actual stocks and profit from the stock market's return through an appreciation in the value of the contracts.

Mr. Mosier explained that about 90% of the Colorado Public Service's $5 million equity portfolio will be held in stocks and 10% or $500,000 in Treasury bills, which will be placed as futures margin for the executing strategies.

Exxon Corporation:[8]

Exxon employed the strategy of buying stock index futures when they are priced below the underlying market index.

This strategy provides an alternative way to maintain a position in the stock market when the fund has cash to invest.

The strategy [. . .] Exxon employs permits it to choose between holding a certain amount in the actual securities, or buying futures and maintaining a cash position that earns interest. Investing either in a portfolio of stocks weighted to track the market or in the futures contract, the investor is subject to roughly the same market risk.

Deciding if stocks or futures are a better buy rests on a comparison between the expected dividends earned by holding the actual stocks and the interest earned on the cash portfolio when futures are bought. Both factors are reflected in the pricings of the futures and actual markets.

Overall, despite the fact that portfolio managers are expected to be the last entrants into the stock index futures markets, and that to date bond portfolio managers have had only limited participation in the Treasury bond futures contracts, stock portfolio managers have made significant use of stock index futures contracts for commercial hedging and other purposes. This use is likely to increase considerably.

---

[6] "Stock Futures Used in Rally."

[7] "Utility Hires for Futures."

[8] "Stock Futures Strategy Passes Fund's Test," *Pensions & Investment Age,* December 6, 1982, pp. 1, 40.

Comment on Nature of Uses of Stock Index Futures Markets

The investment and hedge uses of the stock index futures markets can be considered in the context of the portfolio management strategies used by stock market professionals and the concepts developed by academic and applied researchers of the stock market. This discussion applies to retail stock market investors as well as professional stock market traders and other institutional participants in the stock market.

In general, there are two types of price risk in the stock market (see Exhibit 11–2). The first has to do with changes in the price level of the overall stock market. The second relates to changes in the prices of individual stocks relative to the price level of the overall stock market. The first type of price risk is called *market risk* or *systematic risk*. The second type of price risk is called *stock-specific risk* or *nonsystematic risk*.

With respect to market risk, some stocks are, on average, as volatile as the overall stock market, while others are, on average, more or less volatile than the overall stock market. A statistic commonly used in stock market analysis to refer to the volatility of a specific stock relative to the volatility of the overall market is called the "beta coefficient." Very volatile stocks are often called "high-beta" stocks, and less volatile stocks are called "low-beta" stocks. The price of a high-beta stock might increase 1½ percent when the overall market increases 1 percent—such a stock has a beta of 1.5. The price of a low-beta stock, on the other hand,

Exhibit 11–2

Two Types of Price Risk in the Stock Market

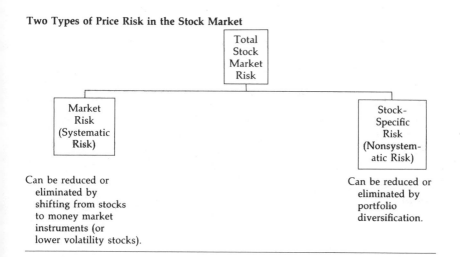

might increase only ½ percent when the overall market increases 1 percent—such a stock has a beta of 0.5.

Given the average volatility of stock prices relative to the market, the prices of some stocks track the trend of the market adjusted for this average volatility very closely (are well correlated with the markets), whereas the prices of other stocks deviate frequently and substantially (are poorly correlated with the market). The former type tracks the market closely and has little stock-specific risk; the latter type tracks the market poorly and has a high degree of stock-specific risk. *So in considering the price behavior of individual stocks relative to the market, two characteristics must be considered: the average volatility of the stock relative to the market (the beta) and how closely the stock tracks the overall stock market when adjusted for the volatility (the correlation).*

In general, a portfolio manager can make his portfolio behave more like the overall market both by making it more highly correlated with the market and by diversifying his portfolio across many stocks so as to give it the same volatility as the market. Obviously, if a portfolio contained stocks representing every stock in an index in the correct proportion, the behavior of the portfolio would be the same as the behavior of the index. However, a high degree of correlation with the overall index and volatility similar to that of the overall index can be achieved by using a number of stocks much smaller than the number of stocks included in the overall index. For example, with respect to volatility, if a stock that increased in price 1.5 percent and a stock that increased 0.5 percent when the market increased 1 percent were combined in equal amounts in a portfolio, the portfolio would move, on average, 1 percent when the market moved 1 percent.

Portfolio managers can deal with stock-specific risk and market risk in two ways. First, they can reduce or eliminate stock-specific risk, as indicated above, by diversifying their portfolios across many stocks. Their portfolios then have only market risk. As indicated, diversifying a stock portfolio properly eliminates stock-specific risk; that is, all changes in the value of the portfolio will reflect movement only in the overall market. Given this, however, the portfolio may still be more volatile than the overall market, less volatile than the overall market, or as volatile as the overall market, depending on the volatilities of the specific stocks in the portfolio. For example, the value of a portfolio may always change by 130 percent, 70 percent or 100 percent of the change in the value of the overall stock market. However, portfolios can be constructed that not only reflect the overall stock market risk but in addition are as volatile as the overall market; that is, the value of such portfolios changes by 100 percent of the change in the value of the overall stock market. In any of these cases, however, the diversified portfolio will reflect only market risk.

Portfolio managers deal with market risk, if at all, in a very different way. In times of expected bull markets, that is, in times of expected stock market price increases, they adjust their portfolios to include more volatile stocks so that the value of the portfolios increases more than the overall stock market.

On the other hand, in times of expected bear markets, that is in times of expected stock market price decreases, they may adjust their portfolios to include less volatile stocks so that the value of their portfolios decreases by less than the overall stock market. In the limit, during times of expected bear markets, portfolio managers liquidate stocks and make less risky investments, such as investments in money market instruments. Of course, to the extent that they do this, they are not in the stock market at all.

Basically, portfolio managers implement two distinct types of strategies. The first is "stock selection," that is, trying to select specific stocks to purchase that will outperform the market and, to a lesser extent, trying to select specific stocks to short that will underperform the market. The second type of strategy has to do with "market timing," that is, shifting to very volatile stocks during times of expected bull markets and to low-volatility stocks or even to money market instruments during times of expected bear markets. Of course, such a strategy may interfere with stock selection strategies or reduce the effectiveness of portfolio diversification. Obviously, in order to implement the market timing strategy, stock-specific risk is first diversified away.

There may, however, be strategic problems both in stock selection and market timing strategies using only the stock market. First, assume that an individual or an institution wishes to make a stock selection decision. They thus purchase a specific stock on the assumption that the price of that stock will increase because it will outperform the market. Again, assume that they are correct and that the price of that stock does outperform the market. But assume that the overall market declines so that even though the stock outperforms the market, the price of the stock also declines. Thus the investors are correct in their assessment, but they lose money.

Consider the following variation on this theme. Assume that an investor believes a stock will outperform the overall stock market on the basis of the fundamentals of the specific stock but that the stock, with respect to systematic risk, is more volatile than the market. For example, assume that a stock is more volatile than the overall market and has a beta of 1.5. Assume also that the market is expected to decline by 5 percent. Then the stock would be expected to decline by 7.5 percent. Suppose, however, that even though the market declines by 5 percent, the stock declines by only 2 percent. This stock, then, would have outperformed the market since its actual return (−2 percent) was greater than its expected return given its level of systematic risk (−7.5 percent). This fact, however, would be of little consolation to the investor since the value of the stock did decline.

Assume that for a particular high-beta stock the investor is concerned that the overall market will go down and that the price of this stock will decline along with the market despite the fact that the fundamentals of the specific stock are better than the market. In this case, even though the investor thought that the stock might outperform the market due to its specific fundamentals, the investor might not buy the stock because of the expected bear market and the high volatility of the stock relative to the market.

Second, assume that an individual or an institution wants to make the market timing investment based on the expectation of a rising market. To do so, they would most likely buy one or a few stocks. Assume that they are correct and that the stock market does rise. Assume also, however, that the stock or stocks they purchase underperform the market and that the prices of the stocks fall, even though the stock market rises. In this case, despite the fact that their assessment is correct and the stock market rises, they experience a loss.

Thus, there may be problems in implementing both stock selection and market timing strategies in the stock market. With stock index futures contracts, however, the problems in implementing both types of strategies can be reduced or eliminated.

First, consider the implementation of a stock selection strategy, that is, the strategy of an investor who wishes to purchase a stock that he believes will outperform the market. To implement this strategy, he could, under certain circumstances for some stocks, buy the stock and short the futures contract. Then, if he is right and the stock outperforms the market, he will earn a net profit even if there is a decline in the market. This would occur because any declines in the overall market would generate a profit on the short futures position that would countervail the effect of the market on the price of the individual stock, leaving a net profit due to the stock outperforming the market. Under these circumstances, stock selection strategies could be implemented without having to be concerned with market or systematic risk. This strategy would permit an investor to buy a very volatile stock during the time of an expected bear market.[9]

Second, consider the market timing decision. If an investor thought

---

[9] The effectiveness of being able to implement this hedged stock selection strategy depends on the correlation of the price of the stock with the price of the overall market. The average volatility of the price of the specific stock relative to the overall market can be adjusted for in this type of strategy by varying the dollar value of the futures contract sold relative to the dollar value of the specific stock being hedged in a way that depends on the relative volatility.

the stock market would go up but was uncertain as to the price behavior of a specific stock, the investor could buy a stock index futures contract, thus sharing in the price movement of the overall stock market without being affected by the price of any individual stock relative to the market.[10] Contrariwise, if the investor thought the market would go down, he could sell the stock index futures contract.

Thus both individuals and stock market professionals can use stock index futures contracts to separate market risk from stock-specific risk and to implement either a stock selection strategy or a market timing strategy, without having unintended effects reduce the effectiveness of the strategy. In these cases, if the investor were right in his assessment, he would profit.

Data on Users

Very little information is available on the amount of open interest or trading volume resulting from the various categories of users. The only publicly available source is the "Commitments of Traders in Commodity Futures," published by the Commodity Futures Trading Commission (CFTC). Tables 11–2 and 11–3 show the tables from this document for New York Futures Exchange and Chicago Mercentile Exchange stock index futures contracts. These data are based on open interest, for which all positions of 25 and over are "reportable to the CFTC." All of a trader's open interest is classified as "commercial" if the trader uses the futures contract for hedging as defined in the CFTC's regulations.

As indicated in Table 11–2, 54.2 percent of the New York Futures Exchange long positions and 51.4 percent of the short positions are reportable, that is, held by traders with 25 or more positions. Commercial reportable open interest is responsible for 11.2 percent of the total long open interest and 20.6 percent of the total short open interest. Thus, of the reportable positions, commercials are responsible for 20.7 percent (11.2/54.2) of the long open interest and 40.1 percent (20.6/51.4) of the short open interest. Commercials would be expected to be responsible for more short than long open interest.

---

[10] Due to the higher leverage of the futures contracts relative to stock purchases, the difference between what is desired to be invested in equities and what must be put up in margin for futures contracts could be placed in Treasury bills to earn the risk-free interest rate. For example, if an investor desires to invest $80,000 in "the market," he could buy two New York Stock Exchange Composite Index futures contracts, which have a total value of approximately $80,000 but only require a margin deposit of approximately $7,000, and place the difference of $73,000 in risk-free Treasury bills.

Table 11-2

Stock Index Futures, NYSE Composite, New York Futures Exchange: Commitments of Traders in All Futures Combined and Indicated Futures, December 31, 1982

	Total Open Interest	Reportable Positions								Nonreportable Positions	
		Noncommercial				Commercial		Total			
		Long or Short Only		Long and Short (spreading)							
Futures		Long	Short	Long	Short	Long	Short	Long	Short	Long	Short
All	5,273	1,495	852	772	772	591	1,088	2,858	2,712	2,415	2,561
Old	5,226	1,525	867	717	717	591	1,088	2,833	2,672	2,393	2,554
Other	47	25	40	0	0	0	0	25	40	22	7

Percent of open interest represented by each category of traders

	Long	Short	Long	Short	Long	Short	Long	Short	Long	Short
All	28.4	16.2	14.6	14.6	11.2	20.6	54.2	51.4	45.8	48.6
Old	29.2	16.6	13.7	13.7	11.3	20.8	54.2	51.1	45.8	48.9
Other	53.2	85.1	*	*	*	*	53.2	85.1	46.8	14.9

Number of traders in each category

	Long	Short	Long	Short	Long	Short	Long	Short
All	42	17	7	7	6	7	23	27
Old	42	16	6	6	6	7	22	27
Other	2	1	0	0	0	0	1	1

Concentration Ratios:

Percent of Open Interest Held by the Indicated Number of Largest Reportable Traders

| | By Gross Position | | | | By Net Position | | | |
| | Four or Less Traders | | Eight or Less Traders | | Four or Less Traders | | Eight or Less Traders | |
	Long	Short	Long	Short	Long	Short	Long	Short
All	30.1	24.1	40.8	32.6	27.0	19.5	34.1	26.1
Old	30.4	23.5	41.2	32.1	27.3	19.7	34.4	26.3
Other	53.2	85.1	53.2	85.1	53.2	85.1	53.2	85.1

* Less than 0.05 percent.
Source: "Commitments of Traders in Commodity Futures," Commodity Futures Trading Commission, December 1982.

Table 11-3

Stock Index Futures, S&P 500, International Monetary Market: Commitments of Traders in All Futures Combined and Indicated Futures, December 31, 1982

		Reportable Positions									Nonreportable Positions	
		Noncommercial				Commercial		Total				
	Total Open Interest	Long or Short Only		Long and Short (spreading)								
Futures		Long	Short	Long	Short	Long	Short	Long	Short		Long	Short
All	11,666	3,292	4,192	311	311	2,305	1,207	5,908	5,710		5,758	5,956
Old	11,666	3,292	4,192	311	311	2,305	1,207	5,908	5,710		5,758	5,956
Other	0	0	0	0	0	0	0	0	0		0	0

Percent of open interest represented by each category of traders

		Long	Short	Long	Short	Long	Short	Long	Short		Long	Short
All	100.0	28.2	35.9	2.7	2.7	19.8	10.3	50.6	48.9		49.4	51.1
Old	100.0	28.2	35.9	2.7	2.7	19.8	10.3	50.6	48.9		49.4	51.1
Other	100.0	*	*	*	*	*	*	*	*		*	*

Number of traders in each category

All	92	36	39	7	7	11	5	52	49			
Old	92	36	39	7	7	11	5	52	49			
Other	0	0	0	0	0	0	0	0	0			

Concentration Ratios:
Percent of Open Interest Held by the Indicated Number of Largest Reportable Traders

	By Gross Position				By Net Position			
	Four or Less Traders		Eight or Less Traders		Four or Less Traders		Eight or Less Traders	
	Long	Short	Long	Short	Long	Short	Long	Short
All	17.7	22.7	26.5	29.8	17.5	22.7	26.3	28.9
Old	17.7	22.7	26.5	29.8	17.5	22.7	26.3	28.9
Other	*	*	*	*	*	*	*	*

* Less than 0.05 percent.
Source: "Commitments of Traders in Commodity Futures," Commodity Futures Trading Commission, December 1982.

Summary

This chapter discusses the types of uses and the nature of the users of stock futures contracts. The users are described in terms of the extent of their participation in stock futures markets and of the time they enter these markets.

Even though the stock index futures markets are quite new, in view of their growth in trading volume and open interest, and also of the types of users, they have achieved considerable maturity as futures contracts.

CHAPTER 12

Hedging

Frank J. Fabozzi, Ph.D., C.F.A.
Professor of Economics
Fordham University

Hedging is the employment of a futures position as a temporary substitute for transactions to be made in the cash market at a later date. Hedging attempts to eliminate price risk by trying to fix the price of a transaction to be made at a later date. If cash and futures prices move together, any loss realized by the hedger from one position (whether cash or futures) will be offset by a profit on the other position. When the profit and loss from each position are equal, the hedge is called a *perfect hedge*.

In practice, hedging is not that simple. The amount of the loss and profit from each position will not necessarily be identical. As will be explained below, whether there is an overall profit or loss from a particular hedge will depend on the relationship between the cash price and the futures price when a hedge is placed and when it is lifted. The difference between the cash price and the futures price is called the *basis*. Consequently, hedging involves the substitution of basis risk for price risk.

Some commodities do not have existing futures contracts. When a hedger assumes a futures position in a commodity different from that in which a cash position is held or will be held, the hedge is referred to as a *cross-hedge*. A hedger who seeks protection against potential adverse price movement for a commodity that does not have an existing futures contract will use a futures contract on an underlying commodity that he hopes will track the price of the commodity being hedged. For example, a party seeking to hedge against adverse price movements in okra will use a futures contract for some agricultural product rather than a futures contract on a precious metal such as gold or silver.

Consequently, cross-hedging adds another dimension to basis risk. The future cash price of the commodity that is being hedged may not be tracked well by the commodity that is being used for the hedge.

Cross-hedging with futures is the name of the game in portfolio management. Other than the few interest rate futures contracts currently traded, there are no futures contracts for specific debt instruments and common stock shares. For example, suppose that a portfolio manager wants to hedge a position in a long-term corporate bond of a particular issuer against adverse price movements due to an increase in market yields. He would have to use an existing futures contract on long-term Treasury bonds since futures contracts on corporate bonds are not available. Because interest rates for all fixed-income obligations move in the same direction, the future cash price of the Treasury bond may track the future cash price of the corporate bond well. The only way to use a futures contract so as to hedge the price of a given issuer's common stock or the price of a common stock portfolio is by using a cross-hedge. Underlying a stock index futures contract is a specific index. How well the price of a stock or the price of a portfolio of common stocks tracks the index will determine the success of the hedge. Unlike debt obligations that have price movements in the same direction as interest rates change, the price of an individual stock or a portfolio of stocks may move in a direction opposite to that of the overall market.

The foregoing points will be made clearer in the illustrations presented later in this chapter.

Short Hedge and Long Hedge

A *short hedge* is used by a hedger to protect against a decline in the future cash price of a commodity or a financial instrument. To execute a short hedge, the hedger sells a futures contract (agrees to make delivery of the underlying commodity or financial instrument). Consequently, a short hedge is also known as a *sell hedge*. By establishing a short hedge, the hedger has fixed the future cash price and transferred the price risk of ownership to the buyer of the contract. Three examples of who may want to use a short hedge follow:

1. A corn farmer will sell his product in three months. The price of corn, like the price of any commodity, will fluctuate in the open market. The corn farmer wants to lock in a price at which he can deliver his corn in three months.

2. A corporate treasurer plans to sell bonds in two months to raise $85 million in capital. The cost of the bond issue to the corporation will depend on interest rates at the time the bond issue is sold. The

corporate manager is uncertain of the interest rates that will prevail two months from now and wants to be sure that they are no higher than today's rates.

3. A pension fund manager knows that the beneficiaries of the fund must be paid a total of $3 million four months from now. This will necessitate liquidating a portion of the fund's common stock portfolio. Should the value of the shares that he intends to liquidate in order to satisfy the benefits to be paid be lower in value four months from now, a larger portion of the portfolio would have to be liquidated. The pension fund manager would like to lock in the price of the shares that will be liquidated.

A *long hedge* is undertaken to protect against the purchase of a commodity or financial instrument in the cash market at some future time. In a long hedge, the hedger buys a futures contract (agrees to accept delivery of the underlying commodity or financial instrument). A long hedge is also known as a *buy hedge*. The following three examples are instances where a party may use a long hedge:

1. A food processing company projects that in three months it must purchase 30,000 bushels of corn. The management of the company does not want to take a chance that the price of corn may increase by the time the company must make its acquisition. It wants to lock in the price of corn today.

2. A bond portfolio manager knows that in two months $10 million of his portfolio will mature and must be reinvested. Prevailing interest rates are high but may decline substantially by the time the funds are to be reinvested. The portfolio manager wants to lock in a reinvestment rate today.

3. A pension fund manager expects a substantial contribution from participants four months from now. The contributions will be invested in the common stock of various companies. The pension fund manager expects the market price of the stocks in which she will invest the contributions to be higher in four months. She therefore wants to lock in the price of those stocks.

Hedging Illustrations

To explain hedging, we shall present several numerical illustrations from the commodities area.

Assume that a corn farmer expects to sell 30,000 bushels of corn three months from now. Assume further that the management of a food processing company plans to purchase 30,000 bushels of corn three months from now. Both the corn farmer and the management of the food processing company want to lock in today's price. That is, they want to eliminate the price risk associated with corn three months from now. The cash or spot price for corn is currently $2.75 per bushel. The futures price for corn is currently $3.20 per bushel. Each futures contract is for 5,000 bushels of corn.

Since the corn farmer seeks protection against a decline in the price of corn three months from now, he will place a short, or sell, hedge. That is, he will promise to make delivery of corn at the current futures price. He will sell six futures contracts since each contract calls for the delivery of 5,000 bushels of corn.

The management of the food processing company seeks protection against an increase in the price of corn three months from now. Consequently, it will place a buy, or long, hedge. That is, it will agree to accept delivery of corn at the futures price. Since it is seeking protection against a price increase for 30,000 bushels of corn, it will buy six contracts.

Let's look at what happens under various scenarios for the cash price and the futures price of corn three months from now, when the hedge is lifted.

1. Cash Price of Corn Decreases and No Change in Basis   Suppose that at the time the hedge is lifted the cash price has declined to $2 and the futures price has declined to $2.45. Notice what has happened to the basis under this scenario. Recall that the basis is the difference between the cash price and the futures price. At the time the hedge is placed, the basis is −$0.45 ($2.75 − $3.20). When the hedge is lifted, the basis is still −$0.45 ($2.00 − $2.45).

The corn farmer at the time the hedge was placed wanted to lock in a price of $2.75 per bushel of corn, or $82,500 for 30,000 bushels. He sold six futures contracts at a price of $3.20 per bushel, or $96,000 for 30,000 bushels. When the hedge is lifted, the value of his corn is $60,000 ($2.00 × 30,000). He realizes a decline in the cash market in the value of his corn of $22,500. However, the futures price has declined to $2.45, so that the cost to the corn farmer to liquidate his futures position is only $73,500 ($2.45 × 30,000). He realizes a gain in the futures market of $22,500. The net result is that the gain in the futures market matches the loss in the cash market. Consequently, the corn farmer does not realize an overall gain or loss. When this occurs, the hedge is said to be a *perfect* or *textbook* hedge. The results of this hedge are summarized in Exhibit 12–1.

The outcome for the food processing company of the buy or long hedge is also summarized in Exhibit 12–1. Because there was a decline in the cash price, the food processing company would gain in the cash market by $22,500 but would realize a loss of the same amount in the futures market. Therefore, this hedge is also a *perfect* or *textbook* hedge.

Exhibit 12–1

Perfect Hedge: Cash Price Decreases

Assumptions

Cash price at time hedge is placed	$2.75 per bu.
Futures price at time hedge is placed	$3.20 per bu.
Cash price at time hedge is lifted	$2.00 per bu.
Futures price at time hedge is lifted	$2.45 per bu.
Number of bushels to be hedged	30,000
Number of bushels per futures contract	5,000
Number of futures contracts used in hedge	6

Short (Sell) Hedge by Corn Farmer

Cash Market	*Futures Market*	*Basis*
At time hedge is placed		
Value of 30,000 bu.:	Sell 6 contracts:	
30,000 × $2.75 = $82,500	6 × 5,000 × $3.20 = $96,000	−$0.45
At time hedge is lifted		
Value of 30,000 bu.:	Buy 6 contracts:	
30,000 × $2.00 = $60,000	6 × 5,000 × $2.45 = $73,500	−$0.45
Loss in cash market = $22,500	Gain in futures market = $22,500	
Overall gain or loss = $0		

Long (Buy) Hedge by Food Processing Company

Cash Market	*Futures Market*	*Basis*
At time hedge is placed		
Value of 30,000 bu.:	Buy 6 contracts:	
30,000 × $2.75 = $82,500	6 × 5,000 × $3.20 = $96,000	−$0.45
At time hedge is lifted		
Value of 30,000 bu.:	Sell 6 contracts:	
30,000 × $2.00 = $60,000	6 × 5,000 × $2.45 = $73,500	−$0.45
Gain in cash market = $22,500	Loss in futures market = $22,500	
Overall gain or loss = $0		

This scenario illustrates two important points. First, for both participants there was no overall gain or loss. The reason for this result was that we assumed that the basis did not change when the hedge was lifted. Consequently, if the basis does not change, a perfect hedge will be achieved. Second, notice that the management of the food processing company would have been better off if it had not hedged. The cost of corn would have been $22,500 less in the cash market three months later. This, however, should not be interpreted as a sign of poor planning by management. Management is not in the business of speculating on the price of corn in the future. Hedging is a standard practice to protect against an increase in the cost of doing business in the future.

2. Cash Price of Corn Increases and No Change in Basis Suppose that when the hedge is lifted the cash price of corn has increased to $3.55 and that the futures price has increased to $4. Notice that the basis is unchanged at −$0.45. Since the basis is unchanged, the cash and futures price we have assumed in this scenario will produce a perfect hedge.

The corn farmer will gain in the cash market since the value of 30,000 bushels of corn is $106,500 ($3.55 × 30,000). This represents a $24,000 gain compared to the cash value at the time the hedge was placed. However, the corn farmer must liquidate his position in the futures market by buying six futures contracts at a total cost of $120,000, which is $24,000 more than the cost when the contracts were sold. The loss in the futures

Exhibit 12–2

Perfect Hedge: Cash Price Increases

Assumptions

Cash price at time hedge is placed	$2.75 per bu.
Futures price at time hedge is placed	$3.20 per bu.
Cash price at time hedge is lifted	$3.55 per bu.
Futures price at time hedge is lifted	$4.00 per bu.
Number of bushels to be hedged	30,000
Number of bushels per futures contract	5,000
Number of futures contracts used in hedge	6

Short (Sell) Hedge by Corn Farmer

Cash Market	Futures Market	Basis
At time hedge is placed		
Value of 30,000 bu.:	Sell 6 contracts:	
30,000 × $2.75 = $82,500	6 × 5,000 × $3.20 = $96,000	−$0.45
At time hedge is lifted		
Value of 30,000 bu.:	Buy 6 contracts:	
30,000 × $3.55 = $106,500	6 × 5,000 × $4.00 = $120,000	−$0.45
Gain in cash market = $24,000	Loss in futures market = $24,000	
Overall gain or loss = $0		

Long (Buy) Hedge by Food Processing Company

Cash Market	Futures Market	Basis
At time hedge is placed		
Value of 30,000 bu.:	Buy 6 contracts:	
30,000 × $2.75 = $82,500	6 × 5,000 × $3.20 = $96,000	−$0.45
At time hedge is lifted		
Value of 30,000 bu.:	Sell 6 contracts:	
30,000 × $3.55 = $106,500	6 × 5,000 × $4.00 = $120,000	−$0.45
Loss in cash market = $24,000	Gain in futures market = $24,000	
Overall gain or loss = $0		

market offsets the gain in the cash market, and we have a perfect hedge. The results of this hedge are summarized in Exhibit 12–2.

The food processing company would realize a gain in the futures market of $24,000 but would have to pay $24,000 more in the cash market to acquire 30,000 bushels of corn. The results of this hedge are summarized in Exhibit 12–2.

Notice that under this scenario the management of the food processing company saved $24,000 in the cost of corn by employing a hedge. The corn farmer, on the other hand, would have been better off if he had not used a hedging strategy and simply sold his product on the market three months later. However, it must be emphasized that the corn farmer, just like the management of the food processing company, employed a hedge to protect against unforeseen adverse price changes in the cash market.

3. Cash Price Decreases and Basis Widens   In the two previous scenarios we have assumed that the basis does not change when the hedge is lifted. There is no reason why this must occur. In the real world the basis does in fact change between the time a hedge is placed and the time it is lifted. In the following four scenarios we shall assume that the basis does change and look at the impact on the hedger.

Assume that the cash price of corn decreases to $2, just as in the first scenario; however, assume further that the futures price decreases to $2.70 rather than $2.45. The basis has now widened from −$0.45 to −$0.70 ($2.00 − $2.70).

The results are summarized in Exhibit 12–3. For the short (sell) hedge, the $22,500 loss in the cash market is only partially offset by the $15,000 gain realized in the futures market. Consequently, the hedge resulted in an overall loss of $7,500. There are several points to note here. First, if the corn farmer did not employ the hedge, the loss would have been $22,500, since the value of his 30,000 bushels of corn is $60,000 compared to $82,500 three months earlier. Although the hedge is not a perfect hedge because the basis widened, the loss of $7,500 is less than the loss of $22,500 that would have occurred if no hedge had been placed. This is what we meant earlier in the chapter when we said that hedging substitutes basis risk for price risk. Second, the management of the food processing company faces the same problem from an opposite perspective. An unexpected gain for either participant results in an unexpected loss of equal dollar value for the other. That is, the participants face a zero-sum game. Consequently, the food processing company would realize an overall gain of $7,500 from its long (buy) hedge. This gain represents a gain in the cash market of $22,500 and a realized loss in the futures market of $15,000.

Exhibit 12–3

Hedge: Cash Price Decreases and Basis Widens

Assumptions

Cash price at time hedge is placed	$2.75 per bu.
Futures price at time hedge is placed	$3.20 per bu.
Cash price at time hedge is lifted	$2.00 per bu.
Futures price at time hedge is lifted	$2.70 per bu.
Number of bushels to be hedged	30,000
Number of bushels per futures contract	5,000
Number of futures contracts used in hedge	6

Short (Sell) Hedge by Corn Farmer

Cash Market	Futures Market	Basis
At time hedge is placed		
Value of 30,000 bu.:	Sell 6 contracts:	
30,000 × $2.75 = $82,500	6 × 5,000 × $3.20 = $96,000	−$0.45
At time hedge is lifted		
Value of 30,000 bu.:	Buy 6 contracts:	
30,000 × $2.00 = $60,000	6 × 5,000 × $2.70 = $81,000	−$0.70
Loss in cash market = $22,500	Gain in futures market = $15,000	
Overall loss = $7,500		

Long (Buy) Hedge by Food Processing Company

Cash Market	Futures Market	Basis
At time hedge is placed		
Value of 30,000 bu.:	Buy 6 contracts:	
30,000 × $2.75 = $82,500	6 × 5,000 × $3.20 = $96,000	−$0.45
At time hedge is lifted		
Value of 30,000 bu.:	Sell 6 contracts:	
30,000 × $2.00 = $60,000	6 × 5,000 × $2.70 = $81,000	−$0.70
Gain in cash market = $22,500	Loss in futures market = $15,000	
Overall gain = $7,500		

The results of this scenario demonstrate that when *(a)* the futures price is greater than the cash price at the time the hedge is placed, *(b)* the cash price declines, and *(c)* the basis widens, then:

The short (sell) hedger will realize an overall loss from the hedge.

The long (buy) hedger will realize an overall gain from the hedge.

4.   Cash Price Increases and Basis Widens   Suppose that the cash price increases to $3.55 per bushel, just as in the second scenario, but that the basis widens to −$0.70. That is, at the time the hedge is lifted the futures price has increased to $4.25. The results of this hedge are summarized in Exhibit 12–4.

Exhibit 12–4

Hedge: Cash Price Increases and Basis Widens

Assumptions

Cash price at time hedge is placed	$2.75 per bu.
Futures price at time hedge is placed	$3.20 per bu.
Cash price at time hedge is lifted	$3.55 per bu.
Futures price at time hedge is lifted	$4.25 per bu.
Number of bushels to be hedged	30,000
Number of bushels per futures contract	5,000
Number of futures contracts used in hedge	6

Short (Sell) Hedge by Corn Farmer

Cash Market	Futures Market	Basis
At time hedge is placed		
Value of 30,000 bu.:	Sell 6 contracts:	
30,000 × $2.75 = $82,500	6 × 5,000 × $3.20 = $96,000	−$0.45
At time hedge is lifted		
Value of 30,000 bu.:	Buy 6 contracts:	
30,000 × $3.55 = $106,500	6 × 5,000 × $4.25 = $127,500	−$0.70
Gain in cash market = $24,000	Loss in futures market = $31,500	
Overall loss = $7,500		

Long (Buy) Hedge by Food Processing Company

Cash Market	Futures Market	Basis
At time hedge is placed		
Value of 30,000 bu.:	Buy 6 contracts:	
30,000 × $2.75 = $82,500	6 × 5,000 × $3.20 = $96,000	−$0.45
At time hedge is lifted		
Value of 30,000 bu.:	Sell 6 contracts:	
30,000 × $3.55 = $106,500	6 × 5,000 × $4.25 = $127,500	−$0.70
Loss in cash market = $24,000	Gain in futures market = $31,500	
Overall gain = $7,500		

As a result of the long hedge, the food processing company will realize a gain of $31,500 in the futures market but only a $24,000 loss in the cash market. Therefore, there is an overall gain of $7,500. For the corn farmer, there is an overall loss of $7,500.

The results of this scenario demonstrate that when *(a)* the futures price is greater than the cash price at the time the hedge is placed, *(b)* the cash price increases, and *(c)* the basis widens, then:

The short (sell) hedger will realize an overall loss from the hedge.

The long (buy) hedger will realize an overall gain from the hedge.

These two results are identical to the results we found in the previous scenario, where we assumed that the cash price declined. The magnitude of the overall gain or loss, $7,500, is the same in both scenarios because in each scenario it was assumed that the basis widened to −$0.70.

5. Cash Price Decreases and Basis Narrows   In the two previous scenarios it was assumed that the basis widened. In this scenario and the one that follows, we will assume that the basis narrows to −$0.25.

Suppose that the cash price declines to $2. Since we are assuming that the basis narrows to −$0.25, the futures price at the time the hedge is lifted is assumed to be $2.25. Exhibit 12–5 summarizes the outcome for the hedge. The corn farmer realizes an overall gain of $6,000. The food processing company, on the other hand, realizes an overall loss of $6,000.

Exhibit 12–5

Hedge: Cash Price Decreases and Basis Narrows

Assumptions

Cash price at time hedge is placed	$2.75 per bu.
Futures price at time hedge is placed	$3.20 per bu.
Cash price at time hedge is lifted	$2.00 per bu.
Futures price at time hedge is lifted	$2.25 per bu.
Number of bushels to be hedged	30,000
Number of bushels per futures contract	5,000
Number of futures contracts used in hedge	6

Short (Sell) by Corn Farmer

Cash Market	Futures Market	Basis
At time hedge is placed		
Value of 30,000 bu.:	Sell 6 contracts:	
30,000 × $2.75 = $82,500	6 × 5,000 × $3.20 = $96,000	−$0.45
At time hedge is lifted		
Value of 30,000 bu.:	Buy 6 contracts:	
30,000 × $2.00 = $60,000	6 × 5,000 × $2.25 = $67,500	−$0.25
Loss in cash market = $22,500	Gain in futures market = $28,500	
Overall gain = $6,000		

Long (Buy) Hedge by Food Processing Company

Cash Market	Futures Market	Basis
At time hedge is placed		
Value of 30,000 bu.:	Buy 6 contracts:	
30,000 × $2.75 = $82,500	6 × 5,000 × $3.20 = $96,000	−$0.45
At time hedge is lifted		
Value of 30,000 bu.:	Sell 6 contracts:	
30,000 × $2.00 = $60,000	6 × 5,000 × $2.25 = $67,500	−$0.25
Gain in cash market = $22,500	Loss in futures market = $28,500	
Overall loss = $6,000		

The results of this scenario demonstrate that when *(a)* the future price is greater than the cash price at the time the hedge is placed, *(b)* the cash price decreases, and *(c)* the basis narrows, then:

The short (sell) hedger will realize an overall gain from the hedge.

The long (buy) hedger will realize an overall loss from the hedge.

6. Cash Price Increases and Basis Narrows Exhibit 12–6 summarizes the outcome of the hedge if the cash price increases to $3.55, as in scenario 4, and the basis narrows to −$0.25 (that is, the futures price when the hedge is removed is $3.80). The food processing company realizes an overall loss of $6,000. The corn farmer realizes an overall gain of $6,000.

Exhibit 12–6

Hedge: Cash Price Increases and Basis Narrows

Assumptions

Cash price at time hedge is placed	$2.75 per bu.
Futures price at time hedge is placed	$3.20 per bu.
Cash price at time hedge is lifted	$3.55 per bu.
Futures price at time hedge is lifted	$3.80 per bu.
Number of bushels to be hedged	30,000
Number of bushels per futures contract	5,000
Number of futures contracts used in hedge	6

Short (Sell) Hedge by Corn Farmer

Cash Market	Futures Market	Basis
At time hedge is placed		
Value of 30,000 bu.:	Sell 6 contracts:	
30,000 × $2.75 = $82,500	6 × 5,000 × $3.20 = $96,000	−$0.45
At time hedge is lifted		
Value of 30,000 bu.:	Buy 6 contracts:	
30,000 × $3.55 = $106,500	6 × 5,000 × $3.80 = $114,000	−$0.25
Gain in cash market = $24,000	Loss in futures market = $18,000	
Overall gain = $6,000		

Long (Buy) Hedge by Food Processing Company

Cash Market	Futures Market	Basis
At time hedge is placed		
Value of 30,000 bu.:	Buy 6 contracts:	
30,000 × $2.75 = $82,500	6 × 5,000 × $3.20 = $96,000	−$0.45
At time hedge is lifted		
Value of 30,000 bu.:	Sell 6 contracts:	
30,000 × $3.55 = $106,500	6 × 5,000 × $3.80 = $114,000	−$0.25
Loss in cash market = $24,000	Gain in futures market = $18,000	
Overall loss = $6,000		

The results of this scenario demonstrate that when *(a)* the futures price is greater than the cash price at the time the hedge is placed, *(b)* the cash price increases, and *(c)* the basis narrows, then:

The short (sell) hedger will realize an overall gain from the hedge.

The long (buy) hedger will realize an overall loss from the hedge.

This outcome is the same as that of the previous scenario, in which the cash price decreased.

Table 12–1 summarizes the outcome of the overall gain or loss for a short hedge and a long hedge for all possible changes in the cash and futures price.

Cross-Hedging

Not all commodities have a futures market. Consequently, if a hedger wants to protect against the price risk of a commodity in which a futures contract is not traded, he may use a commodity that he believes has a close price relationship to the one he seeks to hedge. This adds another dimension of risk when hedging. The cash market price relationship between the commodity to be hedged and the commodity used to hedge may change.

Since cross-hedging is involved when stock index futures are used to hedge an individual common stock or a portfolio of common stocks, we will first illustrate the key elements associated with a cross-hedge for a commodity.

Suppose that an okra farmer plans to sell 37,500 bushels of okra three months from now and that a food processing company plans to purchase

Table 12–1

Summary of Basis Relationships for a Hedge

Price		Absolute Change in Basis	Overall Gain (+) or Loss (−) When at Time Hedge Is Placed Cash Price Is Less than Futures Price	
Cash	Futures		Short Hedge	Long Hedge
Decreases	Decreases by same amount	No change	0	0
Decreases	Decreases by a smaller amount	Widens	−	+
Decreases	Decreases by a greater amount	Narrows	+	−
Increases	Increases by same amount	No change	0	0
Increases	Increases by a smaller amount	Narrows	+	−
Increases	Increases by a greater amount	Widens	−	+
Decreases	Increases	Widens	−	+
Increases	Decreases	Narrows	+	−

the same amount of okra three months from now. Both parties want to hedge against price risk. However, okra futures contracts are not traded. Both parties believe that there is a close relationship between the price of okra and the price of corn. Specifically, both parties believe that the cash price of okra will be 80 percent of the cash price of corn. The cash price of okra is currently $2.20 per bushel, and the cash price of corn is currently $2.75 per bushel. The futures price of corn is currently $3.20 per bushel.

Let's examine various scenarios to see how effective the cross-hedge will be. In each scenario, the difference between the cash price of corn and the futures price of corn at the time the cross-hedge is placed and at the time it is lifted will be assumed to be unchanged at −$0.45. This is done so that we may focus on the importance of the relationship between the two cash prices at the two points in time.

Before proceeding, we must first determine how many corn futures contracts must be used in the cross-hedge. The cash value of 37,500 bushels of okra at the cash price of $2.20 per bushel is $82,500. To protect a value of $82,500 using corn futures with a current cash price of $2.75, the price of 30,000 bushels of corn ($82,500/$2.75) must be hedged. Since each corn futures contract involves 5,000 bushels, six corn futures contracts will be used.

1. Cash Price of Both Commodities Changes in the Same Direction and by the Same Percentage Suppose that the cash prices of okra and corn decrease to $1.60 and $2 per bushel, respectively, and that the futures price of corn decreases to $2.45 per bushel. The relationship between the cash price for okra and the cash price for corn that was assumed when the cross-hedge was placed holds when the cross-hedge is lifted. That is, the cash price of okra is 80 percent of the cash price of corn. The basis for the cash price of corn and the futures price of corn is still −$0.45 at the time the cross-hedge is lifted. The outcome for the short and long cross-hedge is summarized in Exhibit 12–7.

The short cross-hedge produces a gain of $22,500 in the futures market and an exact offset loss in the cash market. The opposite occurs for the long cross-hedge. There is neither an overall gain nor a loss from the cross-hedge in this case. That is, we have a perfect cross-hedge. The same would occur if we assume that the cash price of both commodities increases by the same percentage and the basis does not change.

2. Cash Price of Both Commodities Changes in the Same Direction but by a Different Percentage Suppose that the cash price of both commodities decreases but the cash price of okra falls by a greater percentage than the cash price of corn. For example, suppose that the cash price of okra falls to $1.30 per bushel, while the cash price of corn falls to

Exhibit 12-7

Perfect Cross-Hedge: Cash Price Decreases for Both Commodities by Same Percentage

Assumptions

Price of okra	
Cash price at time hedge is placed	$2.20 per bu.
Cash price at time hedge is lifted	$1.60 per bu.
Price of corn	
Cash price at time hedge is placed	$2.75 per bu.
Futures price at time hedge is placed	$3.20 per bu.
Cash price at time hedge is lifted	$2.00 per bu.
Futures price at time hedge is lifted	$2.45 per bu.
Number of bushels of okra to be hedged	37,500
Number of bushels of corn to be hedged	
assuming ratio of cash price of okra to corn is 0.8	30,000
Number of bushels per futures contract for corn	5,000
Number of corn futures contracts used in hedge	6

Short (Sell) Cross-Hedge by Okra Farmer

Cash Market	Futures Market	Basis*
At time hedge is placed		
Value of 37,500 bu.:	Sell 6 contracts:	
37,500 × $2.20 = $82,500	6 × 5,000 × $3.20 = $96,000	−$0.45
At time hedge is lifted		
Value of 37,500 bu.:	Buy 6 contracts:	
37,500 × $1.60 = $60,000	6 × 5,000 × $2.45 = $73,500	−$0.45
Loss in cash market = $22,500	Gain in futures market = $22,500	
Overall gain or loss = $0		

Long (Buy) Cross-Hedge by Food Processing Company

Cash Market	Futures Market	Basis*
At time hedge is placed		
Value of 37,500 bu.:	Buy 6 contracts:	
37,500 × $2.20 = $82,500	6 × 5,000 × $3.20 = $96,000	−$0.45
At time hedge is lifted		
Value of 37,500 bu.:	Sell 6 contracts:	
37,500 × $1.60 = $60,000	6 × 5,000 × $2.45 = $73,500	−$0.45
Gain in cash market = $22,500	Loss in futures market = $22,500	
Overall gain or loss = $0		

* Basis = Cash price of corn − Futures price of corn.

$2.00 per bushel. The futures price of corn falls to $2.45 so that the basis is not changed. The cash price of okra at the time the cross-hedge is lifted is 65 percent of the cash price of corn rather than the 80 percent that was assumed when the cross-hedge was constructed. The outcome for the long and short cross-hedge is shown in Exhibit 12–8.

For the short cross-hedge, the loss in the cash market exceeds the

Exhibit 12–8

Cross-Hedge: Cash Price of Commodity to Be Hedged Falls by a Greater Percentage than the Commodity Used for the Hedge

Assumptions

Price of okra	
Cash price at time hedge is placed	$2.20 per bu.
Cash price at time hedge is lifted	$1.30 per bu.
Price of corn	
Cash price at time hedge is placed	$2.75 per bu.
Futures price at time hedge is placed	$3.20 per bu.
Cash price at time hedge is lifted	$2.00 per bu.
Futures price at time hedge is lifted	$2.45 per bu.
Number of bushels of okra to be hedged	37,500
Number of bushels of corn to be hedged	
assuming ratio of cash price of okra to corn is 0.8	30,000
Number of bushels per futures contract for corn	5,000
Number of corn futures contracts used in hedge	6

Short (Sell) Cross-Hedge by Okra Farmer

Cash Market	Futures Market	Basis*
At time hedge is placed		
Value of 37,500 bu.:	Sell 6 contracts:	
37,500 × $2.20 = $82,500	6 × 5,000 × $3.20 = $96,000	−$0.45
At time hedge is lifted		
Value of 37,500 bu.:	Buy 6 contracts:	
37,500 × $1.30 = $48,750	6 × 5,000 × $2.45 = $73,500	−$0.45
Loss in cash market = $33,750	Gain in futures market = $22,500	
Overall loss = $11,250		

Long (Buy) Cross-Hedge by Food Processing Company

Cash Market	Futures Market	Basis*
At time hedge is placed		
Value of 37,500 bu.:	Buy 6 contracts:	
37,500 × $2.20 = $82,500	6 × 5,000 × $3.20 = $96,000	−$0.45
At time hedge is lifted		
Value of 37,500 bu.:	Sell 6 contracts:	
37,500 × $1.30 = $48,750	6 × 5,000 × $2.45 = $73,500	−$0.45
Gain in cash market = $33,750	Loss in futures market = $22,500	
Overall gain = $11,250		

* Basis = Cash price of corn − Futures price of corn.

realized loss in the futures market by $11,200. For the long cross-hedge, the opposite is true. There is an overall gain of $11,200 from the cross-hedge.

Had the cash price of okra fallen by less than the decline in the cash price of corn, the short cross-hedge would have produced an overall gain, while the long cross-hedge would have generated an overall loss.

3. Cash Price of Both Commodities Moves in the Opposite Direction

Suppose that the cash price of okra falls to $1.60 per bushel, while the cash price and the futures price of corn rise to $3.55 and $4, respectively. The results of the cross-hedge are shown in Exhibit 12–9.

The short cross-hedge results in a loss in both the cash market and the futures market. The overall loss is $46,500. Had the okra farmer not used the cross-hedge, his loss would have been limited to the decline

Exhibit 12–9

Cross-Hedge: Cash Price of Commodity to Be Hedged Falls while the Cash Price of Commodity Used for the Hedge Rises

Assumptions

Price of okra	
Cash price at time hedge is placed	$2.20 per bu.
Cash price at time hedge is lifted	$1.60 per bu.
Price of corn	
Cash price at time hedge is placed	$2.75 per bu.
Futures price at time hedge is placed	$3.20 per bu.
Cash price at time hedge is lifted	$3.55 per bu.
Futures price at time hedge is lifted	$4.00 per bu.
Number of bushels of okra to be hedged	37,500
Number of bushels of corn to be hedged assuming ratio of cash price of okra to corn is 0.8	30,000
Number of bushels per futures contract for corn	5,000
Number of corn futures contracts used in hedge	6

Short (Sell) Cross-Hedge by Okra Farmer

Cash Market	Futures Market	Basis*
At time hedge is placed		
Value of 37,500 bu.:	Sell 6 contracts:	
37,500 × $2.20 = $82,500	6 × 5,000 × $3.20 = $96,000	−$0.45
At time hedge is lifted		
Value of 37,500 bu.:	Buy 6 contracts:	
37,500 × $1.60 = $60,000	6 × 5,000 × $4.00 = $120,000	−$0.45
Loss in cash market = $22,500	Loss in futures market = $24,000	
Overall loss = $46,500		

Long (Buy) Cross-Hedge by Food Processing Company

Cash Market	Futures Market	Basis*
At time hedge is placed		
Value of 37,500 bu.:	Buy 6 contracts:	
37,500 × $2.20 = $82,500	6 × 5,000 × $3.20 = $96,000	−$0.45
At time hedge is lifted		
Value of 37,500 bu.:	Sell 6 contracts:	
37,500 × $1.60 = $60,000	6 × 5,000 × $4.00 = $120,000	−$0.45
Gain in cash market = $22,500	Gain in futures market = $24,000	
Overall gain = $46,500		

* Basis = Cash price of corn − Futures price of corn.

in the cash price, $22,500 in this instance. The long hedger, on the other hand, realizes a gain in both the cash and futures market, and therefore an overall gain.

Exhibit 12–10 shows the outcome for the short and long cross-hedge if the cash price of okra increases to $3 per bushel, while the cash price and the futures price of corn decline to $2 and $2.45, respectively. In this case the long cross-hedge results in a loss in both the cash and futures

Exhibit 12–10

Cross-Hedge: Cash Price of Commodity to Be Hedged Rises while the Cash Price of Commodity Used for the Hedge Falls

Assumptions

Price of okra	
Cash price at time hedge is placed	$2.20 per bu.
Cash price at time hedge is lifted	$3.00 per bu.
Price of corn	
Cash price at time hedge is placed	$2.75 per bu.
Futures price at time hedge is placed	$3.20 per bu.
Cash price at time hedge is lifted	$2.00 per bu.
Futures price at time hedge is lifted	$2.45 per bu.
Number of bushels of okra to be hedged	37,500
Number of bushels of corn to be hedged	
assuming ratio of cash price of okra to corn is 0.8	30,000
Number of bushels per futures contract for corn	5,000
Number of corn futures contracts used in hedge	6

Short (Sell) Cross-Hedge by Okra Farmer

Cash Market	Futures Market	Basis*
At time hedge is placed		
Value of 37,500 bu.:	Sell 6 contracts:	
37,500 × $2.20 = $82,500	6 × 5,000 × $3.20 = $96,000	−$0.45
At time hedge is lifted		
Value of 37,500 bu.:	Buy 6 contracts:	
37,500 × $3.00 = $112,500	6 × 5,000 × $2.45 = $73,500	−$0.45
Gain in cash market = $30,000	Gain in futures market = $22,500	
Overall gain = $52,500		

Long (Buy) Cross-Hedge by Food Processing Company

Cash Market	Futures Market	Basis*
At time hedge is placed		
Value of 37,500 bu.:	Buy 6 contracts:	
37,500 × $2.20 = $82,500	6 × 5,000 × $3.20 = $96,000	−$0.45
At time hedge is lifted		
Value of 37,500 bu.:	Sell 6 contracts:	
37,500 × $3.00 = $112,500	6 × 5,000 × $2.45 = $73,500	−$0.45
Loss in cash market = $30,000	Loss in futures market = $22,500	
Overall loss = $52,500		

* Basis = Cash price of corn − Futures price of corn.

markets. The total loss is $52,500. The loss would have been only $30,000, the loss in the cash market, had the management of the food processing company not employed a cross-hedge with corn.

Hedging with Stock Index Futures

So far in this chapter we have demonstrated that a successful hedge strategy will depend on what happens to the basis between the time the hedge is placed and the time it is lifted. The basis is a function of the pricing of the futures relative to the cash price. Moreover, when cross-hedging is employed, the cash price relationship between the product to be hedged and the product underlying the futures contract will determine the degree of success of a cross-hedge.

How successful stock index futures will be for hedging the price risk of an individual stock or a portfolio of common stocks will depend on the pricing of the futures relative to the underlying cash or spot stock index. The pricing of the futures relative to the stock index is discussed in Section Two of the book. Since a stock index futures contract may be used to hedge a stock or a portfolio of common stocks that is not identical in composition to the underlying stock index, any hedge employing stock index futures is a cross-hedge. Therefore, a relationship between the value of the stock index and the individual stock or portfolio of common stocks must be estimated.

Before illustrating how stock index futures can be used for hedging, we will explain the relationship between an individual common stock or a portfolio of common stocks and a market index. How the relationship is statistically estimated is explained in most investment textbooks.

The Relationship between the Price Movement of an Individual Stock or a Portfolio of Common Stocks and a Market Index

The statistical technique of regression analysis is used to estimate the relationship between the price of an individual stock or a portfolio of common stocks and a market index. The relationship estimated is as follows:

Percentage change in price of a stock (or value of a portfolio) in period t

$$= \text{Alpha} + \text{Beta} \left(\begin{array}{l} \text{percentage change in} \\ \text{the value of the market} \\ \text{index in period } t \end{array} \right) + \begin{array}{l} \text{Error term in} \\ \text{period } t \end{array}$$

This relationship is known as the *market model*. Strictly speaking, the market model shows the relationship between rates of return (price changes plus cash dividends) rather than price changes. However, one study has demonstrated that the estimate of beta will be for all practical purposes the same whether the relationship involves rates of return or simply price changes.[1]

The data to estimate the parameters of the model, alpha and beta, are the observed price changes for the stock (or market value change for the portfolio) and the change in the market index value over some time period.

In practice, the market model has been estimated by using monthly and weekly data. The value of the parameters estimated will differ depending on whether monthly or weekly data are employed. The value of the parameters will also differ depending on the number of observations (e.g., two years of monthly or weekly data versus one year of monthly or weekly data) used to estimate the market model.

The parameter of interest to us is beta, the slope of the market model. This parameter tells us how volatile the individual stock or the portfolio of common stocks is relative to the market index. A value of beta greater than one indicates that the stock or the portfolio is more volatile than the market index. If beta is less than one, the stock or portfolio is less volatile than the market index. If beta is one, the stock or portfolio mirrors the market index. It is rare to find a beta that is negative.

However, the value of beta is not the only important piece of information that we must have in order to assess the likelihood of success of a hedge. We must know how good the relationship is. Look back at the last term in the expression for the market model. The size of the error term indicates how well the stock or portfolio tracks the movement of the market index. If there is a strong relationship between the movement of the stock or portfolio and the market index, the error term will be small.

A statistical measure of the strength of the relationship is the coefficient of determination, or "R-squared" (R^2). This measure indicates the percentage of the variation in the movement of the stock or portfolio explained by the market index. The coefficient of determination can range from zero to one. The closer the coefficient of determination is to one, the stronger is the statistical relationship. The coefficient of determination is directly related to a concept that most individuals are familiar with— the correlation coefficient. The correlation coefficient is equal to the square root of the coefficient of determination. Whether the correlation coefficient is positive or negative is determined by the sign of beta. For example, if the coefficient of determination is .7 and the beta is 1.2, the correlation coefficient is +.84.

---

[1] William F. Sharpe and Guy M. Cooper, "Risk-Return Classes of New York Stock Exchange Common Stocks," *Financial Analysts Journal*, March–April 1972, pp. 46–54, 81.

A major problem with the market model for individual common stocks is that the coefficient of determination is small, typically between .01 and .65. Statistical techniques are available to determine whether the relationship is statistically significant, that is, whether beta is significantly different from zero. For example, depending on the number of observations used to estimate the market model, a coefficient of determination of .2 may be statistically significant. That is, even though the market model indicates that only 20 percent of the variation in the movement of the price of the stock is explained by the market index, from a purely statistical perspective such a relationship is significant. However, a portfolio manager may have serious reservations about using the relationship to hedge a stock.

As the number of stocks in a portfolio increases, the error term tends to decrease. In the jargon of the portfolio manager, price movements not associated with the movement in the market, the error term, are diversified away as the number of issues in the portfolio increases. One study has shown that only 12 to 18 issues are needed to diversify the risk not associated with the movement of the market.[2] Consequently, a diversified common stock portfolio does a better job of tracking the market index than does an individual stock issue. In statistical terminology, the coefficient of determination approaches one as the number of issues in the portfolio increases. However, keep in mind that even if the coefficient of determination is one for a portfolio relative to a market index, this does not mean that the beta for the portfolio will equal one. The beta tells us how volatile the portfolio is relative to a market index. The coefficient of determination and the correlation coefficient indicate how good the relationship is.

Table 12–2 presents the beta, the coefficient of determination, and the correlation coefficient for 19 randomly selected NYSE stocks. The market model was estimated using weekly price changes for the 33-week period October 5, 1981, to May 17, 1982, and estimated for both the S&P 500 Composite Index and the NYSE Composite Index. Also shown on Table 12–2 are the corresponding values for a portfolio consisting of an equal number of shares of each of the 19 issues. Notice that the correlation for the portfolio is considerably higher than the correlation for any of the stocks comprised by the portfolio and that the correlation is close to one.

When a hedge is constructed, the beta will tell the investor the contract value of the futures position that should be taken to hedge the stock or portfolio. It plays the same role in hedging a stock or portfolio that the relationship between the cash price of okra and the cash price of

---

[2] John L. Evans and Stephen H. Archer, "Diversification and the Reduction of Dispersion: An Empirical Analysis," *Journal of Finance*, December 1968, pp. 761–67.

Table 12-2

Estimates of Beta, Coefficient of Determination, and Correlation Coefficient for 19 Randomly Selected Stocks*

Company	Based on S&P 500 Composite Index			Based on NYSE Composite Index		
	Beta	Coefficient of Determination (R^2)	Correlation Coefficient	Beta	Coefficient of Determination (R^2)	Correlation Coefficient
Amerada Hess	1.883	.460	.678	1.960	.472	.687
American Brands	0.412	.158	.397	0.418	.154	.393
American Broadcasting	0.911	.152	.390	0.983	.168	.409
CP National	0.595	.164	.405	0.649	.185	.430
CSX	1.150	.333	.577	1.221	.356	.597
Crown Zellerbach	1.614	.458	.677	1.722	.494	.703
Crum & Foster	0.982	.171	.414	0.942	.149	.387
Ford	0.635	.063	.250	0.645	.061	.248
Procter & Gamble	0.595	.390	.625	0.615	.396	.629
Rohr Industries	1.054	.206	.453	1.104	.214	.462
Rollins	1.690	.400	.632	1.710	.388	.623
Schering Plough	0.994	.315	.561	1.036	.325	.570
Schlumberger Ltd.	1.812	.647	.804	1.790	.599	.774
Scott Paper	1.075	.339	.582	1.113	.344	.587
G. D. Searle	0.711	.243	.493	0.754	.260	.509
Sears Roebuck	0.618	.155	.394	0.666	.170	.413
Stokely-Van Camp	0.482	.043	.207	0.568	.056	.237
Eastman Kodak	0.891	.479	.692	0.934	.499	.706
Eaton	0.623	.147	.383	0.625	.140	.374
Portfolio†	0.940	.860	.927	0.976	.878	.937

* Weekly data used to estimate the market model—October 5, 1981, to May 17, 1982.
† Portfolio consisting of one share of the common stock of each company.

corn did in our cross-hedging example earlier in this chapter. The coefficient of determination will indicate how good the relationship is and will allow the hedger to assess the likelihood of success of the hedge.

Examples of Hedging Using Stock Index Futures

To demonstrate how stock index futures can be used to hedge the price risk of an individual stock or a portfolio, actual cases will be used. Suppose that on May 17, 1982, an investor owned 10,000 shares of Crown Zellerbach. On that day the closing price of the stock was $21 per share and therefore the market value of 10,000 shares was $210,000. Suppose that the investor needed to hold the shares until August 9, 1982, in order to qualify for long-term capital gain treatment. However, the investor anticipated that the market, and therefore his stock, would decline in value by August 9. To protect himself against a decline in the price of the stock, the investor decided to enter into a sell or short hedge using the September S&P 500 futures contract.

The first thing that the investor has to determine is how many contracts to purchase. This depends on Crown Zellerbach's beta and on the dollar value of the cash index at the time the hedge is placed. The steps for determining the number of contracts are as follows:

Step 1   Determine the "equivalent market index units" of the market by dividing the market value of the stock (portfolio) by the current cash index underlying the futures contract.

$$\text{Equivalent market index units} = \frac{\text{Market value of stock (portfolio)}}{\text{Current cash index value}}$$

Step 2   Multiply the equivalent market index units by beta to obtain the "beta-adjusted equivalent market index units."

$$\text{Beta-adjusted equivalent market index units} = \text{Beta} \times \text{Equivalent market index units}$$

Step 3   Divide the beta-adjusted equivalent market index units by the multiple specified in the futures contract. Since stock index futures contracts are for $500 times the value of the index, divide by $500.

$$\text{Number of contracts} = \frac{\text{Beta-adjusted equivalent market index units}}{\$500}$$

In our illustration, since the S&P 500 index on May 17, 1982, was 118.01 and the beta for Crown Zellerbach was equal to 1.614 (see Table 12–2), the number of S&P 500 futures contracts required to hedge 10,000 shares of Crown Zellerbach was 5.7443, as shown below:

Step 1

$$\text{Equivalent market index units} = \$210,000/118.01$$
$$= \$1,779.5102$$

Step 2

$$\text{Beta-adjusted equivalent} = \$1,799.5102 \times 1.614$$
$$\text{market index units} = \$2,872.1295$$

Step 3

$$\text{Number of contracts} = \frac{\$2,872.1295}{\$500}$$

$$= 5.7443$$

Although it is not possible to purchase fractional portions of a futures contract, in the illustrations presented in this chapter fractional portions will be used.

The value of the futures position of the investor is equal to the number of contracts times the current futures price of the contract times the contract multiple ($500). Suppose that the investor sold 5.7443 S&P 500 futures contracts for 118.30 on May 17, 1982. Then the value of the investor's short futures position would be $339,775 (5.7443 × 118.30 × $500).

On August 9, 1982, the time the stock was to be sold, the price of Crown Zellerbach declined to $16.50 per share. Consequently, the market value of the shares declined $45,000, from $210,000 to $165,000 ($16.50 × 10,000).

The futures price of the September S&P 500 contract on August 9, 1982, was 102.60. Hence 5.7443 contracts could be purchased for $294,683; therefore, closing out the futures position produced a profit of $45,092 ($339,775 − $294,683). Since the loss in the cash market was $45,000 and the gain in the futures market was $45,092, the overall result of the short hedge was a trivial gain of $92. This short hedge is summarized in Exhibit 12–11.

Let us analyze this hedge to determine why it was successful. As explained earlier in this chapter, in a cross-hedge there are two risks—basis risk and the risk that the relationship assumed between the product used for the hedge and the product to be hedged fails to materialize precisely as hypothesized. Consider the basis risk. At the time the hedge was placed, the cash price was 118.01 and the futures price was 118.30. The basis at the time the hedge was placed was −0.29 (the futures price

Exhibit 12–11

Short (Sell) Hedge of 10,000 Shares of Crown Zellerbach Using S&P 500 Futures Contracts

Situation

Own 10,000 shares of Crown Zellerbach common stock on May 17, 1982.
Need to hold shares until August 9, 1982, in order to qualify for long-term capital gain.
Want to hedge against a decline in the price of the stock when the stock will be sold on August 9, 1982.

Facts

	May 17, 1982	*August 9, 1982*
Price per share	$ 21.00	$ 16.50
Cash price for S&P 500 index	118.01	103.71
Futures price for S&P 500 index	118.30	102.60

Beta = 1.614.
Coefficient of determination (R²) = .46.
Correlation coefficient = .68.

Cash Market	*Futures Market*	*Basis**
May 17, 1982—time hedge is placed		
Own 10,000 shares at $21 per share = $210,000	Sell 5.7443 September S&P futures contracts†	−0.29
	Value of short position = $339,775 (5.7443 × 118.30 × $500)	
August 9, 1982—time hedge is lifted		
Sell 10,000 shares at $16.50 per share = $165,000	Buy 5.7443 September S&P futures contracts	1.11
	Cost to close out position = $294,683 (5.7443 × 102.60 × $500)	
Loss in cash market = $45,000	Gain in futures market = $45,092	
Overall gain = $92		

* Basis = Cash price − Futures price.
† The computation of the number of contracts is explained in the chapter.

sold at a premium to the cash price). Had the basis been unchanged at −0.29 at the time the hedge was lifted, the futures price would have been 104.00 (103.71 + 0.29). The cost of closing out the futures position would have been $298,704 (5.7443 × 104.00 × $500), and the profit from the futures position would have been $41,071 ($339,775 − $298,704).

At the time the hedge was lifted, the cash value for the index was 103.71, so the basis was 1.11 (103.71 − 102.6). That is, the futures price sold at a discount to the cash price. The change in the basis was 1.40 (1.10 − (−0.29)). The change in the basis was in favor of the short hedger (see Table 12–1), resulting in a gain in the futures market of $700 per contract (1.4 × $500), or $4,021 for 5.7443 contracts.

In the cash market, the S&P 500 index declined by 12.11762 percent, from 118.01 to 103.71. Since the beta of Crown Zellerbach is 1.614, the price of the stock should have decreased by 19.55783 percent (12.11762 percent × 1.614) to $16.8929 per share, or $168,929. This would have resulted in a loss of $41,071 in the cash market. Notice that the loss of $41,071 in the cash market had the price of the stock declined by the hypothesized relationship (as indicated by beta) would have been exactly equal to the gain in the futures market had the basis remained constant. That is, there would have been a perfect hedge.

The stock, in fact, declined by more than the amount suggested by its beta. It fell from $21 to $16.50, or $0.3929 more per share than was predicted by its beta. Thus the loss in the cash market was $3,929 more than it would have been if the stock price had fallen to only $16.8929. Since the additional gain in the futures market because of a change in the basis was $4,021 and the additional loss in the cash market because the stock price fell more than predicted by its beta was $3,929, there was an overall gain of $92 ($4,021 − $3,929). This, of course, agrees with our earlier analysis of the outcome of the hedge.

To summarize, the change in the basis and the decline of the stock price by an amount different from that predicted by beta resulted in a less than perfect hedge. The hedge turned out to be successful, resulting in a trivial gain of $92. The reason for the success was a basis change that moved in favor of the investor, despite the fact that the stock declined by more than the amount predicted by beta.

Exhibit 12–12 shows the results of hedging 10,000 shares of Crown Zellerbach on May 17, 1982, using the NYSE Composite futures contract and the beta based on the NYSE Composite Index. The number of contracts needed to hedge the 10,000 shares of Crown Zellerbach was 10.6187. The overall result of the hedge was a gain of $6,235. The reason for the overall gain was a profit in the futures market of $51,235 and a loss in the cash market of $45,000. The basis changed from −0.19 to 1.04, or by 1.23 in favor of the short hedger. This meant a gain of $615 per contract (1.23 × $500), or $6,530 for 10.6187 contracts. Given the estimated beta of 1.722, the stock price fell by more than the amount predicted, resulting in a greater loss of $295 in the cash market. The favorable movement in the basis resulted in a gain of $6,530 in the futures market and the greater loss of $295 in the cash market resulted in the overall gain of $6,235.

Tables 12–3 and 12–4 summarize the results of a short hedge placed on May 17, 1982, and lifted on August 9, 1982, for 10,000 shares of 19 randomly selected stocks using the September S&P 500 and NYSE futures contracts, respectively. The results are broken down to indicate the gain or loss due to a change in the basis and a price change for the stock that differed from that predicted by its beta. Notice the importance of the beta estimate in the final outcome of the hedge. It should be clear that the success of the hedge will be tied to how reliable the estimate of beta is.

Exhibit 12-12

Short (Sell) Hedge of 10,000 Shares of Crown Zellerbach Using NYSE Composite Index Futures Contracts

Situation
Own 10,000 shares of Crown Zellerbach common stock on May 1?, 1982.
Need to hold shares until August 9, 1982, in order to qualify for long-term capital gain.
Want to hedge against a decline in the price of the stock when the stock will be sold on August 9, 1982.

Facts	*May 17, 1982*	*August 9, 1982*
Price per share	$21.00	$16.50
Cash price for NYSE Composite Index	68.11	59.69
Futures price for NYSE Composite Index	68.30	58.65
Beta = 1.722.		
Coefficient of determination (R²) = .49.		
Correlation coefficient = .70.		

Cash Market	Futures Market	Basis*
May 17, 1982—time hedge is placed		
Own 10,000 shares at $21 per share = $210,000	Sell 10.6187 September NYSE Composite futures contracts† Value of short position = $362,628 (10.6187 × 68.30 × $500)	−0.19
August 9, 1982—time hedge is lifted		
Sell 10,000 shares at $16.50 per share = $165,000	Buy 10.6187 September NYSE Composite futures contracts Cost to close out position = $311,393 (10.6187 × 58.65 × $500)	1.04
Loss in cash market = $45,000	Gain in futures market = $51,235	
Overall gain = $6,235		

* Basis = Cash price − Futures price.
† The computation of the number of contracts is explained in the chapter.

The last column of these two tables presents the overall hedge results if transaction costs are considered. The transaction costs are assumed to be $50 per transaction or $100 for a round trip. Transaction costs for institutions are considerably less—approximately $15–40 for a round trip. As can be seen, transaction costs are trivial.

Table 12–5 shows the percentage change in the value of the 10,000 shares for each of the 19 stocks with and without hedging. For the time period for which these results were simulated, the outcome was always better by short hedging since all but two of the issues declined in value. However, had the hedge been used for a long, or buy, hedge in anticipation of purchasing the stock on August 9, 1982, then for the two issues that increased in value, American Broadcasting and Schering Plough, the long

Table 12-3

Summary of Short Hedge Results for 10,000 Shares Using S&P 500 Futures Contracts

Stock	Beta	R²	Number of Contracts	Value of Stock-Unhedged 5/17/82	8/9/82	Gain or Loss	Cash Market	Futures Market	Overall	Due to Stock Price Change ≠ Beta*	Due to Change in Basis†	Overall after Transaction Costs‡
Amerada Hess	1.883	.46	6.9410	$217,500	$163,750	−$ 53,750	−$ 53,750	$ 54,487	$ 737	−$ 4,122	$ 4,859	$ 43
American Brands	0.412	.16	2.8977	415,000	385,000	− 30,000	− 30,000	22,747	− 7,253	− 9,281	2,028	− 7,543
American Broadcasting	0.911	.15	5.5775	361,250	382,500	21,250	21,250	43,783	65,033	61,129	3,904	64,475
CP National	0.595	.16	2.4706	245,000	241,250	− 3,750	− 3,750	19,394	15,644	13,914	1,729	15,397
CSX	1.150	.33	8.3319	427,500	366,250	− 61,250	− 61,250	65,406	4,156	− 1,677	5,832	3,322
Crown Zellerbach	1.614	.46	5.7443	210,000	165,000	− 45,000	− 45,000	45,092	92	− 3,929	4,021	482
Crum & Foster	0.982	.17	4.7016	282,500	222,500	− 60,000	− 60,000	36,907	− 23,093	− 26,384	3,291	− 23,563
Ford	0.635	.06	2.5425	236,250	218,750	− 17,500	− 17,500	19,958	2,458	679	1,780	2,204
Procter & Gamble	0.595	.39	8.4831	841,250	832,500	− 8,750	− 8,750	66,592	57,842	51,904	5,938	56,994
Rohr Industries	1.054	.21	1.8309	102,500	92,500	− 10,000	− 10,000	14,373	4,373	3,091	1,282	4,190
Rollins	1.690	.40	4.5469	158,750	108,750	− 50,000	− 50,000	35,693	− 14,307	− 17,490	3,183	− 14,762
Schering Plough	0.994	.31	4.9906	296,250	307,500	11,250	11,250	39,177	50,427	46,933	3,493	49,927
Schlumberger Ltd.	1.812	.65	14.6637	477,500	358,750	− 118,750	− 118,750	115,110	− 3,640	− 13,905	10,265	− 5,106
Scott Paper	1.075	.34	3.0289	166,250	137,500	− 28,750	− 28,750	23,777	− 4,973	− 7,094	2,120	− 5,276
G. D. Searle	0.711	.24	4.2476	352,500	322,500	− 30,000	− 30,000	33,343	3,343	370	2,973	2,919
Sears Roebuck	0.618	.15	2.0686	197,500	185,000	− 12,500	− 12,500	16,238	3,738	2,290	1,448	3,531
Stokely-Van Camp	0.482	.04	2.5119	307,500	305,000	− 2,500	− 2,500	19,718	17,218	15,460	1,758	16,967
Eastman Kodak	0.891	.48	11.1366	737,500	715,000	− 22,500	− 22,500	87,422	64,922	57,126	7,796	63,808
Eaton	0.623	.15	3.2203	305,000	227,500	− 77,500	− 77,500	25,280	− 52,220	− 54,475	2,254	− 52,543

* Projected market value minus actual market value on 8/9/82.

$$\text{Projected market value} = \left[1 - \left(\frac{\text{Index on } 8/9/82}{\text{Index on } 5/17/82} - 1\right)\text{Beta}\right](\text{Market value on } 5/17/82)$$

† Change in basis = 1.40 × Number of contracts × $500.
‡ Overall hedge results − Transaction costs.

Transaction costs = 2 × $50 × Number of contracts

Table 12-4

Summary of Short Hedge Results for 10,000 Shares Using NYSE Composite Futures Contracts

| Stock | Beta | R² | Number of Contracts | Value of Stock—Unhedged | | | Overall | Cash Market | Futures Market | Results of Hedge—Gain or Loss | | |
				5/17/82	8/9/82	Gain or Loss				Due to Stock Price Change ≠ Beta*	Due to Change in Basis†	Overall after Transaction Costs‡
Amerada Hess	1.960	.47	12.5180	$217,500	$163,750	−$53,750	$ 6,649	−$ 53,750	$ 60,399	−$ 1,049	$ 7,699	$ 5,397
American Brands	0.418	.15	5.0938	415,000	385,000	− 30,000	− 5,422	− 30,000	24,578	− 8,555	3,133	− 5,932
American Broadcasting	0.983	.17	10.4275	361,250	382,500	− 21,250	71,563	− 21,250	50,313	65,150	6,413	70,520
CP National	0.649	.19	4.6691	245,000	241,250	− 3,750	18,778	− 3,750	22,528	15,907	2,871	18,311
CSX	1.222	.36	15.3400	427,500	366,250	− 61,250	12,766	− 61,250	74,016	3,332	9,434	11,232
Crown Zellerbach	1.722	.49	10.6187	210,000	165,000	− 45,000	6,235	− 45,000	51,235	− 295	6,531	5,173
Crum & Foster	0.942	.15	7.8143	282,500	222,500	− 60,000	− 22,296	− 60,000	37,704	− 27,102	4,806	− 23,078
Ford	0.645	.06	4.4746	236,250	218,750	− 17,500	4,090	− 17,500	21,590	− 1,338	2,752	3,642
Procter & Gamble	0.615	.40	15.1922	841,250	832,500	− 8,750	64,552	− 8,750	73,302	55,209	9,343	63,033
Rohr Industries	1.104	.21	3.3229	102,500	92,500	− 10,000	6,033	− 10,000	16,033	3,989	2,044	5,701
Rollins	1.710	.39	7.9713	158,750	108,750	− 50,000	− 11,538	− 50,000	38,462	− 16,441	4,902	− 12,336
Schering Plough	1.036	.32	9.0123	296,250	307,500	11,250	54,735	11,250	43,485	49,192	5,543	53,833
Schlumberger Ltd.	1.790	.60	25.0984	477,500	358,750	− 118,750	2,350	− 118,750	121,100	− 13,086	15,436	160
Scott Paper	1.113	.34	5.4335	166,250	137,500	− 28,750	2,534	− 28,750	26,216	5,875	3,342	3,077
G. D. Searle	0.754	.26	7.8046	352,500	322,500	− 30,000	7,657	− 30,000	37,657	2,857	4,800	6,877
Sears Roebuck	0.666	.17	3.8624	197,500	185,000	− 12,500	6,136	− 12,500	18,636	3,761	2,375	5,750
Stokely-Van Camp	0.568	.06	5.1288	307,500	305,000	− 2,500	22,246	− 2,500	24,746	19,092	3,154	21,733
Eastman Kodak	0.934	.50	20.2268	737,500	715,000	− 22,500	75,095	− 22,500	97,595	62,655	12,440	73,072
Eaton	0.625	.14	5.5976	305,000	227,500	− 77,500	− 50,492	− 77,500	27,008	− 53,934	3,443	− 51,052

* Projected market value minus actual market value on 8/9/82.

Projected market value $= \left[1 - \left(\frac{\text{Index on } 8/9/82}{\text{Index on } 5/17/82} - 1 \right) \text{Beta} \right]$ (Market value on 5/17/82).

† Change in basis = 1.23 × Number of contracts × $500.
‡ Overall hedge results − Transaction costs.

Transaction costs = 2 × $50 × Number of contracts

Table 12-5

Change in Portfolio Value: Unhedged and Short Hedged

		Hedged—No Transaction Costs (%)		Hedged—Transaction Costs (%)	
Stock	Unhedged (%)	S&P 500	NYSE Composite	S&P 500	NYSE Composite
Amerada Hess	−24.71	+ 0.34	+ 3.06	+ 0.02	+ 2.48
American Brands	− 7.23	− 1.75	− 1.31	− 1.82	− 1.43
American Broadcasting	+ 5.88	+18.00	+19.81	+17.85	+19.52
CP National	− 1.53	+ 6.39	+ 7.66	+ 6.28	+ 7.47
CSX	−14.33	+ 0.97	+ 2.99	+ 0.78	+ 2.63
Crown Zellerbach	−21.43	+ 0.04	+ 2.97	− 0.23	+ 2.46
Crum & Foster	−21.24	− 8.17	− 7.89	− 8.34	− 8.17
Ford	− 7.41	+ 1.04	+ 1.73	+ 0.93	+ 1.54
Procter & Gamble	− 1.04	+ 6.88	+ 7.67	+ 6.77	+ 7.49
Rohr Industries	− 9.76	+ 4.27	+ 5.89	+ 4.09	+ 5.56
Rollins	−31.50	− 9.01	− 7.27	− 9.30	− 7.77
Schering Plough	+ 3.80	+17.02	+18.48	+16.85	+18.17
Schlumberger Ltd.	−24.87	− 0.76	+ 0.49	− 1.07	− 0.03
Scott Paper	−17.29	− 2.99	− 1.52	− 3.17	− 1.85
G. D. Searle	− 8.51	+ 0.95	+ 2.17	+ 0.83	+ 1.95
Sears Roebuck	− 6.33	+ 1.89	+ 3.11	+ 1.79	+ 2.91
Stokely-Van Camp	− 0.81	+ 5.60	+ 7.23	+ 5.52	+ 7.07
Eastman Kodak	− 3.05	+ 8.80	+10.18	+ 8.65	+ 9.91
Eaton	−25.41	−17.12	−16.55	−17.23	−16.74

hedge would not have performed well. The long, or buy, hedge would have resulted in a considerably greater cost of acquiring 10,000 shares of each issue compared to the cost of an unhedged position. Had the investor not hedged, it would have cost 5.9 percent more to acquire American Broadcasting and 3.8 percent more to acquire Schering Plough on August 9, 1982, than on May 17, 1982. By comparison, the long hedge resulted in a cost of acquiring 10,000 shares of the two issues that would have been 17 to 19 percent greater on August 9, 1982, than on May 17, 1982.

Because of the higher correlation between a diversified portfolio of common stock and the market index, one would expect a hedge to perform better for a diversified portfolio than for an individual common stock. To see this, suppose that on May 17, 1982, a portfolio consisting of 10,000 shares of each of the 19 stocks shown in Table 12-3 was to be hedged against an adverse price movement.

The beta for the portfolio is 0.94, and the correlation with the S&P 500 is .93. The market value of the portfolio on May 17, 1982, was $6,337,500. The number of September S&P 500 futures contracts that had to be sold to hedge this portfolio was 100.9618. The value of the futures contracts was therefore $5,971,891 (100.9618 × 118.30 × $500).

On August 9, 1982, the market value of the portfolio was $5,737,500, resulting in a loss in the cash market of $600,000. Since the futures price of the September S&P 500 declined to 102.60, the futures position could be closed out for $5,197,340 (100.9618 × 102.60 × $500), for a gain in the futures market of $792,550 ($5,737,500 − $5,197,340). The overall result of the hedge was a gain of $192,550. Considering the dollar value of the portfolio that was hedged, the short hedge performed well. The portfolio value increased by only +3 percent compared to a decline of 9.5 percent that would have occurred had the short hedge not been placed. Had a long hedge been placed, the hedged position would have produced a portfolio value 3 percent less than the market value at the time the hedge was placed. Once again, the transaction costs are trivial. These costs would not have exceeded $11,000 ($100 round-trip commission per contract). The results of the short hedge using the September S&P 500 futures contracts are summarized in Exhibit 12–13.

Exhibit 12–13

Short (Sell) Hedge of a Portfolio Using S&P 500 Futures Contracts

Situation

Own 10,000 shares of each of 19 issues of common stock with a portfolio value of $6,337,500 on May 17, 1982.
Want to hedge against a decline in the value of the portfolio when the portfolio is to be liquidated on August 9, 1982.

Facts

	May 17, 1982	*August 9, 1982*
Value of portfolio	$6,337,500	$5,737,500
Cash price for S&P 500 index	118.01	103.71
Futures price for S&P 500 index	118.30	102.60

Beta = 0.94
Coefficient of determination (R^2) = .860
Correlation coefficient = .93

Cash Market	*Futures Market*	*Basis**
May 17, 1982—time hedge is placed		
Market value of portfolio = $6,337,500	Sell 100.9618 September S&P 500 futures contracts† Value of short position = $5,971,891 (100.9618 × 118.30 × $500)	−0.29
August 9, 1982—time hedge is lifted		
Market value of portfolio = $5,737,500	Buy 100.9618 September S&P 500 futures contracts Cost to close out position = $5,179,340 (100.9618 × 102.60 × $500)	1.11
Loss in cash market = $600,000 Overall gain = $192,550	Gain in futures market = $792,550	

* Basis = Cash price − Futures price.
† The computation of the number of contracts is explained in the chapter.

An analysis of the outcome of the hedge would be insightful. Because of the change in the basis in favor of the short hedger, there was a gain in the futures market of $70,673 (100.9618 × 1.4 × $500). Based on a portfolio beta of 0.94, the market value of the portfolio should have declined by 11.39056 percent since the market declined by 12.11762 percent. Had the decline been 11.39056 percent, the market value of the portfolio on August 9, 1982, would have been $5,615,623. The predicted market value for the portfolio was less than its actual market value of $5,737,500 by $121,877. The reduced loss in the cash market by $121,877 and a gain of $70,673 in the futures market due to a favorable change in the basis produced an overall gain of $192,550 for the short hedge.

Exhibit 12–14 summarizes the results of a short hedge for the portfolio using the September NYSE futures contract.

Exhibit 12–14

Short (Sell) Hedge of a Portfolio Using NYSE Composite Index Futures Contracts

Situation

Own 10,000 shares of each of 19 issues of common stock with a portfolio value of $6,337,500 on May 17, 1982.
Want to hedge against a decline in the value of the portfolio when the portfolio is to be liquidated on August 9, 1982.

Facts

	May 17, 1982	*August 9, 1982*
Value of portfolio	$6,337,500	$5,737,500
Cash price for NYSE Composite Index	68.11	59.69
Futures price for NYSE Composite Index	68.30	58.65

Beta = 0.976
Coefficent of determination (R^2) = .88.
Correlation coefficient = .94.

Cash Market	*Futures Market*	*Basis*[*]
May 17, 1982—time hedge is placed		
Market value of portfolio = $6,337,500	Sell 181.6297 September NYSE Composite futures contracts[†] Value of short position = $6,202,654 (181.6297 × 68.30 × $500)	−0.19
August 9, 1982—time hedge is lifted		
Market value of portfolio = $5,737,500	Buy 181.6297 September NYSE composite futures contracts Cost to close out position = $5,326,291 (181.6297 × 58.65 × $500)	1.04
Loss in cash market = $600,000 Overall gain = $276,363	Gain in futures market = $876,363	

* Basis = Cash price − Futures price.
† The computation of the number of contracts is explained in the chapter.

Margin

As explained in Chapter 4, an investor who wants to employ stock index futures contracts for hedging must be prepared to meet the initial margin requirement and must make provisions to furnish variation margin.

Summary

Stock index futures can be employed to hedge against adverse stock price movements of an individual stock issue or a portfolio of common stocks. However, because hedging with stock index futures involves cross-hedging, a strong relationship must exist between the price movement of the stock or portfolio to be hedged and the market index that underlies the futures contract and a good estimate of that relationship must be made. The well-known beta of a stock or portfolio is used to indicate the relationship between its price movement and a market index. Beta is estimated using a statistical technique known as regression analysis. The strength of the relationship is measured by the correlation coefficient or the coefficient of determination. Since a diversified portfolio will have a higher correlation with a market index than will an individual stock issue, the likelihood of hedging successfully will be greater for a diversified portfolio than for an individual stock issue. In addition to depending on the relationship between the stock or portfolio and a market index, the success of a hedge will depend on how the basis changes between the time the hedge is placed and the time it is lifted.

CHAPTER 13

Creating an Index Fund

Frank J. Fabozzi, Ph.D., C.F.A.
Professor of Economics
Fordham University

T. Dessa Garlicki
Instructor
The College of Staten Island, CUNY

Index funds represent a passive equity approach to portfolio management. The manager of the portfolio does not attempt to identify under- or overvalued stock issues based on fundamental security analysis. Nor does he attempt to forecast general movements in the stock market and to structure the portfolio so as to take advantage of those movements. Instead, index funds are designed to track the total return performance of a visible market index of stocks. For the reasons explained in the next section of this chapter, the index fund approach to portfolio management has received a great deal of attention since the mid-1970s.

In this chapter we will demonstrate how under certain pricing conditions for the futures relative to the actual index, a portfolio manager can use stock index futures contracts and Treasury bills to create an index fund. An index fund so created will have lower transaction costs and can therefore be expected to outperform an actual index portfolio. Furthermore, if the futures are sufficiently underpriced, the index fund created by the futures and Treasury bills will outperform the target market index, including dividends.

Reasons for the Growth of Index Funds

The indexing approach to portfolio management found its beginning in studies of the efficiency of the equity market in the late 1960s and early

1970s. The first category of studies of market efficiency concerned whether investors could use historical price patterns to develop trading rules for earning consistent abnormal risk-adjusted rates of return. This is the so-called "weak form" of the efficient market hypothesis. All empirical studies found support for the hypothesis that the market is efficient in the weak form. The implication of these findings is that technical analysis, that is, analysis based on the belief that stock prices move in trends that persist, will·not be useful in enhancing investment performance.

A second class of empirical studies investigated whether stock prices fully discounted not only information about historical prices but also all other publicly available information, such as earnings and dividends. This is called the "semistrong" form of efficiency. The evidence of these studies on balance supports the view that the stock market is efficient in the semistrong form. The implication is that if the prices of securities embody all publicly available information, then fundamental security analysis will not enhance a portfolio's return.

The "strong form" of market efficiency contends that stock prices reflect all information, both public and private. A third class of empirical studies examined this form of market efficiency by looking at the performance of corporate insiders, stock exchange specialists, and professional money managers. The results were mixed. Corporate insiders and stock exchange specialists did outperform the market on a risk-adjusted basis. However, the performance of professional money managers supported the strong form of market efficiency. Since compared to the information available to corporate insiders and stock exchange specialists, the information available to professional money managers is more indicative of the information available to the average market participant, these studies furnished strong evidence for some observers that the market is efficient in the strong form.

At the outset many of the studies were dismissed as mere academic exercises. Yet no evidence was submitted by the investment community that provided financial services to counter these findings. Instead, highly respected market researchers found support for the academic findings. In 1975, for example, Charles D. Ellis, president of Greenwich Research Associates, estimated that over the preceding decade approximately 85 percent of professionally managed portfolios failed to perform as well as the Standard & Poor's 500. James R. Vertin, senior vice president of Wells Fargo Investment Advisors, an organization that established the first equity index portfolio in 1971, noted that

> Between 1968 and 1977, according to the Becker Securities Funds Evaluation Service, the S&P 500 Index portfolio ranked on average in the 37th percentile of annual equity portfolio investment returns. In terms of cumulative ranking over the 1968–77 period, the S&P 500 Index portfolio was in

the 17th percentile, which means that 83 percent of the managers surveyed failed to outperform the Index over this period.[1]

William S. Gray III, senior vice president of Harris Trust & Savings Bank, noted that "the median experience of actively managed equity portfolios has been well below (1 to 2 percent) the S&P 500 in most years during the 1970s and early 1980."[2]

If the findings of market efficiency are accepted, then the costs associated with active equity portfolio management may not enhance the return on a portfolio. These costs consist of the research costs associated with uncovering mispriced stocks, the transaction costs in buying and selling stocks to take advantage of mispricing, and the transaction costs associated with trying to time the market. Consequently, a passive approach to equity portfolio management may be more appropriate for the typical sponsor of a fund.

Further impetus to the use of index funds was provided by the passage of the Employee Retirement Income Security Act in 1974. John H. Langbein and Richard A. Posner reach the following conclusion concerning the use of index funds under investment trust Law:

> Courts may one day conclude that it is imprudent for trustees to fail to use such vehicles. Their advantages seem decisive: at any given risk/ return level, diversification is maximized and investment costs minimized. A trustee who declines to procure such advantages for the beneficiaries of his trust may in the future find his conduct difficult to justify.[3]

Growth of Index Funds

In the early 1970s three major index fund services were developed. Wells Fargo Investment Advisors, a division of Wells Fargo Bank in San Francisco, created the first equity index portfolio in June 1971. The fund was designed to track the performance of the New York Stock Exchange Composite Index on an equal-dollar-weighted basis. The fund was subsequently changed to track the Standard & Poor's 500 Composite Index. The other index fund services were created by American National Bank and Trust Company of Chicago and Batterymarch Financial Management Corporation of Boston. Both of these services use the S&P 500 as their target.

---

[1] James R. Vertin, "Passive Equity Management Strategies," in *The Investment Manager's Handbook,* ed. Sumner Levine (Homewood, Ill.: Dow Jones-Irwin, 1980), p. 286.

[2] William S. Gray III, "Portfolio Construction: Equity," in *Managing Investment Portfolios: A Dynamic Process,* ed. John L. Maginn and Donald L. Tuttle (New York: Warren, Gorham & Lamont, 1983), p. 402.

[3] John H. Langbein and Richard A. Posner, "Market Funds and Trust-Investment Law," *American Bar Foundation Research Journal,* 1975, p. 2.

According to a 1980 survey by *Pensions & Investment Age,* index fund assets were $9.6 billion as of May 1980 compared to $6.9 billion the year earlier.[4] These amounts probably substantially underestimated the assets actually indexed. This is because there were probably a great number of "closet" indexers whose assets were not reported in the survey. A closet indexer is a fund manager who does not state that he follows an indexing policy but whose portfolio, by accident or by design, performs similarly to some market index.[5] In recent years pension fund managers have been employing a combination of active and passive equity portfolio management. A core of the portfolio is indexed, and the noncore is actively managed. Although the pension and trust areas are the principal domains of index funds, there is a mutual fund—First Index Investment Trust— that is managed as an index fund. How many closet index investment companies there are is, of course, not known.

Problems Associated with Constructing an Index Fund

The index fund approach is only one form of passive portfolio management. The view that a portfolio designed to replicate the performance of the "market" is the best approach to passive portfolio management is supported by the work of Harry Markowitz in 1952 on the construction of optimal and efficient portfolios[6] and by capital market theory as developed by William F. Sharpe[7] and John Lintner.[8] The Sharpe-Lintner analysis demonstrated that a market portfolio offers the highest level of return per unit of risk in an efficient market. The theoretical market portfolio consists of all risky assets. Each risky asset is given a weight in the market portfolio equal to its percentage of the aggregate market value of all risky assets. That is, the market portfolio is a capitalization-weighted portfolio of all risky assets.

When applying the concept of an index fund to manage an equity portfolio, the manager of the fund cannot be totally passive. The first decision that he must make is to select the target market index. Most index funds are indexed to the S&P 500. Of course, this is not the "theoretical" market portfolio used in the development of capital market theory,

---

[4] Cathy Capozzoli, "Indexed Assets Up to $9 Billion as of May 1980," *Pensions & Investment Age,* July 7, 1980, p. 41.

[5] Nancy Belliveau, "The Pension Funds vs. The Closet Indexers," *Institutional Investor,* March 1978.

[6] Harry M. Markowitz, "Portfolio Selection," *Journal of Finance,* March 1952, pp. 77–91.

[7] William F. Sharpe, "Capital Asset Prices: A Theory of Market Equilibrium under Conditions of Risk," *Journal of Finance,* September 1964, pp. 425–42.

[8] John Lintner, "Security Prices, Risk, and Maximal Gains from Diversification," *Journal of Finance,* December 1965, pp. 587–616.

because it does not consist of all risky assets (common stock, bonds, real estate, etc.) or of all equity shares.

Once a target market index has been selected, the manager of the index fund must decide whether to replicate the target market index exactly (full-capitalization weighting approach) or to select only a sample of issues from the target market index (stratified sampling approach). Either approach will entail transaction costs associated with (1) the purchase of the shares held to construct the index, (2) the reinvestment of cash dividends, and (3) the adjustment of the portfolio if the composition of the issues in the target market index changes.[9] Although the full-capitalization approach will track the target index better, the transaction costs will be higher. Thus the fund manager must evaluate the costs and benefits of this approach. If the stratified sample approach is adopted, the cost of the initial construction of the index fund is reduced. However, transaction costs will be incurred to rebalance the index fund over time. These costs would not be incurred with the full-capitalization weighting approach.

The transaction costs plus management fees result in a divergence between the return on the target market index and that of the index fund. In the case of full-capitalization weighting, the return will be less than that of the index. Whether the return on the index will be greater than or less than that of the index fund constructed using the stratified sampling approach depends on whether the issues excluded underperform or outperform the issues included in the sample.

Constructing an Index Fund Using Stock Index Futures and Treasury Bills

If stock index futures contracts are priced according to their theoretical value, a portfolio consisting of a long position in stock index futures and Treasury bills will produce the same portfolio return as that of a portfolio of common stock constructed to replicate the underlying index. To see this, suppose that a fund manager who wishes to index his portfolio has $9 million in new money to invest and seeks to replicate the performance of the S&P 500. Also assume the following:

1. The S&P 500 is currently 150.
2. The S&P futures index with six months to settlement is currently selling for 156.

---

[9] For example, if the S&P 500 has been used as the target index in 1976, the fund manager would have had to restructure because of the dramatic change in the components of the index. Specifically, the industrial component of the S&P 500 was reduced from 425 issues to 400 issues, the utility component was reduced from 60 to 40 issues, and a finance component was introduced.

3. The expected dividend yield for the S&P 500 for the next 6 months is 2 percent.
4. Six-month Treasury bills are currently yielding 6 percent for six months.

Recall from Chapter 6 that the theoretical price for the futures contract is the current index value times the net carry adjustment. The net carry adjustment is essentially the difference between the Treasury bill yield and the expected dividend yield multiplied by the current value of the index. In our illustration the net carry adjustment is 4 percent (6 percent minus 2 percent) times 150, or 6. The theoretical price is then 156, which in our example is the current price for the S&P 500 futures contract.

The construction of the futures/T bill portfolio first requires the determination of the number of contracts to purchase. In terms of the underlying index, to purchase $9 million of equivalent equity if the current index is 150, 120 contracts must be purchased, since each contract is $500 times the value of the current index. Consequently, the two strategies that the index fund manager may select are:

Strategy 1:   Direct purchase of $9 million of equity in such a way as to replicate the performance of the S&P 500.

Strategy 2:   Buy 120 S&P 500 futures contracts with a settlement six months from now at 156 and buy $9 million of six-month Treasury Bills.[10]

We can now examine the portfolio value for each strategy under various scenarios for the price of the index when the contracts settle six months from now. Three scenarios will be investigated: the S&P 500 increases to 180, remains unchanged at 150, and declines to 126. At settlement the futures price converges to the value of the index. Exhibits 13–1 through 13–3 show the value of the portfolio for both strategies for each of the three scenarios. As can be seen, for a given scenario Strategy 1 (long position in the stock portfolio) and Strategy 2 will produce the same value for the portfolio.

There are several points that should be noted. First, in Strategy 1 the ability of the portfolio to replicate the S&P 500 depends on how well the portfolio is constructed. On the other hand, assuming that expected dividends are correct, the futures/T bill portfolio (Strategy 2) will mirror the performance of the S&P 500 exactly. Second, the cost of transacting is less for Strategy 2. For example, if the cost of one S&P contract is $50, then the transaction costs for Strategy 2 would be $6,000 (120 contracts times $50 per contract). This would be considerably less than the

---

[10] In this illustration, margin requirements are ignored. The T bills can be used for initial margin as explained in Chapter 4.

Exhibit 13-1

Comparison of Portfolio Value From Purchasing Stocks to
Replicate an Index and a Futures/T Bill Strategy when
There Is No Mispricing and Market Increases

Assumptions
1. Amount to be invested = $9 million
2. Current value of S&P 500 = 150
3. Value of the S&P 500 at settlement (six months later) = 180
4. Current value of S&P 500 futures contract = 156
5. Expected dividend yield = 2 percent
6. Yield on Treasury bills = 6 percent

Strategy 1: Direct Purchase of Stocks

Increase in value of index = 180/150 − 1 = 0.20

Market value of portfolio		
that mirrors the index	=	
1.20 × $9,000,000	= $10,800,000
Dividends	=	
.02 × $9,000,000	= $180,000
Value of portfolio	= $10,980,000
Dollar return	= $1,980,000

Strategy 2: Future/T Bill Portfolio

Number of S&P 500 contracts to be purchased = 120

Gain from sale of one contract	
Purchased for	156
Sold for	180
Gain per contract	24

Gain for 120 contracts	=	
120 × $500 × 24	= $1,440,000
Value of Treasury bills	=	
$9,000,000 × 1.06	= $9,540,000
Value of portfolio	= $10,980,000
Dollar return	= $1,980,000

transaction costs associated with the acquisition of a broadly diversified equity portfolio constructed to replicate the S&P 500. Finally, in the analysis of the performance of each strategy, the dollar value of the portfolio at the end of the six-month period is the amount in the absence of taxes. For Strategy 1, no taxes will be paid if the securities are not sold, though taxes will be paid on dividends. For Strategy 2, taxes must be paid on the interest from the Treasury bills and on any gain from the disposal of the futures contract.[11] Because of this complication, the use of the futures/T bill strategy would be more appropriate for funds not subject to taxation.

---

[11] Interest income is taxed as ordinary income. The tax treatment of futures contracts is discussed in Chapter 19.

Exhibit 13–2

Comparison of Portfolio Value from Purchasing Stocks to
Replicate an Index and a Futures/T Bill Strategy when
There Is No Mispricing and Market Does Not Change

Assumptions

1. Amount to be invested = $9 million
2. Current value of S&P 500 = 150
3. Value of the S&P 500 at settlement (six months later) = 150
4. Current value of S&P 500 futures contract = 156
5. Expected dividend yield = 2 percent
6. Yield on Treasury bills = 6 percent

Strategy 1: Direct Purchase of Stocks

Change in value of index = 150/150 − 1 = 0

Market value of portfolio that mirrors the index =	
1.00 × $9,000,000	= $9,000,000
Dividends =	
0.02 × $9,000,000	= $180,000
Value of portfolio	= $9,180,000
Dollar return	= $180,000

Strategy 2: Futures/T Bill Portfolio

Number of S&P 500 contracts to be purchased = 120

Loss from sale of one contract

Purchased for	156
Sold for	150
Loss per contract	6

Loss for 120 contracts =	
120 × $500 × 6	= ($360,000)
Value of Treasury bills =	
$9,000,000 × 1.06	= $9,540,000
Value of portfolio	= $9,180,000
Dollar return	= $180,000

Enhancing Returns When the Futures Contract Is Undervalued

The use of stock index futures and Treasury bills to construct an index fund that would reproduce the performance of the underlying index if the futures were priced according to their theoretical value was demonstrated above. However, when the futures price is less than the theoretical price, the index fund manager can enhance the portfolio return by buying the index and Treasury bills. That is, the return on the futures/T bill portfolio will be greater than that on the underlying index.

To see this, suppose that in our previous illustration the current futures price were 153 instead of 156; that is, the futures contract is undervalued.

Exhibit 13-3

Comparison of Portfolio Value from Purchasing Stocks to Replicate an Index and a Futures/T Bill Strategy when There Is No Mispricing and Market Declines

Assumptions

1. Amount to be invested = $9 million
2. Current value of S&P 500 = 150
3. Value of the S&P at settlement (six months later) = 126
4. Current value of S&P 500 futures contract = 156
5. Expected dividend yield = 2 percent
6. Yield on Treasury bills = 6 percent

Strategy 1: Direct Purchase of Stocks

Decrease in value of index = 126/150 − 1 = −0.16

Market value of portfolio		
that mirrors the index	=	
0.84 × $9,000,000	=	$7,560,000
Dividends	=	
0.02 × $9,000,000	=	$180,000
Value of portfolio	=	$7,740,000
Dollar return	=	($1,260,000)

Strategy 2: Futures/T Bill Portfolio

Number of S&P 500 contracts to be purchased = 120

Loss from sale of one contract	
Purchased for	156
Sold for	126
Loss per contract	30

Loss for 120 contracts	=	
120 × $500 × 30	=	($1,800,000)
Value of Treasury bills	=	
$9,000,000 × 1.06	=	$9,540,000
Value of portfolio	=	$7,740,000
Dollar return	=	($1,260,000)

Exhibit 13-4 shows the value of the portfolio from each strategy for each scenario. As can be seen, the value of the portfolio is $180,000 (or 200 basis points) greater by buying the futures contracts and Treasury Bills.[12]

Several market observers have found that there have been periods in which the futures contract has been underpriced. In one study, for example, the authors found that on October 1, 1982, the December 1982 S&P futures contract was undervalued by nearly 1.75 percentage points. If new funds had been invested in a portfolio constructed with a long posi-

---

[12] The gain on each contract will be $1,500 greater (3 times $500) for each scenario. Since there are 120 contracts, the gain will be $180,000 greater. When there is a loss as a result of the decline in the index value at settlement, the loss is $1,500 less per contract, or $180,000 for 120 contracts.

Exhibit 13–4

Enhancement of Portfolio Return for a Futures/T Bill Portfolio when Futures Contract Is Underpriced

Assumptions
1. Amount to be invested = $9 million
2. Current value of S&P 500 = 150
3. Current value of S&P 500 futures contract = 153
4. Expected dividend yield = 2 percent
5. Yield on Treasury bills = 6 percent
6. Theoretical price of futures contract = 156

If value of index at settlement is 180

Value of portfolio for Strategy 1 (direct purchase of stocks)
(from Exhibit 13–1) = $10,980,000

Value of portfolio for Strategy 2 (futures/T bill portfolio)
Gain per contract = 180 − 153 = 27

Gain for 120 contracts = 120 × $500 × 27	$ 1,620,000
Value of Treasury bills	9,540,000
Value of portfolio	$11,160,000

If value of index at settlement is 150

Value of portfolio for Strategy 1 (direct purchase of stocks)
(from Exhibit 13–2) = $9,180,000

Value of portfolio for Strategy 2 (futures/T bill portfolio)
Loss per contract = 150 − 153 = 3

Loss for 120 contracts = 120 × $500 × 3	$ (180,000)
Value of Treasury bills	9,540,000
Value of portfolio	$9,360,000

If value of index at settlement is 126

Value of portfolio for Strategy 1 (direct purchase of stocks)
(from Exhibit 13–3) = $7,740,000

Value of portfolio for Strategy 2 (futures/T bill portfolio)
Loss per contract = 126 − 153 = 27

Loss for 120 contracts = 120 × $500 × 27	$(1,620,000)
Value of Treasury bills	9,540,000
Value of portfolio	$7,920,000

tion in the contract and Treasury bills, the investor could have outperformed the S&P 500 by 1.75 percentage points for the period October 1, 1982, to December 16, 1982 (the settlement date of the December contract).[13]

---

[13] Nicholas Hanson (with Louis L. Margolis), *Futures Contracts on Stock Indexes—The First Year* (New York: Salomon Brother, Inc., May 11, 1983), p. 5. For an excellent discussion of why the difference in tax treatment of futures contracts and equities may cause underpricing of the former, see Jonathan C. Jankus, *Stock Index Futures—Research Focus: Tax-Free Institutional Investors* (New York: Kidder, Peabody & Co., May 13, 1983), pp. 6–10.

Index Swaps

Thus far we have illustrated how a strategy consisting of stock index futures and Treasury bills can be used to construct a portfolio *from additional cash contributions* to mirror the market or outperform the market when the futures price is undervalued. Suppose instead that an index fund manager has a portfolio of $200 million. If a futures contract is underpriced, the fund manager may be able to enhance returns by liquidating the existing portfolio and buying futures and Treasury bills. That is, the fund manager could "swap" an index fund for a long position in the underlying futures contract and Treasury bills. Once the futures contract becomes overpriced by a sufficient amount, the fund manager could swap out of the futures/T bill portfolio and back into a stock portfolio designed to replicate the index.

Whether an index swap strategy will enhance the portfolio return depends on the degree of mispricing and the transaction costs associated with (1) liquidating an existing portfolio, (2) buying it back if the contract becomes overpriced, and (3) acquiring a long position in the stock index futures. These transaction costs coupled with the costs associated with monitoring and executing an index swap must be assessed before the swap is undertaken. As noted earlier in this chapter, the construction of a portfolio of equities to create an index fund also has transaction and monitoring costs. Therefore, it is imperative to examine portfolio returns under either strategy for indexing after all associated costs are considered.[14]

Summary

Index funds have gained in popularity in recent years. Although the construction of an index fund is simple in principle, a good deal of judgment on the part of the fund manager is required to design a portfolio that will track the target index. Stock index futures provide a fund manager with a less costly alternative strategy for constructing a portfolio to mirror the performance of the index when the price of the futures contract is equal to its theoretical price. When the futures contract is underpriced, a futures/T bill portfolio will outperform the underlying index. Under certain circumstances, index swaps may enhance portfolio returns.

---

[14] As discussed earlier, one study suggested that on October 1, 1982, the December S&P 500 futures contract was underpriced by 1.75 percentage points. On October 31, the futures contract became overpriced. By swapping out of the futures/T bill portfolio and into the long equity position on October 31, an investor could have earned a return over the one-month period that would have outperformed the S&P 500 by 3 percentage points (300 basis points) after transaction costs. (See Hanson, *Futures Contracts on Stock Indexes*, p. 5.)

CHAPTER 14

Active Portfolio Management

Stanley J. Kon, Ph.D.
Associate Professor of Finance
Graduate School of Business Administration
University of Michigan

The recent availability of stock index futures contracts has provided portfolio managers and individual investors with a unique set of investment opportunities that were nonexistent prior to the new contract. These opportunities will allow investment managers to obtain the maximum benefits from their special skills and enhance the risk-adjusted return to their clients.

It is well recognized that the return on a common stock investment can be attributed to both firm-specific and market-wide events. The inherent advantage of using stock index futures contracts in portfolio management lies in the fact that such contracts make it possible to unbundle and manage these two sources of return on investment separately. Without stock index futures contracts a manager might pass over an incremental investment in a new security because its contribution to the stock selection performance of the fund may be contrary to its contribution to the market timing performance of the fund. For example, an investment in a high–market risk stock that the manager believes to be undervalued due to a new technological discovery or the introduction of superior management skills might be passed over because of a bear market forecast and the unfavorable high-beta characteristic of the stock.[1] With a position in stock index futures contracts the manager can have his cake and eat it

---

[1] Beta measures the sensitivity of a security's return relative to the market.

too. That is, he can purchase the undervalued stock to achieve positive stock selectivity performance and simultaneously sell the index futures contract to hedge away the effect of general market movements. If he is very confident that the general market will move downward, he can sell more contracts than are required to eliminate market risk and thus make a profit if the market declines. All of this can be done at a trivial commission cost. Consequently, managers can no longer blame general market movements for their lack of success in selecting undervalued securities, since bearing market risk is no longer a prerequisite to bearing and profiting from the management of firm-specific risk.

In order to analyze the contribution that positions in stock index futures contracts can make to the performance of a managed portfolio, we begin in the next section by introducing the principles of both stock selectivity and market timing performance. The balance of the chapter discusses the risk-return properties of using index futures relative to a specific common stock portfolio and presents the solution to the optimal futures position for a managed pension portfolio of undervalued stocks.

Performance Measurement

The investment management process can be dichotomized into the activities of stock selection and market timing. Stock selection is based on forecasts of company-specific events, and hence the prices of individual securities. Market timing, however, refers to forecasts of future realizations of the market (index) portfolio. If an investment manager believes he can make better than average forecasts of market portfolio returns, he will adjust his portfolio risk level in anticipation of market movements. If the manager can also make better than average predictions of firm-specific events for a group of stocks, then this portfolio will be levered up in anticipation of a bull market and down in anticipation of a bear market. If successful, he will earn abnormal returns relative to an appropriate benchmark for each activity.

Consider an investment manager of a $100 million stock portfolio that he believes is undervalued by $5 million and that he believes the marketplace will revalue within one year. Assuming that prices are determined by the Sharpe-Lintner capital asset pricing model,[2] then:

$$E(R) = r + \beta[E(R_M) - r] \qquad (14\text{–}1)$$

---

[2] William F. Sharpe, "Capital Asset Prices: A Theory of Market Equilibrium under Conditions at Risk," *Journal of Finance,* September 1964, pp. 425–42; and John Lintner, "The Valuation of Risk Assets and the Selection of Risky Investments in Stock Portfolios and Capital Budgets," *Review of Economics and Statistics,* February 1965, pp. 13–37.

That is, the expected rate of return on any security or portfolio, $E(R)$, is equal to the riskless rate, r, plus a risk premium that depends on its level of systematic risk, β, and the excess return on the market portfolio, $[E(R_M) - r]$.

Equation (14–1) is known as the ex ante security market line (SML) and is illustrated in Exhibit 14–1 as the ray rA. Risk-averse investors will set prices today such that the greater the systematic (nondiversifiable) risk of an asset, the greater the expected return must be to compensate them. For example, if the current rate on one-year treasury issues is 0.1 (10 percent) and the expected return on the market portfolio is 0.2, then the expected return on a portfolio with a β of 0.8 is 0.18 [= 0.1 + 0.8 (0.2 − 0.1)]. This is point P in Exhibit 14–1.

A model that describes the actual or ex post returns on securities or portfolios, R, over the next year is:

$$R = r + \beta(R_M - r) + \epsilon \qquad (14\text{–}2)$$

One difference between Equations (14–1) and (14–2) is the replacement of the expected return on the market portfolio, $E(R_M)$, with what actually occurred, R_M. This determines the effect on a security's return from market-wide events, and the magnitude depends on the security's sensitivity to these events. The measure of this sensitivity is its level of systematic risk, or beta (β). Therefore, $R = r + \beta(R_M - r)$ represents the ex post security market line. Ray rU in Exhibit 14–1 is an example of a bull market outcome of 0.3, in which all stocks will do better than expected just due to the general market movement.

It is this ex post return on the market portfolio that market timers are forecasting and betting on. A shift to a higher level of sensitivity to market outcomes will magnify the portfolio's return in a bull market. For example, it would be preferable to have selected portfolio G with a $\beta = 1.2$ rather than P in a bull market, since the ex post return at G' of 0.34 [= 0.1 + 1.2(0.3 − 0.1)] is considerably greater than the 0.26 = [0.1 + 0.8(0.3 − 0.1)] at P'. The difference of 0.08 (= 0.34 − 0.26) has two components: compensation for the incremental risk increase from 0.8 to 1.2 and the timing performance gain for correctly predicting the bull market. The change in expected return for an additional 0.4 of systematic risk can be calculated with the risk premium term in Equation (1), $\beta(E(R_M) - r)$. Therefore, one expects 0.04 [= 0.4 (0.2 − 0.1)] as compensation for bearing the additional 0.4 of systematic risk. The gain for a correct market forecast will depend on the size of the market turn and the magnitude of the change in the risk level. The market timing performance resulting from the decision to depart from the assumed target risk level of 0.8 must be measured relative to the gain or loss that would have occurred had the manager decided to remain at the target level (passive or no timing decision). Hence the net gain is that from point G

Exhibit 14–1

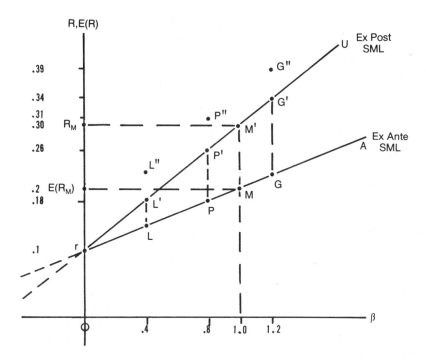

to G' (for having selected a portfolio risk level of 1.2 during a bull market of 0.3) less the gain from point P to P' that would have occurred anyway had the manager maintained the target risk level of the fund. Therefore, the market timing performance is measured by the distance $G'G = 0.12$ ($= 0.34 - 0.22$) less the distance $P'P = 0.08$ ($= 0.26 - 0.18$). The difference of 0.04 ($= 0.12 - 0.08$) represents the gain for this correct market timing decision. The *market timing performance* component can be generalized to the following equation.[3]

$$\tau = [(\beta_A - \beta_T)(R_M - E(R_M))]$$

Note that the timing performance measure does depend on the magnitude of the risk-level change from the target level, β_T, to the actual risk level selected, β_A. The target risk-level value depends on the stated objectives

[3] See Eugene F. Fama, "Components of Investment Performance," *Journal of Finance,* May 1972, pp. 551–67; Stanley J. Kon and Frank C. Jen, "The Investment Performance of Mutual Funds: An Empirical Investigation of Timing, Selectivity, and Market Efficiency," *Journal of Business,* April 1979, pp. 263–89; Stephen Figlewski and Stanley J. Kon, "Portfolio Management with Stock Index Futures," *Financial Analysts Journal,* January–February 1982, pp. 52–60; and Stanley J. Kon, "The Market Timing Performance of Mutual Fund Managers," *Journal of Business,* July 1983, pp. 323–47.

of the managed portfolio. The actual risk level selected will deviate from the target level based on the magnitude of the bull or bear market prediction, the degree of confidence in the prediction (forecast error), and the risk-return trade-off that the fund is willing to assume based on its stated objectives.[4] The size of the market turn is also included in this timing measure by the deviation of the actual return on the market portfolio, R_M, from its expected level, $E(R_M)$. In the numerical example τ is again equal to 0.04 [= $(1.2 - 0.8)(0.3 - 0.2)$].

Furthermore, note that Equation (14–3), the timing performance equation, is symmetric. That is, if the manager was predicting a bear market and moved the risk level of the fund to 0.4 during a bull market return of 0.3, then $\beta_A - \beta_T = 0.4 - 0.8 = -0.4$ and the performance would be -0.04. This is the distance of $L'L$ minus the distance $P'P$ in Exhibit 14–1. Therefore, penalties for inferior market timing performance will also be assessed. This measure captures the manager's ability to predict bear markets as well. In Exhibit 14–2 ray rA is the same ex ante security market line as in Exhibit 14–1 and ray rD in the ex post security market line for a bear market of $R_M = -0.2$. The performance measure for having predicted a bull market and selected a high risk level of 1.2 in a bear market is -0.16 [= $(1.2 - 0.8)(-0.2 - 0.2)$]. This is the negative distance $G'G$ minus the smaller negative distance $P'P$ in Exhibit 14–2. If the manager had correctly predicted a bear market and lowered the portfolio risk level to a beta of 0.4, the performance would be a positive 0.16 [= $(0.4 - 0.8)(-0.2 - 0.2)$]. This is the negative distance $L'L$ less the larger negative distance $P'P$ in Exhibit 14–2.

The last term in Equation (14–2), ϵ, represents the effect on a security's return due to firm-specific events that will occur over the next year. This is the variable that is being forecast in the stock selectivity activity. Today the consensus of investors is that the value of ϵ will be zero for all stocks. Our hypothetical investment manager, however, *expects* his portfolio of undervalued stocks with a β of 0.8 to have an ϵ of 0.05 ($5 million/$100 million). If he has no special information concerning general market movements and the target risk level of the fund is also 0.8, then if he is exactly right about the firm-specific events and there is a bull market ($R_M = 0.3$), the total return on the portfolio will be 0.31. This is represented by point P'' in Exhibit 14–1. The 0.31 return is made up of a 0.26 return associated with the bull market outcome and the systematic risk level of the portfolio and a 0.05 return from the previous selection of undervalued securities. It is this 0.05 return that is known as the "Jensen

[4] See Michael C. Jensen, "Optimal Utilization of Market Forecasts and the Evaluation of Investment Performance," in *Mathematical Methods in Investment and Finance*, ed. G. P. Szego and K. Shell (Amsterdam: North-Holland, 1972); and Kon and Jen, "Investment Performance of Mutual Funds."

Exhibit 14–2

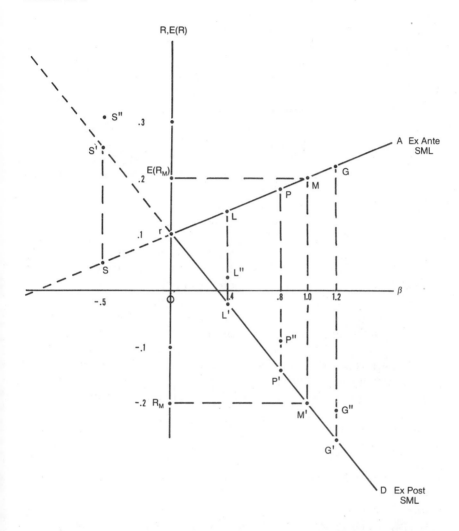

measure" of superior selectivity performance.[5] Since the final decision was to select a portfolio risk level equal to the target level, the market timing performance was zero, as indicated by Equation (3) and the definition of a passive timing policy.

Now we can examine some of the conflicts of interest that can arise when investment managers participate in timing and selectivity activities simultaneously. In our continuing example, if the manager still believes

[5] Michael C. Jensen, "The Performance of Mutual Funds in the Period 1945–1964," *Journal of Finance*, May 1968, pp. 389–416.

that the portfolio of stocks with a beta of 0.8 is undervalued by a 0.05 return and that there will be a bull market, then financial *theory* tells us to lever up that stock portfolio by borrowing at the riskless rate and investing the proceeds and initial wealth in the undervalued portfolio until the risk level reaches a beta of 1.2. In general, however, regulated funds are restricted from borrowing for speculation, so that in practice a manager must sell low-risk securities and buy high-risk securities to achieve the high-beta position. First, this more realistic alternative requires large transaction costs and presents possible liquidity problems for large positions in some stocks. Second, no manager wants to sell undervalued stocks and purchase correctly priced stocks. A manager will engage in this trade-off only if the perceived benefits of the timing activity exceed those of the selectivity activity.

But why give up either, since it will be shown that the purchase of stock index futures can be used as a perfect substitute for levering up the undervalued stock portfolio with a beta of 0.8 to a beta of 1.2 at trivial commission charges. Therefore, correct stock selectivity and bull market forecasts will yield a total return of 0.39. The result is represented by point G'' in Exhibit 14–1. This point is obtained by levering portfolio P to point G with index futures contracts and obtaining a market timing performance of 0.04 from the bull market outcome at G' (return of 0.34) and a 0.05 selectivity performance from the revaluation of securities in the portfolio to reach G''. Then a total (timing plus selectivity) investment performance of an incremental 9 percent can be achieved without sacrificing one activity for another.

Similar conflicts of interest can be resolved with the index futures contract even when fund managers are being passive with respect to market timing. For example, stock index futures can be used if the research analysts are currently finding that most of the undervalued securities are low-beta stocks such that an optimal portfolio of these stocks would have a beta of 0.4, whereas the stated objectives of the fund are more consistent with a portfolio having a beta of 0.8. In the absence of special information about general market movements, it is the obligation of the investment manager to select a portfolio with a constraint that the beta be equal to the target level. This is crucial to fund clients who have other wealth invested elsewhere and are making an optimal personal account portfolio decision based on the manager's adherence to stated objectives concerning risk. Rather than forgo selectivity profits by selling some low-beta undervalued stocks and buying high-beta correctly priced stocks to achieve a portfolio beta of 0.8, the manager can buy stock index futures contracts to lever up the undervalued stocks and maintain the gains to selectivity performance. In Exhibit 14–1 this is illustrated by levering portfolio L to obtain point P. If the manager is correct about the individual security events, in a bull market point P'' will result.

Another interesting portfolio strategy that is not readily attainable without index futures contracts involves taking maximum advantage of bear market forecasts. In principle, a bear market forecast is usually implemented by selling high-beta stocks and purchasing low-beta stocks. As noted before, this may involve giving up positive selectivity performance. But more interestingly, the strategy is limited by the lack of negative beta stocks available and is only considered a loss-minimizing strategy. This is illustrated by the rule of thumb of selling stocks and buying Treasury securities with a zero beta in anticipation of a bear stock market. This is equivalent to selecting point r in Exhibit 14–2 and giving up any expected positive selectivity performance. However, being able to construct portfolio S with a beta of -0.5 will result in an outcome of S' in a bear market, and if this can be done by selling index futures and holding undervalued portfolio P, then the final outcome of the strategy will be point S'', with the selectivity performance of 0.05 still intact. The additional market timing performance will be 0.52 [$= (-0.5 - 0.8)(-0.2 - 0.2)$] for a bear market of -0.2. This is a total investment performance of 57 percent *above* the performance required to compensate investors for risk bearing.

Portfolio Opportunities with Stock Index Futures

In an article by Figlewski and Kon the pricing and risk-return properties of the index futures contract are analyzed by considering a portfolio of cash holdings of an index fund and enough sales of the index futures contracts to eliminate all risk.[6] A riskless portfolio must earn the rate of return that exists for other risk-free assets, such as Treasury bills. Otherwise, arbitrageurs will step in and engage in a strategy to earn riskless returns above the riskless rate. This will bid the prices in the cash and futures markets to values at which there are no further arbitrage opportunities. At this point the pricing relations will hold.

An investor holding the index portfolio can lock in a future value by *selling* stock index futures and *transferring* the full risk of fluctuations in the market to the buyer, who requires compensation for risk bearing. It is clear from the security market line in Exhibit 14–1 and Equation (14–1) that for the market index with a $\beta_M = 1.0$, the risk premium required is $E(R_M) - r$. Therefore, given a specific stock portfolio, the change in expected portfolio return for an incremental long position in the index future is:

$$E(R_F) = E(R_M) - r \tag{14–4}$$

[6] Stephen Figlewski and Stanley J. Kon, "Portfolio Management with Stock Index Futures."

For example, if an investment manager is currently holding portfolio P in Exhibit 14–1 on the security market line and is forecasting a bull market, he can attain point G without selling any of his undervalued stocks by buying index futures contracts. If the manager is forecasting a bear market, point S in Exhibit 14–2 can be attained by selling enough index futures contracts. Since the risk premium on the index futures return is the same as the slope of the security market line, all points on the line are obtainable with positions in the index futures from any cash market position. Furthermore, since all fluctuations in the index are being transferred from the seller to the buyer of the index futures contract, the variance of the index futures' return (σ_F^2) is the same as that of the market (σ_M^2),

$$\sigma_F^2 = \sigma_M^2; \qquad (14\text{–}5)$$

the beta of the index futures return (β_F) is the same as the cash market index return (β_M),

$$\beta_F = \beta_M = 1.0; \qquad (14\text{–}6)$$

and the covariance of the return on any stock portfolio J (R_J) with the index futures' return (R_F) is the same as that with the index itself,

$$Cov(R_J, R_M) = Cov(R_J, R_F) \qquad (14\text{–}7)$$

Since there is no initial investment in an index futures contract, the rate of return on a futures position can only be measured relative to the cash value of a specific stock portfolio.[7] A convenient standardization is to measure the stock portfolio value and the position in the index futures market in index units based on the current value of the index. Therefore, define N_J as the number of index units in the given stock portfolio J. This is the current market value of portfolio J divided by the current value of the index. Define N_F as the number of index units sold short in the index futures market. N_F will be negative for long positions in the index futures market. Then,

$$h = N_F / N_J \qquad (14\text{–}8)$$

is the hedge ratio, which can be varied to obtain an entire set of portfolio risk-return combinations with the following characteristics.

The portfolio consisting of stock portfolio J and hedge position h in the index future has an expected return of

$$E(R) = E(R_J) - hE(R_F), \qquad (14\text{–}9)$$

---

[7] For index futures the margin requirement is essentially a modest collateral requirement that can be satisfied with a portion of the portfolio's existing assets (e.g., with Treasury bills). Since there is no reduction in the return from the collateral asset, the margin requirement for index futures does not represent any additional cash outlay.

variance of return of

$$\sigma^2 = \sigma_J^2 + h^2\sigma_F^2 - 2hCov(R_J,\ R_F)$$
$$= \sigma_J^2 + h^2\sigma_M^2 - 2hCov(R_J,\ R_M), \qquad (14\text{--}10)$$

and portfolio systematic risk of

$$\beta = \beta_J - h\beta_F$$
$$= \beta_J - h \qquad (14\text{--}11)$$

Now we can see how the choice of hedge ratio affects the β of the portfolio of stocks and index futures. If h is selected to equal β_J, then the portfolio $\beta = 0$ and all market risk is hedged away and only nonmarket (diversifiable) risk remains. Recall that ex post returns can be described by the equation

$$R = r + \beta(R_M - r) + \epsilon \qquad (14\text{--}2)$$

Hence a portfolio with $\beta = 0$ will have returns equal to the riskless rate plus deviations due solely to firm-specific events. Therefore, an investor who believes that a mutual fund contains a positive $E(\epsilon)$, but does not want to incur the fund's level of systematic risk, can hedge the market risk away by selecting a hedge ratio equal to the beta of the fund and keep the expected positive selectivity performance. The variance of the return process in Equation (14–2) is

$$\sigma^2 = \beta^2\ \sigma_M^2 + \sigma_\epsilon^2 \qquad (14\text{--}12)$$

so that only the last term associated with firm-specific risk is left when all market risk is hedged away ($\beta = 0$). The important result here is that market risk can be controlled *independently* of the firm-specific return and risk. If the manager in our earlier example, with stock portfolio P in Exhibit 14–1 with a beta of 0.8, wants to lever up to a β of 1.2 in anticipation of a bull market and keep his undervalued stocks, he can do so by purchasing enough futures contracts to make $h = -0.4$. From Equation (14–8), the number of index units in the futures market to be purchased would be $N_F = hN_J = (-0.4)(\$100\ \text{million}/165) = \$242{,}424.2424$, where 165 is the current value of the S&P 500 index. This means that if the futures price delivery of an index unit in one year is 170, then the manager wants to purchase ($\$242{,}424.2424)(170) = \$41{,}212{,}121.21$ worth. Since futures contracts in the S&P 500 index sell for 500 times the futures price, this requires a purchase of $\$41{,}212{,}121.21/(\$500 \times 170) = 484.85$, or approximately 485 contracts. Then, from Equation (14–11) the final portfolio will have a $\beta = 0.8 - (-0.4) = 1.2$.

If the investment manager is predicting a bear market and wants to create a final portfolio with a beta of -0.5, as in point S of Exhibit 14–2, while preserving the firm-specific ϵ, he can sell enough index futures contracts to make the hedge ratio equal to 1.3. Then, from Equation (14–11) the market risk exposure will be $\beta = -0.5 = 0.8 - 1.3$. The number of index units in the futures market to be sold to achieve a portfolio β of -0.5 is $N_F = hN_J = 1.3(\$100 \text{ million}/165) = \$787,878.78$. This is implemented by selling $N_F/500$, which is approximately 1,576 index futures contracts.

Optimal Index Futures Position for a Pension or Trust Fund

In the previous sections of this chapter we have discussed performance measurement and optimal index futures positions when the relevant measure of portfolio risk is the systematic, or beta, risk of the managed portfolio. This is appropriate for the many cases in which the investors in the fund only allocate a relatively small proportion of their wealth to the managed fund. If these investors are well diversified on personal account, then the beta concept of relative contribution to the variance of total portfolio returns is a reasonable approximation. This is frequently the case for mutual fund shareholders. However, in many cases an individual's entire wealth is being managed by one investment adviser. Pension funds, trusts for widows and orphans, and personal investors are some possible examples. Then variance or standard deviation of portfolio returns is the relevant measure of risk.

This problem has been explored by Figlewski and Kon and will be elaborated on here.[8] The ray rA in Exhibit 14–3 is the capital market line (CML), which represents all efficient portfolio opportunities as perceived by the consensus of all investors. The consensus views portfolio P as inefficient, with an expected value of returns to firm-specific events of zero. However, our superior skilled investment manager believes that this portfolio is undervalued and has an expected return on firm-specific events of 10 percent. He has considerable confidence in his prediction, so that his assessment of the firm-specific standard deviation is about one half that of the consensus. Hence the manager's view of the risk-return dimensions of this portfolio is represented by P' in Exhibit 14–3. In the absence of an index futures market, the manager would select a point on ray rB that is consistent with the investors' risk preferences. For example, portfolio R' is preferred to the passive strategy denoted by R at the same level of target risk, σ_R.

Now we can introduce the opportunities that would be available by making the index futures contract available. The curve GH represents the portfolio opportunities of combining stock portfolio P' and the index futures contract. This curve is defined by Equations (14–9) and (14–10)

---

[8] Stephen Figlewski and Stanley J. Kon, "Portfolio Management with Stock Index Futures."

Exhibit 14-3

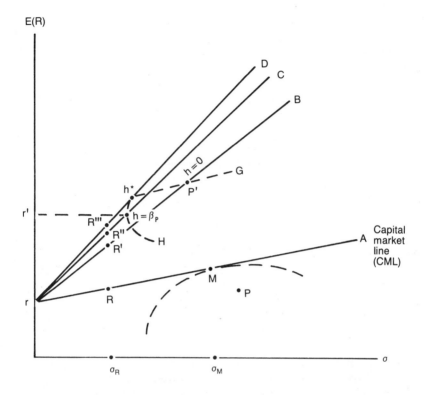

for various choices of the hedge ratio h where the parameters described by portfolio J are replaced by the manager's assessment of P'. At point P' $h = 0$ with no position in the index futures contract. At the point where $h = \beta_P = \beta_{P'}$, all market risk is hedged away and the expected return to that strategy, r', is equal to the riskless rate plus the return that the fund manager expects on firm-specific events. That is, the distance r to r' represents $E(\epsilon)$, the Jensen measure of expected selectivity performance, discussed earlier. Then points along ray rC are obtainable by combinations of the riskless asset, portfolio P', and a position in the index futures market to hedge away all the market risk in P'. Clearly, these opportunities dominate those along ray rB without a position in the index futures contract. This is illustrated by R'' with its dominance of more return than R' at the same level of target risk. However, the most efficient set of opportunities requires the solution to an optimal hedge ratio h^* on the positively sloped segment of the opportunity set offered by P' and positions in the index future. This dominant efficient set as perceived by the fund manager is ray rD. Combinations of the riskless asset, stock portfolio P', and hedge position h^* in the futures contract can be used to construct any portfolio along ray rD, including the preferred risk position in which R''' dominates all others at the target risk level.

If there are restrictions on borrowing at the riskless rate and investing the proceeds in portfolio P', then the perceived efficient frontier becomes the portfolio opportunities along $rh^*P'G$. Portfolios along the segment from r to h^* involve the optimal hedge position in the futures market with portfolio P' and lending at the riskless rate. Portfolios along the curve from h^* to G involve combinations of portfolio P' and a hedge position in the index futures contract with h less than h^*.

The optimal h^* is obtained by selecting the value of h that maximizes the "Sharpe measure" of investment performance.[9] That is,

$$\text{Max } \theta = [E(R) - r]/\sigma$$
$$= \frac{[E(R_{P'}) - hE(R_F) - r]}{[\sigma_{P'}^2 + h^2\sigma_F^2 - 2hCov(R_P, R_F)]^{1/2}} \qquad (14\text{-}13)$$

By taking the derivative of θ with respect to h and setting it equal to zero, we have the optimality condition. Then solving for h yields

$$h^* = \beta_P - [\sigma_\epsilon^2/E(\epsilon)][(E(R_M) - r)/\sigma_M^2] \qquad (14\text{-}14)$$

Note that as the manager's assessment of selectivity performance, $E(\epsilon)$, increases, h^* increases toward the fully hedged against the market position, $h = \beta_P$. This occurs because the curve HG moves up the graph. When the manager is more confident about his forecast, σ_ϵ decreases and the curve moves to the left, so that the optimal solution h^* also moves toward $h = \beta_P$. If the manager is less confident about his forecast or if he perceives less selectivity performance, then h^* will decrease toward G. Note that Equation (14-14) is only appropriate for positive values of expected selectivity performance. The optimal portfolio decision in the absence of special information concerning individual stock prices is along the capital market line (i.e., portfolio R).

---

[9] William F. Sharpe, "Mutual Fund Performance," *Journal of Business*, Supplement, January 1966, pp. 119–38.

Chapter 15

Speculating

Ira G. Kawaller, Ph.D.
Director
New York Office, Chicago Mercantile Exchange

The most straightforward application for stock index futures is speculation. Ultimately, this use boils down to placing the proper bet on the direction of the market. In other words, it's the old "buy low, sell high." In spite of the simplicity of the strategy, a high degree of sophistication may be employed. It is the purpose of this chapter to identify a number of valuation practices—both quantitative and subjective—to help in the speculative trading strategy.

The first step in designing a speculative strategy is understanding the instruments. Chapter 3 presented the specifications of the stock index futures contracts currently being traded. Chapter 5 described the respective underlying indexes. Here this background information is assumed. The organization of this chapter is as follows. First, we will examine the trading history of the Standard & Poor's 500 Composite Index, the New York Stock Exchange Composite Index, and the Value Line Average Composite. That history and other structural conditions have a bearing on the choice of a contract for speculative purposes. Second, we will identify and evaluate several basic speculative strategies. The chapter concludes with a summary and some cautionary remarks concerning speculative activities.

Factors Bearing on the Choice of a Contract for Speculative Purposes

Trading History

Despite the conceptual and practical differences among the underlying stock indexes, a historical view of the price performance of these indexes shows no *consistent* bias in the way the three comprehensive indexes— NYSE, S&P 500, and Value Line—perform. Virtually no general rule can be made as to which of the underlying indexes will exhibit the greatest move at a particular time—in either bull or bear markets. This conclusion is supported by Exhibits 15–1 and 15–2.

For Exhibit 15–1, quarter-end data are used for the period 1971 through 1982. Each of the three indexes is reindexed, with March 31, 1971, set equal to 1.00. Shown on the chart are the plots of the natural logs of the rebased indexes. When the plotting is done in natural logarithm form,

Exhibit 15–1

Stock Market Indexes, Natural Logarithm End-of-Quarter Close*

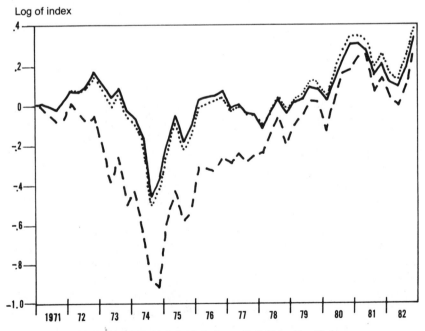

Note: Standard & Poor's (line), New York Stock Exchange (dot), Value Line (dash).

* Reindexed: March 31, 1971 = 100.

Exhibit 15–2

Stock Market Indexes, Percent change, daily close

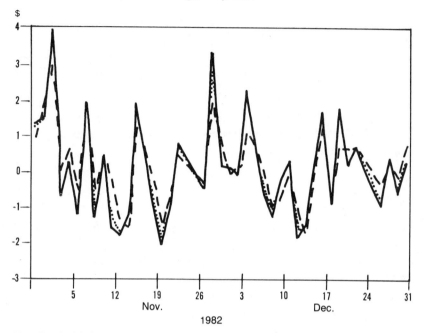

Note: Standard & Poor's (line), New York Stock Exchange (dot), Value Line (dash).

the slopes of the lines reflect the respective rates of growth of the three underlying indexes. The steeper the slope, the faster the rate of change of the underlying index, and vice versa.

Two conclusions stand out. First, the S&P index and the NYSE index performed in very similar fashions, while the Value Line index showed numerous periods of contrary movement. Second, and more subtle, the behavior of the Value Line index relative to that of the other two indexes is inconsistent. Look, for example, at the periods in which both the S&P index and the NYSE index declined (1973–74, 1977, and 1980–82). In the first decline, the Value Line index dropped most steeply; in the second, the Value Line actually rose; and in the third, all three indexes experienced comparable declines. The reasons for the difference between the price performance of the Value Line index and that of the other two indexes are discussed in Chapter 5.

Shifting the focus to the short run, Exhibit 15–2 shows daily percentage changes for each of the three comprehensive (unadjusted) indexes. On a daily basis, hardly any difference in the performance of the indices is noticeable for the period July–December 1982. They all behaved similarly. The point is that with any single speculative effort, none of the underlying indexes can be counted upon with certainty to have the largest percentage change in its value. Sometimes the largest change will occur for one index, sometimes for another. Put differently, from the price history it appears that any of the three indexes can be used for speculative purposes, and one cannot tell before the event which of the indexes will move the most for any given market change.

If price performance does not seem to be a helpful differentiating factor for deciding which contract should be traded, how should the decision be made? Two factors are suggested below relating to liquidity and margin requirements and their impact on leverage.

Liquidity

To compare liquidity for the three contracts, two different indicators are used: *volume* and *open interest.* Volume measures the number of contracts

Exhibit 15–3

Stock Market Indexes, Average Volume

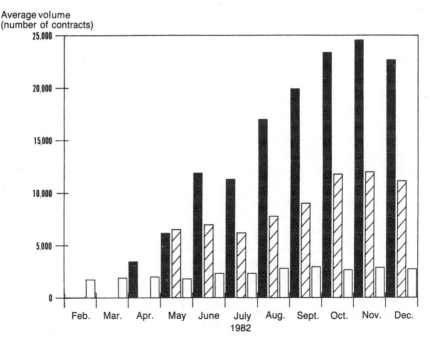

Note: Standard & Poor's (solid), New York Stock Exchange (stripe), Value Line (clear).

that are traded in the course of a day, while open interest gives a reading on the depth of the market by counting the number of contracts outstanding at the end of the day. Exhibit 15–3 plots the average daily volume of the three contracts from the onset of trading through the end of 1982.

Clearly, the Standard & Poor's contract has the highest trading volume. The New York Stock Exchange contract has grown in volume, too, albeit at a more modest pace; but volume at the Kansas City Board of Trade, where the Value Line contract trades, appears to have leveled out. In Exhibit 15–4 open interest is shown. By this measure of liquidity, the Standard & Poor's contract is again the most liquid of the three, the NYSE contract is next, and the Value Line contract is third.

These two measures of liquidity are relevant because they give an indication of a capacity to enter and exit from a futures position without disrupting the market. As a general rule, as volume and open interest rise, there is a decline in the potential of any single market order to affect the price of futures. For this reason, all else being equal, market participants prefer to trade in markets with higher volume and open interest. They also tend to shy away from relatively less active markets because

Exhibit 15–4

Stock Market Indexes, Average Open Interest

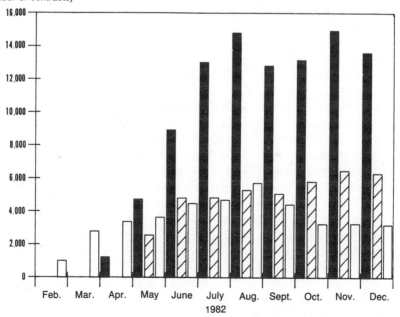

Note: Standard & Poor's (solid), New York Stock Exchange (stripe), Value Line (clear).

liquidity is dynamic. That is, although sufficient volume and open interest exist at the time the futures position is initiated, during any period in which that position is open, one faces the risk that liquidity will diminish by the time termination of the position is desired.

Given market participants' preference for trading in the market with the highest volume, order flow naturally tends to gravitate to that market, reinforcing the liquidity of ordering. Therefore, as the most liquid contract, the S&P future has a clear advantage over the two other stock index futures.

Margin and Leverage

A second differentiating factor among the index futures contracts relates to margin requirements—the initial margin requirement and the ratio between the value of the margin and the value of the underlying contracts. The initial margin requirement is important because it reflects the capital needed to initiate a futures position. The minimum initial margins required for the three contracts at the time of this writing (all margins are subject to change) are as follows:

Value Line	$6,500
S&P	6,000
NYSE	3,500

Thus those speculators who want to commit the smallest amount of capital will favor the NYSE contract.

Aside from the issue of the amount of capital needed in order to speculate, initial margin is important because it has a bearing on leverage. The lower the ratio of the initial margin requirement to the value of the underlying contract, the greater is the leverage offered by the contract. The reciprocal of this ratio indicates the amount of contract value that can be purchased for a given dollar of initial margin. For example, suppose that the Value Line, S&P, and NYSE indexes were trading at 167.40, 145.72, and 84.16, respectively. Since each contract is equal to 500 times the underlying index, the contract values would be $83,700, $72,860, and $42,080.[1] The ratio of the initial margin to the contract value would be 7.77 percent for the Value Line contract, 8.23 percent for the S&P 500 contract, and 8.32 percent for the NYSE contract. The reciprocals of the ratios are 12.99, 12.15, and 12.02, respectively. This means that given the assumed index value and the present initial margin requirements,

---

[1] The author recognizes that he is taking some liberty by valuing the indexes rather than the futures, but this practice eliminates the complications of theoretical time values appropriate to different settlement dates.

the Value Line contract allows the purchase of about $13 in contract value for each dollar of initial margin, while the two other contracts allow the purchase of about $12 for each dollar of initial margin.

As the market moves or as initial margin requirements change, the degree of leverage associated with the three contracts will vary. Historically, the leverage afforded by the Value Line contract has been slightly higher than that afforded by two other contracts.

More leverage, of course, means greater rewards for a given movement in the futures price; however, it also means more risk. Therefore, it is not clear whether the higher leverage that has been historically associated with the Value Line contract means that it should be favored by speculators. The preference will be highly individual.

The foregoing discussion focused on structural considerations that speculators should confront: how the respective underlying stock indexes move, liquidity, and margin requirements and their impact on leverage. Now we turn to more quantitative and strategic concerns.

Speculative Strategies

First, let us review the opening position in the futures market that should be taken based on the speculator's expectations about the movement of "the market." If the speculator expects a rise in the market, the speculator should buy the futures contract (that is, take a long position). On the other hand, if the speculator expects that a decline in the market, the speculator should sell the futures contract (that is, take a short position). The speculator will realize a gain if the market moves in the direction anticipated, but he will pay the piper if the market moves in the opposite direction.

In discussing speculative trading strategies, it is helpful to focus on the duration of the holding period. One who intends to speculate on broad market moves that are expected over weeks and months will base his trading decisions on technical and fundamental considerations (i.e., analysis of existing conditions and trends in the stock market and in the economy as a whole). It is not the intention of this chapter to explain this type of research and the long-term position taken. Rather, we focus on those who trade with a more rapid round-trip period—for example, intraday or an overnight basis. Such traders will employ additional considerations in their trading decisions. In this chapter two specific strategies are suggested for the short-term speculator. Both of these strategies involve tracking the underlying stock index for any of the three stock futures; and therefore to speculate with these strategies, one must have access to a quote vending machine—either directly or through a broker.

The first strategy simply relies on a traditional commodity trading maxim—"Go with the trend." Although the market may have a number of peaks and troughs during any given day, by and large it is fairly easy to categorize the short-run action as rising, flat, or declining. A tick-by-tick chart (see Exhibit 15–5) shows the relative smoothness of an underlying index, in this case the S&P, compared to the future. The idea, then, is simply to *determine the direction of the trend in the stock market. Go long the future on market rises and short the future on market declines. The position should be maintained only as long as the actual market continues its trend.* At any market leveling or trend reversal, the futures position should be liquidated. As Exhibit 15–5 demonstrates, this strategy is not without its pitfalls. Specifically, profits cannot be realized unless the market undergoes a sustained move, and short run ups and downs may result in a rapid turnover of futures positions that could generate cumulative losses. Moreover, even when the market does move decidedly in one direction, sometimes the futures move perversely. A good case in point occurred around 2 P.M. on the day shown on Exhibit 15–5.

The second strategy involves a more selective process of timing futures positions and mitigates some of the above shortcomings. In Chapter 6 the traditional cash-and-carry strategy was described and it was shown that within certain parameters the futures price and the underlying index price are related. Those parameters, however, provide ample leeway for expectations to affect the difference between the futures price and the cash price—the basis.[2]

First, let us consider a bull market scenario, where the basis is at a premium. Even in bull markets, there tend to be short-run periods where the actual stock market goes into a decline. When this happens, the basis usually shrinks. *The strategy, therefore, is to wait for basis conditions in which the basis appears to be atypically high (judgmentally) and then to enter a short futures position as soon as the market moves downward. The short position should be maintained only as long as the downward direction of the actual stock market is observed.* If the uptrend resumes or if the market stays flat, the short position should be dropped.

This strategy works in reverse during a bear market. The speculator waits until the basis is atypically wide—at a discount this time—and exercises a long position during an upward correction. Again, the position is liquidated when the underlying stock market resumes its bearish direction. Returning again to Exhibit 15–5, at least two and possibly three opportunities to implement this strategy arose on the day shown—at about 11, after 2, and perhaps near the close, at about 3:40. In each case the suggested strategy would have been successful.

---

[2] There is no universally accepted definition of the basis. While some authors define it as we have defined it here, some prefer to define it as the difference between the cash price and the futures price. The reader is advised to be careful.

Exhibit 15–5

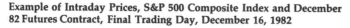

Example of Intraday Prices, S&P 500 Composite Index and December 82 Futures Contract, Final Trading Day, December 16, 1982

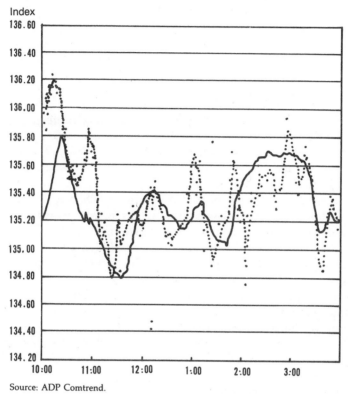

Source: ADP Comtrend.

Characteristically, the transition from bear market to bull market, or vice versa, comes with little advance notice. Thus this strategy would conceivably put someone in position to capture a downward move from the peak or an upward move from the trough, earning the original atypically wide basis in addition to the magnitude of the market move. Moreover, it is conceivable that aside from earning the initial basis, a second advantageous basis could be captured as the change in expectations moves the basis from premium to discount in going from a bull market to a bear market (or from discount to premium going from a bear market to a bull market).

In both of these strategies one must literally follow the index recalculations as they occur (about once every minute). Moreover, the speculator must recognize that he or she is essentially playing probabilities. Clearly, there will be times when markets are choppy and when, because the market never undergoes any significant change, futures positions will be executed with little or no profit. The speculator must be prepared, therefore, to withstand a certain amount of loss in order to be positioned for major moves when they do develop. Either of the two strategies, if described above, if adhered to with discipline, will tend to limit losses and allow profits to accumulate. In the long run, both strategies should lead to desirable results.

Concluding Remarks

This chapter considers short-run speculative trading strategies, focusing on three fundamental decisions (1) which of the available index futures contracts should be chosen as the vehicle for speculation, (2) upon which direction of the market one should speculate, and (3) when one should enter (and exit from) the market.

With respect to the issue of which contract to choose, the speculator must evaluate trade-offs between liquidity and margin requirements (and their impact on leverage opportunities). Two specific strategies are explained that emphasize the trends of the underlying indexes and the opportunities created by a variable basis—the difference between the future and its underlying stock index.

Despite the reasonableness of the strategies outlined, no chapter on speculation would be complete without ample words of caution. Stock index futures offer some very attractive opportunities, but seeking potential gains always involves an element of risk. Among the most extreme categories on the risk-reward spectrum is speculating in futures—and stock index futures are no exceptions. In this chapter, however, an effort has been made to try to mitigate some of the risk facing the speculator in these futures. If the speculator uses the strategies suggested, there is no question that some—perhaps even many or most—of the trades made may end in losses, but the hope is that the strategies will enable the speculator to approach these futures markets intelligently and will offer a discipline that limits losses on losing trades while allowing profits on winning trades to run. The approaches suggested *should* be profitable in the long run; but no matter how reasonable or sophisticated the strategies may be, the risk is still present that the long run won't arrive until it's too late!

CHAPTER 16

Intermarket Spreading

Gregory M. Kipnis
Vice President
Donaldson, Lufkin & Jenrette, Inc.

Steve Tsang, Ph.D.
Analyst
Donaldson, Lufkin & Jenrette, Inc.

A spread trade is not arbitrage in its purest sense. In this chapter we examine a number of approaches to intermarket spread trading in stock index futures. By intermarket spreads we mean trades involving two or more combinations of the Standard & Poor's 500 (S&P) Composite Index, the New York Stock Exchange (NYSE) Composite Index, or the Value Line Average Composite (VLA). Most of the emphasis focuses on the fundamentals that will cause the indexes to move differentially; however, later in the chapter we discuss a purely technical approach to trading the intermarket spreads.

To understand the difference between a spread and arbitrage trade, consider the following examples. Spread trades between two *identical* markets are implemented to arbitrage price aberrations. These aberrations are usually random and short-lived. A spread between *similar,* but not identical, markets is governed by different factors. For example, a spread between Chicago and Kansas City wheat futures contracts reflects supply/demand judgments about different types of wheat. A more complex example involves a spread between *related* markets, such as soybean and soybean meal. In this case the spread measures the price of a derivative product— soybean oil, net of gross crushing margins.

A spread between two different (though related) stock index futures contracts is conceptually similar to a soybean/soybean meal spread. In this analysis we point out that the NYSE index (soybeans in this word equation) is a proxy for the value-weighted performance of all stocks, that the S&P 500 index (soybean meal) measures the prices of large-capitalization stocks, and that the Value Line Average (soybean oil) is a proxy for the stock prices of small companies. Therefore, to the extent that the stock prices of small and large companies behave identically, trading spreads between the indexes would be an arbitrage. However, to the extent that they behave differently (as they often do), trading the spreads requires fundamental analysis and judgments about the relative price outlook for small and large companies.

As the number of stock index futures contracts expand and the markets become more active, it becomes increasingly important for hedgers, arbitrageurs, or spread traders to have a clear idea of the price behavior differences between different index contracts. Once the historical and theoretical price relationships are well defined, then risk and opportunities can be identified. In the early sections we discuss the fundamental determinants of two spread relationships: the NYSE index versus the S&P 500 index and the NYSE index versus the VLA index. In a later section we look at a technical approach to spread-trading the S&P 500 index against VLA. *Because of insufficient futures trading history, the long-term price relationships examined are based on actual index closing values.*

Index Differences[1]

The VLA index, traded on the Kansas City Board of Trade (KCBOT), is a broadly based stock price index consisting of nearly 1,700 stocks. It is calculated by multiplying the previous day's index by the geometric mean of the daily stock price relatives of the component stocks. The geometric mean is defined as the Nth root of the product of the N items. This method gives equal importance to each stock and thus dampens the effect of large percentage changes.

The S&P 500 index, traded on the Chicago Mercantile Exchange, consists of 500 large-capitalization stocks, most of which are listed on the NYSE and a few of which are traded on the American Stock Exchange and the over-the-counter markets. This index measures the total current capitalization, that is, the market value of all the outstanding shares, relative to the market value in the base period. In effect, this method weights price changes according to the market value of each security.

The NYSE Composite Index, traded on the New York Futures Exchange (NYFE), is also a market-weighted index. It comprises all of the more than 1,500 stocks listed on the New York Stock Exchange.

---

[1] See Chapter 5 for a more detailed explanation.

Exhibit 16–1

Selected Major Stock Indexes: S&P 500 (Thin Line), NYSE (Dot), and VLA (Thick Line) (base = 100 on 1/1/75)

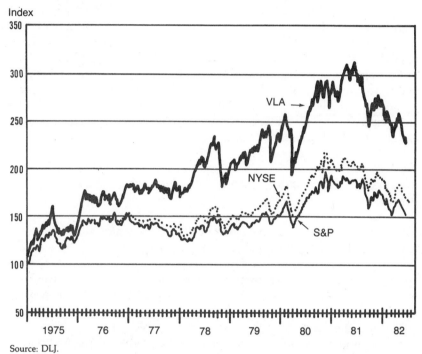

Source: DLJ.

Because of the differences in either computational method or stock coverage, the broad historical behavior for the three stock indexes has not been identical, though it has been reasonably close (see Exhibit 16–1). The indexes were rebased to 100 on January 1, 1975, to facilitate ease of comparison. The correlation analysis results, shown in Table 16–1, indicate that the simple correlation coefficients between any two of the three indexes are all higher than .87, comparing price levels, price

Table 16–1

Correlation between Selected Stock Indexes, 1975–82

	NYSE/S&P 500	NYSE/VLA	VLA/S&P 500
Level	.992	.967	.932
Daily price changes	.987	.907	.875
Daily percentage changes	.986	.905	.875

Source: DLJ.

differences, or percentage changes, for the 1975–82 period on a daily basis.

Because the NYSE and the S&P 500 indexes are both market weighted and the S&P 500's total capitalization accounted for nearly 80 percent of the market values of the NYSE index, the correlation should be very high. Since a different computational method is used for the VLA, its correlation with the NYSE and the S&P 500 indexes is somewhat lower. However, the higher correlation between the VLA and the NYSE, relative to the correlation between the VLA and the S&P 500 (.968 versus .932), is due to the fact that both the VLA and the NYSE also cover a large number of smaller and more volatile stocks. The correlation disparities are even more prominent when comparing daily price changes or percentage changes (.907 versus .875 and .905 versus .875, respectively).

Intermarket Stock Index Spreads Are Not What They Appear to Be

Since the historical price behavior of the three major stock indexes is not identical, trading the spreads between them is not as simple as arbitraging price aberrations. Therefore, a fundamental understanding of the spread difference between these indexes is important. Proper weighting is essential in determining the correct interpretation of an intermarket spread position.

Because the S&P 500 index can be considered a subset of the NYSE index, a properly weighted spread difference between them should be viewed as a new or "synthetic" index that measures the market capitalization of the nearly 1,000 stocks other than the S&P 500 stocks on the NYSE. To prove this point, we constructed a weighted spread position between the NYSE and the S&P 500 that virtually duplicates the performance of the non–S&P 500 stocks traded on the NYSE, with a correlation coefficient higher than .999, measured either on price levels or on daily price changes (see Exhibit 16–2)! We have dubbed the market value index for the approximately 1,000 smaller companies traded on the NYSE, but not included in the S&P 500 index, the "small 1,000." The correlation analysis, based on daily closes between 1975 and 1982, indicated that the small-stock index (small 1,000) is much more highly correlated with the VLA index (.994) than with either the NYSE index (.974) or the S&P 500 index (.939). This point can be seen graphically in Exhibit 16–3.

The spread difference between the VLA and the S&P 500 indexes, on the other hand, may be viewed as a measurement of the relative performance of small-capitalization stocks versus large-capitalization stocks, because the S&P 500 stocks account for less than 30 percent of

Exhibit 16–2

Small-Stock Index* versus NYSE–S&P 500 Ratio Spread

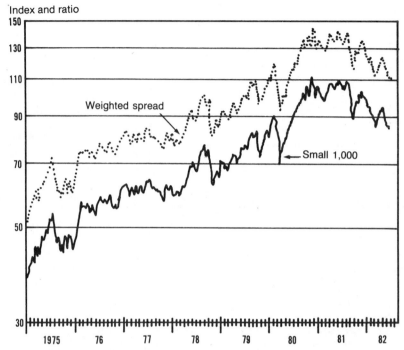

* Over 1,000 NYSE Non–S&P 500 Stocks.
Source: DLJ.

the weights in the VLA index. Since the VLA comprises more volatile (risky) stocks than does the S&P 500 index, it has the tendency, in the long run, to make larger moves over major market swings. For example, during the major bear market of 1972–74 the VLA declined by 65.08 points (57 percent), from 114.05 to 48.97. During the same period the S&P 500 index declined by 49.49 points (42 percent), from 118.05 to 68.56. During the major bull market of 1974–76, the VLA moved from 48.97 to 93.47, for a 44.5-point gain (90.9 percent), while the S&P 500 moved from 68.56 to 107.45, for a 38.98-point (56.7 percent) gain. In the bull market of 1978–80, the VLA also outgained the S&P 500 index. On an annual basis, however, this tendency occurred only six times in the past 11 years.

The spread between the NYSE and VLA indexes, if weighted properly, would closely approximate the S&P 500. If the spread is not properly

Exhibit 16-3

Small-Stock Index (Line) versus Value Line (Dot) (base = 100 on 1/1/75)

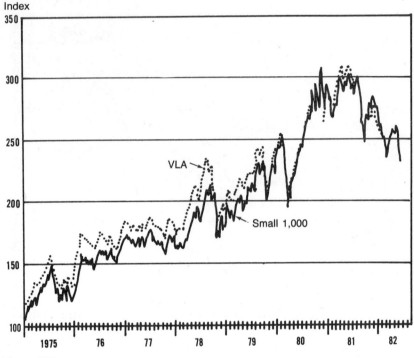

Source: DLJ.

weighted, however, its meaning would be difficult to interpret because both the VLA and NYSE indexes consist of a large number of stocks. Since the weighting scheme used in the NYSE index is slanted heavily toward large-capitalization stocks, the spread between the NYSE and VLA indexes may also be viewed as a measure of the performance of large stocks versus small stocks.

This brief discussion and interpretation of the meaning of the intermarket stock index spreads should be treated as an approximation because of the distortions introduced by different weighting schemes and differences in stock components. Furthermore, it should be pointed out that the commonly used spreads between exchanges, such as a 2:1 ratio recognized by the NYFE and the KCBOT, perform differently from the properly weighted spreads.

In the following sections we discuss the historical intermarket spread relationship between the NYSE, S&P 500, and VLA indexes for the past several years. Since the dollar value of the NYSE index contract is about one half the size of the S&P 500 or VLA contract, for simplicity, an intermarket spread ratio of 2 to 1 is used (i.e., 2 times the NYSE index value versus either the S&P 500 index or the VLA index. For the S&P 500 and VLA spread, we discuss a ratio that is technically determined.

Spread Trading

NYSE versus S&P 500

As shown in Exhibit 16–4, the movements of the NYSE index and the S&P index were almost identical during the 3½-year period. (The actual NYSE index is only one half of the value shown on the left scale but was doubled to facilitate comparison and preserve the 2:1 ratio de-

Exhibit 16–4

NYSE Index (2×, Line) versus S&P 500 Index (Dot)

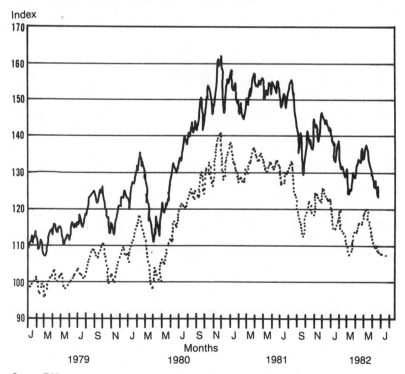

Source: DLJ.

scribed above.) The close association between the two indexes should not be a surprise, for the reasons discussed earlier. However, upon closer examination, the seemingly identical index movements are found not to be exactly the same.

The spread difference (2:1 ratio), as shown in Exhibit 16–5, clearly moves with the market indexes (i.e., the spread widens as the market moves higher, and the spread narrows as the market moves lower). The result is largely due to the fact that the 2:1 ratio gives the NYSE index more weight than the S&P 500 index and partly due to the fundamental differences between the two indexes. The correlation analysis indicates that the spread difference is much more highly correlated with the VLA index (.988) than with either the NYSE index (.941) or the S&P 500 index (.892). This is clear statistical support for the view expressed earlier that the spread difference approximates the performance of the smaller-

Exhibit 16–5

Spread: NYSE Index (2×) Less S&P 500 Index

Index points

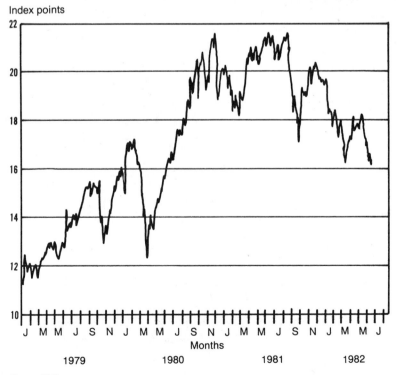

Months

1979   1980   1981   1982

Source: DLJ.

capitalization stocks, which tend to have higher volatilities. For example, between January 1979 and November 1980 the S&P 500 moved from about 100 to 140, for a 40 percent gain, while the spread differences moved from around 12 points to around 21 points, for a 75 percent gain. During the same period the small 1,000 index of smaller NYSE stocks (i.e., other than the S&P 500 stocks), estimated by us, moved from 68.8 to 111.7, for a 62 percent gain!

It is also revealing to note that the NYSE and the S&P 500 both peaked in November 1980; however, both the index spread and the VLA peaked in June 1981, seven months later. The closer association of the spread with the VLA is shown in Exhibit 16–6 for the period between 1975 and 1982.

The scatter diagram in Exhibit 16–7 amplifies the historical NYSE/S&P 500 spread in relation to the market levels, as measured by the S&P 500 index. The tight cluster band, with a width approximately equal to 2 index points measured vertically, emphasizes the strong positive correlation between the spread and movements in the level of the market.

Exhibit 16–6

Value Line Average versus NYSE/S&P 500 Spread (2:1)

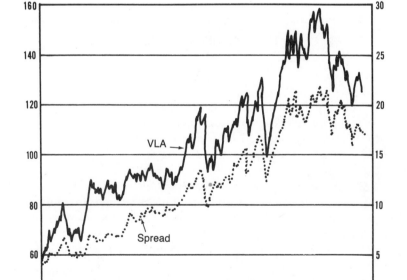

Source: DLJ.

Exhibit 16–7

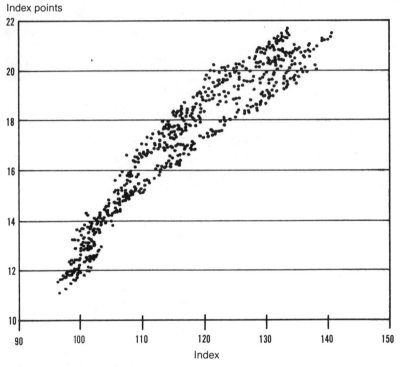

Scatter: NYSE/S&P 500 Spread (2:1) versus S&P 500 Index

Index points

Index

Source: DLJ.

The slight curvature in the cluster band indicates that the change in the spread has greater acceleration at lower index levels than at higher levels.

The NYSE/S&P 500 spread relationships shown in Exhibits 16–4 through 16–7 clearly indicate that if the market is expected to move higher, the spread should be bought (i.e., buy two NYSE contracts and sell one S&P 500 contract). On the other hand, if the market is expected to move lower, the reverse trade should be implemented. In addition to observing this fundamental trading rule, the reader should refer to the section below entitled "Technical Approach to Spread-Trading the S&P 500 and VLA," which discusses how to identify low-risk trading opportunities.

VLA versus NYSE

The movements of the NYSE index, as shown in Exhibit 16–8, are also highly correlated with the VLA index, but the similarity between

Exhibit 16–8

NYSE Index (2×, Line) versus Value Line Average (Dot)

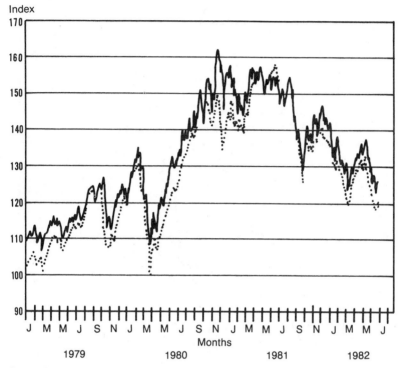

Months

| 1979 | 1980 | 1981 | 1982 |

Source: DLJ.

the two indexes is significantly lower than the similarity between the NYSE index and the S&P 500 index. Again, the actual NYSE index value is doubled for ease of comparison. The divergence of the index movements is due to the fact that they differ in their mathematical construction even though both indexes consist of more than 1,500 stocks.

As indicated in Exhibit 16–9, the spread difference between the VLA and NYSE indexes (1:2 ratio) generally moves in the same direction as the market movements. The dramatic divergence between the spread and the stock index movements that occurred during late 1980 and early 1981 can be largely attributed to the major relative price collapse of the petroleum and related stock groups. Because of the implied weighting differences, a major price shift in large-capitalization stocks would cause significant differences between index changes. As is quite visible in Exhibit 16–8, the VLA index did not respond to the peaking and contraction in the NYSE index during this period. As a result, the volatility of the VLA/NYSE spread was much higher than that of the NYSE/S&P 500 spread.

Exhibit 16–9

Spread: Value Line Average less NYSE Index (2×)

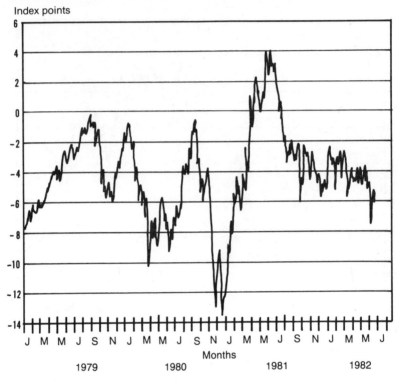

Source: DLJ.

For example, the average for the NYSE/S&P 500 spread (2:1 ratio) during the period was 17.1 points, with a standard deviation of 2.9 points. However, the average VLA/NYSE spread difference (1:2 ratio) for the same period was −4.1 points, with a standard deviation of 3.0 points. Also, the maximum/minimum range was 10.6 points for the NYSE/S&P 500 spread and 17.8 points for the VLA/NYSE spread.

The higher volatility for the VLA/NYSE spread can be seen clearly in Exhibit 16–10. The scatter has a much wider dispersion than that shown in Exhibit 16–7. Except for the small outlying group, the spread difference also shows a tendency to move with the market.

When Exhibit 16–9 is compared with Exhibit 16–5, it becomes clear that the VLA/NYSE spread provides more interesting but also riskier trading opportunities. If one believes that smaller (riskier) stocks will outperform or underperform the large-capitalization stocks, then spread trading could offer some interesting trading opportunities. In the following section we outline one such potential spread trade.

Exhibit 16–10

Scatter: VLA/NYSE Spread (1:2 ratio) versus Value Line Average

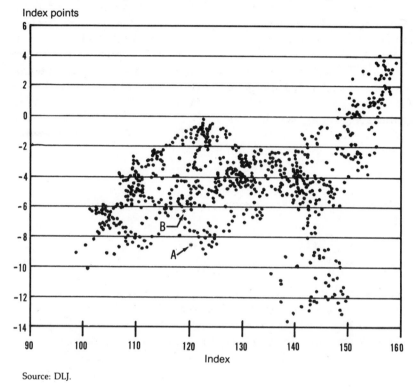

Source: DLJ.

Example

On June 23, 1982, the closing values for NYSE and VLA stock index futures contracts were shown in Table 16–2.

As is clear from the spread differences in the last column of Table 16–2, the deferred VLA futures contracts were underpriced relative to the NYSE contracts. Referring to the historical spread scatter in Exhibit

Table 16–2

	Stock Index Prices		Spreads (1:2 ratio)
Contract Month	VLA	NYSE	VLA/NYSE
Spot (actual)	120.35	63.26	−6.17
June	121.15	63.35	−5.55
September	121.05	64.35	−7.65
December	121.10	64.70	−8.30

Source: DLJ.

16–10, the −8.30 point spread difference for the December 1982 contract (see point A, Exhibit 16–10) represented a relatively low-risk entry point. Also, compared with the −6.17-point spread difference between the spot (actual) indexes (see point B), the VLA futures market offered a 2.13-point discount advantage to attract spread traders. Furthermore, the NYSE contract expired only one day earlier than the VLA contract; thus the existing 2.13-point discount could disappear just prior to the contract expiration. Therefore, if one had a neutral to mildly bullish market opinion about the stock market the potential spread would have been: buy one December VLA contract; sell two December NYSE contracts. The risk for this spread trade was that the stock market could decline to significantly lower levels or that the large-capitalization stocks might outperform the small stocks in the near future.

Technical Approach to Spread-Trading the S&P 500 and VLA

Basic Relationship

In this section we discuss some basic technical approaches to spread trading. Although we use the VLA and S&P 500 as an example, the techniques discussed are equally applicable to other spread positions.

As indicated in Exhibit 16–11, the VLA and S&P 500 moved very closely to each other during the period 1980 to April 1982. However, the major market turning point (peak) was reached in November 1980 for the S&P 500, while the major peak for the VLA was reached seven months later, in June 1981. As shown in Exhibit 16–12 (in conjunction with Exhibit 16–11), the spread between the VLA and the S&P 500 tends to move with the market (i.e., the VLA gains on the S&P 500 during uptrends and loses to the S&P during downtrends). The dramatic exception that occurred in late 1980 was similar to the NYSE/VLA spread discussed earlier.

The scatter diagram in Exhibit 16–13 emphasizes the strong linear correlation between the VLA and the S&P 500. The distribution of the two index values on each date is roughly bounded by a linear band with a width approximately equal to 11 points, measured vertically. The upper (U) and lower (L) boundaries can be approximated, in functional form, as follows:

$$\text{VLA (U)} = 1.3(\text{S\&P}) - 17.0$$
$$\text{VLA (L)} = \text{VLA (U)} - 11.0$$

The least squares equation may not go through the center of the linear

Exhibit 16–11

S&P 500 (Line) versus Value Line (Dashes)

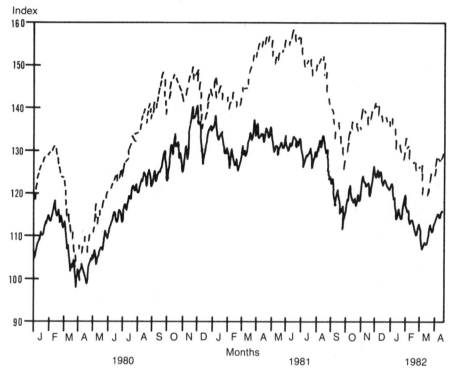

Source: DLJ.

band because of a slight distortion due to heteroscendasticity (i.e., the few observations that are outside the lower boundary at higher index levels would pull a regression slope slightly downward).

Constructing the Spread Trade

Using Boundaries   The wide band in Exhibit 16–13 covers more than 95 percent of the corresponding values for the selected period. The observations that are close to either side of the boundaries indicate arbitrage opportunities. For example, in January 1980 the S&P 500 index was around 110 and the VLA index was close to the estimated upper boundary, at around 126 (see point 1 in Exhibit 16–13). The arbitrage trade would

Exhibit 16–12

Spread: VLA less S&P 500

Months

1980   1981   1982

Source: DLJ.

have been to sell 10 VLA contracts and buy 13 S&P contracts. The 10:13 ratio is suggested by the functional form indicated above. A trading profit of $45,000 (i.e., 90 points × $500) could have been taken three months later, in late March 1980, as the S&P 500 was at about 100 (for a 130-point loss, i.e., 13 × [100 − 110]) and the VLA at about 104 (for a 220-point gain, i.e., 10 × [126 − 104]), a position near the opposite boundary line (see point 2).

Since the scatter values did not move outside the upper boundary during the whole period, the spread position would not result in any noticeable trading losses, even when the spread widened significantly. For example, the S&P 500 was at around 133 and the VLA at 155.9 in late June 1981. Starting from the January 1980 positions (point 1), the 299-point trading loss in the VLA position (i.e., 10 × [155.9 − 126]) would have been offset by the 299-point gain in the S&P position (i.e.,

Exhibit 16–13

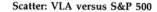

Scatter: VLA versus S&P 500

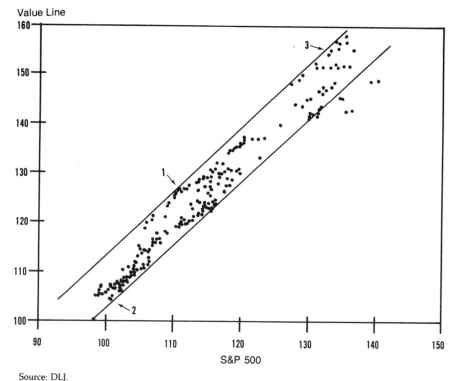

Source: DLJ.

13 × [133 − 110]), despite the widening of the index difference from 16 points to 22.9 points (see point 3).

Using Ratios   The historical ratios between the VLA and the S&P 500 for the selected period, as shown in Exhibit 16–14, reflected the relative price changes between the two indexes. The large ratio movements during the 1980–82 period ranged from 1.025 to 1.195, indicating that the price relationship between large stocks and small stocks was not very stable. However, the scatter diagram of the ratios in relation to the S&P 500 index level, as shown in Exhibit 16–15, indicates that the ratio was positively correlated with the S&P 500 index level (i.e., the VLA tended to move faster than the S&P 500).

If a trader has a firmly established market opinion on large stocks versus small stocks, spread trading based on price ratios can be placed using the balanced contract value approach—that is, the proper number

Exhibit 16–14

Ratio: VLA to S&P 500

Source: DLJ.

of contracts is determined by balancing the values between the two index
contracts. This process is equivalent to rebasing the two indexes to 100
at the initiation of the spread. Trading profits should result if price gains
faster on the long leg than the short leg, if it falls proportionately less
on the long leg than on the short leg, if either leg moves in the right
direction while the other remains unchanged, or if both legs move in
the right direction. In other words, spread trading based on ratios insulates
the spread position from price-level risk.

The deficiency of this trading approach is that some of the profitability
is sacrificed because of the extra weights assigned to one leg. However,
trading profit is always assured if the ratio moves in the right direction,
while the same price moves may not be profitable when an equal contrast
spread is initiated.

In the following section we outline one potential trade based on the

Exhibit 16-5

Scatter: VLA/S&P Ratio versus S&P 500

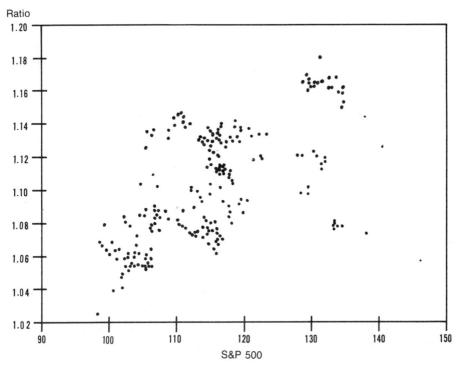

Source: DLJ.

historical boundary and ratio relationship between the VLA and the S&P 500.

Example

The April 27, 1982, closing values for the VLA futures contract and the S&P 500 index contract are shown in Table 16-3.

Based on the historical relationship as shown by the exhibits, the current price levels do not present extremely low-risk spread trading opportunities because the spread differences or the ratio levels are toward the middle of the clustered trading ranges in relation to the S&P 500 index values (see Exhibits 16-13 and 16-15). However, the June 1982 spread is relatively closer to the upper boundary and the March 1983

Table 16–3

VLA and S&P 500 Closing Values, April 27, 1982

Contract	VLA	S&P 500	Spreads	Ratios	VLA Boundaries*
Spot	131.47	118.00	13.47	1.11	136.4–125.4
June	133.05	118.85	14.20	1.12	137.5–126.5
September	133.80	120.75	13.05	1.11	140.0–129.0
December	134.80	122.50	12.30	1.10	142.3–131.2
March	135.55	124.00	11.55	1.09	144.2–133.2
June	136.30	—	—	—	

* Calculated by using the S&P 500 index closing values.
Source: DLJ.

spread is relatively closer to the lower boundary. Thus a potential spread would be to sell VLA/buy S&P in the June 1982 contracts and buy VLA/sell S&P in the March 1983 contracts.

Conclusion

The historical relationship between stock indexes illustrated in this report should be helpful to spread traders in identifying the intermarket trading opportunities. However, the stock index futures contracts are new and the spread relationship for futures contracts may differ significantly from the behavior of the spot indexes before futures contracts reach their maturity. Furthermore, one should be careful to avoid possible illiquidity problems in the deferred contracts.

Also, spreading strategies should be periodically reevaluated to ascertain whether structural shifts in the price relationships between two markets are taking place.

It must be pointed out again that the different expiration dates for the different stock index futures contracts could significantly distort the futures price relationship relative to the spot indexes. The futures price distortions may not automatically disappear, even if only one day separates the contract expirations. Only if both the stock index futures contracts expired on the same day could the futures spread distortions be significantly reduced.

SECTION FOUR

Options on Stock Indexes and Stock Index Futures

CHAPTER 17

Introduction to Options on Stock Indexes and Stock Index Futures Contracts

Frank J. Fabozzi, Ph.D., C.F.A.
Professor of Economics
Fordham University

Gary L. Gastineau
Manager of the Options Portfolio Service
Kidder, Peabody & Co., Inc.

R. Steven Wunsch
Vice President
Kidder, Peabody & Co., Inc.

In early 1983 options on stock index futures contracts began trading on the Chicago Mercantile Exchange (S&P 500) and the New York Futures Exchange (NYSE Composite). By midyear these options on futures contracts had been joined by cash settlement options for two synthetic stock indexes. Unlike a stock index futures contract, which requires the investor to make a cash settlement at the expiration date of the contract, an option on a stock index futures contract grants the buyer of the option the right, but not the obligation, to exercise the option.

In this chapter we shall discuss the basic elements that an investor who is contemplating using options on stock indexes and stock index futures contracts should be familiar with. No matter how intricate an option investment strategy the investor may adopt, *the principal result of any option purchase or sale is to modify the risk characteristics of an investor's position.*

This feature of options can have an important impact on portfolio structure and on the investor's overall risk exposure. In the next chapter the factors that affect the price of an option, option evaluation, and the use of options in risk management are discussed. Options provide the investor with a unique way to modify a common stock portfolio's exposure to market risk. This statement appears at odds with the popular view of options as speculative tools that permit an investor to obtain superior leverage on a small amount of capital. Options can satisfy much more important functions in an investment portfolio than this popular view suggests. Options can be of substantial aid to investors, large and small, who wish to modify the exposure of their portfolios to market fluctuations and improve their risk-adjusted return on investment.

At the time of this writing, options on stock index futures contracts appear to be less popular with investors than cash settlement options on the indexes themselves. The success of the CBOE 100 (renamed the S&P 100) index options, as measured by the number of contracts traded, suggests that the stock index futures options will face heavy competition from direct options. There are several reasons for this.

Options on stock index futures are regulated by the Commodities Futures Trading Commission. In order to trade options on stock index futures, brokers must register with the CFTC. However, options on stock indexes are considered by the Securities and Exchange Commission to be securities and are therefore regulated by that agency. Consequently, a broker registered to trade options on common stock, which are regulated by the SEC, may also trade options on stock indexes. Because of the greater number of salespersons who may trade options on stock indexes compared to those who may trade options on stock index futures, the options on stock indexes have a competitive advantage.

The principles discussed in this chapter and the one that follows are, for the most part, equally applicable to cash settlement options on stock indexes (also referred to as index options or cash index options) and stock index futures options. Differences will be pointed out.

Definitions and Contract Specifications

An option is a negotiable contract in which the writer of the option grants the buyer of the option the right to purchase from or sell to the writer a designated instrument at a specified price or receive a cash settlement within a specified period of time. The writer grants this right to the buyer for a certain sum of money, called the *option premium.* The price at which the option may be executed is called the *exercise or strike price.* The date after which an option is void is called the *expiration date.*[1]

---

[1] An American option may be exercised at any time before the expiration data. A European option, on the other hand, may be exercised only at the expiration date.

When an option grants the buyer the right to purchase the designated instrument from the writer, it is called a *call option*. When the option buyer has the right to sell the designated instrument to the writer (seller), the option is called a *put option*.

Most investors are familiar with exchange-listed options on common stock. Options on common stock were first listed on the Chicago Board Options Exchange (CBOE) in 1973, followed by trading on the American Stock Exchange in January 1975. Since then, common stock options have traded on several regional exchanges.

An option on a stock index futures contract gives the buyer the right to buy from or sell to the writer a designated stock index futures contract at a designated price at any time during the life of the option (which is equal to the life of the future). Upon exercise, both common stock options and stock index futures options require delivery of the underlying instrument. Since it would be impractical to deliver an index that represents a basket of common stock, the exercise of cash index options requires cash settlement. At this time there are two exchanges trading options on the stock index futures contracts that they trade—the Chicago Mercantile Exchange (Standard & Poor's 500 Composite Index) and the New York Futures Exchange (NYSE Composite Index).

If the option on a stock index futures contract is a call option, the buyer has the right to purchase one of the designated stock index futures contracts at the exercise (strike) price. That is, the buyer has the right to acquire a long futures position in the designated stock index at the exercise (strike) price (cash settlement in the case of an index option). If the call option is exercised by the buyer, the writer acquires a short position. For example, on April 5, 1983, a December 90 call option on the NYSE Composite Index futures sold for 4.25 points. The buyer of the call option had the right to purchase from the writer (seller) of the option a December NYSE Composite futures contract at 90. If this call option holder exercised the option, he would have been in a long futures position with respect to the December NYSE Composite futures contract. The writer (seller) of this call option would have been in a short position with respect to the December NYSE Composite futures contract. The option premium or price is $500 times the quoted price. For the December 90 call option, the quoted price on April 5, 1983, was 4.25 points; the dollar price was $2,125 (4.25 × $500).

If the option on a stock index futures contract is a put option, the buyer has the right to sell one of the designated stock index futures contracts to the writer at the exercise (strike) price. That is, the buyer has the right to acquire a short futures position in the designated stock index futures contract at the exercise price (again, cash settlement in the case of a cash index option). If the put option is exercised, the writer acquires a long position. For example, on April 5, 1983, a September 150 put option on the S&P 500 futures contract sold for 7 points. The put option granted its holder the right to sell to the writer (seller) of the option a September S&P 500 futures contract at 150 points. By exercising this option, the option buyer accepted a short futures position in the September S&P 500 futures contract at 150. The writer (seller) on the other hand, had to accept a long position in the September S&P 500 futures contract at 150. Since the option premium or price is $500 times the quoted price, the dollar price for the September 150 S&P 500 futures contract put option was $3,500 (7 × $500).

Exhibits 17–1 and 17–2 provide basic information about the two currently traded options on stock index futures contracts. Further information about the underlying stock index futures contracts for these two options is provided in Exhibits 3–1 and 3–2 in Chapter 3. Exhibits 17–3 and

Exhibit 17–1

Contract Summary for Options on Standard & Poor's 500 Index Futures Contracts

Exchange: Chicago Mercantile Exchange.

Trading Hours: 10 A.M.–4:15 P.M. (New York), 9 A.M.–3:15 P.M. (Chicago) (4 P.M. on last day of trading for expiring contract).

Contract Unit: Put or call on one Standard & Poor's 500 Composite Index futures contract (see Exhibit 3–1 of Chapter 3 for futures contract specifications).

Price Quotation: Options are quoted on the basis of the Standard & Poor's 500 Composite Index futures contract. Premiums (the value or actual cost of the options contract that must be paid when the option is bought) are quoted in points, and each full point is worth $500/contract, or $25 per 0.05. A premium quoted at 2.60 is $1,300 (2.60 × $500). The payment of the premium entitles the buyer to enter a long (if a call is bought) or short (if a put is bought) position at the strike or exercise price in one S&P index futures contract at any time prior to expiration of the option. Strike prices are set at five-point intervals.

Minimum Price Change: 0.05 of one point, or $25 ($500 × 0.05 = $25).

Daily Price Change Limit: None.

Delivery Months: Options will trade on the nearest three futures contracts in the March, June, September, and December cycle.

Exercise: The buyer of an S&P 500 index futures option may exercise the option on any business day prior to the expiration by giving notice to the clearing corporation by 5 P.M. The clearing corporation, through its clearing members, will then assign the notice to an option seller.

The clearing corporation will then establish a futures position for the buyer (long if the option is a call and short if the option is a put) and an opposite futures position for the seller (short if the option is a call and long if the option is a put) at the strike price before the opening of trading on the following business day.

Contract Trading Termination: Trading in the expiring option contract ends simultaneously with its underlying future at the close of trading on the third Thursday of the contract month.

Expiration: An unexercised S&P 500 index futures option expires at 4 P.M. on the last trading day of the underlying futures contract. In-the-money options are automatically exercised at expiration and are settled in cash as futures. (See Exhibit 3–1 of Chapter 3 for futures contract specifications.)

Exhibit 17–2

Contract Summary for Options on New York Stock Exchange Composite Index Futures Contracts

Exchange: New York Futures Exchange.

Trading Hours: 10 A.M.–4:15 P.M. (New York) (4 P.M. on last day of trading for expiring contract).

Contract Unit: Put or call on one New York Stock Exchange Composite Index futures contract (see Exhibit 3–2 of Chapter 3 for futures contract specifications).

Price Quotation: Options are quoted on the basis of the NYSE Composite Index futures contract. Premiums (the value or actual cost of the options contract that must be paid when the option is bought) are quoted in points, and each full point is worth $500/ contract or $25 per 0.05. A premium quoted at 2.60 is $1,300 (2.60 × $500). The payment of the premium entitles the buyer to enter a long (if a call is bought) or short (if a put is bought) position at the strike or exercise price in one NYSE Composite Index futures contract at any time prior to expiration of the option. Strike prices are set at two-point intervals.

Minimum Price Change: 0.05 of one point, or $25 ($500 × 0.05 = $25).

Daily Price Change Limit: None.

Delivery Months: Options will trade on the nearest three futures contracts in the March, June, September, and December cycle.

Exercise: The buyer of an NYSE Composite Index futures option may exercise the option on any business day prior to the expiration by giving notice to the clearing corporation by 5 P.M. The clearing corporation, through its clearing members, will then assign the notice to an option seller.
   The clearing corporation will then establish a futures position for the buyer (long if the option is a call and short if the option is a put) and an opposite futures position for the seller (short if the option is a call and long if the option is a put) at the strike price—before the opening of trading on the following business day.

Contract Trading Termination: Trading in the expiring option contract ends simultaneously with its underlying future at 4 P.M. (New York) on the second to last business day of the contract month.

Expiration: An unexercised NYSE Composite Index futures option expires at 4 P.M. on the last trading day of the underlying futures contract. In-the-money options are automatically exercised at expiration and are settled in cash as futures. (See Exhibit 3–2 of Chapter 3 for futures contract specifications.)

17–4 summarize contract information for the options on the CBOE 100 and the Major Market Index, respectively.

Price Quotation

The premium or price of the option is quoted in points. For the two options on stock index futures contracts traded at this time, each full point is equal to $500. Consequently, an option quoted at 2.60 points is selling for $1,300 (2.60 × $500). For the two index options traded at

Exhibit 17-3

Contract Summary for Options on the CBOE 100 (S&P 100 Index Option)

Exchange: Chicago Board Options Exchange.

Trading Hours: Opens when capitalization weighted 50% of stocks in index have traded. Closes at 4:10 (New York).

Contract Unit: Put or call on the CBOE 100 Index. Each index option contract represents $100 times the current value of the CBOE 100 Index. For example, when the index is at 160, the dollar value of the index will equal $16,000 ($100 × 160).

Price Quotation: Options are expressed in terms of dollars and fractions per unit of the index. Each full point represents $100. A premium quoted at 2.6 is $260 ($100 × 2.6). Strike prices are set at five-point intervals to bracket the current value of the S&P 100.

Minimum Price Change: $\frac{1}{16}$ (or $6.25) for option series trading below $3 and $\frac{1}{8}$ (or $12.50) for all other series.

Daily Price Change Limit: None

Delivery Months: Introduced with terms of three, six, and nine months, expiring in the months of March, June, September, and December.

Exercise: The final expiration date for the buyer of a CBOE 100 Index option is the Saturday following the third Friday of the expiration month.

Upon exercise, the CBOE 100 Index options are settled by the payment of cash and not by the delivery of the securities that the index comprises. The exerciser of a call/put receives upon exercise a cash amount equal to the difference between the closing dollar value of the index on the exercise date and the aggregate exercise price of the option. In effect, the exerciser receives the in-the-money amount for the option.

Exhibit 17-4

Contract Summary for the Major Market Index Option

Exchange: American Stock Exchange.

Trading Hours: 10 A.M.–4:10 P.M. (Eastern Time).

Contract Unit: Put or call on the Major Market Index. Each index option contract represents $100 times the current value of the MMI. For example, when the index is at 110, the dollar value of the index will equal $11,000 ($100 × 110).

Price Quotation: Options are expressed in terms of dollars and fractions per unit of the index. Each full point represents $100. A premium quoted at 2.6 is $260 ($100 × 2.6). Strike prices are set at five-point intervals to bracket the current value of the MMI.

Minimum Price Change: $\frac{1}{16}$ (or $6.25) for option series trading below $3 and $\frac{1}{8}$ (or $12.50) for all other series.

Daily Price Change Limit: None

Delivery Months: Introduced with terms of three, six, and nine months, expiring in the months of January, April, July, and October.

Exercise: The final expiration date for the buyer of an MMI option is the Saturday following the third Friday of the expiration month.

Upon exercise, the MMI options are settled by the payment of cash and not by the delivery of the securities that the index comprises. The exerciser of a call/put receives upon exercise a cash amount equal to the difference between the closing dollar value of the index on the exercise date and the aggregate exercise price of the option. In effect, the exerciser receives the in-the-money amount for the option.

this time, each full point is equal to $100 per contract. Therefore, an option quoted at 2.60 is selling for $260 (2.60 × $100).

Exercise Price

For all stock index futures options and index options contracts, there are put and call options trading with several different exercise prices. Exercise prices are set at five-point intervals for all options except the NYSE futures option. For the NYSE futures option, the exercise price is set at two-point intervals. Generally, a minimum of four exercise prices is set at all times: one "in-the-money," one "at-the-money," and two "out-of-the-money." These three terms are discussed in the next section.

Minimum Price Change

The minimum price change for an option is specified by the exchange. For all options on stock index futures contracts currently traded, the minimum price change, or "tick," is 0.05 of an index point. A 0.05 change is equivalent to $25 (0.05 × $500). There are no daily limits imposed on the maximum price change. For the two index options, the minimum price change is $\frac{1}{16}$ for option series trading below $3 and $\frac{1}{8}$ for all other series. A $\frac{1}{16}$ change is equivalent to $6.25 ($\frac{1}{16}$ × $100), and a $\frac{1}{8}$ change is equivalent to $12.50. The minimum price change for the index options is the same as for options on common stock.

Contract Trading Termination

An option on a stock index futures contract ends simultaneously with its underlying futures contract. For the NYSE Composite this is the next to the last business day of the contract month. For the S&P 500, the last trading day is the third Thursday of the contract month.

The Option Premium (Price)

The cost of an option to the buyer and the return to the seller are primarily a reflection of the option's *intrinsic* value and any premium over its intrinsic value.[2] Each is discussed below.

---

[2] Intrinsic value is sometimes referred to as *parity value*. The premium over intrinsic value is sometimes referred to as *time value*. Do not confuse the option premium, which is the price of the option, with the component of the option premium that represents the premium over the intrinsic value.

Intrinsic Value

The intrinsic value of a call option is the difference between the current price of the futures contract and the exercise price. For example, if the exercise price for a call option is 78 and the current price of the futures contract is 81, the intrinsic value is 3 (81 − 78). That is, if the option buyer exercised the option and simultaneously sold the underlying futures contract, the option buyer would realize 81 from the short position, which would be covered by acquiring an offsetting long position at 78 through exercise of the option—thereby netting 3 points. Since each point is $500 per contract, the intrinsic value is $1,500 (3 × $500).

When a call option has intrinsic value, it is said to be "in-the-money." When the exercise price of a call option exceeds the current price of the futures contract, the call option is said to be "out-of-the-money" and has no intrinsic value. An option for which the exercise price is equal to the current price of the futures contract is said to be "at-the-money."

For a put option, the intrinsic value is equal to the amount by which the futures price is below the exercise price. For example, if the exercise price of a put option is 78 and the current price of the futures contract is 71, the intrinsic value of the put option is 7, or $3,500 (7 × $500). When the put option has intrinsic value, the option is said to be "in-the-money." A put option is "out-of-the-money" when the current price of the futures contract exceeds the exercise price.

Premium over Intrinsic Value

The premium over intrinsic value is whatever amount buyers are willing to pay over and above any intrinsic value that the option may have. The option buyer hopes that at some point prior to expiration, changes in futures prices will further increase the value of the rights conveyed by the option.

For example, if the premium (price) for a call option with an exercise price of 78 is 9 when the current price of the underlying stock index futures contract is 81, then the premium over intrinsic value of this option is 6 (9 − the intrinsic value of 3), or $3,000 (6 × $500). If the current price of the underlying stock index futures contract is below 78, the premium over intrinsic value of an option priced at 9 is 9, or $4,500, since the option has no intrinsic value.

There are two ways in which an investor may realize the value of a position taken in an option. (1) He may exercise the option giving him a position in the futures market and simultaneously take an offsetting position in the futures market. For example, for our hypothetical call option with an exercise price of 78 and an option price of 9 and in which the current price of the underlying futures contract is 81, the option buyer can exercise the option. This will give him a long position in the futures market at 78. By simultaneously selling a futures contract for 81, the option holder will realize 3 points, or $1,500. (2) Alternatively, the option buyer may sell the call option for 9, or $4,500. Obviously, the latter is the preferable alternative. Because the exercise of an option will cause the immediate loss of any premium over intrinsic value that the option has left (in this case 6 points), options are not likely to be exercised very often. Furthermore, unlike the analogous exercise of an option on common stocks, which results in ownership of (or a short position in) a lasting asset, the exercise of an option on a stock index futures contract results only in a futures position that is itself due to expire.

In the next chapter the factors that affect the premium are discussed.

Margin Requirements

There are no margin requirements for the buyer of an option on stock index futures contracts once the premium has been paid in full. Because that premium is the maximum amount that the investor can lose no matter how far the price of the futures contract falls (in the case of a call option) or rises (in the case of a put option), there is no need for additional margin.

On the other hand, because the writer (seller) of an option has agreed to accept all of the risk (and none of the reward) of the underlying futures position, the writer (seller) is required to put up not only the margin required on the futures contract position but also, with certain exceptions, the option premium that he is paid for the option.

In addition, as prices adversely affect the writer's position, the writer would be required to deposit additional margin on the increased premium as it was marked-to-market.[3]

An exception occurs when the option is out-of-the-money, in which case the premium-plus-futures margin requirement is reduced depending on the futures contract. For options on the S&P 500 futures contracts, the amount of the premium that must be posted is reduced by one half of the out-of-the-money amount. For options on the NYSE Composite futures contract, it is reduced by all of the out-of-the-money amount.

The following examples will illustrate the initial margin requirements for an option writer (seller). On April 5, 1983, the settlement prices for a September 1983 futures contract for the S&P 500 and the NYSE Compos-

---

[3] The mark-to-market procedure is illustrated in Chapter 4.

ite were 152.60 and 87.90, respectively. Suppose that on that trading day an option writer (seller) could have sold the following call options:

Exercise Price	Futures Contract	Option Premium
140	S&P 500	14.90
160	S&P 500	3.90
84	NYSE Composite	6.20
92	NYSE Composite	2.50

The initial margin for an S&P 500 futures contract is $6,000. The premium for the September 140 call is $7,450 (14.90 × $500). Since the September 140 call is in-the-money, the required initial margin for the option writer is $6,000 plus the premium of $7,450, or $13,450. The premium for the out-of-the-money September 160 call option is $1,900 (3.90 × $500). The amount by which this call option is out-of-the-money is $3,700 (the difference between 152.60 and 160 multiplied by $500). Therefore, the amount of the premium that is required as margin is reduced by one half of $3,700, or $1,850. The required initial margin is then $6,000 plus $1,900 minus $1,850, or $6,050.

The initial margin required for an NYSE Composite futures contract is $3,500. Since the option premium for the in-the-money September 84 call option is $3,100 (6.20 × $500), the initial required margin for this call option seller is $6,600. For the out-of-the-money September 92 call option, the option premium is $1,250 (2.50 × $500). The amount by which this call option is out-of-the-money is $2,050 (the difference between 87.90 and 92 multiplied by $500). The initial margin required for the September 92 call option is therefore $3,500 plus $1,250 minus 2,050 (the entire amount by which the call option is out-of-the-money), or $2,750.

Risk-Return Parameters for Selected Option Strategies

Speculative positions in stock index futures contracts require initial margin deposits of less than 10 percent of contract value. This means that stock index futures positions may have more than 10 times the leverage and risk of the overall stock market. In addition, buying options on stock index futures can greatly increase this already substantial leverage, though the risk of a purchased option is limited to the amount paid for the option.

In this section the risk-return parameters associated with the four basic option positions—buying call options, writing (selling) call options, buying put options, and writing (selling) put options—are illustrated. In the next section the uses of options on stock index futures for risk management are illustrated.

Buying Call Options

The most straightforward option strategy for participating in an anticipated upward move of the market is to buy a call option. The investor
who buys a call option is said to be in a "long call" position.

To illustrate this strategy, consider the following data for the NYSE
Composite December futures contract and call options on April 5, 1983.

December futures contract	88.00
December 86 call option	6.30
December 88 call option	5.35
December 94 call option	3.00

Suppose the investor purchases the December 88 call for 5.35. The
option premium is $2,675 (5.35 × $500). The option premium represents
the maximum loss that the option buyer faces by buying a call. If the
settlement price of the December NYSE Composite futures contract is
88 or less at expiration, the buyer of this call option will lose the entire
option premium, $2,675. The investor will break even if the settlement
price of the futures contract at expiration is 93.35 (the exercise price
plus the premium). Any settlement price between 88 and 93.35 reduces
the investor's loss to an amount less than the option premium. On the
other hand, should the settlement price of the futures contract at expiration exceed 93.35, the option buyer will realize a profit of $500 for each
point by which the settlement price exceeds 93.35.

Exhibit 17-5 graphically portrays the profit profile of an investor who
buys the at-the-money December 88 NYSE Composite call option at 5.35.
For comparative purposes, Exhibit 17-5 also shows the profit profile of
an investor who buys an NYSE Composite December futures contract
at 88. An investor who takes a long futures position will realize a $500
gain for each point by which the settlement price of the futures contract
exceeds 88 and a $500 loss for each point by which the settlement price
of the futures contract falls below 88.

The unlimited return potential and limited risk position of the buyer
of a call option versus the unlimited return and risk potential of the
long futures position can be seen from Exhibit 17-5. Exhibit 17-6 shows
both the dollar profit and the percentage return for the long call and
long futures positions. In the case of the call buyer, the investment is
the option premium of $2,675. For the long futures position, the invest-
ment is the initial $3,500 margin required for an NYSE Composite futures
contract. The lower investment required for the call buyer provides greater
leverage as prices advance, while limiting the loss to 100 percent of the
investment. If the price declines, the long futures position requires not
only an initial margin but also a maintenance margin if the equity in
the account falls below $1,500 (a drop of four points from 88 to 84).

Exhibit 17-5

Profit Profile of a Long Call Option versus a Long Futures Position

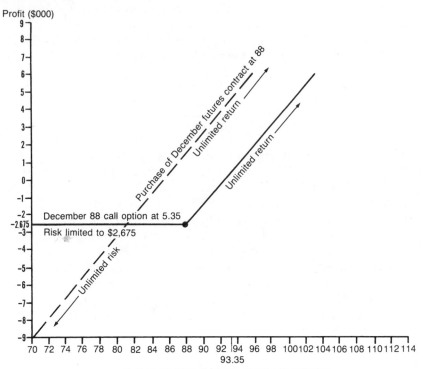

Settlement price of futures contract at expiration

The investor could have selected any one of five call options on the NYSE Composite December futures contract. Exercise prices were available for 86, 88, 90, 92, and 94. The December 86 was in-the-money; the December 88 was at-the-money; and the last three were out-of-the-money. Exhibit 17–7 graphically portrays the profit profile for the December 86 call option at 6.30, the December 88 call option at 3.35, and the December 94 call option at 3.00. Exhibit 17–6 shows the dollar profit and the percentage return on investment for all three call options. Because the premium paid for call options with high exercise prices will be lower than the premium paid for call options with low exercise prices, higher prices have both a higher potential return per investment (premium paid) and a smaller maximum dollar loss. Of course, higher exercise prices are also farther out of reach than lower exercise prices.

Buying Put Options

The most straightforward option strategy for benefiting from an anticipated market decline is to buy a put option. The investor who purchases a put option is said to be in a "long put" position.

To illustrate this strategy, consider the following data for the NYSE Composite December futures contract and put options on April 5, 1983.

December futures contract	88.00
December 84 put option	3.20
December 88 put option	4.95
December 92 put option	7.30

Suppose an investor buys the at-the-money put option December 88 for a premium of $2,475 (4.95 × $500). Should the settlement price of the NYSE Composite December futures contract at expiration be greater than the exercise price of 88, the put option will expire worthless and the investor will lose the entire premium of $2,475. The investor will recover the premium but show no profit or loss if the settlement price of the futures contract is 83.05 (the exercise price of 88 minus the premium of 4.95). For any settlement price for the futures contract between 83.05 and 88 at expiration, the investor will reduce his loss below the premium of $2,475. The investor will realize a $500 profit for each point by which the settlement price of the futures contract at expiration is below the break-even price of 83.05.

The profit profile of the December 88 put option and the short position in a December futures contract are shown in Exhibit 17–8. Once again, it can be seen that the option buyer has unlimited return potential but limited risk potential, whereas the futures position offers a potential for both unlimited return and unlimited risk. Exhibit 17–9 shows both the dollar profit and the percentage return per dollar invested for both the long put and short futures positions. As can be seen, while fixing the maximum loss at 100 percent of the dollar invested, the long put provides greater leverage to allow the investor to benefit from favorable price movements in the price of the futures contract. Also shown in Exhibit 17–9 are the dollar profit and the percentage return on investment for the December 84 and December 92 put options. The lower the exercise price, the higher is the leverage for the put option.

Writing Call Options

An investor who believes that the market will decline or stay flat can, if his expectations are correct, realize income by writing (selling) a call option. A call writer is said to be in a "short call" position.

Exhibit 17-6

Profit Profile for a Call Buyer (Long Call Position) and Outright Purchase of a Futures Contract (Long Futures Position)

Futures Price at Expiration	Purchase of NYSE Composite December 88 Call at 5.35		Purchase of NYSE Composite December 86 Call at 6.30		Purchase of NYSE Composite December 94 Call at 3.00		Purchase of NYSE Composite December Futures Contract at 88	
	Profit	Percent Return*	Profit	Percent Return*	Profit	Percent Return*	Profit	Percent Return†
70	–$ 2,675	–100%	–$ 3,150	–100%	–$1,500	–100%	–$ 9,000	–257%
71	– 2,675	–100	– 3,150	–100	– 1,500	–100	– 8,500	–242
72	– 2,675	–100	– 3,150	–100	– 1,500	–100	– 8,000	–228
73	– 2,675	–100	– 3,150	–100	– 1,500	–100	– 7,500	–214
74	– 2,675	–100	– 3,150	–100	– 1,500	–100	– 7,000	–200
75	– 2,675	–100	– 3,150	–100	– 1,500	–100	– 6,500	–185
76	– 2,675	–100	– 3,150	–100	– 1,500	–100	– 6,000	–171
77	– 2,675	–100	– 3,150	–100	– 1,500	–100	– 5,500	–157
78	– 2,675	–100	– 3,150	–100	– 1,500	–100	– 5,000	–142
79	– 2,675	–100	– 3,150	–100	– 1,500	–100	– 4,500	–128
80	– 2,675	–100	– 3,150	–100	– 1,500	–100	– 4,000	–114
81	– 2,675	–100	– 3,150	–100	– 1,500	–100	– 3,500	–100
82	– 2,675	–100	– 3,150	–100	– 1,500	–100	– 3,000	– 85
83	– 2,675	–100	– 3,150	–100	– 1,500	–100	– 2,500	– 71
84	– 2,675	–100	– 3,150	–100	– 1,500	–100	– 2,000	– 57
85	– 2,675	–100	– 3,150	–100	– 1,500	–100	– 1,500	– 42
86	– 2,675	–100	– 3,150	–100	– 1,500	–100	– 1,000	– 28
87	– 2,675	–100	– 2,650	– 84	– 1,500	–100	– 500	– 14
88	– 2,675	–100	– 2,150	– 68	– 1,500	–100	0	0
89	– 2,175	– 81	– 1,650	– 52	– 1,500	–100	500	14
90	– 1,675	– 62	– 1,150	– 36	– 1,500	–100	1,000	28
91	– 1,175	– 43	– 650	– 20	– 1,500	–100	1,500	42
92	– 675	– 25	– 150	– 4	– 1,500	–100	2,000	57

93	175	6	350	11	−1,500	−100	2,500	71
94	325	12	850	26	−1,500	−100	3,000	85
95	825	30	1,350	42	−1,000	−66	3,500	100
96	1,325	49	1,850	58	−500	−33	4,000	114
97	1,825	68	2,350	74	0	0	4,500	128
98	2,325	86	2,850	90	500	33	5,000	142
99	2,825	105	3,350	106	1,000	66	5,500	157
100	3,325	124	3,850	122	1,500	100	6,000	171
101	3,825	142	4,350	138	2,000	133	6,500	185
102	4,325	161	4,850	153	2,500	166	7,000	200
103	4,825	180	5,350	169	3,000	200	7,500	214
104	5,325	199	5,850	185	3,500	233	8,000	228
105	5,825	217	6,350	201	4,000	266	8,500	242
106	6,325	236	6,850	217	4,500	300	9,000	257
107	6,825	255	7,350	233	5,000	333	9,500	271
108	7,325	273	7,850	249	5,500	366	10,000	285
109	7,825	292	8,350	265	6,000	400	10,500	300
110	8,325	311	8,850	280	6,500	433	11,000	314
111	8,825	329	9,350	296	7,000	466	11,500	328
112	9,325	348	9,850	312	7,500	500	12,000	342
113	9,825	367	10,350	328	8,000	533	12,500	357
114	10,325	385	10,850	344	8,500	566	13,000	371
115	10,825	404	11,350	360	9,000	600	13,500	385

* Profit/option premium.
† Profit/initial margin requirement of $3,500.

Exhibit 17–7

Profit Profile for Three Long Call Positions

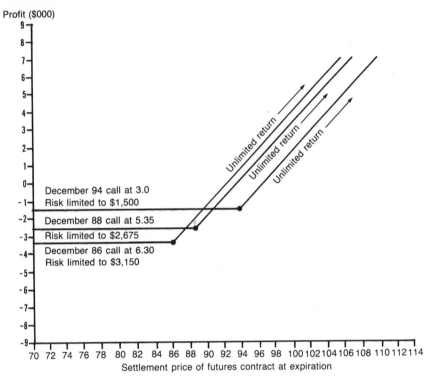

Profit ($000)

December 94 call at 3.0
Risk limited to $1,500

December 88 call at 5.35
Risk limited to $2,675

December 86 call at 6.30
Risk limited to $3,150

Settlement price of futures contract at expiration

To illustrate this option strategy, we shall use the three December call options on the NYSE Composite December futures contract that were used to illustrate the strategy of buying a call option.

The profit profile of the call writer is the mirror image of the profit profile of the call buyer. As in the case of a long futures and short futures position, we have a zero-sum game. That is, the profit position of the writer is of the same dollar magnitude but in the opposite direction of the profit position of the buyer.

Exhibit 17–10 graphically portrays the profit profile of the December 88 call option writer. The maximum profit that the call writer can realize is the amount of the premium, $2,675. As long as the settlement price of the futures contract is less than 93.35 (the exercise price of 88 plus the premium of 5.35), the writer will realize a profit. If the settlement price of the futures contract at expiration is greater than 93.35, the call writer will realize a $500 loss for each point above 93.35. Also shown

Exhibit 17–8

Profit Profile of a Long Put versus a Short Futures Position

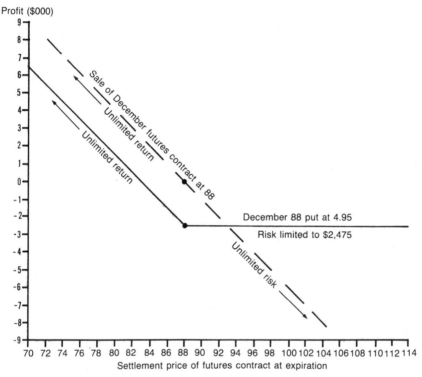

Profit ($000)

Sale of December futures contract at 88

Unlimited return

Unlimited return

December 88 put at 4.95

Risk limited to $2,475

Unlimited risk

Settlement price of futures contract at expiration

in Exhibit 17–10 is the profit profile of a call buyer (long call position). Exhibit 17–11 graphically depicts the profit profile for the writer of a December 86, December 88, and December 94 call option.[4]

Writing Put Options

An investor who believes that the market will advance or stay flat can, if his expectations are correct, realize income by writing (selling) a put option. A put writer is said to be in a "short put" position.

---

[4] Notice that we have not discussed the return on investment for the call option writer, and we shall not do so in our discussion of the put option writer. The reason is that return on investment is a fuzzy concept when it is applied to uncovered option writing. The reason is explained in appendix B of Gary L. Gastineau, *The Stock Options Manual* (New York: McGraw-Hill, 1979). Furthermore, the margin requirement varies as prices change.

Exhibit 17-9

Profit Profile for a Put Option Buyer (Long Put Position) and Outright Sale of a Futures Contract (Short Futures Position)

Futures Price at Expiration	Purchase of NYSE Composite December 88 Put at 4.95		Purchase of NYSE Composite December 92 Put at 7.30		Purchase of NYSE Composite December 84 Put at 3.20		Sale of NYSE Composite December Futures Contract at 88	
	Profit	Percent Return*	Profit	Percent Return*	Profit	Percent Return*	Profit	Percent Return†
70	$6,525	263%	$7,350	201%	$5,400	337%	$9,000	257%
71	6,025	243	6,850	187	4,900	306	8,500	242
72	5,525	223	6,350	173	4,400	275	8,000	228
73	5,025	203	5,850	160	3,900	243	7,500	214
74	4,525	182	5,350	146	3,400	212	7,000	200
75	4,025	162	4,850	132	2,900	181	6,500	185
76	3,525	142	4,350	119	2,400	150	6,000	171
77	3,025	122	3,850	105	1,900	118	5,500	157
78	2,525	102	3,350	91	1,400	87	5,000	142
79	2,025	81	2,850	78	900	56	4,500	128
80	1,525	61	2,350	64	400	25	4,000	114
81	1,025	41	1,850	50	— 100	— 6	3,500	100
82	525	21	1,350	36	— 600	— 37	3,000	85
83	25	1	850	23	— 1,100	— 68	2,500	71
84	— 475	— 19	350	9	— 1,600	— 100	2,000	57
85	— 975	— 39	— 150	— 4	— 1,600	— 100	1,500	42
86	— 1,475	— 59	— 650	— 17	— 1,600	— 100	1,000	28
87	— 1,975	— 79	— 1,150	— 31	— 1,600	— 100	500	14
88	— 2,475	— 100	— 1,650	— 45	— 1,600	— 100	0	0
89	— 2,475	— 100	— 2,150	— 58	— 1,600	— 100	— 500	— 14
90	— 2,475	— 100	— 2,650	— 72	— 1,600	— 100	— 1,000	— 28
91	— 2,475	— 100	— 3,150	— 86	— 1,600	— 100	— 1,500	— 42
92	— 2,475	— 100	— 3,650	— 100	— 1,600	— 100	— 2,000	— 57

93	− 2,475	−100	− 3,650	−100	− 1,600	−100	− 2,500	− 71
94	− 2,475	−100	− 3,650	−100	− 1,600	−100	− 3,000	− 85
95	− 2,475	−100	− 3,650	−100	− 1,600	−100	− 3,500	−100
96	− 2,475	−100	− 3,650	−100	− 1,600	−100	− 4,000	−114
97	− 2,475	−100	− 3,650	−100	− 1,600	−100	− 4,500	−128
98	− 2,475	−100	− 3,650	−100	− 1,600	−100	− 5,000	−142
99	− 2,475	−100	− 3,650	−100	− 1,600	−100	− 5,500	−157
100	− 2,475	−100	− 3,650	−100	− 1,600	−100	− 6,000	−171
101	− 2,475	−100	− 3,650	−100	− 1,600	−100	− 6,500	−185
102	− 2,475	−100	− 3,650	−100	− 1,600	−100	− 7,000	−200
103	− 2,475	−100	− 3,650	−100	− 1,600	−100	− 7,500	−214
104	− 2,475	−100	− 3,650	−100	− 1,600	−100	− 8,000	−228
105	− 2,475	−100	− 3,650	−100	− 1,600	−100	− 8,500	−242
106	− 2,475	−100	− 3,650	−100	− 1,600	−100	− 9,000	−257
107	− 2,475	−100	− 3,650	−100	− 1,600	−100	− 9,500	−271
108	− 2,475	−100	− 3,650	−100	− 1,600	−100	− 10,000	−285
109	− 2,475	−100	− 3,650	−100	− 1,600	−100	− 10,500	−300
110	− 2,475	−100	− 3,650	−100	− 1,600	−100	− 11,000	−314
111	− 2,475	−100	− 3,650	−100	− 1,600	−100	− 11,500	−328
112	− 2,475	−100	− 3,650	−100	− 1,600	−100	− 12,000	−342
113	− 2,475	−100	− 3,650	−100	− 1,600	−100	− 12,500	−357
114	− 2,475	−100	− 3,650	−100	− 1,600	−100	− 13,000	−371
115	− 2,475	−100	− 3,650	−100	− 1,600	−100	− 13,500	−385

* Profit/option premium.
† Profit/initial margin requirement of $3,500.

Exhibit 17–10

Profit Profile of a Short Call Position versus a Long Call Position

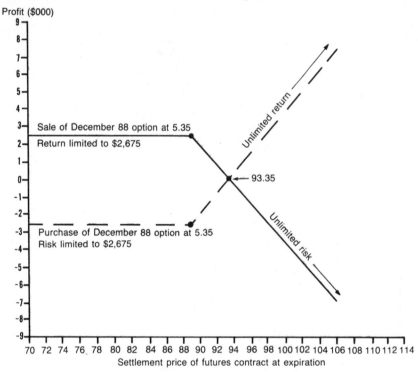

Profit ($000)

Settlement price of futures contract at expiration

The three December put options on the NYSE Composite December futures contract that were used to illustrate the strategy of buying a put option shall be used here to illustrate the risk-return parameters of a put writer.

It should be no surprise that the profit profile of the put writer is the mirror image of the profit profile of the put buyer. What the put buyer gains (loses) the put seller loses (gains). The profit profile of the December 88 put option writer is depicted in Exhibit 17–12 along with the long put position. The maximum profit that the option writer can realize is the amount of the premium.

As long as the settlement price of the futures contract is greater than 83.05 (the exercise price of 88 minus the premium of 4.95), the put writer will realize a profit. If the settlement price of the futures contract at expiration is 83.05, the put writer will break even. Any settlement price

Exhibit 17–11

Profit Profile for Three Short Call Positions

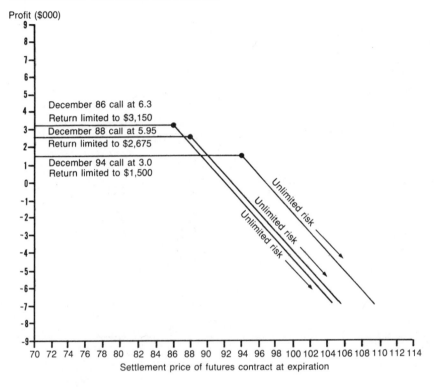

Profit ($000)

December 86 call at 6.3
Return limited to $3,150

December 88 call at 5.95
Return limited to $2,675

December 94 call at 3.0
Return limited to $1,500

Settlement price of futures contract at expiration

for the futures contract at expiration that is less than the break-even price will produce a $500 loss for each point below 83.05.

Exhibit 17–13 compares the profit profile for a short position in the three December put contracts—December 84, December 88, and December 92.

Summary

In this chapter we provided basic information about options contracts currently traded on broad market indices and the basic profit and loss position resulting from an options position. As this book goes to press, new index options have begun trading on particular industry indices, such as the Oil and Gas Index and the Computer Technology Index, both traded on the American Stock Exchange. The principles we discussed in this chapter are equally applicable to options on industry indices.

Exhibit 17–12

Profit Profile of a Short Put Position versus a Long Put Position

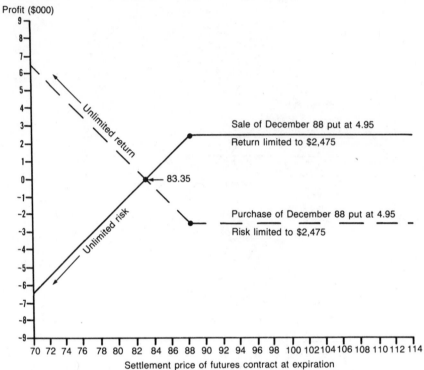

Exhibit 17–13

Profit Profile for Three Short Put Positions

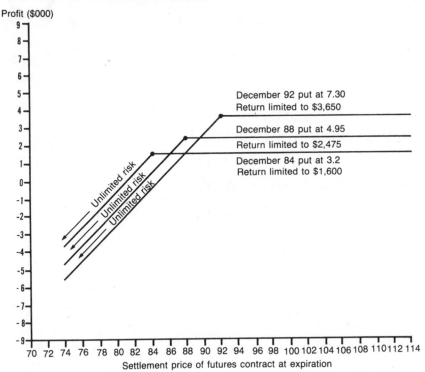

Profit ($000)

December 92 put at 7.30
Return limited to $3,650

December 88 put at 4.95
Return limited to $2,475

December 84 put at 3.2
Return limited to $1,600

Unlimited risk
Unlimited risk
Unlimited risk

Settlement price of futures contract at expiration

CHAPTER 18

Options on Stock Indexes and Stock Index Futures: Pricing Determinants, Role in Risk Management, and Option Evaluation

Frank J. Fabozzi, Ph.D., C.F.A.
Professor of Economics
Fordham University

Gary L. Gastineau
Manager of the Options Portfolio Service
Kidder, Peabody & Co., Inc.

Albert Madansky, Ph.D.
Professor of Business Administration
University of Chicago

In the previous chapter, background information about options on stock indexes and stock index futures contracts was furnished. In this chapter we shall discuss (1) the factors that affect the price of an option, (2) the role of options in risk management, and (3) option evaluation. The concepts discussed in this chapter are, for the most part, equally applicable to options on both stock indexes and stock index futures. Any differences will be highlighted.

Factors That Affect the Option Price

The five major factors affecting the option premium are (1) the current price of the futures contract (or the index) relative to the exercise price,

(2) the time remaining until the expiration of the option, (3) the anticipated volatility of the price of the underlying futures contract or index, (4) the level of interest rates, and (5) cumulative dividends before expiration or settlement.

1.   *Current Price of the Futures Contract relative to the Exercise Price*   As explained in the previous chapter, the current price of the futures contract relative to the exercise price determines whether the option has intrinsic value. But the relationship is also important for the premium over intrinsic value component of the option premium.

All other factors equal, an at-the-money option generally has the greatest premium over intrinsic value. For an in-the-money option in which the current price of the futures contract differs substantially from the exercise price, the premium over intrinsic value is usually small. One of the reasons is the reduced leverage provided by purchasing the option compared to directly acquiring a futures position. For a substantially out-of-the-money option, the premium over intrinsic value is generally small in spite of the substantial leverage afforded by purchasing the option. This is because there is a lower probability that it will be profitable to exercise the option.

2.   *Time Remaining to the Expiration of the Option*   An option is a "wasting asset." That is, after the expiration date the option has no value. All other factors equal, the longer the time to expiration of the option, the greater is the option premium. This is because as the time to expiration decreases, less time remains for the value of the index to change so as to compensate the option buyer for any premium over intrinsic value that he has paid. Consequently, as the time remaining until expiration decreases, the option price approaches its intrinsic value.

3.   *Anticipated Volatility of the Underlying Stock Index or Stock Index Futures Contract*   All other factors equal, the greater the anticipated volatility of the underlying stock index or stock index futures contract, the more an investor would be willing to pay for the option and the more an option writer would demand for it. This is because the greater the volatility, the greater is the probability that the price of the underlying trading unit will move in favor of the option buyer before expiration.

4.   *Level of Interest Rates*   To illustrate how the level of interest rates and the cumulative dividends before expiration-settlement affect the option premium, we shall use an option on one share of common stock instead of a stock index futures contract or a stock index. Consider the following two investment strategies.

Strategy 1:   Purchase a share of XYZ stock for S dollars.

Strategy 2:   (a) Purchase a call option on XYZ stock for P dollars with an exercise price of E dollars and with T months to expiration; and b) place funds in a bank account sufficient to exercise the option at expiration and to pay all dividends that would be paid on XYZ stock prior to expiration of the option.

Assume (1) that the interest that could be earned on the funds placed in the bank account for T months is r percent and (2) that XYZ stock will pay only one dividend one day prior to expiration of the option in the amount of D dollars. Then the amount to be placed in the bank account, A, is simply the present value of the exercise price plus the present value of the dividends to be paid. That is,

$$\begin{matrix} \text{Investment under} \\ \text{Strategy 2} \end{matrix} = A = \frac{E}{1+r} + \frac{D}{1+r}$$

Let us investigate Strategy 2. This strategy will produce the same outcome as Strategy 1 at the end of the expiration date if it is beneficial for the investor to exercise the call option (i.e., if the price of XYZ is greater than the exercise price). There will be just enough funds to reproduce the dividends paid on XYZ stock and to pay the exercise price. Hence, if it is beneficial to exercise the call option at expiration, then S at most should be equal to the option premium plus the present value of the dividends plus the strike price, or:[1]

$$S = P + \frac{E}{1+r} + \frac{D}{1+r}$$

Solving for the option premium, P, we have

---

[1] Note that if it is not beneficial to exercise the call option because the price of XYZ is less than the exercise price, Strategy 2 would be better than Strategy 1. Consequently, whether or not it pays to exercise the call option, we know that the value of Strategy 2 must be greater than or equal to the value of the price of XYZ stock (Strategy 1) at expiration. Thus,

$$P + \frac{E}{1+r} + \frac{D}{1+r} \geq S$$

Solving for the option premium, P, we have

$$P \geq S - \frac{E}{1+r} - \frac{D}{1+r}$$

The above relationship places a lower bound on the option premium for a call. Although the foregoing relationship has been developed for the two strategies at expiration, which would be true for a European call option, since an American call option is at least as valuable as a European call option, the relationship still holds for an American call option.

$$P = S - \frac{E}{1+r} - \frac{D}{1+r}$$

As can be seen from the above relationship, as the level of interest rates increases, the present value of the exercise price and dividends decreases and the option premium for a call increases. The opposite occurs for a put. That is, the higher the level of interest rates, the lower is the option premium for a put.

5. Cumulative Dividends before Expiration or Settlement   The relationship developed above clearly indicates that as the cumulative dividends before expiration-settlement increase, then, other factors equal, the option premium for a call decreases.

For an option on stock index futures, there are no dividends received by holding the stock index futures contract. For a cash index option, however, cumulative dividends are a factor to be considered in determining the option premium. This factor is discussed later in the chapter.

The Use of Options in Risk Management

The principles behind the use of options in risk management are well established as a result of academic work on option theory and a decade of experience with listed stock options. Every option contract, whether the option is an index or index futures option, a stock option, or a bond option, has what is variously called an *equivalence ratio,* a *neutral hedge ratio,* a *delta factor,* or an *elasticity.* Whatever the designation, the number represents the fractional change in the price of the option in response to a one-point change in the price of the underlying instrument subject to the option. This number, which we will call here the *hedge ratio,* is used to translate any option into its risk equivalent in the underlying instrument.

We will illustrate the hedge ratio in terms of a simple stock option. If an option changes in price by one-half point when the underlying stock changes in price by one point, that half-point price change on an option on 100 shares of stock is a change in the option's value of $50. The $50 equals the exact change in value that a holder of 50 shares of stock would experience if the stock price changed by $1. Therefore, the option is the risk equivalent of 50 shares of stock. In constructing a portfolio, we use the option as if it were actually 50 shares. If another option changed in price by one-quarter point in response to a one-point move in the stock price, that option would be the equivalent of 25 shares of stock. Every option—stock, bond, or index; in-the-money or out-of-the-money; put or call—can be translated into a fractional equivalent of the underlying instrument. If the fractional price change is one-half point on the option for a one-point change on the underlying instrument, it is simply a matter of multiplying that fraction by the number of units covered by the option contract, be it 100, 500, or some other number selected for the contract. The hedge ratio can be calculated for puts as well as calls and can be used to evaluate and control the degree of risk taken on or laid off in the options market.

Obviously, a certain amount of care must be taken in using this number because the hedge ratio will change as the market moves up and down. An option moving in-the-money or out-of-the-money will have a different hedge ratio than an option that is at-the-money. In a properly constructed stock option portfolio, the net stock-equivalent exposure of the portfolio may change relatively slowly because the risks of long and short option positions usually change in offsetting directions. In a portfolio using index options to control risk, the hedge ratio may change relatively quickly in periods of high market volatility because the portfolio will usually be long or short one type of index options, rarely on both sides of the option contract. A position that seems to provide an appropriate degree of risk may turn out to have too much or too little risk in the aftermath of a significant market move. Frequent adjustments of the index equivalence of an option position may be necessary.

Once the technique of using the hedge ratio is thoroughly understood, most investors find this approach more useful than the traditional option diagrams used in the previous chapter to show the profit or loss of an option relative to a position in the underlying instrument. The hedge ratio provides a dynamic risk analysis in contrast to the static analysis of the profit-loss lines.

The concept of beta is useful in analyzing differences in portfolio volatility and calculating the appropriate adjustment to be obtained from stock index futures or index options contracts. If a portfolio has a high beta (i.e., if it responds more dramatically than the average portfolio to changes in the market averages), hedging that portfolio against market risk on a dollar-for-dollar equivalent basis will not be adequate. The value of the portfolio should be multiplied by the beta. The resulting figure is the appropriate hedge target that the index-equivalent hedge position should offset. If an investor is attempting to use index options as a substitute for a long common stock portfolio and the investor is in the habit of investing in stocks with below-average beta, the lower portfolio beta should be taken into account in constructing the option position. The combination of beta and the hedge ratio should help fine tune the risk control. Beta is discussed in Chapter 12.

Option Evaluation

The hedge ratio is of value in understanding the concept of option evaluation. Option valuation discrepancies are the major reason, if not the only reason, for using options rather than futures contracts. Evaluation of stock index and index futures options is beyond the scope of this chapter, but any investor using options should be certain that he or she has a thorough understanding of the principles of option evaluation. There is no reason why every option investor should understand the mechanics of an option evaluation model or be prepared to develop detailed volatility estimates for the underlying optionable instrument. Every option investor should, however, understand that the principal decision variable in the process of option evaluation is the price volatility of the underlying instrument, be it a common stock, a debt instrument, or an index.

The major gains from astute evaluation of common stock options are possible in part because common stocks tend to have greater price volatility than do debt instruments and indexes. The fact that the underlying instrument in debt and index options is inherently less volatile means that the scope for significant over- and underevaluation is less pronounced. Also, stock market and interest rate volatilities tend to be more widely analyzed than does the volatility of an individual stock. If a typical stock option is mispriced by 15 to 25 percent, careful analysis of that degree of over- or underpricing should enable an astute portfolio manager to add several percent per year to the total return of a portfolio compared to the return on a stock-equivalent portfolio created using underlying common stocks alone. Because the index is less volatile than the stocks that it comprises, a similar degree of mispricing on the index options would provide a far smaller potential for improved return. If closer analysis of market volatility leads to more efficient markets for index options, the potential is further reduced. In addition, the transaction costs associated with the use of index options would be increased by the fact that an index option position will probably have to be adjusted more frequently than a stock option position that is part of a diversified portfolio of stock and option positions. On balance, most users of index options will probably find that the most they can expect from their activities in these options is to achieve the desired degree of risk adjustment and cover their transaction costs through astute use of option evaluation. Because transaction costs (the bid-asked spread as well as commissions) will be material, option evaluation is worthwhile. The investor who is on the wrong side of the option contract (e.g., short calls rather than long puts to offset the risk of a long stock portfolio) will be creating a risk adjustment position inefficiently. Transaction costs *and* the valuation premium or discount will be working against this investor. Thus, while option evaluation is unlikely to do as much for an investor in stock index or stock index futures options as it will for an investor in stock options, the transaction cost offset opportunity alone makes the evaluation exercise worthwhile.

Futures contracts can also be mispriced, but the mispricing is different from option mispricing and can either add to or offset it. If a futures contract is the underlying instrument, it is theoretically possible that a mispriced futures contract alone (without any option position) might be a more efficient way of undertaking a given degree of risk adjustment. When the calculation lag and related effects leading to futures contract mispricing are taken into account, what at first appears to suggest the purchase of an undervalued put may actually call for the sale of an over-valued call.[2]

There are relatively minor differences in valuation between options on index futures and cash settlement options priced on the indexes themselves. The circumstances that are likely to give rise to early exercise are similar but not identical. Given the pattern of ex-dividend dates, there is perhaps a somewhat greater possibility of early exercise of stock index options than of stock index *futures* options. When remaining dividends are high relative to the level of interest rates, there may be an incentive to exercise in the money cash settlement index calls to capture remaining dividends. When interest rates are high relative to dividends, the opposite effect may encourage exercise of in-the-money puts to capture cash that is likely to return more interest than the remaining likelihood of a decline in the index is worth.

Calculation lag also adds to the possibility of early exercise of stock index options should these options be significantly in-the-money. If index options are priced as if the settlement price were a futures price corrected for calculation lag and so forth, the actual closing price may encourage early exercise of some in-the-money options. This will probably not happen with stock index futures options because the futures contract price can adjust more quickly than the cash index value.

The slightly different nature of the incentive for early exercise complicates the analysis of both index and index futures options relative to options on common stocks and fixed-income securities. While the mathematics of the problem are complex, an analogy in the stock options market might be difficulties in making appropriate adjustments for dividends if (1) the underlying stock pays a dividend at least every other day, (2) the dividend varies greatly from one day to the next, and (3) the underlying stock is quoted in several different currencies.

As if these difficulties were not enough, there is another problem in the evaluation of stock index and stock index futures options. Many stock option evaluation models assume that the distribution of common

---

[2] Calculation lag is discussed in Chapter 8.

stock returns is lognormal.[3] Regardless of the shape of the underlying stock return index, problems occur when a variety of stocks with different volatilities (standard deviations) but similarly shaped distributions are combined in a weighted index. The resulting index will have not only a different variance or standard deviation (invariably lower than that of the average of the component common stock distributions) but also a different shape. The widely used Black-Scholes model is less useful in evaluating stock index and stock index futures options than in evaluating the stock options for which it was originally devised.[4]

An investor who is called upon to accept a model to evaluate stock index or stock index futures options should ask the following questions:

1. *What is the nature of the model used?*   If the answer is that it is a Black-Scholes or similar model adapted from stock option evaluation, the investor should use the results with a healthy degree of skepticism.[5] As a practical matter, numerical integration is probably the only way to handle a distribution problem that does not lend itself to a closed-form solution.

2. *How is the dividend adjustment handled?*   The answer to this question should reflect some of the material contained in Chapters 6, 7, and 8, and explicit adjustments should be made for dividends for each day of the life of the option.

3. *How are interest rate levels handled?*   The answer to this question should be complex. The way an interest rate adjustment is handled for a futures option is different from the way an interest rate adjustment is handled for a stock index option with cash settlement. The significance of the difference is related to the value of the underlying instrument and the probability of early exercise.

4. *What volatility estimate is being used, and how was it developed?*   The answer to this question should include more than a discussion of historic and implied volatilities. No specific approach to volatility estimation is inherent to any model, and mechanically derived volatility estimates should be viewed with suspicion. For example, any weighting of historic and implied volatility is arbitrary at best. Analysis of the underlying factors affecting volatility should be incorporated.

---

[3] Common stock prices are said to have a lognormal distribution if the logarithm of the price has a normal distribution. Thus, if a stock is priced at $100 and prices have a normal distribution, then the distribution of prices is the familiar bell-shaped curve centered at $100. But if the prices have a lognormal distribution, then it is the logarithm of the price which has a bell-shaped distribution about log 100 = 4.6051702. The logarithm of the prices is equally likely to be 5.2983174 or 3.912023, i.e., 4.6051702 ± .6931472 corresponding to prices of $200 and $50, respectively. If the probability density curve is plotted as a function of price, rather than as a function of the logarithm of price, the curve will appear skewed and with tails more nearly depicting the actual observed behavior of stock prices.

[4] Fischer Black and Myron Scholes, "The Pricing of Options and Corporate Liabilities," *Journal of Political Economy,* May–June 1973, pp. 637–54.

[5] For a discussion of option evaluation models, see Gary L. Gastineau, *The Stock Options Manual* (New York: McGraw-Hill, 1979), pp. 214–63.

The investor should ask anyone who provides a stock index or stock index futures option model the same questions that would be asked of anyone providing a common stock option model. While investors have a right to expect that these questions have been answered by the services that provide a commercial option evaluation model, these services are rarely up to the state of the art. Many services are guilty of misleading their subscribers, and skepticism is appropriate.

SECTION FIVE

Regulation, Tax, and Accounting Considerations

CHAPTER 19

Taxation of Stock Index Futures

Andrew G. Balbus, J.D.
Paul, Weiss, Rifkind, Wharton & Garrison

One of the most attractive features of trading in stock index futures is the favorable rate of taxation—a maximum federal income tax rate of 32 percent—available to most traders. This favorable rate was enacted as part of the Economic Recovery Tax Act of 1981 (the 1981 Act), which introduced into the Internal Revenue Code (the Code) a number of new concepts and rules as well as an entirely unique system for the taxation of certain commodity futures contracts known as "regulated futures contracts." The impetus behind the enactment of this legislation was the desire of Congress to eliminate abusive tax shelter transactions involving straddles in commodity futures contracts.[1] The impact of the 1981 Act has been a fundamental alteration in the manner in which all commodity futures contracts are taxed.

Although a stock index differs significantly from the type of commodity generally traded, such as gold, coffee, or pork bellies, the taxation of stock index futures is governed by the general rules of commodity futures taxation introduced by the 1981 Act and by certain amendments to those rules that were enacted as part of the Technical Corrections Act of 1982.[2]

This chapter will describe and illustrate with examples some of the basic concepts and rules of commodity futures taxation as they apply to the taxation of stock index futures. The description contained herein is not intended to be an exhaustive review of all the factors affecting

---

[1] The term *straddle* is defined later in this chapter.

[2] Technical Corrections Act of 1982, P.L. 97–448, 97th Cong., 2d Sess.

the taxation of stock index futures, nor does it take into account particular circumstances that might produce different results for certain taxpayers. This chapter should be used only as a guide and not as a substitute for careful planning by a professional tax adviser.

There are two kinds of traders in the world of commodity futures: speculators and hedgers. Most traders, including individuals, partnerships, and corporations, are speculators. Speculators trade contracts in commodity futures in order to profit from price movements in those contracts. Very often speculators trade commodity futures as a hobby, but professional traders are also speculators, unless they are hedgers.

Hedgers trade commodity futures in the normal course of their business in order to protect present or anticipated transactions in the underlying commodity against adverse price movements. Hedgers are interested primarily in profiting from sales to customers of the underlying commodity and not from transactions in commodity futures. A good example of a hedger involving stock index futures would be a securities dealer who trades stock index futures to protect his inventory of stock against a decline in the price of the stock.

Speculators and hedgers engage in different activities with respect to commodity futures. The tax laws reflect this. The taxation of stock index futures differs depending on whether the taxpayer is a speculator or a hedger. For that reason, the description that follows is divided into two parts: taxation of speculators and taxation of hedgers.

Taxation of Speculators

In 1981 Congress reacted to the growing use of tax shelters involving commodity futures straddles, which had threatened to prove half wrong the old adage that nothing is certain except death and taxes, by enacting as part of the 1981 Act a number of interrelated provisions concerning the taxation of commodity futures. These provisions were designed to prevent taxpayers from using straddles to defer recognition of income and to convert short-term capital gain into long-term capital gain. The favorable tax rate was part of the carrot used by Congress to win acceptance of the remedial legislation, which involves certain sacrifices by taxpayers, including the recognition of gain and loss in the absence of a closing transaction and the forfeiture of long-term capital gain and short-term capital loss treatment.

Although the loopholes closed by Congress in the 1981 Act did not involve stock index futures, which were not traded until 1982, many of the corrective provisions do apply to stock index futures. The following explanation of some of the interrelated concepts and rules introduced by those new provisions provides the basis for an understanding of the taxation of stock index futures held by speculators.

"Regulated Futures Contract"

The first concept is the "regulated futures contract," known simply as the RFC. An RFC is a contract that (1) is traded on or is subject to the rules of a domestic board of trade designated as a contract market by the Commodity Futures Trading Commission, or of any other exchange approved by the secretary of the Treasury; and that (2) is marked-to-market under a daily cash flow system of the type used by U.S. commodity futures exchanges.[3] A third requirement, that the contract require the delivery of specially defined personal property or an interest in such personal property, was removed by the Technical Corrections Act of 1982 to enable cash settlement contracts, which do not provide for the delivery of personal property, to be classified as RFCs.

The principal beneficiary of this amendment is the stock index futures contract, which is a cash settlement contract and otherwise qualifies as an RFC. Stock index futures are traded on three approved boards of trade or exchanges: the Chicago Mercantile Exchange (Standard & Poor's 500 Composite Index), the New York Futures Exchange (NYSE Composite Index), and the Kansas City Board of Trade (Value Line Average Composite). All of the stock index futures contracts traded on these exchanges are valued at 500 times the index number. For example, if the NYSE Composite Index were 78, the price of the NYSE Composite Index futures contract would be $39,000 (500 × 78).

On all of these exchanges the stock index futures contract is subject to a system of marking-to-market. This system determines the amount that must be deposited, in the case of loss, or the amount that may be withdrawn, in the case of gain, by comparing the price of the contract with the settlement price for the same contract on the exchange at the close of every business day. In other words, at the end of each business day the fair market value of each futures contract on that exchange is compared with the fair market value of the futures contract at the end of the previous day. Gain is credited to the margin account and may be withdrawn in cash each day. Conversely, loss is charged to the margin account and must be deposited in cash each day.

As a result of being traded on approved exchanges under a mark-to-market system, the stock index futures contract satisfies the two requirements for being an RFC. Under the law existing before the passage of the Technical Corrections Act of 1982, stock index futures would not have qualified as RFCs because they did not provide for the delivery of personal property. Unlike futures contracts in commodities such as gold, Treasury bills, and pork bellies, which provide for the delivery of the physical commodity upon expiration of the contract, the delivery of the underlying commodity upon expiration of a stock index futures contract

---

[3] Internal Revenue Code of 1954, as amended, Section ("I.R.C. §") 1256(b).

is virtually impossible. It would require the delivery of shares of stock in each of the corporations that are comprised by the index. Consequently, instead of providing for delivery of the underlying commodity, the stock index futures contract provides for a final marking-to-market of the contract on the last day of its trading, known as cash settlement.

Realization of Gain or Loss and the 60/40 Rule

There is a general principle of taxation that gain or loss is not realized for tax purposes until there is a taxable event. There are three taxable events that cause the realization of gain or loss with respect to stock index futures. These are: (1) a sale, known as a closing transaction; (2) cash settlement; and (3) year-end marking-to-market. Under no other circumstances is gain or loss realized. This means that any payments required under the mark-to-market system, either to enter into a position (initial margin) or to reflect a decrease in value of the position during the time it is held (maintenance margin), do not give rise to taxable losses in the absence of one of the above three taxable events. The same holds true for initial margin received on entering into a short position and maintenance margin received to reflect an increase in value of the position during the time it is held; neither of these receipts constitutes a taxable event.

A closing transaction is the equivalent of a sale. Instead of actually selling an unwanted position, a speculator disposes of it by entering into an opposite position, also known as an offsetting position, on the same exchange. For example, a speculator closes out a long NYSE Composite Index futures contract having a September 1984 maturity by entering into a short stock index futures contract for the same index (the NYSE Composite Index) and having the same maturity (September 1984). The short sale, in effect, cancels out the long position, thereby closing out the speculator's position in the same way that positive one combined with negative one produces a sum of zero.

The closing transaction is a taxable event. It produces taxable gain or loss in an amount equal to the difference between the contract price on the date of sale of the short position and the contract price on the date of acquisition of the long position. For example, if a speculator acquires a long September 1984 contract at a price of $39,500 (500 × index of 79) and closes it out with a short September 1984 contract when the price is $42,000 (500 × index of 84), he would recognize a gain (before commissions) of $2,500 [500 × (84 − 79)]. The identical result occurs if an initial short sale is closed out by the acquisition of a long stock index futures position.

In the hands of a speculator, a stock index futures contract is a *capital* asset. This is true whether those hands belong to a dentist or to a professional trader.[4] Any gain or loss realized with respect to such a contract is capital gain or loss, but is taxed under a special rule. The rule, known as the 60/40 rule, applies to all RFCs and treats 60 percent of the gain or loss as long-term capital gain or loss and the remaining 40 percent of the gain or loss as short-term capital gain or loss.[5] The 60/40 rule is applied to the net RFC gain or loss derived by adding together all of the RFC gains and losses realized during the taxable year. The 60/40 rule applies regardless of how long the stock index futures contract was held by the speculator and regardless of whether the stock index futures contract constituted a short or a long position. The maximum rate of federal income tax applicable to stock index futures and all RFCs under this rule is 32 percent.[6]

To illustrate the computation of a capital gain resulting from a closing transaction and the 60/40 rule, consider the following example: On September 1, 1983, the Standard & Poor's 500 Composite Index is at 134. Sam Speculator, D.D.S., expecting the index to go even higher, calls his broker and places an order to buy a Standard & Poor's 500 futures contract having a March 1984 maturity at a price of $67,000 (500 × index of 134), a long position. Under the rules of the Chicago Mercantile Exchange, the exchange on which the trade is placed, a good faith deposit (initial margin) must be deposited in order to guarantee that the speculator has sufficient funds to cover adverse price movements. Accordingly, Sam deposits the required amount with his broker. There is no tax consequence to entering into this position. Had Sam placed an order to sell a Standard & Poor's 500 futures contract, a short position, he would still be required to deposit initial margin. There would be no tax consequence to entering into that position either.

On September 2 the Standard & Poor's 500 goes up to 136.50. Sam's stock index futures contract is marked-to-market; the price of the contract is compared with the closing or settlement price of the contract on the exchange at the close of the day. If Sam's contract has increased in value, his account is credited for that amount. Generally, Sam has the right to withdraw cash from his account in the amount of gain credited to it. In this example, Sam's account is credited with $1,250 [500 × (136.50 − 134.00)] of gain, which he can withdraw immediately. If Sam's contract

---

[4] *Faroll* v. *Jarecki,* [56–1 USTC ¶ 9367] 261 F.2d 281 (7th Cir. 1956). In contrast, stock in the hands of a broker is ordinary income property unless specifically designated as held for investment. § 1221(1) and § 1236.

[5] § 1256(a)(3).

[6] The maximum federal income tax rate on long-term and short-term capital gains in 1983 was 20 percent and 50 percent, respectively. Consequently, the maximum federal income tax rate on stock index futures and all RFCs was:

$$60\% \times 20\% + 40\% \times 50\% = 32\%.$$

had decreased in value, his account would have been charged for that amount. If the equity in his account had fallen below the minimum exchange requirement, Sam would have been required to deposit additional cash before the next trading day. The cash that flows into and out of Sam's account in accordance with daily changes in the value of his contract is maintenance margin. There is no tax consequence to the receipt or payment of maintenance margin under the mark-to-market system except at the end of the taxable year.

On September 4 the Standard & Poor's 500 goes up to 138. Happy with his killing in the market, Sam closes out his long position by entering into an offsetting short position. A closing transaction is a taxable event. Sam realizes gain in an amount equal to the difference between the price at which he entered into his short position $69,000 (500 × index of 138) and the price at which he entered into his long position $67,000 (500 × index of 134), for a gain of $2,000 [500 × (138 − 134)].

At the end of Sam's taxable year, his net gain or loss must be recognized and taxed in accordance with the 60/40 rule: 60 percent long-term and 40 percent short-term capital gain or loss. If Sam has no other trades during the year, his gain is $2,000, of which 60 percent, or $1,200, is long-term capital gain and 40 percent, or $800, is short-term capital gain.

The result produced by the 60/40 rule is quite different from the result produced by the sale of stock. In the hands of most taxpayers, stock is a capital asset.[7] Any gain or loss realized upon the sale of stock is capital gain or loss but is long-term, or short-term capital gain or loss depending on how long the stock was held by the taxpayer before it was sold.[8] The present holding period for long-term capital gain or loss taxation is any period over 12 months.[9] Long-term capital gains receive preferential treatment; 60 percent of such gains are deductible, leaving only 40 percent to be taxed.[10] This produces a maximum rate of tax of 20 percent on long-term capital gains. Short-term capital gains are taxed in their full amount without deduction at a maximum rate of 50 percent.

Instead of entering into a closing transaction, a speculator in stock index futures may decide to keep his position open until the trading for a contract expires. Upon expiration, because delivery of the underlying commodity, a stock index, is virtually impossible, cash settlement occurs. Cash settlement is a taxable event. The tax consequences of cash settlement are exactly the same as those of a closing transaction on the last day of trading for the particular contract. Gain or loss is recognized in

---

[7] § 1221.

[8] § 1222.

[9] § 1222(3). Legislation has been introduced in Congress that would reduce the holding period for long-term capital gain or loss from the current holding period of over 12 months to a holding period of over 6 months.

[10] § 1202.

an amount equal to the difference between the price of the contract upon expiration and the price of the contract at the time it was entered into and is taxed under the 60/40 rule.

At year-end, each stock index futures position (as well as every other RFC) held by a speculator that has not been disposed of either by way of a closing transaction or by cash settlement is marked-to-market and treated as sold for its fair market value on the last business day of the taxable year.[11] This is known as the mark-to-market rule. Gain or loss realized by the marking-to-market of each stock index futures position is recognized and taxed under the 60/40 rule: 60 percent long-term capital gain or loss and 40 percent short-term capital gain or loss. This gain or loss is taken into account in determining gain or loss when the position is finally disposed of through a closing transaction or cash settlement in the following taxable year.[12]

To illustrate the foregoing rule, suppose that instead of closing out his position on September 4, Sam Speculator, D.D.S., a calendar-year taxpayer, holds his long Standard & Poor's 500 Composite Index futures position through the end of the year. On the last business day of that year, the index is 140.20. For tax purposes, Sam is treated as if he had sold the position for $70,100 (500 × index of 140.20). Sam recognizes gain in an amount equal to the difference between the amount he is considered to have constructively received, $70,100, and the amount he paid for his position, $67,000 (500 × index of 134), or $3,100 [500 × (140.20 − 134.00)]. The gain is taxed in accordance with the 60/40 rule. Of the $3,100 gain, 60 percent, or $1,860, is long-term capital gain and 40 percent, or $1,240, is short-term capital gain. Sam's $3,100 gain is taken into account in determining subsequent gain or loss with respect to his long position in the next taxable year.

If Sam allows his long futures position to expire on the last day of trading for his contract, the third Thursday in March 1984, when the Standard & Poor's 500 is at 139.20, cash settlement will occur. Sam will recognize a loss of $500 [500 × (139.20 − 140.20)]. Had Sam not previously recognized a gain of $3,100 with respect to his long position, he would have recognized a gain of $2,600 pursuant to the cash settlement transaction. The gain would have been computed as follows: $69,600 (500 × index of 139.20), the settlement price of the contract on the last day of trading, minus $67,000 (500 × index of 134), the price at which Sam entered into his long position. However, a gain of $3,100 has already been recognized with respect to the long position in the prior taxable year under the mark-to-market rule. An adjustment must be made to reflect the economic reality that gain of only $2,600 has been realized

---

[11] § 1256(a)(1).

[12] § 1256(a)(2).

with respect to Sam's long position. That adjustment is the recognition of a $500 loss at the time of the cash settlement. The $3,100 gain in the first year combined with the $500 loss in the second year net out to equal the $2,600 economic gain realized on the long position during the entire period it was held by Sam. The $500 loss is taxed under the 60/40 rule: 60 percent, or $300, is long-term capital loss and 40 percent, or $200, is short-term capital loss.

Carry-back and Carry-forward of Loss Rules

If the combination of all gains and losses realized during the taxable year with respect to stock index futures and all other RFCs from closing transactions, cash settlement, or year-end marking-to-market produces a net loss and insufficient capital gain is realized from other sources to offset that loss, speculators other than corporations, trusts, and estates can elect to carry back the loss, known as the net commodities futures loss, to the three previous taxable years and apply it against any net commodities futures gain recognized during those years.[13] The exact manner in which the net commodities futures loss is computed, carried back, and applied against net commodities futures gain, a set of rules no easier to describe than Rubik's Cube is to solve, is set out in the Code.[14] The earliest year to which a net commodities futures loss may be carried back is 1981, the first year in which there could be any net commodities futures gain against which the loss could be applied. If no net commodities futures gain exists in any of the three prior years, the net commodities futures loss can be carried forward indefinitely.[15] Capital losses attributable to assets other than RFCs do not receive this special three-year carry-back treatment.

Straddle Transactions

The tax rules described above pertaining to the taxation of stock index futures as RFCs are relatively simple. More complex rules apply where a speculator engages in a straddle transaction. For those who understood calculus more readily than the above rules governing the taxation of stock index futures as RFCs, don't despair; most of the rules concerning the taxation of straddle transactions will not apply to stock index futures. The rules will be discussed in brief, however, because they play an integral

---

[13] § 1212(c).
[14] § 1212(c)(4) and (5).
[15] § 1212(c)(6).

role in the taxation of commodity futures in general and because under certain circumstances the straddle rules might apply to stock index futures.

The straddle is another new concept introduced into the tax laws by the 1981 Act to prevent taxpayers from deferring the recognition of income and from converting short-term capital gain into long-term capital gain. A straddle is defined as a combination of two or more offsetting positions with respect to personal property.[16] A position is an interest in personal property with the exception of exchange-traded stock options with exercise periods of 12 months or less.[17] Personal property means any personal property that is actively traded except stock.[18] To simplify, the limitations pertaining to straddle positions apply to interests in all property except stock, short-term stock options, and real estate.

Positions are offsetting when the risk of loss from holding one position is substantially diminished by holding the other position or positions.[19] Offsetting positions are like two sides of a seesaw: one side goes up as the other side goes down. Loss realized on one position is offset by gain realized on the other position. The most basic straddle consists of a long position and a short position in the same commodity on the same exchange for delivery in different months. Delivery must not be in the same month; otherwise, the two positions will cancel each other out. Any increase in value of one position will be matched by an approximately equal decrease in value of the other position. The risk of loss from holding the long position is substantially diminished by holding the short position, because any loss on the long position will be offset by an approximately equal gain on the short position, and vice versa.

Stock index futures are positions that can constitute a straddle. Whether another position held by a speculator is an offsetting position with respect to a stock index futures contract is a question of fact; however, several rebuttable presumptions of situations in which positions will be considered offsetting are identified in the Code.[20] In general, if the value of the stock index futures contract ordinarily varies inversely with the value of one or more other positions, even if they actually do not vary inversely, those positions will be presumed offsetting and the rules governing the taxation of straddles will apply.

Stock index futures are new instruments, and the tax laws governing them are also new. Consequently, it is impossible to state precisely which positions will be offsetting with respect to a stock index futures contract, but some situations can be identified. A speculator who holds a long

---

[16] § 1092(c)(1).
[17] § 1092(d)(2).
[18] § 1092(d)(1).
[19] § 1092(c)(2).
[20] § 1092(c)(3).

and a short position in the same stock index futures contract with different delivery months does have offsetting positions that constitute a straddle. Additionally, a speculator who holds a long position and a short position in different stock index futures, such as a long NYSE Composite Index futures contract and a short Standard & Poor's 500 Composite Index futures contract, also holds offsetting positions that constitute a straddle because the value of one position ordinarily varies inversely with the value of the other position, even though the magnitude of those inverse movements may not be identical.

A speculator who holds a short stock index futures position and a portfolio of stock or exchange-traded stock options, with exercise periods of 12 months or less, the movements of which mirror movements of the stock market, does not have a straddle, despite the fact that such positions are offsetting, because stock and such stock options do not constitute positions in personal property.[21] If, on the other hand, the long position was composed of exchange-traded stock options with exercise periods of greater than 12 months (no such options are currently traded), the movements of which mirrored movements of the stock market, the positions would be offsetting and would constitute a straddle.[22]

It is also possible that straddles could be formed with stock index futures and Treasury bills, Treasury bill futures or Treasury bill options provided the value of such Treasury bill positions ordinarily varies inversely with the value of the stock index futures.

For the purpose of determining whether positions are offsetting positions, the Code contains certain attribution rules that treat positions held by a related person as held by the taxpayer. Positions held by the taxpayer's spouse and any other person filing a consolidated return with the taxpayer are treated as held by the taxpayer.[23] In addition, all of the positions held by flow-through entities in which the taxpayer has an interest, such as partnerships, trusts, estates, subchapter S corporations, and regulated investment companies, are treated as held by the taxpayer.[24] Regulations may ameliorate this onerous rule by providing that only a pro rata share of a flow-through entity's positions will be treated as held by the taxpayer.

Straddles can be composed of positions that are all RFCs (RFC straddles), positions that are both RFCs and non-RFCs (mixed straddles), or positions that are all non-RFCs. As explained above, stock index futures

---

[21] § 1092(d)(1),(2).

[22] If the proposed legislation referred to in footnote 9 is enacted, exchange-traded stock options with exercise periods of greater than six months would constitute positions in personal property. Such options are currently traded and together with a concurrently held offsetting stock index futures position would constitute a straddle.

[23] § 1092(d)(3)(A),(B).

[24] § 1092(d)(3)(C).

are RFCs. The only straddles that stock index futures can be a part of are RFC straddles and mixed straddles. Consequently, the taxation of non-RFC straddles will not be addressed in this chapter.

Straddles composed of two or more offsetting stock index futures constitute RFC straddles. So do straddles composed of stock index futures and other offsetting RFCs. If long Treasury bill futures, for example, ordinarily vary inversely in value with short stock index futures, a straddle formed by one or more of each of the two offsetting futures contracts would be an RFC straddle.

RFC straddles are specifically exempt from the application of the rules governing the taxation of straddles (provided such RFC straddles are not part of larger straddles).[25] Thus, for most speculators in stock index futures, the only rules that apply are the mark-to-market rule and the 60/40 rule. RFC straddles are exempt from the following straddle rules because the mark-to-market rule is sufficient to prevent the type of tax shelter arrangements that Congress sought to eliminate.

A mixed straddle consists of at least one RFC position and at least one non-RFC position, provided the two or more positions are identified in the taxpayer's records as forming a mixed straddle before the close of the day on which the first RFC position is acquired.[26] For example, a short NYSE Composite Index futures contract and an offsetting position made up of a number of long exchange-traded stock options with exercise periods of more than 12 months, the movements of which mirror movements of the stock market, constitutes a mixed straddle. The NYSE Composite Index futures contract is an RFC. The stock options are non-RFCs.

The principal rule applying to mixed straddles is the loss deferral rule, which provides that if one of the positions comprised by a straddle is closed out at a loss, the loss is recognized in that taxable year only to the extent that the loss exceeds the unrecognized gain in other open offsetting positions that were acquired before the closing transaction giving rise to the loss.[27] To the extent that the loss does not exceed the unrecognized gain, recognition of the loss is postponed until the first taxable year in which there is no unrecognized appreciation in offsetting positions.[28]

In the case of a mixed straddle, the RFC position is marked-to-market at year-end. Any gain is recognized. Any loss from the closing of the offsetting non-RFC position during the taxable year is recognized in full because there is no unrealized gain in the RFC position. If, on the other hand, loss is realized on the RFC position from a closing transaction,

---

[25] § 1256(a)(4).
[26] § 1256(d)(4).
[27] § 1092(a)(1)(A).
[28] § 1092(a)(1)(B).

year-end marking-to-market, or cash settlement, the loss is deferred to the extent of unrealized gain in the open offsetting non-RFC position.

To illustrate the tax treatment of a mixed straddle, suppose that on September 1, 1983, Sam Speculator, D.D.S., enters into a number of long exchange-traded stock options with exercise periods of over 12 months, the movements of which mirror movements of the stock market. On September 3 Sam enters into a short Value Line Average Composite futures contract. The two positions offset each other and constitute a straddle. The straddle is identified as a mixed straddle before the close of the day. At year-end the long stock option position has a gain of $100. The position is not an RFC, so it is not marked-to-market. The short stock index futures position, which is an RFC, has a year-end mark-to-market loss of $120. Only $20 of that loss is recognized in 1983 because of the loss deferral rule, which requires that loss be deferred to the extent of unrealized gain in other open offsetting positions. Here that amount is $100. The $20 loss is taxed under the 60/40 rule. The $100 deferred loss is carried over into the succeeding taxable year subject to the same restriction. If in the succeeding taxable year the long stock option position is closed out or expires, the deferred loss would be recognized in full.

Taxpayers are given the right to make a one-time election for all years to have the mark-to-market rule not apply to RFC positions in all mixed straddles.[29] The election is revocable only with the consent of the Internal Revenue Service. If the election is made, the RFC position will not be marked-to-market at year-end. In effect, the mixed straddle becomes a non-RFC straddle. If no straddle position has been terminated during the taxable year, either by way of closing transaction or by cash settlement, there is no loss and the loss deferral rule is inapplicable. If one of the positions is terminated at a loss, the loss deferral rule applies: the loss is recognized in that taxable year only to the extent that it exceeds the unrealized gain in other open offsetting positions. To the extent that the loss does not exceed the unrealized gain, recognition of the loss is postponed.

As part of the 1981 Act, Congress granted the secretary of the Treasury the authority to promulgate regulations comparable to the wash sale rule presently covering only stock and securities. The wash sale rule disallows any loss realized on the sale of stock or securities where substantially identical stock or securities are acquired within 30 days before or after the sale.[30] The rule is designed to prevent taxpayers from realizing loss on the sale of property when, in actuality, they continue to hold on to the property. By definition, this rule is inapplicable to RFCs because

---

[29] § 1256(d)(1),(2),(3).
[30] § 1091.

such contracts are not stock or securities.[31] The comparable regulations, which have not been published yet, would cover all positions in mixed straddles (and non-RFC straddles)[32] and would probably disallow loss on the sale of an offsetting position where a substantially identical position is acquired within 30 days before or after the sale. The same provision gives the secretary of the Treasury authority to promulgate a rule comparable to the short sale rule that affects the character of gain or loss and the holding period of stock delivered to close out a short sale. Such a rule probably would not apply to stock index futures, however, because, as RFCs, stock index futures have no holding period and are taxed under the 60/40 rule.

Reporting Requirements

All positions with unrealized gain held at the close of the taxable year must be reported annually, regardless of whether the positions are part of a straddle.[33] In addition, the amount of unrealized gain attributable to each reported position must also be reported annually.[34] There are a few exceptions to this requirement, the three most important of which are (1) positions in property that is inventory, (2) positions that are part of a hedging transaction, and (3) all positions held by the taxpayer if no loss was sustained on any position held during the taxable year or if the only loss sustained was in inventory or in hedging transaction positions.[35]

Holders of long or short positions in stock index futures probably will not be required to make reports with respect to such contracts. Because stock index futures are RFCs, the contracts are marked-to-market and gain is realized at year-end. As a result, there is no unrealized gain to report.

Taxation of Hedgers

A hedging transaction is a transaction entered into by a taxpayer in the normal course of business primarily to reduce the risk of price change with respect to property held or to be held by the taxpayer, provided the gain or loss on the transaction is treated as ordinary income or loss

---

[31] Revenue Ruling 71–568, 1971–2 C.B. 312.

[32] § 1092(b).

[33] § 1092(a)(3)(B)(i)(I).

[34] § 1092(a)(3)(B)(i)(II).

[35] § 1092(a)(3)(B)(ii).

and the transaction is clearly identified as a hedging transaction before the close of the day on which it is entered into.[36] A market maker who, in order to provide continuous bid and ask prices for stocks, is required to maintain an inventory of stocks and who trades in stock index futures to protect that inventory from adverse price changes, would be engaged in hedging transactions with respect to stock index futures.

The tax consequences of a hedging transaction are considerable. All gains and losses are ordinary. The maximum tax rate on such gains and losses is 50 percent. The mark-to-market rule is inapplicable.[37] Thus there is no recognition of gain or loss at year-end for RFCs held as part of hedging transactions, including stock index futures, unless such contracts are terminated through a closing transaction or cash settlement during the year. The loss deferral rule and any forthcoming wash sale rule are also inapplicable.[38] Thus a stock index future held as part of a hedging transaction could be closed out at a loss and that loss would be recognized (at ordinary income rates) despite the fact that there was unrealized gain in the taxpayer's stock inventory. If the taxpayer's transaction qualifies as a hedging transaction but the taxpayer fails to so identify it, the gain or loss will still be ordinary income or loss, but the mark-to-market, loss deferral, and wash sale rules will apply. There is a special rule denying hedging transaction treatment to syndicates. In general, syndicates are partnerships in which more than 35 percent of the losses are allocated to the limited partners.[39]

---

[36] § 1256(e)(2).

[37] § 1256(e)(1).

[38] § 1092(e).

[39] § 1256(e)(3).

CHAPTER 20

Regulation of Users of Stock Index Futures

Stephen F. Selig, LL.B.
Partner
Baer Marks & Upham

The Commodity Exchange Act and regulations thereunder adopted by the Commodity Futures Trading Commission (CFTC) apply to persons and entities that trade futures contracts as well as to market professionals. These regulations are discussed in Chapter 22. However, for many types of entities that propose to trade stock index futures, further regulation is involved. This second layer of regulation comes about because the basic nature of the entity's activities subjects it to substantive supervision by other federal agencies or by state agencies. The entities that are subject to this type of regulation include pension plans, commercial banks, saving and loan associations, credit unions, insurance companies, and common investment vehicles, such as pools. Thus, even though the CFTC has "exclusive jurisdiction" with respect to "accounts, agreements . . . , and transactions involving contracts of sale of a commodity for future delivery," these other agencies may limit the extent to which an entity subject to their jurisdiction may use stock index futures. Indeed, they can—and some do—prohibit an entity from using stock index futures altogether.

This chapter attempts to discuss in general terms the scope of such regulation. It will set forth for each category of entity referred to above, the name of the regulator, the extent to which that regulator permits the use of stock index futures, and the conditions which must be satisfied to obtain such permission.

Three preliminary observations are in order. First, trading in stock index futures commenced only in February 1982. Thus regulators have had but a limited period to address the utility of stock index futures to the entities whose activities they oversee. Accordingly, much of the material in this chapter of necessity is based on the position these regulators have taken regarding futures contracts on financial instruments such as Treasury bills, GNMA certificates, and the like. Indeed, up until the past few years, all futures contracts were regarded as improper for the institutions discussed in this chapter. The regulators took this position because futures contracts entail a high degree of leverage and thus were regarded as inherently dangerous. Recently, however, many regulators have come to understand that financial instrument futures may be used effectively to reduce portfolio risk. This realization in turn has led regulators to replace absolute prohibitions or severe constraints with more objective tests and more reasonable procedural rules. There is no reason why these tests and rules should not be equally applicable to stock index futures.

The second observation flows from the first. This chapter was written at the end of 1982. As regulatory authorities become more knowledgeable with respect to stock index futures, they can be expected to review their regulatory postures.

The third point is that much of the material in this chapter can be presented only in broad general terms.

For these reasons, the reader should obtain a knowledgeable adviser in order to obtain more detailed and more current information regarding these materials.

Private Pension Plans

Private pension plans ("plans") are subject to the Employee Retirement Income Security Act of 1974 (ERISA). ERISA does not talk about the use of stock index futures or, for that matter, any other kind of futures contracts, and until recently the Department of Labor (DOL), which has responsibility for administering ERISA, had not issued any rulings or advisory opinions on the use of futures. Accordingly, for the most part, to learn whether, and to what extent, plans and other deferred compensation plans, such as profit-sharing plans, may use stock index futures, one must look to the general provisions of ERISA.

From the viewpoint of a plan there are three critical questions: whether and to what extent the plan may use stock index futures, whether margin deposits are plan assets, and on whom the plan may rely to obtain advice on how to trade stock index futures.

May a Plan Use Stock Index Futures?

The basic answer to this question is yes. However, there are limits. ERISA requires a person making investment decisions for a plan to diversify plan assets "so as to minimize the risk of large losses" and to act "with the care, skill, prudence and diligence under the circumstances then prevailing that a prudent man acting in a like capacity and familiar with such matters would use in the conduct of an enterprise of a like character and with like aims."

DOL regulations supplementing ERISA provide that this prudence test will be satisfied if the fiduciary gives:

> appropriate consideration to those facts and circumstances that, given the scope of such fiduciary's investment duties, the fiduciary knows or should know are relevant to the particular investment or investment course of action involved, including the role the investment or investment course of action plays in that portion of the plan's investment portfolio with respect to which the fiduciary has investment duties.

The regulation goes on to define "appropriate consideration" to include:

> (A) a determination by the fiduciary that the particular investment or investment course of action is reasonably designed, as part of the portfolio (or, where applicable, that portion of the plan portfolio with respect to which the fiduciary has investment duties), to further the purposes of the plan, taking into consideration the risk of loss and the opportunity for gain (or other return) associated with the investment or investment course of action, and (B) consideration of the following factors as they relate to such portion of the portfolio:
> (i) the composition of the portfolio with regard to diversification;
> (ii) the liquidity and current return of the portfolio relative to the anticipated cash flow requirements of the plan; and
> (iii) the projected return of the portfolio relative to the funding objectives of the plan.

This DOL rule is colloquially known as the "prudent expert" rule. It is different from and it supersedes the so-called prudent man rule, which governs fiduciaries under state law. Under the prudent man rule, each and every transaction is looked at separately to see if it is a prudent investment. If it is not, and the investment has declined in value, the fiduciary may be charged personally with the loss. However, under the ERISA standard, each investment is looked at as part of the overall portfolio and in connection with the plan's objectives and needs. Thus an investment, though possibly imprudent if viewed under the prudent man doctrine, may be acceptable under the ERISA standard.

It seems clear that the prudent expert rule should permit a plan to use stock index futures to hedge an equity portfolio. For example, if the plan fiduciary holds what it regards as an attractive portfolio of equity securities but fears that the market as a whole will soon experience a decline, the fiduciary should be able to hedge that portfolio by going short the appropriate stock index futures rather than being forced to liquidate the portfolio. If the fiduciary's market analysis is correct, the value of the portfolio should decline by less (or at the least by not more) than the gain on the stock index futures position. Even if the fiduciary's market analysis is wrong (that is, the market rises), the gain in value of the portfolio should exceed (or be no less than) the loss on the short stock index futures position.

The alternative to this approach would be to liquidate the portfolio, invest in short-term market instruments, and, when the fiduciary believes the equity market will improve, sell the short-term securities and repurchase equity securities. The problems with this approach are that the transaction costs may be higher and it may be difficult to reconstruct as favorable an equity portfolio as the plan held previously. Of course, it is possible that a plan fiduciary using stock index futures to hedge may find himself in a position where his futures gains are less than his securities losses or his securities gains are less than his hedging losses. This, however, is not necessarily the fault of hedging. It may well be that the fiduciary's selection of securities was at fault.

An anticipatory hedge may also be prudent. If a plan anticipates receiving a substantial cash contribution in three months and would like to be able to invest in equity securities at the present time because price increases are expected over the next three months, the plan in effect can do so by going long a stock index futures now. If the plan fiduciary has accurately forecast prices, the cash contribution received in three months plus the gain on the futures trade should enable the plan to acquire the securities desired even though their prices may have risen.

Finally, it may be prudent to simply take a speculative position. For example, depending on interest rates, it may be possible for a plan fiduciary to be long a stock index futures contract and hold the bulk of its assets in debt securities (remember, most exchanges will permit a customer to use government securities as original margin). If interest rates are sufficiently high, this portfolio may produce a greater return to the plan than would dividends received on a broad equity portfolio. At the same time the plan can benefit from appreciation in the equity market.

How May a Plan Trade Stock Index Futures?

Until September 21, 1982, some plan managers were not sure whether a plan could maintain an account directly with a futures commission merchant (FCM). This concern arose because ERISA requires all plan assets to be held in trust. Thus, if the cash or securities used by a plan as margin for a stock index futures position constitute "plan assets," they would have to be held by a trustee. .

To deal with this perceived problem, some plan managers insisted on using a so-called "procedural understanding," which is an agreement between the plan manager, the FCM, and a bank acting as trustee. Under this agreement, the plan deposited original margin (usually Treasury bills) with the trustee and the FCM could have access to this original margin only if the plan failed to meet a variation margin call on a timely basis. In addition, to avoid the risk that the plan and the FCM could be involved in an improper extension of credit, the agreement usually called for daily payment of variation margin, often by wire transfers.

The procedural understanding, beside adding to the plan's expense of trading futures (the trustee bank charges a fee and daily wire transfers also cost money), might also be in violation of exchange rules requiring FCMs to receive original margin. As noted above, under the procedural understanding, the FCM does not receive and hold original margin; it only has a contractual right to receive the original margin if the plan breaches its agreement to pay variation margin on a timely basis. Under applicable CFTC regulations, this in turn could subject the FCM to charges against its capital.

Happily, these problems ended on September 21, 1982. In response to an application by Futures Industry Association, Inc. (the national association of FCMs), the DOL issued a series of advisory opinions that, in essence, will permit plans to deposit original margin directly with an FCM. The DOL stated that the bundle of rights represented by a futures contract, rather than the amount of margin required to be maintained with respect to that futures contract, constituted the "plan asset."

Accordingly, a plan may now maintain an account directly with an FCM. However, caution still dictates that to avoid extension of credit problems, margin payments by plans and variation margin payments both to and from FCMs should be made promptly.

Who May Make Futures Trade Decisions for a Plan?

Under ERISA, only trustees, fiduciaries named in a plan document, or "investment managers" are permitted to control or manage plan assets. For plans contemplating trading stock index futures and other futures contracts, the problem was that ERISA specified that only banks, insurance companies, and persons registered with the SEC as investment advisors might act as investment managers. This statutory provision excluded FCMs and commodity trading advisors (CTAs), who at this stage of the game may generally be more knowledgeable about trading futures contracts than banks, insurance companies, or security advisers. Of course, there are many banks and insurance companies with extensive experience in futures trading and the number of such institutions becoming involved in these markets is increasing rapidly.

In any event, the DOL has ruled that if an FCM or a CTA is registered with the SEC as an investment advisor, it may be an investment manager for a plan even though the advice it gives is solely with respect to futures trading. This provision may be important to plan fiduciaries because their liability may be reduced to the extent that trading decisions are made by an investment manager.

It is also important to keep in mind that a plan may not have an FCM both act as investment manager and execute transactions for the plan. Indeed, a plan may not hire its FCM to give trading advice. However, if the FCM does not charge a separate fee for rendering advice and does not charge commissions greater than those it charges to comparable customers, it may be able to give such trading advice to a plan without running afoul of ERISA.

These restrictions come about because under ERISA a person who, for a fee or other compensation, renders trading advice to a plan or has control of or discretion with respect to a plan's assets is a "fiduciary." In general, a plan fiduciary may not effect brokerage transactions for the plan. The securities industry has obtained an exemption from the DOL permitting a fiduciary to act as a securities broker provided certain conditions are met. However, the DOL has not yet granted a like exemption for fiduciaries seeking to act as an FCM with respect to stock index futures and other futures.

Thus, at this time a plan fiduciary may not act as an FCM for the plan. However, a person who renders investment advice but does not receive "a fee or other compensation" is outside the definition of a fiduciary. Accordingly, where the FCM renders advice without charge and where its commission charges to the plan do not exceed such charges to comparable customers, it may well be able to render advice and at the same time act as an FCM.

Commercial Banks

Commercial banks are either national banks, state banks that are members of the Federal Reserve System, or state banks that are members of the Federal Deposit Insurance Corporation (FDIC) but not the Federal Reserve System. These commercial banks are subject to regulation as follows:

National banks—U.S. Comptroller of the Currency (Comptroller).

Member banks of Federal Reserve System—Federal Reserve Board (FRB) and banking authorities of state of incorporation.

Member banks of FDIC—FDIC and banking authorities of state of incorporation.

Federal Regulation

The three federal regulators—the Comptroller, the FRB, and the FDIC—have issued a joint policy statement relating to futures activities of banks subject to their respective jurisdictions. Although the policy statement deals with the use of financial instrument futures, the principles contained therein should be equally applicable to stock index futures to the extent that a bank holds a portfolio of equity securities capable of being hedged. Whether and to what extent a commercial bank may hold such a portfolio is basically determined by the banking laws of the jurisdiction in which the bank is organized. That is, federal law applies to national banks and the law of the appropriate state applies to all other commercial banks. A review of all these laws is beyond the scope of this chapter. Rather, it shall be assumed that either through a "market basket" clause (that is, a statutory provision permitting a bank to use a specified percentage of its assets to make "other investments" in addition to other classes of specifically enumerated types of investments specified in the statute) or through a statutory provision expressly permitting investments in equity securities, a commercial bank may invest in equity securities. However, as a matter of prudence, a bank intending to use stock index futures should seek confirmation from its federal regulator (the Comptroller, the FRB, or the FDIC) that the policy statement is also applicable to stock index futures.

In general terms, the policy statement urges each bank to make certain that its interest rate futures transactions are designed to reduce risk in terms of the bank's total assets and liabilities. Specifically, the policy statement sets forth the following guidelines:

a. The Comptroller takes the position that the use of interest rate futures is "neither inherently prudent or imprudent." The FRB and FDIC duck this question. Instead, they request banks organized under state laws to obtain an opinion of counsel concerning the use of interest rate futures under state law. Clearly, the same step should be taken if a bank organized under state law plans to trade stock index futures.

b. The decision to use futures contracts should be made by the bank's board of directors. Action by the board in authorizing the use of futures should be based on written policies that are set forth in sufficient detail to summarize permissible contract strategies and their relationships to other activities engaged in by the bank. In addition, the bank's record-keeping systems should be in such detail that internal auditors and examiners are able to ascertain whether the bank personnel effecting futures transactions are functioning within the parameters of the authorized policies. Bank personnel should be in a position to describe in detail how the bank's futures contract positions are in furtherance of the bank's stated objectives and, where appropriate, documentation of the foregoing should also be available.

c. The bank's board is to establish position limits applicable to futures positions (as well as forward and standby contract positions), and the board (or a board committee or the bank's internal auditors) should review contract positions periodically to make certain that these limits are being adhered to. Periodically means at least monthly.

d. The policy statement also specifies bookkeeping requirements and accounting treatment for futures positions.

e. Financial statements and reports issued by the bank should include a footnote explaining any futures activity that materially affects the financial condition of the bank.

f. Banks should provide for internal controls such as reports to management by operating personnel, separation of function, and internal audits to make certain that policy is being complied with and to guard against abuses.

The FRB has also issued a separate policy statement on the use of interest rate futures by bank holding companies and their nonbank subsidiaries. The reason for this policy statement is that the FRB is of the view that holding companies should serve as a source of strength for their subsidiary banks and that, accordingly, the futures activities of bank holding companies and their nonbank subsidiaries should be risk reducing rather than risk enhancing. Simply put, only hedging transactions should be engaged in.

The detailed aspects of this release are similar to those contained in the joint release concerning written policies, position limits, internal controls, audit programs, record keeping, and accounting.

State Regulation

The common denominator of state banking law is that at present there are no statutes that expressly permit or prohibit the use of futures trading by a state-chartered bank. Rather, state laws cover the following range:

a. Legislation that gives a state bank the same authority as is "authorized or permitted to national banks by an act of Congress." The joint policy statement described above is not an act of Congress, and therefore it cannot be said with any certainty that a bank chartered in a state that refers to federal statutes may engage in futures transactions.

b. Legislation permitting a state bank to make "other investments" in some limited fashion (the market basket clause). It is arguable that a bank organized under the laws of such a state could use stock index futures. However, one state insurance commissioner, in construing a similar clause of the state's insurance law, took the position that one does not "invest" in futures contracts—one speculates. Accordingly, the views of the state banking department on whether the market basket clause permits use of stock index futures should be obtained.

 c. Legislation that permits a state bank to make such additional investments as may be approved by the state official or department or other body that administers the state's banking laws.

 d. Legislation that gives banks the power to take action reasonably necessary to avoid loss on investments already made. This seems to permit a bank to hedge with respect to an existing equity portfolio. However, it does not appear to permit anticipatory hedging or using stock index futures and debt securities as a substitute for ownership of equity securities.

 e. Legislation that gives a bank authority to undertake such further activities as are incidental to or necessary for attaining its business objectives. The Comptroller has expressed the view that the use of financial instrument futures is an activity incidental to banking. From this it could be argued that legislation of this type permits hedging activities.

The banking authorities of New York and California have expressed the view that commercial banks may use financial instrument markets for hedging. California requires prior written approval, and both states require policies and safeguards similar to those contained in the joint policy statements issued by the Comptroller, the FRB, and the FDIC. Logically, there is no reason why, if so requested, the banking authorities of these states would not similarly permit stock index futures transactions by banks subject to their jurisdiction.

In sum, a commercial bank holding an equity portfolio should be able to hedge that portfolio to the same extent that it can use financial futures to hedge a debt instrument portfolio. However, since the policy statements of the Comptroller, FRB, and FDIC speak only of interest rate futures, confirmation should be obtained that the guidelines contained in those statements are equally applicable to stock index futures. Similarly, commercial banks organized under state law must ascertain whether governing legislation or regulations permit such activity. Again, if financial instrument futures are permissible to hedge a debt portfolio, stock index futures should be permissible to hedge an equity portfolio.

Savings and Loan Associations; National Credit Unions

The answers here are shorter and simpler. Neither savings and loan associations nor national credit unions may use stock index futures.

With respect to savings and loan associations, the basic fact is that they do not engage in the type of transactions that would cause them to hold an equity portfolio requiring hedging. Their activities primarily revolve around mortgages and other loans. Because of this, the Federal Home Loan Bank Board has adopted regulations permitting savings and loan associations to engage in interest rate futures transactions as hedgers.

National credit unions are not even permitted to use financial instrument futures, and in any event, they, like savings and loan associations, do not hold equity portfolios requiring hedging.

Insurance Companies

There is no federal legislation or regulation applicable to investments by insurance companies. Accordingly, state law governs the extent to which an insurance company may invest in equity securities and use stock index futures. Like state banking laws, state insurance laws are diverse with respect to permitted investments:

a. Legislation that permits insurance companies to make only those investments that are specifically named in the statute. In such a state, even assuming that the insurance company may invest in equity securities, it will not be permitted to use stock index futures.

b. Legislation that authorizes specified investments but does not state that the specified investments are the only ones that may be made. In such a state, an insurance company may be able to use stock index futures.

c. Legislation that enables insurance companies to make, in addition to enumerated investments, "other investments." Here again, it can be argued that stock index futures may be used as a hedge, but verification from the relevant state authorities should be obtained.

d. Legislation that permits an insurance company to make other investments with the prior approval of the relevant regulator (usually the commissioner of insurance or the superintendent of insurance). In such a state, permission will have to be sought and, as noted below, may be difficult to obtain.

e. Legislation that permits other investments, but only in "good and solvent securities." Stock index futures are probably not "securities" and thus may not be utilized by insurance companies in a state with such legislation.

Although the ability of insurance companies to use stock index futures is limited, such use may increase in the future. The National Association of Insurance Commissioners has a Subcommittee on Valuation that recently issued a report supporting the use of futures contracts by insurance companies for hedging purposes. It is hoped that this report will lead to appropriate legislation. In addition, Illinois has adopted regulations permitting insurance companies to use interest rate futures subject to certain limitations. Analytically, the Illinois Commissioner of Insurance should be willing to permit stock index futures to be used on the same basis. However, an application for this relief will be necessary. In addition, an Advisory Committee on Insurance Regulatory Reform appointed by the governor of New York issued a report recommending that New York's detailed provisions on insurance company investments be replaced with a different set of investment criteria. Specifically, the committee proposes that New York insurance companies be permitted to invest up to 5 percent of their assets in exchange-traded futures for the purpose of reducing their economic risks in connection with their identifiable assets or liabilities.

Common Investment Vehicles

Commodity pools, like mutual funds, are common investment vehicles designed to enable the small investor to participate in a diverse investment and obtain the advantages of professional management. Under the Commodity Exchange Act and CFTC regulations, the person or entity that organizes a pool must be registered with the CFTC as a commodity pool operator and must file a disclosure document concerning the pool with the CFTC. In addition, because participants in a commodity pool (typically units of limited partnership) are regarded as securities, the pool must file a registration statement with the SEC (or be exempt from such registration) and may be required to make appropriate filings under state blue-sky laws.

All of this is fairly straightforward (though if the Futures Trading Act of 1982 is signed into law by the president, the role of the states will be less certain). The more difficult question (and one for which an answer cannot be given with certainty at this time) is whether a commodity pool that trades stock index futures is an investment company within the meaning of the Investment Company Act of 1940 (ICAct) and whether the trading advisor for such a pool must register as an investment advisor under the Investment Advisers Act of 1940 (IAAct). It is beyond the scope of this chapter to enumerate the statutory provisions governing such registrations. Rather, we shall assume that the only reason such registration is *not* required is that futures contracts are not securities. In other words, we are assuming that if stock index futures are deemed to be securities for purposes of the ICAct and the IAAct, such registration would be required.

Thus the specific inquiry becomes: is a stock index futures contract a security for purposes of the ICAct and the IAAct? The answer is that one cannot be sure. Accordingly, prudence dictates that commodity pools refrain from trading stock index futures until the Futures Trading Act of 1982 becomes law.

The problem comes about because the SEC has refused to concede that the CFTC has exclusive jurisdiction with respect to futures contracts where the object underlying the futures contract is a security. These contracts include, in addition to stock index futures, futures contracts for Treasury bills, Treasury notes, Treasury bonds, GNMA certificates, Eurodollars, and bank certificates of deposit. In fact, the SEC has taken the position that financial instrument futures may be "securities" for the purposes of the ICAct and the IAAct even though they are regarded as "commodities" under the Commodity Exchange Act. In a 1979 no-action letter the SEC stated:

> The term "Security," as defined in the Investment Company Act of 1940 . . . and the Investment Advisers Act of 1940 . . . includes a right to purchase a security. For this reason and others, a futures contract on a security may itself be deemed to be a security.

However, the SEC's letter went on to state that the staff would not recommend that the SEC take any action under the ICAct or the IAAct against the pool or its advisors if the pool and its advisors did not register under those acts. However, the SEC staff expressly stated that its no-action position was

> conditioned on any investment by the [pool] in . . . and any advice given by the [advisor] about futures contracts on financial instruments, *being limited to* futures contracts on United States Treasury Bills, United States Treasury Notes, United States Treasury Bonds, Government National Mortgage Association certificates, and commercial paper. (emphasis added)

It could be argued that a stock index futures contract is not a security because it is not a "right to purchase a security," since settlement is by cash rather than by the delivery of securities. In addition, to distinguish between a commodity pool that trades only those financial instrument futures enumerated in the SEC's letter and a pool that also trades stock index futures just does not make sense.

This apparently was recognized by the chairmen of the SEC and the CFTC when, early in 1982, they reached a jurisdictional accord under which the CFTC would be given exclusive jurisdiction with respect to broadly based stock index futures. The three stock index futures now being traded (based on the Value Line, Standard & Poor's, and New York Stock Exchange indexes) meet this criterion.

This jurisdictional accord has been incorporated into the Futures Trading Act of 1982. Accordingly, since that bill was enacted into law in January, 1983, pools should be able to trade stock index futures without fear of SEC involvement.

CHAPTER 21

Accounting for Stock Index Futures

David C. Fisher
Partner
Arthur Andersen & Co., New York

As was the case when trading in interest rate futures contracts began in late 1975, the question of appropriate accounting arose almost immediately when trading in stock index futures contracts began in early 1982. The Financial Accounting Standards Board (FASB) is only now addressing the question of accounting for commodity futures contracts. The FASB's current timetable calls for the release of an exposure draft of a Statement of Financial Accounting Standards (SFAS) on commodity futures accounting in the second quarter of 1983, with a final statement to be issued by the end of 1983. It is anticipated that the exposure draft will cover stock index futures transactions, and therefore the FASB's views may ultimately vary from those expressed in this chapter.

Accounting Issues

Transactions in futures contracts generally involve a margin deposit. This amount should be recorded simply as a deposit, representing a receivable from the futures commission merchant (FCM) with which trades are transacted. This receivable should be increased/decreased for variation margin changes, that is, gains and losses. Thus, at each reporting date the balance in the margin deposit account should represent the amount due from the FCM if all positions were closed out at that time. This amount should normally agree with the amount reflected on the FCM's monthly statement, less commissions accrued on open positions not yet payable.

315

The controversial accounting issue for futures transactions has been whether the increases/decreases in margin deposits (gains/losses) should be reflected in income currently or deferred and recognized in a later period. In 1980 a task force of the American Institute of Certified Public Accountants (AICPA) prepared an accounting issues paper on interest rate futures that recommended current recognition of gains and losses unless the futures contracts were entered into as a hedge of assets, liabilities, or anticipated transactions that were or would be accounted for on other than a market value basis. For these hedging situations, the issues paper recommended a specialized accounting treatment referred to as *hedge* or *deferral accounting*. This specialized accounting is based on a concept of "symmetry" between the accounting for the futures contract and the accounting for the cash position being hedged.

A question has been raised as to whether the recommended accounting set forth in this issues paper also applies to stock index futures contract transactions. That is, should there be a specialized accounting treatment for stock index futures contracts entered into as a hedge? Statement of Financial Accounting Standards No. 12, "Accounting for Certain Marketable Securities," gives guidance.

Overview of Statement of Financial Accounting Standards No. 12

SFAS No. 12, released in December 1975, sets forth accounting standards for marketable equity security transactions. The Statement does not apply to not-for-profit organizations, mutual life insurance companies, or employee benefit plans.

SFAS No. 12 defines an equity security as "any instrument representing ownership shares (e.g., common, preferred and other capital stock), or the right to acquire (e.g., warrants, rights and call options) or dispose of (e.g., put options) ownership shares in an enterprise at fixed or determinable prices." The term *marketable* as applied to an equity security is defined as "an equity security as to which sales prices or bid and ask prices are currently available on a national securities exchange."

Since SFAS No. 12 was released in 1975, before the advent of the stock index futures market, the Statement's definition of *equity security* does not specifically include or exclude stock index futures contracts. However, as seen above, the definition does include instruments representing the right to acquire or dispose of ownership shares in an enterprise. Although stock index futures contracts settle in cash and do not represent rights to acquire or dispose of the stock underlying the contracts (i.e., the stock underlying the index on which trading is based), the contracts, at least for accounting purposes, can be viewed substantively as rights to acquire or dispose of stock. Further, stock index futures contracts can be used for purposes similar to those of other equity security instruments defined under SFAS No. 12, for example, speculation or hedging. Therefore, it is logical to conclude that the accounting standards set forth in SFAS No. 12 apply to stock index futures contracts.

SFAS No. 12 comprises two basic sections. The first addresses accounting principles for marketable equity securities for enterprises in industries that do not have specialized accounting practices with respect to marketable securities. The second addresses such principles for enterprises in industries with specialized accounting practices.

Enterprises in Industries That Do Not Have Specialized Accounting Practices

SFAS No. 12 requires that a marketable equity securities portfolio be carried at the lower of its aggregate cost or market value, determined at each balance sheet date. The amount by which the aggregate cost of the portfolio exceeds its market value is to be accounted for as a valuation allowance. The valuation allowance represents the net unrealized loss (the amount by which the aggregate cost exceeds the market value) in that portfolio.

SFAS No. 12 requires entities with classified balance sheets (those entities that show separate classifications of current assets and liabilities permitting ready determination of working capital) to classify marketable equity security holdings into separate current or noncurrent portfolios to determine the amount, if any, and the disposition of a valuation allowance (i.e., the comparison of aggregate cost and market value for each portfolio). The classification of marketable equity securities into current or noncurrent portfolios is based on existing accounting literature, mainly Accounting Research Bulletin No. 43, chapter 3. For entities with unclassified balance sheets, all marketable equity securities are considered noncurrent. If for some reason the classification of a marketable equity security changes between current and noncurrent, the security is to be transferred between the corresponding portfolios at the lower of its cost or market value at the date of transfer. If a security's market value is less than its cost, its market value becomes the new cost basis. The theretofore unrealized loss should be accounted for as if it were a realized loss and included in net income.

Realized gains and losses on marketable equity security positions are to be included in the determination of income for the period in which they occur. Changes in the valuation allowance for a marketable equity securities portfolio classified as current are to be included in the determination of net income for the period in which the changes occur. On the other hand, accumulated changes in the valuation allowance for a marketable equity securities portfolio classified as noncurrent (including portfolios in unclassified balance sheets) are to be included separately in the stockholders' equity section of the balance sheet.

The provisions of Accounting Principles Board (APB) Opinion No. 11, "Accounting for Income Taxes," should be applied to unrealized gains and losses on marketable securities, whether recognized in net income or included in the stockholders' equity section of the balance sheet. That is, the provisions of APB Opinion No. 11 are to be applied in determining whether net unrealized gain or loss should be reduced by the applicable income tax effect. A tax effect is to be recognized on an unrealized capital loss only when there is assurance beyond a reasonable doubt that the benefit will be realized by an offset of the loss against capital gains.

Enterprises in Industries with Specialized Accounting Practices

SFAS No. 12 recognized that certain industries apply specialized accounting practices with respect to marketable securities. These industries include investment companies, brokers and dealers in securities, stock life insurance companies, and fire and casualty insurance companies. SFAS No. 12 did not alter any industry's specialized accounting practices except for specialized industries that had carried marketable equity securities at cost. These industries are now required to carry marketable equity securities at the lower of aggregate cost or market value, or on a market value basis if the market value basis of accounting is also an accepted specialized practice permissible in the industry.

Applicability of SFAS No. 12 to Stock Index Futures Contract Transactions

Enterprises in Industries That Do Not Have Specialized Accounting Practices

Following the logic of the accounting standards of SFAS No. 12, gains and losses on open stock index futures positions (i.e., unrealized gains and losses) should be considered in determining the aggregate market value of an entity's marketable equity securities portfolio at each reporting date. Thus unrealized gains and losses should be considered in determining the amount, if any, of the valuation allowance.

For example, if on a reporting date an entity held a marketable equity securities portfolio, absent stock index futures contracts, at a cost of $1 million and with a market value of $950,000, SFAS No. 12 would require that entity to establish a valuation allowance of $50,000. However, if the entity also had open stock index futures contracts at the reporting date, the unrealized gains/losses would be subtracted from/added to the required valuation allowance. That is, if over the holding period of the stock index futures contracts, unrealized gains of $50,000 or more had been generated, there would be no valuation reserve requirement; the unrealized gains on the futures contracts would offset the unrealized losses on the securities portfolio. However, if the unrealized gains amounted to only $20,000, a $30,000 valuation allowance would still be required. If the entity had incurred losses on the futures holdings, those losses would require an increase to the valuation allowance.

Changes in the valuation allowance for a marketable equity security portfolio, including gains and losses from open stock index futures contracts, included in current assets should be included in the determination of net income for the period in which the changes occur. Accumulated changes in the valuation allowance for a marketable equity securities portfolio, including open stock index futures positions, included in noncurrent assets or in an unclassified balance sheet should be included in the stockholders' equity section of the balance sheet and shown separately.

Under SFAS No. 12, realized gains and losses are to be included in the determination of net income for the period in which they occur. Therefore, gains and losses on stock index futures contracts closed out should be included in the determination of net income for the period in which they occur.

Some persons familiar with the AICPA's recommended accounting for interest rate futures contracts used in a hedging situation may argue that realized gains and losses on stock index futures contracts used as a hedge should be reflected as an adjustment to the cost basis of the securities portfolio being hedged. In this manner these gains and losses would continue to be included in the determination of the valuation allowance until the security positions making up the portfolio were sold out. This accounting position is consistent with the concepts set forth for interest rate futures contracts used to hedge assets or liabilities accounted for on a historical cost basis. However, as previously noted, SFAS No. 12 encompasses marketable stock option contracts but does not provide for special accounting treatment of realized gains and losses on options used as a hedge (e.g., the purchase of call options to guarantee a minimum price for an anticipated purchase or the purchase of put options to protect against the risk of falling prices on existing security positions). Rather, under SFAS No. 12, gains and losses on all marketable equity positions, whether common, preferred, or other capital stocks or rights to acquire or dispose of ownership shares in an enterprise at fixed or determinable prices, are to be recognized in income when realized, regardless of the intent of the initiation of the transaction.

Enterprises in Industries with Specialized Accounting Practices

For industries with specialized accounting practices, such as investment companies and brokers and dealers in securities that report gains and losses on securities positions on a market value basis, unrealized gains and losses on stock index futures contracts should be included in the determination of net income for the period in which they occur.

The accounting principles for investment security transactions for insurance companies (other than mutual life insurance enterprises, assessment enterprises, or fraternal benefit societies) are set forth in SFAS No. 60, "Accounting and Reporting by Insurance Enterprises." Like SFAS No. 12, SFAS No. 60 does not address stock index futures transactions specifically. However, it can be assumed that the principles of SFAS No. 60 apply. Under SFAS No. 60, realized gains and losses on stock index futures transactions would be reported in the net income statement below operating income and net of applicable income taxes. Unrealized gains and losses, net of applicable income taxes, are to be reported as a separate component of stockholders' equity.

The accounting principles for investments held by pension plans are set forth in SFAS No. 35, "Accounting and Reporting by Defined Benefit Pension Plans." Under SFAS No. 35, plan investments, whether equity or debt securities, real estate, or other (excluding certain contracts with insurance companies), are to be presented at their fair value at each reporting date. Under this method of accounting (commonly referred to as "mark-to-market" accounting), changes in the market value of the plan's investments are recognized currently in the statement of changes in net assets available for plan benefits. Therefore, entities should recognize unrealized gains and losses on futures contracts currently in the statement of changes in net assets.

CHAPTER 22

Regulation of Stock Index Futures Trading*

Howard Schneider
Partner
Rosenman Colin Freund Lewis & Cohen

Fred M. Santo
Partner
Rosenman Colin Freund Lewis & Cohen

Stock index futures, whose economics, mechanics, and ramifications are explained elsewhere in this book, became, in the year of their introduction, the hottest and perhaps most interesting new contract that had ever been developed in the highly innovative world of commodity futures trading. The combination of stock market analysis with futures market hedging and speculative potential captured the imagination of the Wall Street community. To understand the stock index futures markets, it is necessary to have a basic understanding of the futures markets and their regulation. The task of this chapter is to explain the regulation of stock index futures contracts in the broader context of the regulation of futures markets.

Although trading in stock index futures contracts commenced only recently, the regulatory framework for the futures markets in general

---

* This chapter was written at the beginning of 1983. The regulation of futures markets in general and stock index futures in particular are rapidly developing and changing areas of the law. New legislation, new or changed CFTC regulations or interpretations, new rules and regulations adopted by the recently registered National Futures Association, amended exchange rules, various judicial and administrative decisions, and even varied custom and usage of the trade all serve to modify existing regulatory structures. Moreover, the wide scope of the materials covered in this chapter requires summary treatment for most topics. Accordingly, the reader should consult with knowledgeable advisers for an in-depth analysis and an update of the materials included in this chapter.

has been evolving over many years. What makes the subject difficult is that a whole jargon has developed that must be mastered to understand fundamental concepts. The area is further complicated by the rapid pace at which the laws, rules, and regulations that pertain to futures trading are changing. Despite the esoteric and complex nature of the regulation of stock index futures trading, for anyone who is involved in such trading to any degree, some rudimentary knowledge of the regulatory atmosphere in which that trading occurs is essential.

This chapter is divided into four basic sections: "The Regulatory Framework," "Who Is Regulated," "Legal Proceedings Available," and "Miscellaneous Regulatory Matters." The section "The Regulatory Framework" discusses the evolution of the stock index as a "commodity" capable of being the subject of futures trading and the jurisdiction of the Commodity Futures Trading Commission (CFTC), the federal independent regulatory commission established in 1975 to oversee the nation's commodity markets. The section "Who Is Regulated" discusses the many entities involved in commodity matters (exchanges, registered futures associations, floor brokers, futures commission merchants, introducing brokers, commodity trading advisors, commodity pool operators, traders, associated persons, and commodity option dealers) and the various regulations affecting each. The section "Legal Proceedings Available" reviews the remedies available to an aggrieved party in a commodity transaction. First, there is an analysis of the remedies available to the government when it finds violations of the law or its regulations; and second, there is a review of the ultimate forums for individuals involved in commodity disputes—the courts, administrative reparations proceedings, or arbitration. The section "Miscellaneous Regulatory Matters" briefly discusses recently enacted legislation that calls for a study regarding the economic impact of futures trading, including trading in stock index futures contracts and options on such instruments.

The Regulatory Framework

The Evolution of Stock Index Futures Contracts

The Commodity Exchange Act (the CE Act) is the basic federal legislation affecting commodity trading. Prior to 1974 trading in only the agricultural commodities that were specifically enumerated in the CE Act (i.e., wheat, corn, soybeans, etc.) was regulated. The agency responsible for overseeing commodity trading up to that time was the Commodity Exchange Authority, an arm of the U.S. Department of Agriculture.

In 1974 Congress extensively revamped the CE Act, expanding the definition of "commodity" to include all those previously enumerated commodities and "all services, rights and interests in which contracts for future delivery are presently or in the future dealt in." The effect of this broad, all-inclusive definition was to enlarge greatly the universe of possible subjects of futures trading, and it has led to innovative new futures markets, including most recently stock index futures (a term referring to any futures contract that has as its underlying "commodity" a group or index of securities).

The Jurisdiction of the Commodity Futures Trading Commission

The 1974 amendments to the CE Act created the CFTC and gave it extensive jurisdiction over commodity matters. The concept of pervasive jurisdiction was made explicit by a statutory grant of "exclusive jurisdiction" to the CFTC. The congressional intent, as evidenced by page after page of legislative history, was to have a single agency govern the commodity industry, without interference from the Securities and Exchange Commission (SEC), state securities administrators, or any other federal or state governmental agency. The purpose was to avoid duplicative regulation and cut bureaucratic red tape. In addition, the all-encompassing nature of the CE Act meant that under the Supremacy Clause of the U.S. Constitution, Congress had preempted the field and no other regulation might obtain. Even though the grant of exclusive jurisdiction is clearly spelled out in the CE Act, the SEC and the state securities administrators have regularly contested just how exclusive "exclusive jurisdiction" really is.

CFTC versus SEC Jurisdictional problems between the SEC and the CFTC first arose shortly after the CFTC's creation in 1975 in connection with fraud cases related to commodity option sales to the public. These problems were heightened in 1976 and 1977 by disputes over which agency should regulate the then new financial instruments futures markets. Under the broad definition of "security" contained in the federal securities laws, the SEC claimed that although instruments such as U.S. Treasury bills, notes, and bonds, mortgage-backed certificates guaranteed by the Government National Mortgage Association, and commercial paper were exempt from registration under the federal securities laws, a contract for future delivery of such exempt securities was a right to acquire a security and that under federal securities laws such a right was itself a security. Into this general swirl of controversy over which agency should regulate what, the concept of stock index futures inflamed already heated passions. The SEC argued that a stock index futures contract, which would have as its underlying "commodity" a group of securities that were not exempt from registration under the federal securities laws, went to the heart of the SEC's congressionally mandated responsibilities, that is, the oversight of the nation's securities markets. On the other hand, the CFTC viewed the stock index concept as but a logical extension of financial futures trading. The CFTC maintained that it had been granted exclusive jurisdiction over all futures contracts, including futures contracts on any group or index of securities and any option to purchase such contracts. Despite the continued controversy, and notwithstanding repeated requests from the SEC and others for clarifying amendments, when the CE Act was amended by the Futures Trading Act of 1978, there was no change in the provisions regarding the exclusive jurisdiction of the CFTC.

In testimony before a House subcommittee prior to the adoption of the Futures Trading Act of 1978, fears were expressed by the SEC and others that futures contracts based on equity or debt securities of a single issuer, traded either on national securities exchanges or in the over-the-counter market, might be developed in the near future and that trading of such futures contracts might have an adverse impact on the cash market for the underlying equity securities. Although the CFTC had not received an application for designation of a futures contract based on a single issuer's securities as a contract market (it had applications for a broad-based index), there was congressional concern over the ramifications of this potential form of futures trading and grave doubts (which were also shared by the CFTC) were expressed as to whether any such futures contract could satisfy the public interest and economic purpose tests for designation as a futures contract under the CE Act.

Proposals for trading in futures contracts based on an aggregate or pool of a number of different securities or indexes involving such an aggregate were not viewed with the same concern. Prior to the adoption of the Futures Trading Act of 1978, a report of the House Committee on Agriculture made this clear when it stated:

> It appears at least theoretically possible that futures contracts may be developed concerning an aggregate of securities or an index thereon that may reasonably be expected to serve a valid economic function. The Committee expects, however, that the [CFTC] will proceed with extreme caution in its consideration and designation of any contract market to trade a futures contract involving securities and that it will satisfy itself that an economic purpose can be expected to be served by the contract consistent with the proper functioning of the market for the underlying securities. The [CFTC] has assured the Committee that it will proceed with caution in considering any such designation application and will solicit the views of the Securities and Exchange Commission and carefully consider its views before proceeding.

As a result of these types of concerns over the burgeoning development of futures contracts in a variety of financial instruments, the 1978 amendments mandated consultation by the CFTC with sister agencies. The CFTC was required to maintain communication with the Department of the Treasury, the Board of Governors of the Federal Reserve System, and the SEC (1) to keep them fully informed of CFTC activities related to their responsibilities, (2) to consider the relationship between the volume and nature of investment and trading in futures compared to securities and financial instruments under their jurisdiction, and (3) to obtain their views on those activities.

The CFTC was required to deliver promptly to the Department of the Treasury and the Federal Reserve Board a copy of any application for designation as a contract market for contracts for future delivery of securities issued or guaranteed by the United States or any agency thereof. The CFTC was prohibited from approving any such application until it had received the views of these agencies or until 45 days after delivery of the application to these agencies, whichever was sooner. Any comments received from these agencies were required to be included in the public record, and the CFTC was required to consider the views of these agencies in approving, refusing, suspending, or revoking such designations or in taking any emergency action affecting such designated contract markets. The CFTC was also required to consider the effect of designation, suspension, revocation, or emergency action on the debt-financing requirements of the United States and on the continued efficiency and integrity of the underlying market for government securities.

Due in part to the impetus from these provisions, as well as the rapid increase in the number and types of financial instruments traded and proposed to be traded in both the commodities and securities markets, on December 7, 1981, Chairman Johnson of the CFTC and Chairman Shad of the SEC announced a jurisdictional accord (the CFTC/SEC Accord). The Accord, subject to congressional implementation, was intended to put to rest many of the jurisdictional battles that the two agencies had fought since the inception of the CFTC in 1975. Under the CFTC/ SEC Accord, the two agencies agreed that the CFTC would retain exclusive jurisdiction over financial futures and options on financial futures and that the SEC would have exclusive jurisdiction over options on the instruments underlying the financial futures. They further agreed that the CFTC would not approve a futures contract (or option) on a stock index unless (1) the index on which such a contract was based was a widely published and accurate measure of a broad segment of the corporate or municipal securities market, (2) the contract was not susceptible to manipulation of the underlying securities or securities option market, and (3) the contract was settled in cash. Any proposed stock index futures contract (or option thereon) could be objected to by the SEC at a hearing before the CFTC. If the contract were approved despite such objection, the SEC could petition an appellate court for review. Finally, they agreed that futures trading on individual corporate or municipal securities would be prohibited for the foreseeable future.

After the CFTC/SEC Accord was reached, but before congressional passage, the CFTC approved three contract markets to trade stock index futures: the Kansas City Board of Trade Value Line Average Composite, the Chicago Mercantile Exchange Standard & Poor's 500 Composite Index, and the New York Futures Exchange New York Stock Exchange Composite Index and subindexes thereof. Those markets have traded stock index futures since early 1982.

Meanwhile, the CFTC/SEC Accord was submitted to Congress for legislative implementation and was enacted into law through a series of amendments to the Securities Act of 1933, the Securities Exchange Act of 1934, and the CE Act. The provisions relating to the approval of stock index futures contracts were altered, however, from those originally agreed upon by the CFTC and SEC. Differing versions of these provisions were passed by the Senate and the House in the late fall of 1982 in connection with the consideration of the Futures Trading Act of 1982 to amend the CE Act and reauthorize the CFTC beyond September 30, 1982. The Senate provisions mirrored the CFTC/SEC Accord, while the House provisions gave the SEC the right effectively to veto any new stock index futures contract (or option on such contract). Moreover, the House provisions called for a Federal Reserve Board study of stock index futures trading lasting two years. A House-Senate conference committee in late 1982 effected a compromise between these two proposals whereby the Senate provisions would govern applications for approval submitted prior to December 9, 1982, and a modified version of the House provisions would govern applications submitted on or after December 9, 1982. Moreover, provisions of the House bill calling for a specific study of stock index futures by the Federal Reserve Board were modified to require a study by the Federal Reserve Board of the effects on the economy of all futures trading, including trading in stock index futures contracts and options on such contracts. The Futures Trading Act of 1982 (the "1982 amendments") was enacted into law on January 11, 1983.[1]

CFTC versus States The jurisdictional disputes that developed between the CFTC and the state securities administrators since the passage of the 1974 amendments to the CE Act have not yet been fully resolved.

---

[1] See the section "Who Is Regulated" for a description of the applicable provisions of the 1982 amendments relating to the designation of stock index futures contracts and options on said contracts.

These disputes have centered primarily on the ability of the states to enforce their securities antifraud statutes in connection with the purchase or sale of all commodity futures contracts, including those on stock indexes. The 1978 amendments to the CE Act provided for the states to continue to investigate commodity frauds, to bring actions in state courts under their general antifraud statutes (not the CE Act), and to bring actions in the federal courts (not state courts) to enforce the provisions of the CE Act (not state laws) that were designed to combat fraud or otherwise protect the public from the unlawful activities of persons who violated the CE Act. For a myriad of reasons, the states raised objections to the limitations contained in these amendments. As a result, the 1982 amendments expressly permit states, upon notice to the CFTC, to prosecute in *state* courts persons who are registered pursuant to the CE Act under the antifraud provisions of the CE Act or any antifraud rule, regulation, or order issued pursuant to the CE Act. However, the CFTC has the right to intervene in any such proceeding and to file an appeal, and either the CFTC or the defendant may seek removal of the proceeding to a federal district court.

Who Is Regulated

Contract Markets; Exchanges

One of the cardinal tenets of commodity law is that no futures transaction may take place off an exchange. Each particular stock index futures contract, which is uniform as to terms for each group or index of securities and varies only as to price and time of settlement, must be purchased or sold at the place specified on an exchange licensed to trade that contract, during normal trading hours, by open outcry, pursuant to open and competitive bidding. Accordingly, central to the concept of stock index futures trading is the marketplace where such trading occurs.

Designation   In general, under the provisions of the CE Act, each contract for each separate stock index to be traded (or each option on such index) must be approved by the CFTC. When approved, the place where it is to be traded is said to be *designated* (*i.e.,* licensed) as a contract market for that particular commodity. Although not defined in the CE Act, the place where one or more such designated contract markets exist is called an "exchange" and will be so characterized in this chapter. It should be noted that separate and distinct contract markets for the same commodity may be designated for trading on more than one exchange.

   In the case of a stock index futures contract, "designation" is a somewhat more complex procedure than designation of other types of commodity contracts. The designation process differs, depending on whether the application was filed before or after December 9, 1982. The 1982 amendments mandate that, to be designated as a contract market for trading in any futures contract involving a particular group or index of securities, a board of trade must submit an application to the CFTC that demonstrates (and the CFTC must expressly find) that settlement of the contract is in cash; that trading in the contract is not susceptible to manipulation, either as to the price of the contract or as to the underlying group or index of securities; and that the group or index of securities on which the contract is based is a widely published and accurate measure of the corporate or municipal securities markets. These were the standards established in the CFTC/SEC Accord. The CFTC must provide an opportunity for public comment on whether the proposed contract meets these requirements.

With respect to any application submitted by a board of trade prior to December 9, 1982, the SEC is entitled to an oral hearing before the CFTC if the SEC objects to the designation of a futures contract on the ground that it fails to meet these requirements. The SEC must lodge its objection within 15 days following the close of the public comment period, and the hearing must be held not less than 30 and not more than 45 days after the close of the comment period, unless both the CFTC and SEC agree otherwise. If, following the hearing, the SEC fails to withdraw its objections and the CFTC nevertheless issues an order designating the board of trade as a contract market with respect to the contract, the SEC has the right to seek judicial review of the CFTC determination in the federal courts.

With respect to any application for designation as a futures contract submitted by a board of trade on or after December 9, 1982, the SEC is entitled, within 45 days following the close of the public comment period on the application, to make a determination that the proposed contract fails to meet the requirements for designation. In the event of such a determination, the board of trade is entitled to a hearing on the record before the SEC no later than 30 days following the request. The SEC is required to make a final determination within 30 days after the close of the hearing. If a final determination against designation is made, it is then binding on the CFTC. If the SEC does not make such a determination, the CFTC may still disapprove the proposed contract. Any person aggrieved by a determination of the SEC has the right to seek judicial review in the federal courts.

The same procedures are applicable to the designation of options on stock index futures contracts.

The Senate-House conference committee report on the 1982 amendments makes clear that the authority of the SEC in the designation process is limited to making findings that stock index futures contracts and options on such contracts meet the criteria for designation. The CFTC retains exclusive regulatory authority after such contracts are approved.

The Contract   The standardized terms and conditions under which a particular stock index is to be traded are set forth in the rule book of the particular exchange on which it trades. The rule book covers contract terms and conditions, such as trading units, trading months, hours of trading, daily price range, position limits, settlement procedures, and the like.

Membership   Exchanges are primarily voluntary associations of members. A member, of whatever category, has trading privileges that enable him to trade futures contracts and other commodities on the floor of the exchange. A member purchases his "seat" (i.e., membership) on the exchange and may transfer that membership for a price to any person whom the exchange accepts for membership. To qualify for membership, applicants must normally meet certain financial and fitness requirements of the exchange. Certain exchanges, including those trading stock index futures, also allow members to lease their seats to approved persons who meet exchange requirements.

Each exchange rule book contains extensive provisions relating to trading practices, membership, categories of membership, and the governance of the exchange. Exchanges are self-regulatory, quasi-public institutions with responsibilities for the enforcement of their own rules and regulations. Violations of exchange rules can subject members to disciplinary actions, including suspension and fines. All such exchange disciplinary actions are subject to review by the CFTC.

Clearing Organizations   Each exchange provides a clearing mechanism with respect to trades effected on it. The clearinghouse becomes the seller to every buyer and the buyer to every seller. Certain members, meeting stringent financial requirements with back office facilities for processing trades, become clearing members. In that capacity, they act for themselves and other members of the exchange in clearing futures transactions. Again, extensive rules and regulations relating to clearing matters are covered in the rule book of the exchange or its separate clearing organization.

Margins   Each exchange sets minimum initial and variation margin requirements (i.e., good faith deposits) for each contract traded on it. However, the Federal Reserve Board is considering the establishment of margin requirements and has requested public comments on a proposed regulatory framework for this purpose.

Review of Exchange Rules by CFTC   Pursuant to the CE Act, each exchange is required to submit all of its rules to the CFTC. Except for the rules concerning the setting of levels of margin, the CFTC must approve all rules relating to trading and it is authorized to alter or supplement any such exchange rule.

Emergency Action by CFTC   The CE Act empowers the CFTC to direct a contract market, in an emergency, to take action that the CFTC considers necessary to restore orderly trading or liquidate existing contracts. "Emergency" is defined as a potential manipulation or other major market disturbance that prevents the market from accurately reflecting the law of supply and demand. The 1982 amendments provide for limited judicial review by a U.S. Court of Appeals of the CFTC's exercise of its emergency powers.

Volume of Trading   Each exchange is required to report daily the volume of trading for each commodity traded on it, together with settlement and other price information. Most major newspapers and financial journals carry information about commodity prices and trading volume.

Registered Futures Association

In the fall of 1981 the CFTC designated the National Futures Association (NFA) as a "registered futures association," with the purpose of providing self-regulatory functions in the public interest. The NFA began operations on October 1, 1982. The NFA assumed several regulatory functions previously performed by the CFTC, including registration responsibility for the newly created category of introducing brokers and their associated persons. As a result, it was anticipated that all futures professionals (other than floor brokers and floor traders—see below) would become "members" or "associates," including futures commission merchants, commodity pool operators, commodity trading advisors, and introducing brokers. Since the CFTC retains regulatory oversight for exchanges, they do not have to become NFA members, but several have voluntarily chosen to do so. The 1982 amendments contain provisions that will facilitate the assumption of certain CFTC registration functions by the NFA. In addition, the CFTC recently adopted a rule, in response to a petition of the NFA, requiring all persons required to be registered with the CFTC as a futures commission merchant to be members of a registered futures association. Since members of the NFA are expressly prohibited from doing business with nonmembers who are acting as futures professionals, commodity pool operators, commodity trading advisors and introducing brokers will have to join NFA in order to clear trades through futures commission merchants.

The NFA's principal regulatory functions, in addition to registering members and associates, include auditing the financial condition of futures commission merchants (particularly those that are not members of any commodity exchange), arbitrating commodity futures disputes between customers and NFA members, and monitoring and enforcing compliance with the NFA's business conduct rules. Exchanges may also delegate to the NFA, arbitration, audit, and compliance responsibilities with respect to their members, thereby reducing these expenses to the exchanges.

The NFA is required to submit any proposed change in or addition to its rules to the CFTC for its approval. Such proposals are effective automatically after 10 days unless the NFA specifically requests the CFTC to review the proposals or unless the CFTC notifies the NFA within this period of its determination to review the proposals.

Floor Brokers

A floor broker is a person who buys or sells a futures contract (or an option on such a contract) for another at the place provided for transacting such business by the exchange, called a pit or ring. A floor trader, as contrasted with a floor broker, will act only for himself and will do no customer business. As a result, floor brokers are required to be registered with the CFTC, while floor traders need not be so registered. Floor brokers and floor traders are extensively regulated by the exchanges on which they operate with respect to situations affecting their trading, order execution, disputes, and similar matters. In addition, the following provisions apply to floor brokers:

Registration It is unlawful for a person to act as a floor broker unless he or she is registered with the CFTC. Subject to denial for good cause shown, a floor broker will be registered upon application to the CFTC on the proper CFTC form (which requires detailed information about the floor broker) and upon payment of the requisite fee. The 1982 amendments to the CE Act set out a number of grounds on which the CFTC is empowered to deny, condition, suspend, or revoke registration. Generally, registrations expire on March 31 and are renewable upon application unless the floor broker's registration has previously been suspended or revoked or is otherwise denied for good cause shown. The CFTC is empowered to alter the registration period by rule, but in no event may the registration period be for less than a year.

Recordkeeping Floor brokers are required to keep detailed records of their commodity transactions (including, of course, trading cards showing each individual transaction executed on the exchange on a given day), to make such reports as are from time to time required by the exchange or the CFTC, and to have all such information available for inspection for fixed periods of time.

Dual Trading   The CFTC, as mandated by the 1974 amendments to the CE Act, made a determination that the practice of dual trading (i.e., trading for one's own account and for the account of customers) by floor brokers and/or futures commission merchants would be allowed to continue. Certain minimum standards, however, are required of floor brokers engaging in this practice, including the requirements that customer orders must come first, that customer confidentiality must be maintained, and that customer orders may be cross-traded with orders of the broker only with specific customer consent.

Fitness   As yet, no standards of training, experience, or written proficiency examinations, or any other applicable qualifications to be licensed as a floor broker, have been adopted by the CFTC, even though it is empowered to do so by the CE Act.

Orders   A floor broker is required to keep a record (within a minimum 30-minute time bracket) of the time a customer order is executed. All trades must be effected in the pit or ring in an open and competitive manner by open outcry. Customer orders may be crossed by a single broker (i.e., where he holds both the buy and sell order) if this is done by open outcry and in conformity with exchange rules (which have been approved by the CFTC) and with regulatory standards that require the specific consent of the customer to such practices.

Certain Prohibited Transactions   The CE Act specifically prohibits transactions that are, or are commonly known to the trade as, "wash sales," "cross trades" (unless according to exchange and CFTC rules), "accommodation trades," or "fictitious sales" or transactions in which the trader causes a price to be reported that is not a true and bona fide price.

Futures Commission Merchants (FCMs)

FCMs are individuals or entities engaged in soliciting and accepting orders from customers for the purchase or sale of futures contracts (and options on such contracts) *and,* in that connection, accepting money or property to secure those contracts. An FCM may use introducing brokers (i.e., other individuals or entities that solicit the business of customers but do not accept money or property to secure the trades effected for customers).

Registration   It is unlawful for a person to act as an FCM unless registered with the CFTC. Like floor brokers, FCMs, subject to denial for good cause shown, will be registered upon payment of the requisite fee and upon application to the CFTC on the appropriate CFTC form. The 1982 amendments to the CE Act set out a number of grounds upon which the CFTC is empowered to deny, condition, suspend, or revoke the registration of an FCM. In addition, an FCM must meet certain minimum financial requirements, as discussed below. Generally, registrations expire on March 31 and are renewable upon application unless the FCM's registration has previously been suspended or revoked or is otherwise denied for good cause shown. The CFTC may alter the registration period by rule, but that period may not be less than one year. An FCM registration application must contain, among other things, the names and addresses of all branch office managers; the names and business histories of all officers, directors, stockholders, partners, or other similar controlling persons; and a separate report of financial condition (as of a date not more than 45 days prior to the date of the filing, with either the report itself or an annual financial statement certified by independent auditors), which includes computations of minimum capital requirements, a schedule of funds on deposit in segregation, a statement describing the source of current assets, and a representation that the FCM's capital has been contributed in order to operate its business and will be continued to be used for that purpose. An FCM registered as a member of the NFA must comply with the NFA's rules, including its minimum financial requirements (unless the FCM is a member of an exchange and subject to the minimum financial requirements of the exchange).

Minimum Financial Requirements   An FCM must, at the time the application to register is filed and thereafter, meet such minimum financial requirements as the CFTC prescribes. Currently, CFTC regulations and NFA rules generally impose a minimum adjusted net capital requirement on each FCM of the greatest of (1) $50,000, if the FCM is a member of an exchange ($100,000 if it is not a member); (2) 4 percent of the customer funds that an FCM is required to segregate (the segregation requirement is discussed below); or (3) for those FCMs that are also registered as brokers or dealers with the SEC, the amount of net capital required under the SEC's rules. An FCM whose capital falls below the CFTC and NFA imposed minimum net capital requirements must (with limited exceptions) transfer all accounts and immediately cease doing business as an FCM until it is in compliance with those minimum net capital requirements. Where an FCM no longer meets minimum net capital requirements, it is allowed to trade for liquidation only. Unless the FCM can immediately demonstrate its ability to comply with the minimum net capital requirements, its FCM license is likely to be revoked or suspended.

Reporting Financial Requirements   An FCM that is not a member of an exchange and in compliance with an exchange's financial reporting requirements must file quarterly with the CFTC and the NFA on CFTC Form 1–FR (either on a fiscal- or calendar-quarter basis) a statement of financial condition, within 45 days of the end of each reporting period. These reports need not be certified; however, the Form 1–FR that has to be filed as of the end of the FCM's fiscal or calendar year must be certified and filed within 90 days after the close of the year. An FCM that is a member of an exchange and in compliance with that exchange's financial reporting requirements must file with the CFTC true copies of each financial report that it files with the exchange and must also file a Form 1–FR with the CFTC upon special written request.

The Early Warning Financial Reporting System   The CFTC has established an early warning reporting system to afford the CFTC, the NFA, and the exchanges advance notice of an FCM's potential financial problems. If the adjusted net capital of an FCM is less than the greater of 150 percent of the appropriate minimum net capital required or 6 percent of the FCM's segregation requirement, within five business days it must file a notice of that fact with the CFTC and with the exchange of which it is a member, or if it is not a member of an exchange and it is a member of the NFA, it must file such a notice with the NFA. In addition, a Form 1–FR must be filed as of the close of business for the month in which the FCM triggers the early warning system, and for each month thereafter, until three successive months elapse during which the FCM's adjusted net capital is at all times equal to or in excess of 150 percent of the required amounts. In addition, if an FCM knows or should know that its adjusted net capital is at any time less than the minimum amount required, within 24 hours after it falls below the required amount, it must give telegraphic notice of that fact to the CFTC and to the exchange of which it is a member, or if it is not a member of an exchange and it is a member of the NFA, it must give such notice to the NFA. Twenty-four hours after giving notice, the FCM is required to file a statement of financial condition, a statement of computation of its minimum capital requirements, and a schedule of segregation requirements and funds on deposit in segregation (if any).

Segregation of Customers' Funds   A major tenet of commodity law is that all customer funds must be segregated for the benefit of the customer. As a result, FCMs are obligated to keep and maintain separate accounting systems with respect to money, securities, and other property belonging to customers. Commingling customer funds with those of the FCM or utilizing any customer's funds on behalf of other persons, including other customers of the FCM, is prohibited. No FCM may invest funds of a customer except in U.S. government obligations or in obligations fully guaranteed as to principal and interest by the United States. Such investments may be made only through an account or accounts used for the deposit of customers' funds, and proceeds from the sale of any such obligations must be redeposited in such an account or accounts.

Recordkeeping Requirements   Each FCM must prepare and keep current ledgers or similar records that show or summarize (with appropriate references to supporting documents) each commodity transaction affecting its assets, liabilities, income, expenses, and capital accounts and in which all its asset, liability, and capital accounts are classified into either the account classification subdivisions specified on CFTC Form 1–FR or categories that are in accord with generally accepted accounting principles. Each FCM must also keep records of its computations of adjusted net capital and of its minimum financial requirements. FCMs must compute *as of the close of each business day* the amount of money, securities, and other property that must be held in segregated accounts. It is not sufficient to make the determination the next day because if the day's losses deplete the funds in segregation, the FCM must advance its own funds overnight until it can call in funds from a customer incurring losses. Month-end computations must also be provided to each customer. In addition, FCMs must furnish each customer with a written monthly statement and record of that customer's open commodity positions and certain other information, such as a statement of unrealized profit and loss in the account. The CFTC recently adopted a rule that relieves FCMs of the obligation to furnish monthly statements to a commodity futures or option customer whose account has neither open positions at the end of the statement period nor any credits or debits to its balance since the prior statement period, provided that the customer receives a statement containing certain specified information at least once every three months. A monthly point balance must be prepared that accrues or brings to the offered closing (or settlement) price fixed by the clearing organization of an exchange each open contract held in an FCM account. Also required are monthly reports to customers whose accounts are controlled by other parties. An FCM is required to maintain a record of the true name and address of the party owning or controlling any account carried by it. It must also maintain records for each customer in such manner and form as to be identifiable to the trading records of the clearinghouses and exchanges. Moreover, FCMs are required to confirm promptly each futures (and options) trade effected for customers. Each FCM must, in addition, keep a record of its own (i.e., "house" or proprietary) cash commodity, futures, and options transactions. All of the records that FCMs are required to keep must be kept for a fixed period of time and must be available for inspection by appropriate governmental authorities.

Dual Trading   The CFTC, as mandated by the 1974 amendments to the CE Act, made a determination that the practice of dual trading (i.e., trading for one's own account and for the account of customers) by FCMs and/or floor brokers would be allowed to continue. Certain minimum standards, however, are required of FCMs engaging in this practice, including requirements that customer orders must come first, that the confidentiality of customer orders must be maintained, and that FCMs may take the other side of a customer order only with the specific consent of the customer.

Fitness   As with floor brokers, no standard of training, experience, or written proficiency examination, or any other applicable qualification for FCMs to be licensed as such, has yet been adopted by the CFTC, although it is empowered to do so under the CE Act, or by the NFA, to which the CFTC has delegated that responsibility. The NFA contemplates establishing such standards in the near future.

Orders   An FCM is required to time-stamp the receipt of a customer order in its office.

Offsetting Long and Short Positions   An FCM that has both a long and a short position in the same futures contract or options contract for a customer must promptly close out the offsetting positions.

Risk Disclosure Statement   An FCM is prohibited from opening a commodity account for any customer unless the FCM first provides the customer with a risk disclosure statement containing certain specific language required by the CFTC. The FCM is required to obtain a signed acknowledgment from the customer to the effect that the customer received and understood the risk disclosure statement. The CFTC currently is considering whether to amend its rules to make explicit that merely furnishing to the customer the risk disclosure statement does not relieve an FCM from any other obligation it has under the CE Act and the CFTC's rules and regulations, including the obligation to disclose all material information to existing or prospective customers.

Supervision   FCMs are required to supervise diligently the handling of all commodity accounts carried by the FCM and all activities of the FCM's partners, officers, and employees, relating to the firm's commodity business. In this connection, the CFTC suggests (but does not require) that each FCM provide specific supervision of each associated person whose duties are not wholly supervisory and maintain written procedures providing that the designated supervisor grant prior written approval of the opening of each customer account, of a customer's delegation of discretionary authority to an associated person, and of each trade effected pursuant to that authority. Frequent examination of customer accounts and prompt review of customer complaints are also suggested by the CFTC as part of the minimum standards for required supervision.

Authorizations to Trade   Before an FCM can trade for a customer, it is required to have written authorization for any discretionary account or a specific customer direction.

Churning   No specific CFTC or NFA rule with respect to the churning of customer accounts has been adopted, although the concept of not churning a customer's account is implicit in the antifraud provisions of the CE Act, in CFTC regulations, and in NFA rules. Accordingly, cases have held FCMs liable for excessive trading in a customer's account over which FCM employees had actual or de facto control.

Know Your Customer   There is no CFTC rule adopted that requires an FCM to "know your customer" (i.e., to know whether the customer is suitable for trading in commodities). Notwithstanding the lack of a specific rule, many FCMs set suitability standards for their own protection before allowing a customer to trade commodities. Several reparation cases before the CFTC have held that a suitability standard is applicable to the commodity industry.

Reportable Positions   Both FCMs and "foreign brokers" (the latter, a category not required to register or comply with any other CFTC regulations, being defined as entities located outside the United States that carry a customer account in commodity futures or options thereon traded on a U.S. exchange) are obligated to submit reports each day to the CFTC and to the various commodity exchanges with respect to all accounts (both customer and proprietary) carried by them that exceed reportable levels for various commodities as established by CFTC regulations (as discussed later in this chapter). The reportable level for both stock index futures contracts and option contracts thereon is currently established at 25 contracts. The reports are required to show each reportable position separately for each exchange and for each futures or option contract. In addition, FCMs and foreign brokers are required to supply the CFTC with information on positions if there is a special call for such information by the CFTC.

Agent for Foreign Traders   The CFTC has adopted a rule that designates an FCM as the agent for service of CFTC-related communications on behalf of FCM customers that are foreign traders or foreign brokers. Prior to opening an account for such foreign customers, the FCM must inform the foreign customers of the requirements of the rule.

Under another recently adopted rule (whose provisions also require an FCM to explain the rule to customers that are foreign brokers or foreign or domestic traders prior to opening an account for such customers), the CFTC may issue a call for information from an FCM or customer, which that FCM or customer is required to furnish, in connection with the CFTC's efforts to determine whether the threat of a market manipulation, corner, squeeze, or other market disorder exists in any contract market. If such a call is issued to a foreign broker or foreign trader, the FCM that is designated as its agent is required to transmit the call promptly to that foreign broker or foreign trader. An FCM or customer failing to respond to such a call may be prohibited from trading on the exchange specified in the call except for purposes of liquidating open positions.

Introducing Brokers (IBs)

The 1982 amendments define an "introducing broker" as any individual or entity, other than an associated person of an FCM (see below), that solicits or accepts orders for futures contracts *but does not* accept money or property (or extend credit in lieu thereof) to margin, guarantee, or secure the trades or contracts that result or may result for the customer. The CFTC recently adopted a comprehensive series of regulations affecting IBs. Excluded from the IB definition are FCMs, floor brokers, associated persons, commodity trading advisors which solely manage discretionary accounts or which do not receive per trade compensation, and commodity pool operators which solely operate pools.

Registration   It is unlawful for a person to act as an IB unless he or she is registered as such. As set forth above, the NFA has been delegated registration responsibilities over IBs and their associated persons, and will determine the expiration date of registrations which may not be less than one year. IB registrations will be renewable upon application unless the IB's registration has previously been suspended or revoked or is otherwise denied for good cause shown. An IB that becomes a member of the NFA must comply with the NFA's rules, including those rules that the NFA may establish regarding minimum financial requirements (unless the IB becomes a member of an exchange and thereby becomes subject to the minimum financial requirements that may be established by the exchange, subject to CFTC approval).

Financial Requirements   IBs will have to maintain a minimum adjusted net capital of $20,000. An alternative method of satisfying this capital requirement is available whereby an FCM enters into a guarantee agreement for the IB. The guarantee agreement must provide that the FCM (which is a party to the agreement) will guarantee performance of the IB's obligations under the CE Act.

Recordkeeping Requirements   IBs are required to maintain daily trading records for each customer in a manner and form that are identifiable to the trading records of the clearinghouses and exchanges. Such books and records must be available for inspection by appropriate governmental authorities. IBs should have fewer transactions and fewer records relating to each transaction than an FCM due to the differences in the nature of their businesses. Accordingly, an IB's recordkeeping burden should be considerably lighter than an FCM's.

Fitness   As yet, no standard of training, experience, or written proficiency examination, or any other applicable qualification for the licensing of IBs has been adopted by the NFA. The NFA contemplates establishing such standards in the near future.

Commodity Trading Advisors (CTAs)

A CTA is a person or entity that, for compensation or profit, advises others as to the value of commodities or as to the advisability of trading commodity futures and issues or promulgates reports or analyses concerning commodities. The statutory definition of a "commodity trading advisor" specifically excludes persons or entities, such as banks, lawyers, accountants, teachers, newspapers, reporters, FCMs, floor brokers, and exchanges, that may provide technical commodity advice in the course of their business activities but whose advisory activities are solely incidental to other functions. Also excluded from most CTA requirements of the CE Act (including the registration provisions) is any person or entity that furnishes commodity advice to fewer than 15 people within any 12-month period and does not hold itself out to the public as a CTA, or any dealer, processor, broker, seller, or farm organization involved in the cash commodity markets so long as the advisory activities of that person or entity (which would otherwise make it a CTA) are solely incidental to its regular business.

Registration   It is unlawful for a CTA to use the mail or any means of interstate commerce unless the CTA is registered with the CFTC. As with floor brokers and FCMs, registration of a CTA is granted, upon approval, by application to the CFTC on the proper CFTC form (giving detailed information about the CTA and its principals—now including fingerprinting) and by payment of the requisite fee. The 1982 amendments to the CE Act set out a number of grounds upon which the CFTC might deny, condition, suspend, or revoke registration. Registration expires on the June 30 after issuance and is renewable upon application unless the CTA's registration has previously been suspended or revoked or is otherwise denied for good cause shown. A CTA must register as a member of the NFA to do business with an FCM.

As discussed earlier in this chapter, the SEC's position that a contract for future delivery of a security or a group of securities was itself a security led the SEC to the conclusion that a person such as a CTA that gives advice on such contracts would be required to register as a securities investment adviser under the Investment Advisers Act of 1940. In 1979 the SEC issued an interpretive letter in which it announced that registration as an investment advisor would not be required if the advice regarding "securities" were limited to futures contracts on certain specified financial instruments that were then being traded (U.S. Treasury bills, bonds or notes; mortgage-backed certificates guaranteed by the Government National Mortgage Association; and commercial paper). This interpretation, with its express limitation to the enumerated financial futures contracts, created problems for CTAs wishing to advise regarding stock index futures contracts. However, in light of the provisions of the 1982 amendments that implement the CFTC/SEC Accord, the staff of the SEC expanded the position taken in its earlier interpretive letter so as not to require registration under the Investment Advisers Act of 1940 with respect to CTAs that render advice regarding financial futures contracts (or options on such contracts), including stock index futures contracts or options thereon.

Antifraud Regulation　The CE Act explicitly prohibits a CTA from, directly or indirectly, defrauding or engaging in any transaction or practice that operates as a fraud or deceit on any client or prospective client. It also prohibits a CTA from representing or implying that the CTA has been sponsored, recommended, or approved, or that the CTA's qualifications have been passed upon, by any agency of the United States, although the CTA may state that it is registered under the CE Act, if such is the case.

Disclosure to Clients　A CTA may not solicit or enter into agreements with a client whose commodity accounts it controls or seeks to control unless the CTA first delivers a disclosure document to the client. The disclosure document may not be used until it has been on file with the CFTC for 21 days. The document must include information about the CTA and its principals; the prior performance record of the CTA and its principals with respect to all accounts controlled by each of them within the previous three years or the lack of such experience; the fees to be charged; the existence of any actual or potential conflict of interest with respect to the CTA, its principals, and any FCM as regards any aspect of the trading program; whether the CTA or its principals will trade for their own account and whether the client may inspect records of such trades; a statement advising, in verbatim language, of the risks of commodity trading; and certain other required informational statements. The CFTC has specifically exempted CTAs registered under the CE Act from being required to disclose futures positions of the CTA and its principals to clients, though the CTA may provide such information voluntarily. A CTA must cease using any disclosure document that is materially inaccurate or incomplete in any respect until the defect has been corrected, and in any event it may not use a disclosure document dated more than six months prior to its contemplated use. In addition, the NFA requires all registered CTAs to file a current copy of their disclosure document with their application for membership.

Recordkeeping CTAs must keep, and make available to the CFTC, records of the names and addresses of all clients, copies of all literature sent to clients, signed and dated acknowledgments of receipt of a disclosure document for each client, itemized daily records of all transactions by the CTA and its principals (both for itself and its clients), monthly statements received from FCMs, copies of powers of attorney to control clients' accounts, and all advisory agreements with clients.

Commodity Pool Operators (CPOs)

A CPO is a person engaged in a business in the nature of an investment trust, syndicate, or similar form of enterprise that solicits, accepts, or receives funds or property from others for the purpose of trading commodity futures. CPOs range from the small local investment club to large publicly offered mutual fund–type pools. CFTC regulations exempt from most CPO provisions of the CE Act (including registration provisions) any CPO that operates a pool or pools composed of fewer than 15 people with net assets below $200,000 and any CPO that (1) does not receive compensation for operating the pool, (2) operates only one pool at any time, (3) is not otherwise required to register, and (4) does not advertise.

Registration It is unlawful for a CPO to use the mails or any means of interstate commerce unless the CPO is registered with the CFTC. As with floor brokers, FCMs, and CTAs, registration of a CPO is obtained, upon approval, by application to the CFTC on the proper form (giving detailed information about the CPO and its principals—now including fingerprinting) and by payment of the requisite fee. The 1982 amendments to the CE Act set out a number of grounds upon which the CFTC may deny, condition, suspend, or revoke registration. Registration expires on the June 30 after issuance and is renewable upon application unless the CPO's registration has been suspended or revoked or is otherwise denied for good cause shown. A CPO must register as a member of the NFA to do business with FCMs.

Antifraud Regulation As with CTAs, the CE Act explicitly prohibits a CPO from, directly or indirectly, defrauding or engaging in any transaction or practice that operates as a fraud or deceit on any pool participant or prospective participant. It also prohibits a CPO from representing that the CPO has been sponsored, recommended, or approved, or that the CPO's qualifications have been passed upon, by any agency of the United States, although the CPO may state that it is registered with the CFTC, if such is the case.

Disclosure to Participants A CPO may not solicit, accept, or receive funds from a prospective pool participant unless it delivers a disclosure document to the prospective participant. The disclosure document must be on file with the CFTC for 21 days prior to its use. It must include information about the CPO and its principals, any conflict of interest in connection with the pool's activities, the actual performance record of the pool for the past three years, the expenses and fees of the pool, restrictions on transferability, tax ramifications, whether the CPO or its principals will trade for their own account and whether the participant may inspect records of such trades, other similar matters, and a risk disclosure statement advising (in verbatim form) of the risks of commodity trading. The CFTC has specifically exempted CPOs registered under the CE Act from being required to disclose futures positions of the CPO and its principals to participants, though the CPO may provide such information voluntarily. A CPO must cease using any disclosure document that is materially inaccurate or incomplete in any respect until the defect has been corrected, and in any event it may not use a disclosure document dated more than six months prior to its contemplated use. In addition, the NFA requires all registered CPOs to file a current copy of their disclosure document with their application for membership.

Capital Formation Aspects Since the raising of money from the public, for whatever purpose, has traditionally been viewed as a public offering of securities, most commodity pools, involved as they are in solicitations of public participation, have acceded to the applicability of the securities laws to such capital formation aspects of their activities. As a result, pools with widespread public distribution have registered the securities involved (usually in the form of interests in, or units of, a limited partnership) with the SEC. As a corollary, registration with the various state securities administrators has followed. Certain states have adopted stringent guidelines for the registration of commodity pools. Pools involving lesser public distributions have offered the pool participations under SEC

Regulation D or complied with some other SEC exemption from registration as well as applicable state securities laws. The 1982 amendments explicitly preserved the SEC's role in the capital formation aspects of commodity pool offerings. The legislative reports on the 1982 amendments also make clear that the jurisdiction of the states in this area has been preempted.

An additional registration issue has surfaced in the area of commodity pools wishing to invest in stock index futures contracts. As discussed earlier in this chapter, the SEC's position that a contract for future delivery of a security or a group of securities was itself a security led that agency to the conclusion that entities such as commodity pools that engaged in the business of investing in such futures contracts would be subject to extensive regulation by the SEC under the Investment Company Act of 1940 with regard to capital formation, periodic reporting, and other aspects of their activities. In 1979, although it continued to assert that futures contracts on financial instruments were securities, the SEC announced in an interpretive letter that it would not require a commodity pool to register under the Investment Company Act of 1940 if its trading in financial futures were limited to futures contracts on U.S. Treasury bills, notes, and bonds, mortgage-backed certificates guaranteed by the Government National Mortgage Association, and commercial paper (the only financial futures traded at the time), since such underlying securities were themselves exempt from the SEC's registration requirements. This interpretation, with its express limitation to the enumerated financial futures contracts, creates problems for pools that propose to engage in stock index futures trading. However, in light of the provisions of the 1982 amendments that implement the CFTC/SEC Accord, the staff of the SEC expanded the position taken in its earlier interpretive letter so as not to require a commodity pool that trades other types of financial futures or options on such instruments, including stock index futures contracts and options thereon, to register under the Investment Company Act of 1940.

Reporting to Participants   A pool with assets in excess of $500,000 must distribute a monthly account statement disclosing certain information about the pool, in the form of a statement of income or loss and a statement of changes in net asset value. Pools with under $500,000 in net assets must report quarterly. In addition, an annual report certified by an independent auditor (unless the pool has less than $50,000 in assets or is composed of fewer than 15 persons) must be sent to participants and filed with the CFTC.

Recordkeeping   CPOs must keep, and make available to the CFTC, itemized daily records of all transactions, receipts, and disbursements; participants' names and addresses; signed and dated acknowledgments of receipt of a disclosure document for each participant; monthly statements received from FCMs; copies of all literature sent to participants; all financial statements; and similar material. Such materials must be made available for the inspection of participants.

Associated Persons (APs)

An AP is an individual employed by an FCM as a partner, officer, or employee or a person who occupies a similar status or performs similar functions and who acts in any capacity that involves the solicitation or acceptance of customer orders (other than in a clerical capacity) or who supervises any person so engaged. The 1982 amendments to the CE Act contain provisions defining an associated person of a CTA, a CPO, and an IB along the same lines as an AP of an FCM and subject such APs to registration with the CFTC and the NFA and to regulation in much the same manner as APs of FCMs are currently regulated. The CFR has adopted regulations to implement these provisions of the 1982 amendments.

Registration   Subject to denial for good cause shown, an AP who is "sponsored" by an FCM will be registered by filing an application with the CFTC on the proper CFTC form (giving fingerprints and a detailed personal and business history of the AP) and by payment of the requisite fee. The 1982 amendments to the CE Act set out a number of grounds upon which the CFTC may deny, condition, suspend, or revoke registration. Registration of an AP is now made coextensive with the continuation of employment by the sponsoring FCM unless the AP's registration is, in the interim, suspended or revoked, or otherwise denied for good cause shown. If an AP seeks employment at a new FCM, that FCM must "sponsor" the AP and the AP must then reapply for registration. An FCM may not permit an unregistered AP to become or remain associated with it in any capacity that requires AP registration if it knows or should know that the AP is not registered. APs of CTAs, COPs and IBs are subject to the same sponsorship and fingerprinting standards as APs of FCMs.

Multiple Associations   Rules recently adopted by the CFR restrict the ability of APs simultaneously to be associated with an FCM and an IB and with more than one FCM or IB. APs of CTAs and CPOs generally are permitted to be associated with more than one CTA or CPO (or with a CTA and a CPO), provided that such multiple associations are reported to the CFTC. APs of CTAs and CPOs are restricted, however, in their ability simultaneously to be associated with an FCM or IB.

Fitness   As is the case with floor brokers, FCMs, CTAs, and CPOs, no standard of training, experience, or written proficiency examination, or any other applicable qualification for APs, has yet been adopted by the CFTC, although it is empowered to do so by the CE Act, or by the NFA, to which the CFTC has delegated that responsibility. The NFA contemplates establishing such standards in the near future.

Supervision   APs are required to be supervised by their employers—the FCMs. Such supervision extends to areas of customer solicitation, customer suitability, order handling, obtaining proper account documentation, obtaining (in applicable cases) written discretionary powers, churning, handling customer complaints, and similar matters relative to the commodity broker/customer relationship.

Trading for One's Own Account   Many FCMs permit their employees to trade for their own account; others do not. If permitted to trade, APs must do so in accordance with the standards required of FCMs (as discussed earlier in this chapter). They may trade through an account opened at either their own FCM or another FCM. If an AP trades through another FCM, the nonemploying FCM must have an authorization from the employing FCM to open an account for the AP and all such trades must be carefully monitored and time-stamped.

Traders

A trader—whether a hedger or a speculator—is a participant in the commodity markets. There is no requirement that individual traders be registered, nor are they otherwise regulated. Traders holding or controlling reportable positions are required, however, (1) to file Form 40 reports with the CFTC that provide certain information about them; and (2) within one business day after a special call from the CFTC, to file reports concerning their transactions and positions. Traders are also required to maintain books and records showing the details of their commodity futures transactions.

Since 1936, the CE Act has contained a provision stating that "excessive speculation" is detrimental to the markets. As a result, the CFTC is empowered to set speculative limits (i.e., the aggregate amount of futures contracts in each commodity held by any single person or group of persons acting in concert at any given time that may not lawfully be exceeded) and has done so with respect to several agricultural commodities. With respect to all other commodities, including stock indexes, the exchanges have established speculative limits. Some of these have already been approved by the CFTC, and others are still pending before it. The CFTC has approved a speculative limit of 5,000 contracts for all stock index futures contracts currently traded. Spread trading and bona fide hedging transactions are not considered speculative, and so are exempted from speculative limits. The 1982 amendments to the CE Act affirm the authority of exchanges to set speculative limits, as long as they do not exceed any limits that the CFTC has established; make a violation of an exchange limit a violation of federal law, with criminal penalties applying if the violation is in connection with certain types of market manipulation; and strengthen the CFTC's emergency powers by giving it authority to set retroactive speculative limits.

In order to enable the CFTC to know the positions of various participants in the market so as to protect against market manipulations or violations of speculative limits, the CFTC has set a given number of open contract positions as the minimum that, once reached by a trader, must be reported to the CFTC by FCMs on forms denominated by the CFTC as Series '01 reports. Reportable positions for stock index contracts have been set at 100 contracts.

Commodity Option Dealers

Prior to the enactment of the 1974 amendments to the CE Act, options (i.e., the right but not the obligation to acquire or sell) were prohibited on the commodities that were then enumerated in the CE Act. The 1974 amendments to the CE Act continued the options ban on the specifically enumerated commodities but allowed the CFTC to determine whether to extend the options ban to the then newly regulated commodities.

The CFTC initially permitted option transactions (off-exchange) pursuant to a set of regulations that essentially made option vendors conform to the minimum financial and other requirements of an FCM; required all persons working for such vendors to register as APs; and required the vendors to provide customers with detailed disclosure statements (including statements of the risks involved), to segregate customer funds, and to keep detailed books and records regarding all option transactions. Exchange-traded options were prohibited until the CFTC could develop and implement a test program to monitor them. Despite the regulatory environment, it became apparent to the CFTC that a large number of customers were being defrauded of vast amounts of money in what the CFTC characterized as high-pressure, boiler-room commodity option scams by unscrupulous vendors who preyed upon the unsophisticated public. The magnitude of customer losses and the unscrupulous character of the commodity option vendors came to light in a series of highly publicized scandals in late 1977 and early 1978. As a result, the CFTC, with limited exceptions, banned all commodity option sales in the United

States from and after June 1, 1978. Among the exceptions were commodity option dealers that met stringent requirements set forth in the CE Act and in CFTC regulations. Such dealers were permitted to sell options on physical commodities (not futures contracts) only through registered FCMs that met stringent CFTC-imposed requirements.

The 1978 amendments to the CE Act provided that the CFTC could establish rules under which commodity options would be traded in the United States so long as the CFTC submitted those rules in advance to Congress and provided evidence of its ability to regulate the proposed option transactions. As a result, the CFTC has adopted rules designed to regulate commodity options as part of a pilot program to develop commodity option trading on U.S. exchanges. Under these rules, each exchange is initially permitted, upon application and qualification by the CFTC, to trade options on one type of commodity futures contract, the underlying futures contract of which is traded on that exchange. In addition, each exchange has primary regulatory responsibility for policing option "retailing" and is required to establish rules, procedures, and safeguards for such trading. Option trading in certain commodities commenced on October 1, 1982; applications by various exchanges to permit option trading on stock index futures contracts were first approved by the CFTC in January 1983.

The CFTC has also approved rules to permit option trading on physical commodities on exchanges. As part of the CFTC/SEC Accord, however, the 1982 amendments provide that the CFTC has no jurisdiction to designate a board of trade as a contract market in options on stock indexes— the CFTC's jurisdiction in the area being limited exclusively to options on futures contracts on stock indexes.

Legal Proceedings Available

To the CFTC

The CFTC has extensive authority to enforce the nation's commodity laws. It can go to court and obtain injunctive relief; it can impose penalties, after a hearing, of up to $100,000 for each offense; and it has authority to issue cease and desist orders, to prohibit trading by the persons it sanctions, and to suspend or revoke the registration of the persons it regulates.

Fraud Provisions The CE Act makes it unlawful to engage in transactions on exchanges that involve cheating or defrauding or attempting to cheat or defraud another person, willfully making a false report or a false record, willfully deceiving or attempting to deceive another person; or bucketing orders. Most CFTC enforcement actions are premised in one way or another on violations of this basic provision of the CE Act or on provisions relating to fictitious or other noncompetitive trading.

Manipulation   The CE Act also makes it unlawful to engage in transactions that attempt to, or actually, manipulate, corner, or squeeze the commodity futures markets.

Type of Relief Available to the CFTC   The CFTC can bring a proceeding in a federal district court by seeking an injunction against a violator of the CE Act or an aider or abettor of such a violator, or it can seek administrative sanctions before its own administrative law judges against such a violator or against an aider or abettor of that violator. In addition, since many violations of the CE Act are classified as felonies or misdemeanors, the CFTC can make a criminal reference to the Justice Department for prosecution by that Department of criminal law violations. CE Act violations for certain felonies carry jail terms and fines of up to $500,000 per violation.

Investigations   The CFTC begins an enforcement matter with a formal or informal investigation. It has published rules concerning its investigations that relate to such matters as rights of witnesses, transcripts, and subpoenas.

Administrative Actions   In an administrative action the CFTC can obtain cease and desist orders; impose civil fines; deny, suspend, or revoke registrations of exchanges and all registered persons; deny trading privileges on the exchanges; or obtain ancillary relief, usually by consent, that could include agreements to undertake affirmative actions, such as the initiation of a new compliance or training program or the removal of certain personnel.

Injunctive Actions   In injunctive actions the CFTC has sought, in addition to the immediate cessation of violations, a freeze against the dissipation of assets, accountings, immediate access to records, the prevention of records destruction, and the appointment of a receiver. As in administrative proceedings, it has often sought and obtained innovative affirmative actions (e.g., establishing a fund for defrauded customers or disgorgement of illegal profits). The 1982 amendments strengthen the CFTC's enforcement arsenal by permitting it to seek judicial restraining orders as well as injunctions to gain access to records or to prevent destruction of evidence or dissipation of assets.

Subpoenas   The CFTC has the right to issue subpoenas to compel witnesses to testify or to produce documents.

Immunity   The CFTC may grant limited-use immunity from prosecution to witnesses.

To Private Individuals

A person aggrieved in a commodity matter may bring a proceeding in one of three forums: a court proceeding, an administrative law proceeding under the CE Act (called "reparations"), or an arbitration. Generally, judicial procedures are formal, lengthy, and expensive; however, they provide extensive discovery mechanisms and appeal procedures. Reparations proceedings are intended to be conducted by an expert administrative tribunal; presumably, they resolve disputes more quickly than judicial proceedings but more formally than arbitrations. Arbitrations are informal, inexpensive hearings that provide little pretrial discovery or posttrial appeal.

Court Proceedings   Until 1981 there was a split among the federal appellate courts as to whether there was a "private right of action" under the CE Act—that is, whether a person who cited a violation of the CE Act would be entitled to base his cause of action on that alleged wrongdoing. Some courts held that the statutory remedies available to a private litigant, such as reparations, indicated that Congress did not intend a cause of action in federal court to be premised on a violation of the CE Act. In 1981 the U.S. Supreme Court affirmatively held that the CE Act created a private right of action. The 1982 amendments, seeking to clarify the Supreme Court decision, reaffirm the private right of action in commodity cases. These amendments provide that a cause of action may be brought in favor of any person (1) against any other person (other than a contract market, clearing organization, licensed board of trade, or registered futures association) for violations of the CE Act and (2) against any contract market, clearing organization, licensed board of trade, or registered futures association (and officers, directors, governors, or committee members thereof) for failure to enforce any bylaw, rule, or regulation that the contract market, clearing organization, licensed board of trade, or registered futures association is obliged to enforce if it can be established that the person to be charged acted in bad faith and that there was a direct causal link between the action (or failure to act) and the loss.

Reparations   The CE Act establishes a procedure whereby persons complaining of violations of the CE Act or CFTC regulations committed by any CFTC registrant (or person who, though unregistered, was required to be registered) can seek reparations for damages sustained as a result of those violations. If the CFTC believes that there are reasonable grounds for pursuing the matter, it is authorized to investigate or, if necessary, hold a hearing. After an administrative hearing is held (in cases involving claims of over $5,000), a CFTC administrative law judge is authorized to determine whether there has been a violation by a CFTC registrant, and if so (if restitution has not already been made), the law judge is authorized to determine the damages to be awarded to the complainant, who can also enforce the award in the courts. If the person against whom a reparations award has been made fails to comply, the CFTC is authorized to suspend that person's registration and trading privileges until compliance is achieved.

The 1982 amendments to the CE Act make changes in this procedure. First, the procedure is now available only with respect to violations by persons or entities actually registered with the CFTC. Second, in contrast to the earlier provisions, which outlined in substantial detail the procedures that had to be followed in reparations cases, the CFTC now has the responsibility for establishing all rules governing reparations cases, from the form, filing, and service of pleadings to the scope of discovery, grounds for dismissal, and rights of appeal, if any. The CFTC is currently considering proposals that would make reparations less attractive and arbitration more attractive as methods of dispute resolution. See the discussion of these proposals below.

Arbitration   Until the passage of the 1974 amendments to the CE Act, it was fairly commonplace for a commodity dispute to be arbitrated, because FCMs required their customers to agree to arbitrate all disputes as a condition to accepting customer accounts. The 1974 amendments, besides establishing procedures by which customers could seek reparations, permitted the use of arbitration only when such use was voluntary on the part of the customer and only in disputes not exceeding $15,000. The amendments also prohibited compulsory payments except as agreed upon between the parties. In addition, the CFTC promulgated a regulation requiring FCMs to give a customer 45 days after he had been served with a notice of the FCM's intention to seek arbitration in which to decide whether to seek reparations or to arbitrate. Such notice was required even if the customer had chosen to arbitrate in advance. As a result of these provisions, arbitration has seldom been used for dispute resolution between customers and FCMs. The 1982 amendments are likely to result in increased use of this procedure, however, because they eliminate the $15,000 ceiling and the necessity for the parties to agree to the settlement payments. FCMs that are not members of an exchange are now also eligible to use its arbitration facilities. The 1982 amendments also require all registered futures associations to adopt rules establishing expeditious arbitration procedures.

The CFTC recently adopted a series of proposals that would further encourage the use of arbitration by customers. These rules include requiring exchange members and their APs, if they enter into binding "predispute" arbitration agreements with their customers, to agree to absorb all the incremental costs of providing arbitration by a "mixed panel." In addition, such predispute arbitration agreements require the exchange member to give the customer a choice of at least two arbitration forums within 10 days of the demand for arbitration (whether customer or member initiated), the procedures of the arbitration forums must conform to CFTC standards, at least one of the forums must have a majority of persons who are not members of an exchange or associated with any member of an exchange, and at least one of the forums must offer the customer the opportunity to have the arbitration proceeding in a reasonably convenient location. Reparations would still be available to customers choosing it.

Miscellaneous Regulatory Matters

The 1982 amendments to the CE Act require the Board of Governors of the Federal Reserve System to organize a study, by the CFTC and the SEC, with the assistance of the Secretary of the Treasury, on the effects on the economy of commodity futures and commodity options trading, including trading in stock index futures and options on these instruments. Among the areas to be studied are the economic purposes, if any, served by such trading; the impact of such trading on the securities markets; and the consequences that present and anticipated volumes of trading have, if any, on capital formation (particularly long-term), the structure of liquidity in credit markets, interest rates, and inflation. The 1982 amendments require the Board of Governors to submit to Congress by September 30, 1984, a report on the results of the studies, together with any supplementation and recommendations for legislative or regulatory action proposed by the CFTC or the SEC.

Vice President Bush is heading a Task Group on Regulatory and Financial Services whose mission is to determine areas of regulatory overlap among agencies with a view to recommending the elimination of duplicative regulatory structure. The CFTC, the SEC, bank regulatory agencies, the Department of the Treasury, and other governmental agencies involved in the regulation of various financial services are participants in the Task Group. Recommendations from the Task Group may affect CFTC regulation in the future.

Index